The Money Illusion

The Money Illusion

Market Monetarism, the Great Recession, and the Future of Monetary Policy

SCOTT SUMNER

THE UNIVERSITY OF CHICAGO PRESS   CHICAGO AND LONDON

The University of Chicago Press, Chicago 60637
The University of Chicago Press, Ltd., London
© 2021 by The University of Chicago
Published 2021
Printed in the United States of America

31 30 29 28 27 26 25 24 23 22   3 4 5 6 7

ISBN-13: 978-0-226-77368-1 (cloth)
ISBN-13: 978-0-226-77371-1 (e-book)
DOI: https://doi.org/10.7208/chicago/9780226773711.001.0001

Library of Congress Cataloging-in-Publication Data

Names: Sumner, Scott, 1955– author.
Title: The money illusion : market monetarism, the Great Recession, and the future of
    monetary policy / Scott Sumner.
Description: Chicago : University of Chicago Press, 2021. | Includes bibliographical
    references and index.
Identifiers: LCCN 2020056573 | ISBN 9780226773681 (cloth) | ISBN 9780226773711 (e-book)
Subjects: LCSH: Monetary policy—United States. | Recessions—Effect of monetary
    policy on—United States.
Classification: LCC HG540.S94 2021 | DDC 339.5/30973—dc23
LC record available at https://lccn.loc.gov/2020056573

♾ This paper meets the requirements of ANSI/NISO Z39.48-1992 (Permanence of Paper).

Contents

Preface

During the 1930s, 1940s, and 1950s, most economists believed that the Great Depression had been caused by financial distress and that monetary policy had been expansionary but largely ineffective. In the 1960s, research by Milton Friedman and Anna Schwartz convinced the profession that monetary policy during the early 1930s had actually been contractionary, and that this had been a major cause of both the Depression and the banking crisis. Further research (including some of my own) established that the monetary failure had been global in nature and linked to flaws in the international gold standard.

When the Great Recession of 2008–2009 hit the global economy, I immediately noticed that many pundits were once again misdiagnosing the crisis, in ways eerily similar to the original (mistaken) view of the Great Depression. By this time, I had already spent several decades studying and teaching monetary economics. My research had focused on a number of topics with particular relevance to understanding the ongoing crisis, including the Great Depression, the Japanese liquidity trap of the late 1990s, and various proposals for reforming monetary policy. This gave me a unique vantage point in terms of seeing what others had missed.

In some respects, I was an unlikely contrarian, as before 2008, my views were not out of the mainstream. Indeed, for nearly a quarter century I had been reasonably satisfied with Federal Reserve policy. After Lehman Brothers failed, however, I realized that monetary policy had suddenly become much too tight, and I began trying to convince my fellow economists of the need for a much more expansionary policy. More importantly, I tried to show that the conventional wisdom was wrong. It wasn't just that policy had drifted off course in 2008—economists as a profession were thinking about the entire issue in the wrong way.

In early 2009, these convictions pushed me to start a blog called *The-MoneyIllusion*—a move that ended up reshaping my career. By 2010, I and several bloggers who shared a similar outlook had coalesced into a school of thought dubbed *market monetarism*, which focused on the need to provide stable growth in nominal gross domestic product. These writers included David Beckworth, Nick Rowe, David Glasner, Marcus Nunes, and Lars Christensen, among others. The mainstream media started paying more attention to our ideas, and people I met began asking me to recommend books with market-monetarist ideas. Unfortunately, I wasn't able to cite a book that provided the sort of comprehensive treatment of market monetarism that Friedman and Schwartz had provided for the earlier versions of monetarism.

One can think of Friedman and Schwartz's *A Monetary History of the United States* as a treatise on monetarist ideas, a revisionist explanation of the Great Depression, and a rationale for monetarist policy recommendations, all in one big book. In this book, *The Money Illusion*, I intend to provide a treatise on market-monetarist ideas, a revisionist explanation of the Great Recession, and a defense of market-monetarist policy recommendations.

Lots of people have contrarian views about current events. So why should you read this alternative account of the Great Recession? The best answer I can give is to point to the surprising number of instances when recent events played out in a way that supports market monetarism. Here are just a few:

- When I complained in late 2008 that money was too tight, almost no one else was making that claim. Today that view is widely held, and even former chair of the Federal Reserve Ben Bernanke admitted (in his memoir) that the Fed erred in not cutting rates after Lehman Brothers failed.
- When I suggested in early 2009 that Fed policy could be much more expansionary, most observers were skeptical. When the Fed eventually tried unconventional stimulus such as quantitative easing (even if this response was still inadequate), the United States performed much better than the eurozone, which did not try such policies until much later.
- When I proposed that banks adopt negative interest rates for bank reserves in January 2009, the idea was widely viewed as impractical. Today, many important central banks have adopted negative interest rates on bank reserves.
- After I suggested in late 2012 that "monetary offset" would prevent fiscal austerity in the US from having the contractionary impact that was widely

predicted, prominent economists dismissed my argument. My view, though, turned out to be correct: growth picked up in 2013. The consensus view was wrong.

- In early 2009, I advocated *nominal-GDP-level targeting*. In subsequent years, many of the top macroeconomists in America endorsed this policy. Christina Romer, who had been head of the Council of Economic Advisers under President Obama, cited my research as providing the "logic" behind nominal GDP targeting in her *New York Times* piece endorsing the concept.[1]
- An important component of market monetarism is the idea that Fed policy should be guided by market forecasts, not by the Fed's complex mathematical models of the economy. By 2019, it was clear that Fed policy is increasingly guided by market forecasts, because the Fed's internal models have proved unreliable.

These examples don't prove that market monetarists are right about everything. But surely the fact that so many of our claims have become increasingly accepted among respected macroeconomists is reason enough to take the ideas seriously. I hope this book provides readers with a better understanding both of what market monetarism is all about and of why we hold such unconventional views about what went wrong during the Great Recession.

This book has two primary goals. One goal is to provide an explanation of basic monetary theory and of the specific perspective called market monetarism. Fulfilling this goal occupies roughly the first half of the book, which includes some technical material at the level of undergraduate economics students. The second goal (addressed in the second half of this book) is to apply these ideas to the Great Recession, which provides an alternative narrative that I believe is superior to the conventional explanation. This narrative makes it easier to see what is distinctive about the market-monetarist approach.

This book is intended to be accessible to upper-level undergraduate economics students, graduate students, and interested readers with some knowledge of basic economic theory. However, this book doesn't just repackage and recycle existing theories—I present a number of new ideas and perspectives that I hope will also be of interest to professional economists.

The Real Problem Was Nominal

"Tell me," the great twentieth-century philosopher Ludwig Wittgenstein once asked a friend, "why do people always say it was natural for man to assume that the sun went around the Earth rather than that the Earth was rotating?" His friend replied, "Well, obviously because it just looks as though the Sun is going around the Earth." Wittgenstein responded, "Well, what would it have looked like if it had looked as though the Earth was rotating?"
—Richard Dawkins, *The God Delusion*

Many readers of this book will have fairly vivid memories of the financial crisis that followed the failure of the Lehman Brothers investment bank and of the Great Recession that began in 2007. Liberals' and conservatives' interpretations of these events may differ in the details, such as which public policies they blame, but both sides share a common understanding of the basic trajectory of the crisis: The bursting of a major real-estate bubble helped trigger first a banking crisis and then a deep recession. Monetary policy was extraordinarily expansionary during the downturn and recovery, but it was largely ineffective at boosting the economy.[1]

In the next few pages, I present a radically different interpretation of the Great Recession. At first it may seem implausible, even preposterous. Yet this radical view is based almost entirely on standard macroeconomic concepts, as they were understood back in 2007. It is the mainstream of the profession, which abandoned this standard model, that needs to justify its new view of macroeconomics.

Unfortunately, few noneconomists are aware of the state of macroeconomic theory circa 2007, so you may have to initially suspend your disbelief while you examine whether an alternative view of the past decade—*market monetarism*—makes more sense than the mainstream view. Market monetarism developed out of the crisis of 2008, but all of its components are well-established economic principles—although the way we utilize them is novel in certain respects.

In a sense, this book maps my intellectual journey, illustrating how I arrived at my current views on monetary economics (which were well established by 2007). These views have always been heavily informed by both data and theory—one without the other leads nowhere. Thus, I toggle back and forth between the major empirical findings of monetary economics and the models used to make sense out of those findings. I hope it will become clear why I espouse market monetarism rather than one of the alternative approaches to macroeconomics, such as the Keynesian, Austrian, classical, or traditional monetarist schools of thought.

In the second half of the book we return to the crisis of 2008, armed with a broad understanding of monetary economics. At that point I'll ask you a question similar to Ludwig Wittgenstein's famous query (recounted in the epigraph): what might we expect the crisis to have looked like if the market-monetarist view of reality is correct?

As with the solar system, the simplest and most coherent model of the Great Recession is highly counterintuitive—and not at all what many observers thought they saw happening in 2008.

The Conventional View

Here is how Stanford economist Robert Hall started off a survey article in the fall 2010 issue of *Journal of Economic Perspectives*: "The worst financial crisis in the history of the United States and many other countries started in 1929. The Great Depression followed. The second-worst struck in the fall of 2008 and the Great Recession followed."[2]

Although Hall is one of my favorite macroeconomists, I believe he's wrong in this case—and wrong in a very revealing way. There was no significant financial crisis in the United States during 1929. The major financial crisis of the Great Depression occurred in 1931.[3] Now, why is this timeline so important? Because Hall's description makes it seem as if the financial crisis in 1929 triggered the Great Depression, whereas what actually occurred was that the Great Depression led to a severe financial crisis. Debts are harder to repay when national income is falling rapidly because income provides the funds that people and businesses use to repay debts.

I argue that something quite similar occurred in 2008. Admittedly, the 2008 case is more complicated than that of the Great Depression. Whereas the financial system was in good shape in 1929, financial stresses were developing well before the 2008 recession because of problems with sub-prime loans. Even so, the specific financial crisis that Hall is referring to "in the fall of 2008" is the severe crisis post–Lehman failure that began in late September 2008 and intensified in October.

Why is the timing so important? Because the Great Recession began in December 2007 and became severe after June 2008. Just as in the 1930s, a slump in the economy triggered severe financial distress. In 2008, it transformed a modest banking crisis into a major financial crisis. Unfortunately, owing to lags in the collection of data on gross domestic product, at the time no one understood that the country was already in the midst of a severe recession when Lehman failed in September. It looked as though Lehman *caused* the severe recession because the truly horrifying GDP data came out later in 2008 and in early 2009.[4]

Real and Nominal GDP

The research firm Macroeconomic Advisers estimates monthly GDP data derived from the various data series that the US government uses to construct its quarterly GDP estimates. Figure I.1 shows what things looked like during the Great Recession: it clearly shows that the sharp drop in GDP occurred between June and December 2008. Keep that six-month period in the back of your mind, because I will continually refer back to it. Owing to quirks in the relationship between levels and rates of change, even a quarterly data series can be very misleading. For example, real GDP (RGDP) looks pretty level in the first three months of 2009, but quarterly RGDP actually shows a sharp decline from the fourth quarter, even though the *level* of GDP in the first quarter of 2009 was not much different from that of December 2008. That's because GDP during October and November 2008 was far higher than during December.

The bottom dropped out of the economy in the second half of 2008, although it wasn't known that this had happened until very late in the year. Lehman failed about halfway through this steep decline (in September 2008), triggering a major global banking crisis. By December most of the damage had been done: the Great Recession had begun, and the effects would linger for years.

I'm going to argue that the housing bubble and financial crisis did not cause the Great Recession. Rather, the direct cause of the recession was a fall in nominal GDP (NGDP), and the cause of the decline in NGDP

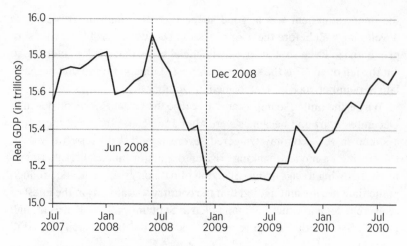

FIGURE I.1. US real GDP, Q3 2007 to Q3 2010

Source: Macroeconomic Advisers monthly real GDP data, https://ycharts.com/indicators/us_monthly_real_gdp.

was an excessively contractionary monetary policy. In a sense, the Federal Reserve was to blame, although it is probably more accurate to say that the entire economics profession was at fault, because economists were operating with a flawed model of monetary policy. The Fed rarely strays very far from the consensus view of elite macroeconomists.

Figure I.2 shows NGDP during the same period of time as is covered in figure I.1: notice the same steep decline in NGDP as in RGDP from June to December 2008. When I compare these two graphs during a lecture, I usually get several questions from the audience: "Isn't this pretty much a tautology?" "Real and nominal GDP are quite similar; obviously if one declines, then the other will as well, right?" "In what sense is a decline in NGDP a cause of a decline in RGDP?" "The real question is what caused them both to decline, isn't it?"

I sympathize with these questions, but they are based on a fundamental misunderstanding of the relationship between real and nominal variables. Although RGDP and NGDP may sound similar, they are radically different concepts, even at an ontological level. Even many economists don't grasp this, because economists are forced to use numbers to measure both aggregates and because RGDP includes many different types of objects. Thus, some sort of "index number" is required to make sense of the concept.

Nonetheless, real and nominal GDP are radically different. Nominal GDP is the total dollar value of all goods and services produced domestically in a given period of time. Real GDP is nominal GDP adjusted for changes in the price level, to factor out the effects of inflation. If you want to picture NGDP, you might visualize a huge pile of dollar bills: a monetary concept. If you want to picture RGDP, you might imagine thousands of factories, shopping malls, office buildings, and homes—and of course, millions of workers providing services.

Figure I.3 shows a Zimbabwe $100 trillion bill. Because of hyperinflation caused by the printing of many such bills, in 2008 Zimbabwe's NGDP soared higher at an astronomical rate. In contrast, Zimbabwe's RGDP is a physical concept; in 2008 its RGDP took the form of abandoned farms and shuttered factories, thanks to inept government policies that punished wealth creators. Real GDP plunged as Zimbabwe fell into depression while NGDP soared higher at the fastest rate in the world.

In the United States, RGDP and NGDP are more closely correlated. But even in the United States, NGDP growth rates soared to double-digit levels in the 1970s, even as RGDP growth was about 3%, lower than during the 1960s. There's no way around it: RGDP and NGDP are very different concepts.

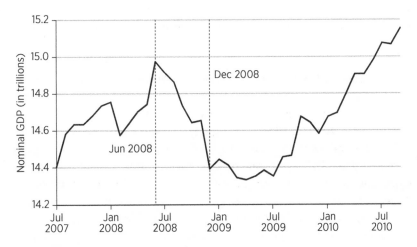

FIGURE I.2. US Nominal GDP, Q3 2007 to Q3 2010

Source: Macroeconomic Advisers monthly GDP data, https://ycharts.com/indicators/us_monthly_gdp.

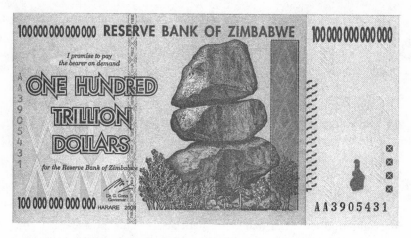

FIGURE I.3. A Zimbabwe $100 trillion bill in 2008

And yet, over shorter periods of time, NGDP and RGDP are indeed highly correlated in the US, although not for the reasons many assume. One of the basic goals of this book, and in some respects the key to macroeconomics, is to understand why NGDP and RGDP are highly correlated in some cases and not at all correlated in others. When we finally figure this out, we'll see that a policy that prevented NGDP from falling in 2008 would most likely also have prevented RGDP from falling, or at least greatly moderated the decline. A mild recession might have been inevitable, but the slump that occurred was far deeper than necessary.

False Assumptions about the Stance of Monetary Policy

Let's say that the decline in NGDP was the proximate cause of the decline in RGDP (later I'll explain exactly how and why these variables are related in the short run). That still leaves open the question of how I can claim that the Fed is to blame for the Great Recession. After all, "everyone knows" that monetary policy was extremely expansionary during 2008. The Fed cut interest rates sharply, to near-zero levels by the end of the year. It also pumped lots of money into the economy. As we will see, however, what "everyone knows" just isn't so.

This is not the first time that economists have confused low interest rates with easy money. The same mistake was made during the 1930s. Not until the publication in the 1960s of the famous *A Monetary History of the United States* by Milton Friedman and Anna Schwartz did economists come to realize that monetary policy was actually quite contractionary, or "tight," during the 1930s, despite near-zero interest rates. Today, even Ben Bernanke accepts Friedman and Schwartz's claim that the Fed was to blame for the Great Depression.

Unfortunately, many economists have continued to judge the stance of monetary policy by looking at interest rates. In December 1997, Friedman expressed dismay that many were forgetting the lessons of *Monetary History*. Interest rates in Japan had fallen to close to zero because of deflationary monetary policies, yet many pundits wrongly assumed that Japan had an easy money policy, despite a falling price level. Friedman wrote in the *Wall Street Journal*:

> Low interest rates are generally a sign that money has been tight, as in Japan; high interest rates, that money has been easy. . . .
>
> After the U.S. experience during the Great Depression, and after inflation and rising interest rates in the 1970s and disinflation and falling interest rates in the 1980s, I thought the fallacy of identifying tight money with high interest rates and easy money with low interest rates was dead. Apparently, old fallacies never die.[5]

Here Friedman is referring to the tendency of interest rates to follow inflation. A tight money policy produces low inflation, which leads to low interest rates, and easy money leads to high inflation, which leads to a high interest rate.[6]

Although Milton Friedman was perhaps the greatest monetary economist of the twentieth century, he was also a monetarist with some unconventional views. Maybe he was wrong about the policy stance in Japan; perhaps Japan did have easy money. But Friedman isn't the only economist to note that low interest rates don't mean easy money. Consider these three key lessons for students from the best-selling monetary policy textbook in 2007:

- "It is dangerous always to associate the easing or the tightening of monetary policy with a fall or a rise in short-term nominal interest rates."
- "Other asset prices besides those on short-term debt instruments contain important information about the stance of monetary policy because they are important elements in various monetary policy transmission mechanisms."
- "Monetary policy can be highly effective in reviving a weak economy even if short-term rates are already near zero."[7]

These points were written by Frederic Mishkin, a highly respected New Keynesian economist who served on the Federal Reserve Board with Ben Bernanke. As an academic, Bernanke also argued that monetary policy has an almost unlimited ability to stimulate the economy when interest rates are stuck at zero.[8]

I had been using Mishkin's textbook to teach for a quarter century before 2008. I believed these three ideas were extremely important, and I always emphasized them in class. Consider my surprise, then, when I looked around in late 2008 and found that few of my fellow economists believed in these assertions. Most economists seemed to think that low interest rates do represent easy money. Most economists also seemed to believe that monetary policy is *not* highly effective when interest rates are close to zero.

This discovery led me to devote my career to trying to change the conventional wisdom back to the ideas in Mishkin's textbook. In this book, I explain why I stuck with the textbook version of monetary economics in 2008 and not the view that caught on with most pundits—that monetary policy became ineffective after rates hit zero in December 2008, if not earlier. Mishkin was right when he claimed that monetary policy remains highly effective at near-zero interest rates.

How Did Asset Markets Move in Late 2008?

Recall that Mishkin claimed that the stance of monetary policy should be measured not by the level of interest rates buy by movements in other asset prices. So let's do that, focusing on the key six-month period in late 2008.

When I point out to other economists that nominal interest rates are not a good indicator of the stance of monetary policy, they often accept my claim but suggest that the real interest rate is a good indicator. So let's look at the real interest rates on five-year Treasury bonds from July to November 2008 (fig. I.4). The graph shows a stunning increase in real interest rates, especially for such a short period of time. Yet few of the economists I have talked to are even aware that real interest rates rose from less than 1% to more than 4% in the teeth of the financial crisis. Why would the Fed allow this to happen?

In fact, the economists who point to the real interest rate are wrong— it's not a good indicator of the stance of monetary policy, for the same basic reason that nominal interest rates are unreliable. Just as nominal

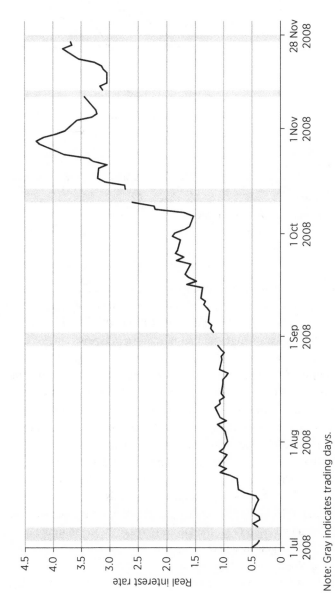

Note: Gray indicates trading days.

FIGURE I.4 US real interest rates, July 2008 to November 2008

Note: Gray indicates trading days.

Source: FRED via Dow Jones & Company and Haver Analytics, https://fred.stlouisfed.org/series/DTP10J14.

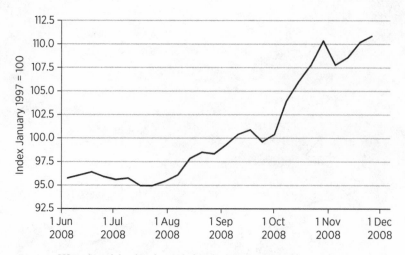

FIGURE I.5. US trade-weighted exchange index, June 2008 to November 2008

Source: FRED via Board of Governors of the Federal Reserve System (US), https://fred.stlouisfed.org/series /TWEXB.

interest rates can be distorted by changes in expected inflation, the real interest rate can be distorted by changes in real output. Ironically, many of the economists who say we should look at the real interest rate seem unaware that this indicator suggests that monetary policy was *highly contractionary* in late 2008.

Another popular asset price is the exchange rate, which measures the value of the dollar in terms of foreign currencies. Once again, it's not always a reliable indicator of the stance of monetary policy, but to the extent that it is useful, it was signaling extremely tight money in late 2008. Indeed, the foreign exchange value of the dollar soared by about 15% (in trade-weighted terms) in late 2008, as shown in figure I.5.

Interestingly, currencies almost always depreciate sharply during a severe financial crisis. Dozens of examples prove this, from Thailand to Mexico to Russia to Iceland. The rare examples when a currency appreciated during a financial crisis (e.g., the US in 1931–1932, Japan in the early 1990s, Argentina in 1998–2001) are cases that we now know involved excessively contractionary monetary policy.

Other asset markets showed the same pattern of sharp decline in late 2008:

- Stock prices crashed in late 2008.
- Commodity prices fell by more than 50% in late 2008.

- Commercial real-estate prices started falling sharply about the same time as NGDP, long after the subprime-lending bubble burst.
- Residential real estate prices in the heartland (e.g., Texas) had been stable during the 2006–2008 subprime crash and started falling in late 2008 along with NGDP.
- Spreads in Treasury Inflation-Protected Securities, or TIPS (i.e., inflation expectations in the bond market), fell sharply.

So if economists are to take seriously what we've been teaching our students for years, then it seems that all the "other asset prices" Mishkin referred to were flashing warning signs in 2008 that money was far too tight.

Of course, not everyone agrees with Mishkin's way of characterizing the stance of monetary policy. I prefer looking at NGDP growth, as does Ben Bernanke:

> The imperfect reliability of money growth as an indicator of monetary policy is unfortunate, because we don't really have anything satisfactory to replace it. As emphasized by Friedman . . . nominal interest rates are not good indicators of the stance of policy. . . . The real short-term interest rate . . . is also imperfect. . . .
>
> Ultimately, it appears, one can check to see if an economy has a stable monetary background only by looking at macroeconomic indicators such as nominal GDP growth and inflation.[9]

If we average out NGDP growth and inflation, we find that monetary policy during the period 2008–2013 was the tightest since Herbert Hoover was president at the onset of the Great Depression. And recall that Bernanke once argued that the Fed's tight money policies caused the Great Depression. Although the stance of monetary policy was extremely contractionary by the criteria Bernanke laid out in 2003, as Fed chair Bernanke suggested that policy was quite *accommodative* during the period 2009–2013.

A well-functioning economy requires NGDP to rise at a fairly steady rate, but not too fast. The Fed has all the tools required to make this happen. When NGDP performs poorly, it means that monetary policy is failing.

Didn't the Housing Bubble Cause the Great Recession?

If macroeconomic theory circa 2007 clearly points to tight money as the cause of the Great Recession, then why do so few economists believe it? One answer is that it didn't look as if tight money was to blame. Even though most economists understand that low rates don't necessarily mean easy money, many don't incorporate the implications of this into their worldview. Instead, they tend to focus on the most visible manifestations of a tight money policy, such as falling asset prices and financial distress. To early humans it looked as if the sun went around the earth as they watched it rise and set—similarly, to most economists it looked as if the housing bust and the subsequent financial crisis caused the Great Recession.

Let's consider the housing "bubble." (I use scare quotes because later we'll see that bubbles are not a useful concept.) The standard view is that American home prices soared to irrational heights during the 2005–2006 housing bubble, so a later sharp decline was almost inevitable. But was it? After all, housing prices soared in many other countries at about the same time. Figure I.6 shows housing prices in six English-speaking countries. Notice that housing prices (in real terms) rose much higher in all six markets, and yet prices later fell sharply in only two of the markets: the US and Ireland. In the other four economies, housing prices moved sideways in real terms (and rose even higher in nominal terms).

Back in 2006, it was difficult to predict which, if any, of these six markets would experience sharp housing price declines. If you correctly predicted the bursting of the housing bubble, then you should consider that's probably because you happen to reside in the US or Ireland, where your prediction turned out to be accurate.

Even if the fall in US housing prices did not represent the bursting of a bubble, it obviously could have caused a recession. After all, there are lots of jobs in home construction and related industries. But did the housing slump actually cause a sharp rise in unemployment? The data suggest that the answer is no. Table I.1 shows how between January 2006 (when housing construction peaked) and April 2008, the US experienced a decline in home building by more than 50%. By the latter date, about 75% of the decline in home building had already occurred. And yet during that twenty-seven-month period, the unemployment rate merely edged up from 4.7% to 5.0% (which was still considered roughly "full employment").

The 2006–2008 period shows exactly how economies are supposed to work, at least in (classical) theory. An economy has a *production possibilities curve*, which shows the maximum possible output in a variety of industries. If more resources are used to produce one type of good, then fewer resources will be available to produce other types of goods. The opportunity cost of more housing, then, is less production of cars, computers, and restaurant meals.

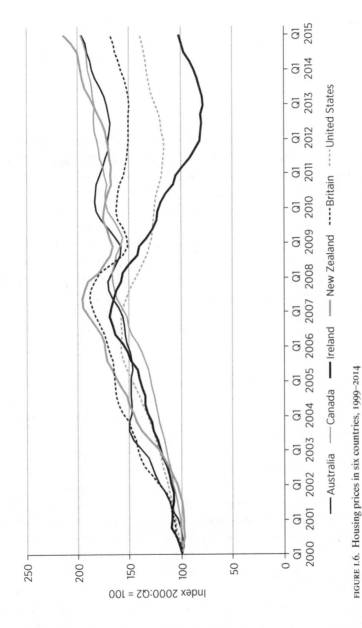

FIGURE 1.6. Housing prices in six countries, 1999–2014

Source: The Economist via OECD; ONS; Reserve Bank of New Zealand; Standard & Poor's; Teranet—National Bank, https://infographics.economist.com/2017/HPI/index.html

— Australia — Canada — Ireland — New Zealand — Britain ---- United States

Index 2000:Q2 = 100

TABLE I.I **US housing statistics versus unemployment rate**

Month and year	Starts	Completions	Average	Unemployment rate
January 2006	2,273,000	2,036,000	2,154,500	4.7%
April 2008	1,013,000	1,022,000	1,017,500	5.0%
October 2009	534,000	746,000	640,000	10.0%

Source: Federal Reserve Economic Data.

The period from January 2006 to April 2008 provides a pretty good example of the classical model in action. As home building slumped, workers shifted into other sectors, such as manufacturing, commercial construction, exports, and services. Because NGDP kept growing (owing to relatively sound monetary policy), the unemployment rate stayed fairly low.

The housing slump did impose some costs on the economy. Workers often find it difficult to switch from one sector to another, and that caused a small rise in the unemployment rate. But these "reallocation" costs are trivial compared to the costs that occur when money is too tight and NGDP falls. Between April 2008 and October 2009, when NGDP fell sharply, the unemployment rate soared from 5.0% to 10.0% (see table I-1). Now jobs were not being lost not just in home building but also in manufacturing, commercial real-estate construction, and even many service industries.

It seems clear, therefore, that the housing bust did not cause the Great Recession. But what about the view that big financial crises always lead to big recessions and slow recoveries? It's not at all surprising that the two are often associated with each other, because people, businesses, and governments can be expected to have more trouble repaying debts when NGDP falls sharply. But that correlation in no way prevents the central bank from promoting a rapid recovery through monetary stimulus. The banking crisis of 1933 was perhaps the worst in American history, but both NGDP and RGDP rose rapidly after March 1933, despite the fact that much of the banking system was shut down at the time.

How did that 1933 growth miracle occur? According to Ben Bernanke, it was FDR's decision to adopt a highly aggressive and unconventional form of monetary stimulus—in the form of dollar devaluation. In 1999, Bernanke wrote a paper entitled "Japanese Monetary Policy: A Case of Self-Induced Paralysis?"—a question he answered in the affirmative. In the final sentence of the paper he implored the Bank of Japan to show

"Rooseveltian resolve" in the face of the zero-interest-rate problem, as FDR had in 1933 after defeating Hoover in a landslide election.[10] Unfortunately, when it was the Fed's turn to show Rooseveltian resolve at the zero-interest-rate boundary, it fell short.

A common misconception is that the Fed "did all it could." Some excuse the Fed by pointing to the political unpopularity of unconventional tools such as qualitative easing and negative interest on bank reserves. But the Fed did not reach the zero bound until mid-December 2008, by which time most of the great NGDP collapse was over. When the Fed met two days after Lehman failed in September 2008, it refused to take even the most basic of conventional monetary policy steps, such as cutting its target interest rate (which was 2% at the time). In his memoir, Bernanke concedes that it was a mistake not to cut rates in September 2008. Later I'll explain why this isn't just Monday-morning quarterbacking; it should have been obvious to policy makers at the time.

Even after interest rates finally were cut to 0.25% in December 2008, the Fed was far from doing all it could. It could have cut them further, to 0.0%, or −0.25%, or −0.5%, or −0.75%. It could have done far more quantitative easing. More importantly, it could have adopted an alternative policy target, such as the "price-level targeting" that Bernanke recommended the Japanese adopt when they were faced with similar circumstances. Interestingly, Bernanke has recently resumed his advocacy of price-level targeting now that he is no longer Fed chair.[11]

In fairness, I think Bernanke did better than most other economists would have in his place. He was not a dictator—he had to work with many other policy makers at the Fed, some of whom had much less enlightened views on monetary policy. The Fed did far better in 2008–2009 than in 1929–1933, and far better than the European Central Bank did. Yet despite the policy of low interest rates and quantitative easing, monetary policy was still effectively tight, and this contributed greatly to an unnecessarily severe recession.

Bernanke has already admitted that the Great Depression was the Fed's fault. He has also asserted that the Fed deserves much of the blame for the Great Inflation of 1966–1981 and much of the credit for producing what he has called the "Great Moderation" of 1984–2007, a period when the economy performed rather well.[12] I agree with all three of these claims: all three "Greats" were strongly linked to Fed policy. So why is it so far-fetched to believe that the Great Recession was also at least partly the Fed's fault?

**Almost Everything You've Heard about the
Great Recession Is Wrong**

In the following chapters we'll go on an intellectual journey. It may involve
unlearning many things you "know" that actually just aren't so. Here are
just a few of the many myths regarding the Great Recession:

- Housing was a bubble that inevitably had to burst.
- The decline in home building caused a big rise in unemployment.
- Beginning in 2008, low interest rates represented easy money.
- Monetary policy was no longer highly effective at zero interest rates.
- NGDP and RGDP declined despite monetary stimulus from the Fed.
- The Fed was unable to stop the decline in GDP during 2008 because interest
  rates had already fallen to zero. (They had not.)
- The Fed cut interest rates as far as it could.
- The financial crisis caused the Great Recession.
- An economy cannot recover rapidly during and after a severe financial crisis.
- After the debt crisis many Americans struggled to make ends meet, and
  therefore it made sense for aggregate demand to decline—for Americans to
  "tighten their belts."

All these and many other misconceptions will be punctured in the following chapters.

Postscript

Just after this manuscript was completed and sent to the publisher, the US
was hit by the COVID-19 epidemic and spiraled into a deep depression of
uncertain duration. The primary cause of the depression was a real shock,
and hence is largely beyond the scope of this book. With nominal (monetary) shocks, the problem can be fixed with more money. When there's a
real shock that prevents people from working or shopping, simply injecting more money into the economy cannot solve the fundamental problem.

Nonetheless, there is a real danger that this epidemic could have secondary effects on nominal spending that end up making the depression
worse than necessary. In that case, expansionary monetary policy can play
a useful role. Early indications are that inflation is likely to fall during 2020

and 2021—exactly the opposite of what is appropriate when aggregate supply declines. Thus, while monetary policy cannot fix the constraints on output caused by COVID-19, a more stimulative monetary policy may be able to reduce the secondary effects of the epidemic on total nominal spending. I suspect that by the time you are reading this book, the problem will have largely shifted from the supply side to the demand side.

While reading this book, you'll notice a few claims that seem a bit out of tune with the COVID-19 slump. I've kept them in the final revision, as I don't wish to shift the focus from the demand shocks that typically drive US business cycles to the highly unusual events of 2020. This book attempts to explain normal business cycles—COVID-19 would require another very different book.

PART I

The Value of Money

CHAPTER ONE

Cognitive Illusions in Economics

Monetary economics is one of the most difficult fields within economics. Like theoretical physicists, monetary economists must be able to master highly abstract models, which seem far removed from reality. But they also need the wisdom and breadth of knowledge of historians. Not many people have both skill sets. In exasperation, Paul Krugman once said that he sometimes felt that he was the only person who understood liquidity traps.

I've devoted much of the past half century to studying money, and here I'll try to guide you through my long education on the subject. I'd like you to see what I saw at each stage of my life, understand what I learned from those events and models, and in the end come to see how I reached a contrarian view of monetary economics.

Think of the field of monetary economics as a vast labyrinth. This book tries to take you on the most direct path to the center of the maze. You'll follow in my footsteps, but without retracing all the wrong turns that I made. When you reach the end of the labyrinth, I hope you'll find that my view of the Great Recession no longer seems bizarre and contrarian— indeed, you might wonder how anyone could see the recession in any other way.

Cognitive Illusions

This book borrows from the title of my blog, *TheMoneyIllusion*. In economics, *money illusion* is one of the reasons that monetary shocks have real effects on the economy. People suffering from money illusion confuse real and nominal changes, and this causes a misallocation of resources, even to the point of affecting the business cycle of the economy. But in my work, I also use the phrase to refer to something else: the way that even many experts misinterpret what's going on with the monetary system.

The monetary system is a sort of "through the looking glass" world, where almost nothing is as it seems. What looks like up may be down, and what looks like left may be right. Thus, if the Fed wants permanently higher interest rates, it needs to first reduce interest rates. Sometimes printing lots of money indicates easy money; at other times it indicates tight money. In this book I devote almost as much effort to disproving common beliefs that just aren't true as I do to introducing new ideas about how the monetary system works.

Much of my blog is devoted to exposing what might be called *cognitive illusions*, the analytical counterpart of optical illusions. For instance, it is well established that our thinking can be distorted or "framed" by a powerful, emotionally charged context. Here is one of my favorite illustrations of this phenomenon: A few years back, a philosopher named Joshua Knobe was interviewed on *Bloggingheads.tv*. During the interview he discussed a fascinating experiment that explored what people mean by the term *intention*. Knobe described how two groups of people were told two slightly different stories and then were asked a question. The first group heard about an engineer who went to the chief executive officer of a company with a project that the engineer said would dramatically boost profits. But the CEO was told there was one drawback: the project would seriously harm the environment. The CEO responded, "I don't care about the environment; I only care about profits. Do the project."[1]

The second group heard a story that was exactly the same except in one detail: the CEO was told that the project would actually *help* the environment. Again, the CEO responded, "I don't care about the environment; I only care about profits. Do the project." In both cases the listeners were asked whether the CEO intentionally hurt (or helped) the environment. Most people in the first group said the CEO did intentionally hurt the environment, but most in the second group said that the CEO did not intentionally help the environment. And yet on closer inspection, it doesn't seem obvious why that distinction is logical.

I frequently saw a similar sort of confused reasoning when I taught economics. It's easy to convince students that when the costs a firm faces rise, the firm will pass at least part of the extra costs on in the form of higher prices. But if you reverse the example and have costs fall, students are much more reluctant to accept the conclusion that firms will cut prices.

But the worst part of this is their reasoning process. Instead of developing a hypothesis that would explain the asymmetry, students always try to tell me that firms are less likely to cut prices because they are greedy. And yet the model is clearly symmetrical. Firms raise prices when costs go up because higher costs make the profit-maximizing price rise. And for the exact same reason, lower costs make the profit-maximizing price fall. When costs fall, firms will cut prices *because they are greedy*.

If you think like an economist, then the correct answer is obvious: profit-maximizing prices are positively correlated with costs.[2] But if you think like most people, using the "moral outrage" part of your brain to interpret cold, hard facts about cause and effect, then you'll get hopelessly lost. That same moral outrage even colors our thinking about the meaning of "intention," as Knobe's example of the heartless CEO nicely illustrates.

Later we will see how these moral intuitions prevented people from seeing clearly what was going on during the housing crash and the Great Recession. We naturally gravitate toward stories with villains, whether they are greedy bankers, dishonest borrowers, or politicians trying to pressure regulators and banks to encourage more lending. There are lots of bad people out there, but that's equally true in poorly functioning and well-functioning economies, and during periods when the US economy is more stable and periods when it is less stable. Why did greed affect the economy in a different way in the year 2008?

Even worse, our puritan instincts lead us to assume that spending needs to fall after a period of excessive investment in housing—which is the worst possible response to the housing bust. Indeed, falling spending was what caused the Great Recession.

The Education of a Coin Collector

As a ten-year-old coin collector, I was already beginning to learn monetary economics without even knowing that the field existed. It was 1965, and there was a sudden shortage of US coins. Up until the end of 1964, all dimes, quarters, and half dollars had been made out of silver. Then the price of silver rose so high that the value of coins melted down into silver bars rose above their face value. Almost immediately the public began to hoard vast quantities of dimes and quarters, and the government had to try to quickly replace them with coins made out of cheaper metals such as copper and nickel. This is Gresham's law at work: bad money drives out good. People spend the bad money (and thus it continues circulating and facilitating transactions) while they hoard the good money, the money worth more than its face value.

In early 1968, the market price of gold in Europe rose above the official price of $35 per ounce. These two milestones, the complete demonetization of gold and silver, can be seen as triggering the Great Inflation of 1966–1981, or they can be seen as largely irrelevant sideshows. It's important, though, to think about these sorts of events from many different angles, in order to see that there isn't necessarily any one right or wrong approach.

The coin shortage of 1965 did not cause even a tiny recession; indeed, the mid-1960s saw a great economic boom. And recall that coins were more important back then, because the price level was far lower than it is today—a quarter in 1965 could buy more than a dollar bill can today. Because many recessions are caused by too little money, the fact that this coin shortage had no visible macroeconomic impact is worth thinking about.

It turns out that most money shortages are not really very important in the modern world, whereas money *scarcity* is very, very important.[3] Economists use the term *shortage* for cases where there is not enough of a good at the going market price: during the gasoline shortage in 1974, people would drive up to a gas station and find that it had no gasoline to sell, or that there was a line two blocks long. In contrast, greater scarcity simply reflects a decline in supply. In 2008 gas prices soared to $4 per gallon in the US, but people had no trouble finding gas to buy, because there were no price controls. The forces of supply and demand were able to find an equilibrium price and quantity. Unlike in 2008, the gasoline scarcity in 1974 turned into an outright shortage because price controls prevented prices from rising to a point at which supply equaled demand.

In 1965, there was enough (paper) money being injected into the economy to keep things booming. The shortage of coins was just a minor annoyance, as it made for a bit more hassle when shopping. In contrast, during late 2007 and early 2008 there was a reduction in the growth rate of the supply of currency, which triggered a recession.[4] There was no shortage of money—people could still access cash from ATMs—but the reduced supply of money depressed spending in the economy. Money was increasingly scarce.

Back in 1965, I was (subconsciously) absorbing another important lesson from coin collecting: the dates of American business cycles. Coins produced in years such as 1921 and 1931 were quite rare, and hence quite valuable. That's because during depression years the government tends not to produce very many new coins. So, on the basis of my comments regarding the 1965 coin shortage, you might assume that the low level of coin production during 1921 and 1931–1933 had no causal effect on the depression—that it was merely a symptom of the depressed economy. But remember, nothing is as it seems in the world of money. Although low coin production is not my preferred explanation for depressions, it is roughly as plausible as the traditional monetarist explanation. Before explaining why, let's briefly discuss the standard monetarist view of the Great Depression. After all, I've been labeled a "market monetarist," so monetarism presumably plays an important role in my views on macroeconomics.

Money and Business Cycles

My introduction to monetary economics was *A Monetary History of the United States, 1867–1960*, by Milton Friedman and Anna Schwartz. Friedman and Schwartz argued that much of the US business cycle could be explained by unstable Federal Reserve policy, which led to ups and downs in the money-supply growth rate. They focused on the broad monetary aggregates, which include not just currency notes and coins but also bank deposits. In their view, a counterfactual monetary policy that led to a much more stable growth path in the money supply would have resulted in much more stable growth in the economy.

Now let's return to the rare coins of 1921 and 1931. The example provided by the 1965 coin shortage shows that the *direct effect* of fewer coins is likely to be trivial. But there is a key difference between the coin shortage of 1965 and the rare coins of 1921 and 1931. In 1965 there was an actual *shortage* of coins, but not in 1921 or 1931. Instead, during a depression there are fewer transactions, and hence less "need" for coins. The government responds by producing fewer coins. The quantity of coins produced in 1921 and 1931 was in "equilibrium."

Friedman and Schwartz argued that the Great Depression was caused by a big drop in what's now called the *M2 money supply*, which includes coins and currency but mostly consists of bank deposits. They reached this conclusion by combining economic theory and statistical correlations. If faced with my example of coin scarcity, they probably would have argued that an economic depression led to fewer coins being produced. Coins had no major causal role, in their view, they were just a side effect.

TABLE 1.1 **Coin production data**

Year	1¢	5¢	10¢	25¢
2000	14,277,420,000	2,355,760,000	3,661,200,000	6,477,470,000
2001	10,334,590,000	1,303,384,000	2,782,390,000	4,806,984,000
2002	7,288,855,000	1,230,480,000	2,567,000,000	3,313,704,000
2003	6,848,000,000	824,880,000	2,072,000,000	2,280,400,000
2004	6,836,000,000	1,445,040,000	2,487,500,000	2,401,600,000
2005	7,700,050,500	1,741,200,000	2,835,500,000	3,013,600,000
2006	8,234,000,000	1,502,400,000	2,828,000,000	2,941,000,000
2007	7,401,200,000	1,197,840,000	2,089,500,000	2,796,640,000
2008	5,419,200,000	640,560,000	1,050,500,000	2,538,800,000
2009	2,354,000,000	86,640,000	146,000,000	533,920,000
2010	4,010,830,000	490,560,000	1,119,000,000	347,000,000
2011	4,938,540,000	990,240,000	1,502,000,000	391,200,000
2012	6,015,200,000	1,023,600,000	1,676,000,000	568,010,000
2013	7,070,000,000	1,223,040,000	2,112,000,000	1,455,200,000
2014	8,146,400,000	1,206,240,000	2,302,500,000	1,580,200,000
2015	9,365,300,000	1,599,600,000	3,041,010,000	2,990,820,000

Sources: US Mint, "Circulating Coins Production," accessed February 8, 2020, https://www.usmint.gov/about/production-sales-figures/circulating-coins-production; R. S. Yeoman, *A Guide Book of United States Coins.*

Just as the Fed doesn't directly control the quantity of coins being produced, however, it doesn't directly control the amount of bank deposits. Instead, Fed policies have an indirect influence on the quantity of bank deposits and the overall M2 money supply. Friedman and Schwartz argued that the Fed's contractionary monetary policy indirectly led to a reduction in M2, and that this depressed the overall economy. Alternatively, *and this is the key takeaway*, they suggested that a counterfactual monetary policy that kept M2 growing at a slow but steady rate would have allowed the US to largely avoid the Great Depression.

So here's a question to think about: Would a hypothetical alternative monetary policy that had the side effect of leading to a slow but steady growth rate in coin production have also allowed the US to avoid the Great Depression? How about the Great Recession? My answer to both questions is "quite likely." And if the answer is yes, does this mean that in some sense the scarcity of coins from 1931 to 1933 "caused" the Great Depression?

Consider the coin production data in table 1.1. Note the large decline in coin production during the Great Recession. Almost all economists would scoff at the notion that too little coin production causes recessions, and they may be right. But if they are right, I'm not sure it is for the right reason. I wonder how many economists have thought through what it means to say something "caused" a depression. Indeed, what does it mean to say any single factor "caused" anything to occur?

For instance, one could list at least four possible causes of Adolf Hitler taking power in 1933: nationalism, punitive war debts, economic distress in Germany, and Hitler's parents' decision to have a child in the first place. Most historians would take the first three causes much more seriously than the fourth, even though it is obviously true that in a counterfactual world where Hitler was never born, he would not have taken power in 1933. So why do we only like the first three of those four examples of "causal explanations"? Perhaps it's the pragmatic side of human nature. For most of our history we struggled to survive in a hostile environment, and we are always on the lookout for practical solutions to problems. Going back in a time machine to prevent someone's parents from procreating is not a practical solution to preventing war. Teaching our children to be less nationalistic, encouraging international cooperation in organizations such as the European Union, establishing magnanimous postwar programs like the Marshall Plan, and trying to prevent a repeat of the Great Depression are all plausible solutions to the problem of war and may well have contributed to the fact that Western Europe today is much less militaristic than it was during the first half of the twentieth century.

Similarly, a government policy could be said to have caused the Great Recession if a very plausible alternative policy setting of *the exact same policy tool that was already being used* would have avoided the recession. As an analogy, a bus driver might be said to have caused the bus to hit a tree if a different position of the steering wheel would have avoided the accident. We don't think of bus drivers as "solving accident problems," though; we hope they will not *cause* accidents.

Thus, if a recession could have been prevented by the Fed's setting of interest rates or the money supply (or both) at a different position, then the actual settings that were associated with a recession could be said to have "caused" the recession. Don't think of the Fed as "solving recession problems." Think of it as finding monetary policy settings that *avoid causing recessions*.

Friedman and Schwartz were probably correct when they argued that a contractionary monetary policy was to blame for the Great Depression in the US, and also that a counterfactual monetary policy that prevented a drop in the M2 money supply would have made any depression in the early 1930s far milder. But one could also make the same argument about a counterfactual policy that prevented a deep drop in coin production.

I've argued that neither causal explanation is best, because there are more *useful* explanations available.[5] That is, it probably doesn't make sense for central banks to target either M2 or coin production, because there are much better indicators to guide monetary policy. And yet, the fact that there are other, more useful causal explanations for the Great Depression doesn't mean that Friedman and Schwartz are completely "wrong," or that a claim that too little coin production caused the Great Depression (and the Great Recession) is incorrect. The test of a model should be its usefulness, including its applicability to a wide range of historical examples.

Earlier I mentioned the rising gold and silver prices during the late 1960s. Those events can also be thought about in two radically different ways. If the Fed had arranged its policy such that the US never stopped using silver coins, and also such that the free-market price of gold in Zurich never rose above $35 per ounce, then there would have been no Great Inflation during 1966–1981. But it's probably not wise to target either gold or silver prices, and so the next few chapters present much better explanations for the cause of the Great Inflation—that is, more *useful* explanations.

Correlation Does Not Prove Causation

In this chapter we've actually gotten ahead of ourselves. I've been suggesting that monetary policy contributes to the business cycle without giving you any good reason to believe this is the case. After all, lots of things are correlated with the business cycle. Steel production almost always drops during recessions; that doesn't mean the steel industry causes business cycles. So we have a lot more work to do to figure out *why* so many people think monetary policy is important. What is the causal mechanism?

Once we identify the root cause of business cycles, we will be able to come up with much better policy indicators than the M2 money supply or the scarcity of coins. Any true causal mechanism is likely to be reliably correlated with the business cycle. In contrast, M2 went out of favor as a policy indicator during the 1980s precisely because its correlation with the economy seemed to weaken over time.

Macroeconomics comprises three basic areas: real variables (e.g., real GDP, employment) in the long run; nominal variables (e.g., inflation, nominal GDP); and the business cycle, which involves short-run fluctuations

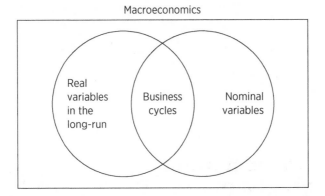

FIGURE 1.1. Components of macroeconomics

in real GDP and employment. Long-run growth is determined by nonmonetary factors such as labor-force growth and technology, inflation is determined by monetary policy, and the business cycle represents the interaction of real and nominal shocks (fig. 1.1).

Even though the business cycle is the most glamorous part of the monetary policy debate, we need to start with a much more basic question: how does monetary policy cause inflation and NGDP growth? Only after we figure out why monetary policy causes an economic problem that our basic economic theories tell us it should cause (inflation) can we begin to understand why monetary policy causes economic problems that our basic economic theories tell us it should not cause (recessions).

CHAPTER TWO

The Value of Money and Money Illusion

I came of age during the Great Inflation, which lasted roughly from 1966 to 1981. In retrospect, it was an ideal time to transition from coin collector to monetary economist. Not only did I have a front-row seat to some of the most dramatic changes in the value of money in American history, but I also learned a lesson in the relationship between the value of money and the value of commodities.

In early 1980, I noticed a Chicago gas station that was advertising gasoline for $.10 a gallon. This was in the midst of the second great oil shock, when most gas stations were charging about $1.20 a gallon. There was just one catch: you had to buy the gas with dimes and quarters minted before 1965.

As we saw in chapter 1, dimes and quarters were made out of silver through 1964. Fast-forward to 1979: silver prices had soared higher and higher throughout the year, and they reached a peak of nearly $50 per ounce in early 1980. (Around the same time, gold peaked at $850 per ounce.) Back in 1964, gold was worth only $35 an ounce, and silver was worth less than $1.50 an ounce.

In 1980, I paid for a portion of my final year of graduate school at the University of Chicago by selling the silver dollars that I'd collected as a child.

The Value of Money

What do we mean by the phrase "value of money"? Isn't a dollar always worth a dollar? Yes, but its ability to purchase other goods, services, and assets changes over time. Unfortunately there's no single way to measure the value of money. When we describe the value of other goods, we typically use money as a sort of measuring stick. But as soon as money itself becomes the item of interest, things get more confusing. For instance, if the price of a British pound in US dollars is $2, then the price of a dollar in British pounds is half a pound. If you are listening to the financial news and you hear something about the dollar falling in value, it's usually in reference to some other currency, such as the pound or euro.

Although foreign exchange rates are the most familiar way of thinking about the value of money, they are not the most useful. You can easily imagine a world with no foreign exchange rates at all—for instance, a world with a single currency. And yet even in that world we would still be very interested in the value of money in terms of its purchasing power.

Perhaps the most widely used definition of the value of money is the inverse of the price level:

$$\text{value of money} = \frac{1}{\text{price level}}.$$

The price level, also known as the *cost of living*, is a weighted average of the prices of all goods and services sold in the economy. Thus, if the price level doubles, then the purchasing power of each dollar bill halves. The inverse of the price level is not the only possible definition of value of money, and I don't even think it is the most useful one, but it's probably the definition that makes it easiest to understand the basic tenets of monetary economics. (Later we'll transition to a definition that involves aggregate nominal spending—the inverse of NGDP—which will prove even more useful.)

The inverse relationship between the value of money and the price level is very similar to what we saw in the foreign exchange example, and for exactly the same reason. Every transaction has two sides: you see yourself as buying gasoline for $4 a gallon; the gas station sees itself as buying dollars for one quart of gasoline per dollar.

If we define the value of money as the inverse of the price level ($1/P$), then changes in the value of money are inversely proportional to changes in the price level. This is a definition, not a theory. This means that any theory of inflation is equivalent to a theory of the value of money. It's not that the two are closely related, or that one causes the other: they are *exactly the same thing*. Inflation is nothing more than depreciation in the value of money. Depreciation is not a side effect of inflation; it *is* inflation—by definition.

This relationship also means that we measure the value of money by measuring the price level. We measure the price level with statistical tools called price indices, such as the consumer price index (CPI), the personal consumption expenditures price index, the producer price index, and the GDP deflator. These various indices represent alternative methods of measuring the value of money.

Economists use price indices to convert nominal or money values into real values:

$$\text{real value} = \frac{\text{nominal value}}{\text{price level}}.$$

For example, consider table 2.1, which reports the income of a hypothetical person—we'll call her Helen—in two different years. Helen's nominal income rose sixfold between 1980 and 2018, and yet her real income increased only twofold. She earned six times as many dollars in 2018 as in 1980, but she could purchase only twice as much in goods and services. This is because the price level also tripled and the value of money fell to one-third of what it had been in 1980. Because the dollar is a sort of measuring stick of value, all sorts of problems occur when the value of the dollar is itself changing over time.

Let's take the measuring stick analogy a bit further with an example. Imagine that a child, Jacob, gets measured in 1980 and is one yard tall. In 2018, he is measured again and is found to have grown to be six feet tall (table 2.2). Jacob's proud father announces that his son has grown sixfold, from one yard to six feet, and you privately think, "What a dummy." The

TABLE 2.1 **Hypothetical Helen's income**

Year	Nominal income	CPI	Real income	Value of money
1980	$20,000	1.0	$20,000	1
2018	$120,000	3.0	$40,000	$\frac{1}{3}$

TABLE 2.2 **Hypothetical Jacob's height**

Year	Height	Average unit length	Real height	Length of measuring stick
1980	1 yard	1.0	1 yard	1 yard
2018	6 feet	3.0	2 yards	$\frac{1}{3}$ yard

measuring stick has changed, and so Jacob actually only experienced a twofold "real growth" in height. It would be silly to say Jacob is six times as tall as he was in 1980.

The example of Jacob is essentially identical to the previous case of real and nominal income. Saying that Helen earns six times as much as in 2018 as in 1980 is just as silly as claiming that Jacob has grown sixfold. Not only would the two claims be equally silly; we would be making *exactly the same mistake* in each case. In both cases the unit of measurement has shrunk by two-thirds between 1980 and 2018. In both cases this makes the average item being measured look three times bigger, merely because of "inflation." But in both cases the specific things being measured actually did increase in real terms: they *really did get bigger*. Helen made twice as much income in real terms, and Jacob grew to twice his original height in real terms. So it's not all inflation.

I like the yardstick analogy because it helps us to better understand what inflation actually *is*. Many people think of inflation as lots and lots of prices going up—but that's not a very useful way to think about it. Suppose that we kept shrinking our measuring sticks by about 5% each year. Would you think, "Gee, it seems like as time goes by the things that I am measuring, on average, keep getting bigger and bigger"? Of course not. You would see that the essential change was a shrinking measuring stick and that the bigger numbers associated with measurements were just an implication of that shorter stick.

Yes, inflation does imply that nominal prices are rising, but at a fundamental level inflation is all about a fall in the value of money. Later chapters will show that it's far easier to understand inflation and deflation if we think in terms of explaining changes in the value of money than if we try to imagine the factors that would be changing the prices of each and every good, service, and asset in the economy.

During much of the Great Inflation, people did try to explain the problem by searching for factors that were pushing up specific wages and prices. Indeed, in a sense the Great Inflation was *caused* by this misconception. Policy makers were treating the symptoms of inflation with failed policies such as price controls rather than treating the root cause by printing less money. Only in the early 1980s, when economists began to recognize rising prices as a *monetary phenomenon*, were policy makers able to figure out how to get inflation under control. Unfortunately, most economists still don't recognize the 2008–2009 deflation as also being fundamentally monetary, an oversight I hope to address.

So far we've defined the value of money in two ways: in terms of foreign exchange rates and in terms of the dollar's purchasing power over goods and services ($1/P$). But there are many other definitions as well. Later we'll see that it might be more useful to define money in terms of a dollar's ability to buy labor or to purchase a share of nominal GDP.

Some people prefer to define the value of money in terms of gold: stable money means a stable price of gold. That doesn't make much sense today, but before 1933 that definition would have been considered standard. During the period of the gold standard, the $1/P$ concept that economists now accept was considered an exotic and controversial definition for the value of money.

Money Illusion

As I explained in chapter 1, economists use the term *money illusion* to refer to cases in which people treat money as a stable measuring stick of value. In his 1928 book *The Money Illusion* (from which I borrowed the title of my blog and this book), Irving Fisher illustrates this concept with a wonderful example of an American woman who owed money on a mortgage in Germany:

> The [First] World War came and she had no communication with Germany for two years. After the war she visited Germany, intending to pay the mortgage. She had always thought of it as a debt of $7000. It was legally a debt of 28,000 marks, in terms of German money. She went to the banker who had the matter in charge and said: "I want to pay that mortgage of $7000." He replied: "The amount isn't $7000; it is 28,000 marks; that sum today is about $250." She said: "Oh! I am not going to take advantage of the fall of the mark. I insist upon paying the $7000." The banker could not see the point; he showed that legally this was not necessary and could not understand her scruples. As a matter of fact, however, she herself failed to take account of the corresponding, though lesser, change in the dollar. She was thinking in terms of American dollars, just as the banker was thinking in terms of German marks. She insisted on paying $7000 instead of paying $250, but she would have rebelled if she had been told that the dollar had also fallen, that the equivalent in buying power of the original debt was not $7000, but $12,000, and that she ought, therefore, to pay $12,000! Then *she* would not have seen the point![1]

In this example the concept of the value of money is moving around so much that it's hard not to get dizzy. American goods that cost $7 before

World War I cost about $12 after the war. But because the dollar was still pegged to gold at a fixed rate, most Americans thought of the value of the US dollar as being stable. As soon as they traveled to another country with much worse inflation and saw the sharply depreciated exchange rate, they could recognize a change in the value of money. In fact, there's no solid ground to stand on here. Values are always shifting in terms of one good or asset, even if they are stable in terms of another good or asset.

There's also a lesson here for gold enthusiasts who insist on measuring values in terms of a fixed weight of gold. Even gold itself has an unstable value that rises and falls with shifts in supply and demand (mostly with changes in demand). So why do gold and silver have a reputation for having relatively stable values?

Gold and silver are examples of *commodity money*, or goods that are often chosen as the measuring stick of value (termed the *medium of account* or *numeraire*). The medium of account is the thing used to measure value, and the unit of account is the name given to one unit of money. Thus, when Fisher wrote *The Money Illusion* in 1928, gold was America's medium of account and the US dollar was the unit of account. In Britain in 1928, gold was also the medium of account and the British pound was the unit of account.[2]

Typically, a commodity does not persistently rise or fall in value against other commodities over very long periods of time. And throughout history, it turns out that gold and silver are pretty typical commodities. In the very long run, their value doesn't change very much against the value of other commodities. Because inflation is a decrease in the value of money, under a gold or silver standard one tends to see relatively little change in the price level over very long periods of time.

In the short run, however, things are often quite different. Shifts in the demand for gold and silver can cause big swings in the value of those commodities. During World War I, gold fell in value as the European powers sold off their gold stocks to pay for weapons. Prices of goods and services rose sharply. In the 1970s, even the *relative* values of gold and silver soared as the public hoarded precious metals as inflation hedges. (Yes, almost all prices rose during the 1970s, but the price of gold rose far more than the prices of most other goods.)

Think about the example from the beginning of this chapter, of buying gasoline with silver coins at $.10 per gallon: it illustrates both sides of the debate over commodity money. To a hard-money enthusiast, it shows how commodity money can hold its purchasing power. A dime could buy a gallon of gasoline in 1980, which means it had even more purchasing power in 1980 than during the Great Depression.[3] In contrast, to a hard-money skeptic this example shows that gold and silver can occasionally be too good a store of value. Back in 1964 (when dimes were still made out of silver), gasoline cost about $.30 a gallon—three dimes. So the fact that a single silver dime could buy a gallon of gas in 1980 meant the value of silver had risen sharply in terms of its purchasing power. When a commodity is used as the medium of account, a gain in its value is called *deflation*.

This is also what happened in the early 1930s: the hoarding of gold (mostly by central banks) led to an increase in the value or purchasing power of gold, which was deflationary for the global economy. In a sense this increase *caused* the Great Depression.[4] In contrast, the rise in the relative values of gold and silver in the 1970s did not lead to deflation, because gold and silver were no longer used as money. It merely drove their nominal prices higher.

Under a gold standard, gold is the one good whose nominal price never changes. Once again, Irving Fisher shares an amusing example in *The Money Illusion*:

> I once jokingly asked my dentist—at a time when people were complaining about "the high cost of living"—whether the cost of gold for dentistry had risen. To my surprise he took me seriously and sent his clerk to look up the figures. She returned and said: "Doctor, you are paying the same price for your gold that you always have."
>
> Turning to me the dentist said: "Isn't that surprising? Gold must be a very steady commodity."
>
> "It's exactly as surprising," I said, "as that a quart of milk is always worth 2 pints of milk."
>
> "I don't understand," he said.
>
> "Well, what is a dollar?" I asked.
>
> "I don't know," he replied. "That's the trouble," I said. "The dollar is approximately one twentieth of an ounce; there are, therefore, twenty dollars in an ounce of gold, and naturally an ounce of gold must be worth $20. The dollar is a unit of weight, just as truly as the ounce is the unit of weight masquerading as a stable unit of value, or buying power."[5]

During my lifetime, the value of the US dollar (i.e., 1/P) has risen only once, in 2009. Later we'll see that this increase contributed to the Great Recession. But first we need to answer a much more basic question: what determines the value of money under a modern fiat system in which we use paper money without any gold or silver backing?

CHAPTER THREE

What Determines the Value of Money?

We have seen already that the value of money is often defined as its purchasing power, which is the inverse of the price level (1/P). That means that we can explain changes in the price level over time by modeling changes in the value of money. Why was there very little change in the price level between 1776 and 1933? Why are consumer prices now nineteen times higher than they were in 1933? Why did the rate of inflation increase sharply in the late 1960s and 1970s, and then fall sharply in the 1980s and 1990s? Why did America experience deflation in 2009 for the first time in more than fifty years?

All of these questions, and many more, can be explained with a fairly simple model of the value of money. What model do you think I plan to use? Here's a hint: suppose we think about the value of something other than money—say apples, or men's haircuts, or single-family homes with 2,400 square feet in Irvine, California. In almost any case, economists would begin an analysis of value with a basic supply-and-demand model.

The Supply and Demand for Commodity Money

At this point you might be scratching your head. Supply and demand tell us the dollar prices of goods and services, but what do we mean by the *price of money*? Isn't a dollar always a dollar? In fact, if you've read the fine print in an Economics 101 textbook, you'll have discovered that the basic model of supply and demand is generally used to explain the *real* or *relative* price of goods. Thus, the variable on a vertical axis is not the dollar price of apples; rather, it is the price of apples relative to other goods. If the overall CPI rose by 5% while the price of apples rose by 7%, then we would say the relative price of apples rose by roughly 2%. That's what the supply-and-demand model explains.

And this is exactly how we will treat the value of money. The nominal price of a $1 bill is always fixed at 1.0, but its real value—that is, its purchasing power—moves inversely to the price level. If prices rise by 3%, then the value of money falls by 3%.

But does this model actually explain anything? For instance, consider figure 3.1, which shows the US price level from the colonial period until 2012. It looks as though prices were pretty flat until the 1930s and have been soaring ever since. But that's a bit misleading, because the scale of the graph makes it hard to see price-level fluctuations during the commodity money period (before 1933). There were sizable price spikes during wartime, but then prices usually fell back after the war. As late as 1933, prices were roughly comparable to what they had been 150 years earlier, when the Revolutionary War ended.

With a logarithmic scale (fig. 3.2), the slope of the line represents the rate of inflation or deflation. At this scale, it's easier to see how price inflation sped up during the Great Inflation of 1966–1981 and slowed afterward. You can also see substantial volatility during the commodity money period, with episodes of inflation typically followed by deflation. But since World War II, the US has experienced almost nonstop inflation. So that's what we need to explain with our basic supply-and-demand model.

Let's first try to explain the long-run near-zero trend rate of inflation during the commodity money period. No change in the price level means no change in the value of money relative to that of other goods and services. Does this seem surprising? Recall that under a commodity money system, money is itself a "good." There is no obvious reason why the particular good chosen as money (gold or silver) should change in value relative to other goods and services. If it's a typical good, then over the very long run its value might well be fairly stable.

But over shorter periods we do see significant price-level volatility prior to 1933, both up and down, despite a long run trend rate of near zero inflation. The volatility during the Civil War is easy to explain: the US temporarily left the commodity money standard and printed lots of "greenbacks." We'll consider fiat money inflation later. But what about the other price-level changes when a gold or silver standard was in effect?

Let's think about this in terms of the supply and demand for silver. Figure 3.3 shows a decline in demand for silver, which means that silver becomes less valuable. If silver is money, then the price level increases.

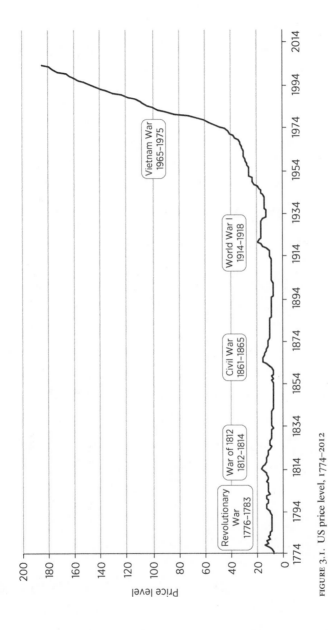

FIGURE 3.1. US price level, 1774–2012

Source: Cambridge, https://hsus.cambridge.org/HSUSWeb/toc/tableToc.do?id=Cc1–2

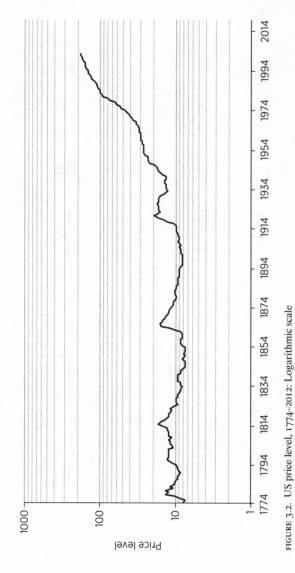

FIGURE 3.2. US price level, 1774–2012: Logarithmic scale

Source: Cambridge, https://hsus.cambridge.org/HSUSWeb/toc/tableToc.do?id=Cc1–3

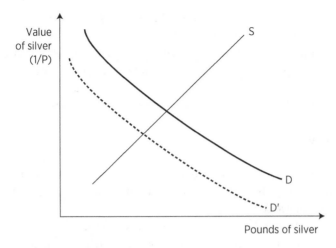

FIGURE 3.3. Supply and demand for silver

When a big silver discovery increases the supply, the value of silver falls and the price level rises in a way that is inversely proportional to the fall in the value of money. Thus, the long European inflation of 1500–1650 was primarily caused by Christopher Columbus, whose discoveries initiated a huge flow of silver from Mexico and Peru to Europe. A greater supply of silver leads to a lower value of silver, which implies higher prices for goods and services purchased with silver.

Eventually, most nations switched from a silver standard to a gold standard. In the US, the unit of account was the dollar, defined (between 1879 and 1933) as 1/20.67 of an ounce of gold. From 1879 to 1897, the demand for gold increased faster than the supply. This raised the value of gold and also reduced prices, and a long deflation resulted. In the late 1890s, new gold discoveries and better mining techniques boosted the supply of gold faster than demand, and prices began to gradually increase.

Because governments generally don't operate gold mines, monetary policy can affect the price level only by shifting the *demand* for gold. The period around World War I offers a good example of this principle. At that time, many European governments sold off gold to pay for the war. This reduced the demand for gold and hence reduced its value, just as in the silver example graphed in figure 3.3. The result was global inflation in any country on the gold standard, even in places such as the US that were not forced to sell gold in order to pay for the war. Under a gold standard, an expansionary monetary policy occurs when a government reduces its demand for gold, which reduces gold's value and boosts prices.

The opposite situation occurred after World War I. European central banks rebuilt their gold stocks, and in the 1930s there were occasional periods of private gold hoarding during crisis periods when investors lost confidence in paper assets. The periods of hoarding by central banks and private individuals did not occur gradually over time but came in bursts: in the early 1920s and again in the early 1930s. In both periods, the increased demand for gold raised gold's value and drove the price level substantially lower. Later we'll consider the impact of deflation on the business cycle.

During 1933, President Roosevelt began devaluing the dollar, and he took it all the way down to 1/35th of an ounce of gold in 1934. (Alternatively, you can think of FDR as raising the dollar price of gold from $20.67 per ounce to $35 per ounce.) Devaluing the dollar is analogous to shortening the measuring stick: because the dollar after 1934 was defined as a smaller chunk of gold than it had been before the devaluation, it did not buy as much as it did before. Prices rose, although the full impact of the rise would not be felt until World War II.

This quasi–gold standard at $35 per ounce lasted from 1934 to 1968, when the US let the free-market price of gold rise above $35 per ounce.[1] The prices of consumer goods rose gradually under this transition regime, despite a stable gold price, mostly because the US government and other governments gradually reduced their demand for gold reserves. After March 1968, however, foreign individuals could no longer exchange US dollars for gold at $35 per ounce, and the price of gold in the free market (in Europe) began to rise above the official price. The US and Europe had fully transitioned to a fiat money standard, with no effective commodity backing for paper money.

The Mysterious World of Fiat Money

Unfortunately, in 1968 the implications of this new fiat money standard were not immediately apparent. The old commodity money system had not been eliminated all at once but rather was being phased out gradually. In 1933, FDR made it illegal for Americans to own gold bullion. In 1968, the gold window was closed to foreign individuals. In 1971, the gold window was closed to foreign central banks. By this time gold seemed an anachronism, or—as John Maynard Keynes had suggested back in 1923—a "barbarous relic."[2] And yet commodities such as gold and silver had been anchoring the price level for centuries. The anchor had occasionally slipped a bit, as when FDR devalued the dollar in 1933, but the commodity anchor had still determined the price level in a fairly understandable way. The price level was determined by the supply and demand for 1/20.67 of an ounce of gold, or 1/35th of an ounce after 1934.

After 1968, however, it wasn't at all clear what determined the price level. Even today economists don't fully agree about how to model fiat money. Policy makers were initially confused by the new system and allowed the inflation rate to soar dramatically higher, peaking at 12% in 1980 (fig. 3.4). During the 1980s, they finally figured out that monetary policy was driving inflation and came up with policies to keep inflation under control. The Fed has done a pretty good job of keeping the inflation rate close to 2% during recent decades. Later we'll look at how it did this, but first let's think about how to model inflation under a fiat money system.

Under a gold standard, the long-run rate of inflation is determined by the fundamentals of the gold-mining industry (gold supply) and by the rate of real economic growth (which affects gold demand).[3] During the US gold-standard period, the average rate of inflation was roughly zero. This was a sort of lucky coincidence, because it just so happens that growth in the supply of gold (which averaged about 2% or 3% per year) was roughly equal to growth in the demand for gold and silver, which was a product of economic growth.[4]

In contrast, under a fiat money system, the long-run rate of inflation is whatever the government wants it to be, selected as someone might choose from a restaurant menu: "Hmmm, I think I'll order (the Fed to produce) 2% annual inflation this century." That's because the government has an essentially unlimited ability to vary the growth rate of paper money. It gets to pick the average inflation rate over extended periods of time, even if month-to-month changes are hard to control.

So far I've also skimmed over one additional complication: there is no generally accepted definition of *money*. Many economists like definitions that focus on the role of money as a medium of exchange; these definitions often include as money assets such as checking-account balances. I prefer to focus on the role of money as a medium of account, the ultimate source of liquidity. Under the gold standard, if you received a $100 bill, you might want to take it to the Treasury to exchange for "real money"—that is, just under five ounces of gold.

In times of stress, such as early 1933, gold was the ultimate liquid asset. Even currency might be devalued—and it *was* devalued in 1933. That's not to say that one cannot model money using cash and bank balances,

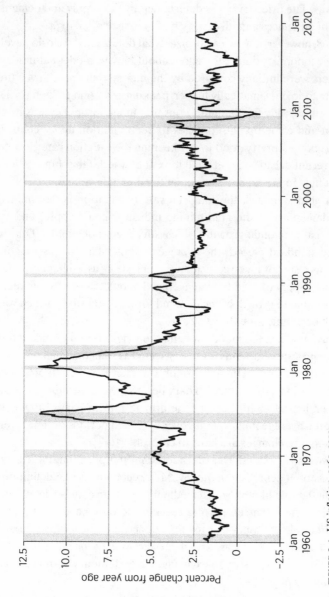

FIGURE 3.4. US inflation, 1960–2019

Note: Gray bars indicate periods of recession.

Source: FRED, via U.S. Bureau of Economic Analysis (BEA), https://fred.stlouisfed.org/series/PCEPI

even under a gold standard. It's just that the gold market offers the most useful method of modeling changes in the price level. Indeed, I wrote a whole book on the Great Depression using exactly that method.[5]

When a government moves from a gold standard to a fiat money regime, the monetary base takes over from gold as the ultimate form of liquidity. The monetary base is composed of cash and bank reserves, and it is the sort of fiat money that people have in mind when they talk about governments "printing money." If you sell something at a garage sale and receive a $100 check, you might take the check to the bank to exchange it for some "real money"—that is, cash.

Before 2008, the monetary base was about 98% cash (paper currency and coins) and about 2% electronic bank reserves at the Fed. I wish that were still the case, because cash is much easier to explain than electronic bank reserves at the Fed, but by 2019 the monetary base was roughly 50% electronic bank reserves. Nonetheless, I'll first give you a simple example of money creation in which the base is entirely paper currency or coins (as was the case before 1913), and then we'll figure out what has changed in the brave new world of quantitative easing.

One advantage of defining *money* as the monetary base is that this definition makes it much easier to explain monetary theory. The Fed clearly has complete control over the supply of base money—full stop. Banks don't "create" this type of money unless they want to be arrested for counterfeiting. This makes it possible to model the price level by simply looking at the interaction between changes in the supply of money, determined by the Fed, and changes in the demand for money, determined by the public.

We'll assume that the supply of money is a vertical line, set by the central bank. This is different from when gold was money, because central banks are not at all like profit-maximizing gold mines, which increase gold production as the value of gold rises. Central banks can set the fiat money supply wherever they like.

Figure 3.5 shows the supply and demand for base money, before and after an increase in the money supply. Readers may notice in this figure two differences from figure 3.3, which modeled supply and demand for silver: (1) the supply of money is now assumed to be vertical (completely inelastic), and (2) the demand for money is assumed to be unit elastic.[6] In contrast, no assumptions were made about the elasticity of demand for silver, except that demand for silver is downward-sloping. So where does this *unit-elastic* assumption come from? And why is it just for fiat money?

As we will see, the key distinction between silver and fiat money is that people like silver for all sorts of reasons, not just because it can be used as

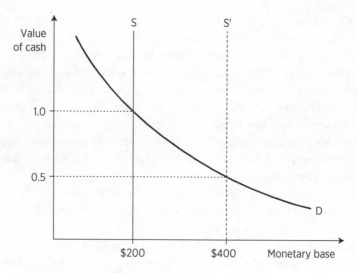

FIGURE 3.5. Supply and demand for fiat money

FIGURE 3.6. Currency note for one US dollar

money. You might want a nice set of silverware, for instance. In contrast, cash has no use other than as money. We don't typically frame currency and put it on the wall (although older currency notes can be quite beautiful; fig. 3.6). Rather, we like currency only because we can buy stuff with it. That assumption turns out to be really important.

Helicopter Drops and the Hot-Potato Model

To better explain the demand for cash, I'm going to start with the famous helicopter-drop thought experiment. Yes, it's unrealistic, and we'll look at more realistic cases. But there's no getting away from the fact that this is a beautiful thought experiment—in my view, the most interesting one in all of macroeconomics. Ben Bernanke used this example so frequently that Wall Street traders gave him the nickname "Helicopter Ben."

Imagine a country with one million people. Each person holds, on average, $200 in cash at any given time. (The people get cash from ATMs and then gradually spend it before restocking.) The total stock of cash in circulation is therefore $200 million.

Why does the average person hold about $200 in cash? The amount of cash one chooses to hold is an economic decision like any other. More cash means more convenience but also a risk of loss or theft plus a little bit of forgone interest from alternative investment options such as certificates of deposit. (We will assume cash pays no interest.) So people weigh the costs and benefits of more cash and find an equilibrium quantity they prefer. We call that quantity the public's "demand for money." It's the aggregate amount of money the public prefers to hold.

Here it might help to visualize yourself as a citizen in this imaginary country. Maybe $200 is enough to buy a week's worth of stuff that you spend cash on. Forget about checks, credit cards, and so forth; I'm interested only in what you spend cash on, no matter how small a share of your spending. The question I want you to think about is this: Who determines how much money you carry in your wallet, you or the chair of the Federal Reserve System? Most people feel that they have free will—that they determine how much money they carry in their wallet. They determine how often they go to the ATM and how much they withdraw each time. But does the public really determine its demand for money? Yes and no.

Now suppose that the central bank of our hypothetical country decides to double the money supply from $200 million to $400 million. The central bank knows that the public prefers to hold only $200 million at the moment, but it doesn't care. It is bound and determined to inject another $200 million into the economy, and no one is going to stop it. It concocts a plan to drop the new money from helicopters, to force it on people who prefer to carry $200 in their wallets, not $400. So what happens to that extra $200 per capita? Does the central bank force the public to hold this extra money or not? Yes and no. (I warned you monetary economics wasn't easy.)

What if you grabbed some of that extra money fluttering in the air—what would you do with it? You might try to get rid of it by spending it. But now the fallacy of composition kicks in—what's true for an individual may not be true for society as a whole. Any single individual can get rid of unwanted cash by spending it. But when you spend it, you literally "pass the buck," saddling other people with excess cash balances so that they now have more than they prefer to hold.

There's no getting around the basic math. If there are one million people and the money supply has doubled from $200 million to $400 million, then the average person's cash holdings have doubled from $200 to $400. The central bank has "forced" people to hold more cash than they wish, or so it seems at first glance. But we have not reached the end of the story. Deep down, you are likely to still believe that the Fed cannot force you to hold more cash. And in a certain sense you are right.

We started by assuming that individuals choose the size of their cash holdings. And that's true, isn't it? *You* decide how much to carry in your wallet, not the Fed. So how can we reconcile these two perceptions? One perception is that we as individuals determine how much cash is in our wallets. And the other perception is that our average holdings, per capita, are determined by the central bank. Don't these perceptions conflict?

The *hot-potato model* provides a resolution to this paradox, and that resolution is the single most important idea in monetary economics. As people attempt to get rid of excess cash balances, they spend their unwanted cash. This increases the demand for goods and services, which is called *aggregate demand*. As demand rises, prices start to move upward. How much higher do prices rise? Take a look at the supply and demand model in figure 3.5. Where is the new equilibrium? Notice that we assume the value of money has fallen in half. That means the price level must have doubled. And that means that a doubling of the supply of cash should lead to a doubling of the price level, at least if we are correct about the demand for money being unit elastic.

Now let's think about why the price level has doubled. We began by assuming that the typical person wishes to hold enough money to do one week's worth of shopping. Then the Fed tries to force the public to hold twice as much money—$400 per person. Initially, the public tries to get rid of these excess cash balances by spending the money. This increase in aggregate demand begins to drive prices higher. Once the price level has doubled, then people are again holding just enough cash to buy one week's worth of purchases. Once again we are in equilibrium.

Earlier I asked whether the public actually determines its demand for money; the answer was yes and no. Now you can see why. The Fed controls the *nominal* quantity of money in the US economy. If it wants to increase the money supply, there's nothing the public can do about it. Unless people want to burn the new money in their fireplaces, they must hold these increased cash balances. But the public determines the *real* demand for money. So if the nominal supply is larger than what the public prefers to hold, people act in such a way that they drive up the price level until real cash balances reach the public's preferred equilibrium.

The preceding example obviously leaves out many aspects of the real world. For instance, do people actually have to hold on to the extra money created by the Fed, in aggregate? Couldn't they just burn it in their fire-places or throw it in the trash? More plausibly, how about putting it in the bank? That's an interesting question, which we will explore in future chapters. Cash put into banks is called *reserves*, and recall that the monetary base is the sum of cash held by the public and reserves, at any given moment. The Fed actually injects base money, and the public (including banks) decides whether to hold it in the form of cash or bank reserves.

In the end, however, banks don't really prevent the hot-potato effect, at least when interest rates are positive. That's because banks also have a preferred level of cash balances—that is, a preferred level of reserves. Until 2008, banks preferred to hold very low levels of bank reserves, be-cause reserves did not earn interest and thus were not profitable to hold. So the hot-potato effect didn't end with cash being deposited in banks; bankers moved the money out into circulation as quickly as possible.

The helicopter-drop thought experiment may seem fanciful, but it il-lustrates the single most important concept in all of macroeconomics. Nothing else in macroeconomics will make any sense until you under-stand it. The hot-potato effect results from the interaction of two factors. One is the idea that the public has a well-defined "demand for money" and that people demand money solely because it has purchasing power. Entire books have been written on the demand for money, and we'll learn much more about that in the next chapter. The other factor is the central bank monopoly on the production of fiat money, and in particular the idea that central banks like the Fed have a virtually unlimited ability to adjust the size of the monetary base. The interaction of these two factors means that the Fed controls the price level and, by implication, *all nominal val-ues in the economy*. That's right, the Fed even controls the nominal allow-ance you give your daughter each week (assuming that the real allowance is what you care about).

Go back and look at figure 3.5. The Fed can generate any price level it wants by making a suitable adjustment in the money supply. There's a rea-son that inflation in the US has averaged about 1.95% since 1990: the Fed has been targeting inflation at 2%. Before it did so, the US had decades with much higher inflation (the 1940s and 1970s) and decades with serious deflation (the 1880s, 1920s, and 1930s).

It's Not Rocket Science—But Is It Easier or Harder?

Back in 1752, David Hume described something very much like a helicopter drop:

> Suppose four-fifths of all the money in GREAT BRITAIN to be annihilated in one night, and the nation reduced to the same condition, with regard to specie [gold and silver], as in the reigns of the HARRYS and EDWARDS, what would be the consequence? Must not the price of all labour and commodities sink in proportion, and every thing be sold as cheap as they were in those ages? . . . Again, suppose, that all the money of GREAT BRITAIN were multiplied fivefold in a night, must not the contrary effect follow?[7]

Although Hume was a brilliant philosopher (and also an economist), it doesn't take a genius to understand the basic idea. Try presenting a version of the helicopter drop to a child, perhaps a ten- or twelve-year-old. "Would it be a good idea for the government to print up a million dollars for each American, and just give people the money for free? We'd all be rich!" In my experience, even young children are able to guess that this is too good to be true. My daughter was able to do so at an age when she was much too young to know any real economics. This stuff isn't rocket science.

On the other hand, there are probably very few people who fully understand the helicopter drop—probably far fewer than the number who understand rocket science (i.e., Newtonian mechanics). For instance, in 2009 the US government did something that was quite similar to our imaginary helicopter drop. It borrowed more than a trillion dollars and then had the Fed buy up that extra debt with new base money. By the end of 2009, the base had more than doubled from its mid-2008 level. And yet there was no inflation, which surprised even some distinguished economists. To understand why prices didn't rise, we need to explore the concept of demand for money in greater depth. In the next chapter we begin that process by focusing on the example provided by the Great Inflation that swept most of the world from the 1960s to the 1980s.

CHAPTER FOUR

The Quantity Theory of Money and the Great Inflation

Fiat money is not like gold or silver; it is valued only to the extent that it has purchasing power. This has a very interesting implication. If you suddenly double the quantity of cash in circulation, people will initially try to get rid of their excess cash balances. Equilibrium won't be restored until the price level has doubled, and the public again is holding its preferred real cash balances. The intuition behind the famous helicopter-drop thought experiment is what underlies the quantity theory of money (QTM). But exactly what do economists mean by the *quantity theory of money*? I'm not entirely sure, but here are five possibilities:

1. The theory that an X% change in the money supply will be associated with an X% change in the price level.
2. The theory that an X% change in the money supply will be associated with an X% change in nominal GDP.
3. The theory that an X% change in the money supply will *cause* the price level and NGDP to be X% higher than otherwise, in the long run.
4. The theory that rapid, sustained periods of money supply growth are a necessary and sufficient condition for rapid, sustained periods of high inflation.
5. The theory that inflation and NGDP growth are best analyzed by modeling the supply and demand for money.

In each case, we can employ many different definitions of the money supply, including the monetary base (which I use), M1 (which also includes checking account balances), and M2 (which includes all types of bank account balances).

In the social sciences, theories are almost never exactly true. I'm interested not in which version is the "actual" quantity theory of money, but in
which ones are useful. As we will see, versions 1 and 2 are not very useful.
We cannot reliably expect a 10% rise in the money supply to be associated
with a 10% rise in the price level, or in NGDP. The latter three versions,
though, are pretty useful. In this chapter we'll look at the sort of data that
sold me on these three versions of the QTM back when I was in college.

The Equation of Exchange Is Not the Quantity Theory of Money

Most textbooks try to explain the QTM using the following equation, called
the *equation of exchange*:

$$M \times V = P \times Y.$$

As a result, many students end up wrongly thinking that the equation of
exchange *is* the quantity theory of money. Not only is MV = PY not the
QTM; it's not a theory at all. It's an identity, which has *nothing at all* to do
with the QTM. It's sort of the monetary version of confusing Y = C + I + G
with Keynesian economics.

So MV = PY is not the QTM. Then what is it? Most explanations go
as follows: M is the money supply, P is the price level, and Y is real GDP.
That means that P × Y is nominal GDP, the total value of spending on
final goods, during a given year. Suppose the money supply is $1 trillion.
Also suppose that NGDP is $52 trillion. Then it stands to reason that V
must be 52, which represents (supposedly) the average number of times
each dollar is spent on goods and services, in a given year. That's why V is
called the *velocity of circulation*. If there is $1 trillion in money supply and
$52 trillion in spending, then each dollar must be spent 52 times per year,
or about once a week.

At least that's the story. But is it true? Right away we should be suspi-
cious, because there are many definitions of the money supply, but only
one P × Y. Can the equation be true for all of them? And what about
money spent on goods that are not a part of GDP? What about barter?
In fact, we can never measure V directly. Instead, we measure the other
three variables and insert the value of V than makes the equation work. It
would have been better to call V the multiplier, but unfortunately that term
is already employed elsewhere in economics. So we are stuck with a misleading term for a very useful equation.

Another point of confusion relates to the fact that $M \times V = P \times Y$ is an identity; that is, it is true by definition. It's often argued that identities are not useful because they cannot establish causal relationships. It's true that they don't show causation, but nonetheless they are quite useful. Indeed, economics is full of identities, and many people who hate the $MV = PY$ identity love the $Y = C + I + G$ identity.

The key is to never make causal claims without good evidence. Thus, we cannot simply assume that because the equation of exchange always holds true, an increase in M will lead to an increase in P—just as in Keynesian economics we cannot simply assume that an increase in G (government output) will lead to an increase in Y (real GDP). In either case, there are two other variables that might also change. But then why do I insist that the equation is so useful?

The equation of exchange gives us hints about how to model inflation and how to model changes in NGDP. In chapter 3 we took a first pass at the question by considering the helicopter-drop thought experiment. In that case, we doubled the money supply, holding the demand curve for money fixed. In the new equilibrium, the value of money fell in half and the price level doubled. Now we can see that this thought experiment was equivalent to assuming that both V and Y were fixed, and that an increase in the money supply (M) led to a proportional increase in the price level (P). Now that we have the equation of exchange, we can immediately see that any discrepancy between the change in M and the change in P will be due to a change in real GDP or a change in velocity (or both). Thus, we can "explain" inflation by explaining M, V, and Y. And that's what I intend to do.

Sherlock Holmes Investigates the Great Inflation

To make this a bit more interesting, let's treat it as a detective story. I'm going to give you my all-time favorite data set, and you and I will figure out all the key ideas in monetary economics, merely by looking for *clues* to support our model of money supply and demand.

Before beginning, let me point out that economists are usually more interested in data expressed as rates of change. When was the last time the news media told you the current level of the CPI? Probably never. Rather, they tell you the percentage rate of change in the CPI, called the rate of inflation (or deflation, if negative). Here's what the equation of exchange looks like expressed as rates of change:

$$\frac{\Delta M}{M} + \frac{\Delta V}{V} = \frac{\Delta P}{P} + \frac{\Delta Y}{Y}.$$

The money growth rate plus the percentage change in velocity equals inflation plus real GDP growth. This is actually an approximation. If you have 10% money growth and 10% velocity growth, then the total is 21%, because there is also an interaction term. As an analogy, two years of earning 10% interest on a bank account compounds to 21%, which is 10% plus 10% plus another 10% of 10% (i.e., 1%). But it's close enough for an inexact field like economics, at least when rates of change are low.[1]

The data set shown in table 4.1 presents us with changes in three of the four variables: M, P, and Y. With those, we can easily calculate the other variable: V. But I'm not interested in proving identities; I want to look for evidence of causation. Let's do so one step at a time. First, we'll look for evidence in support of the helicopter-drop thought experiment—if we double the money supply, the price level will also double. And then, if we find any discrepancies (flash alert—we will!), we'll round up the usual suspects, one at a time and put them under intense interrogation. We'll look at both motive (theory) and circumstantial evidence (correlations). But alas, there will be no smoking gun. With this data set, theory plus correlation is the best we can do.

The data in table 4.1 are from seventy-nine countries and represent average growth rates over a long period of time. The countries are arranged from highest inflation rate to lowest. The exact period differs from one country to another depending on data availability. (In most cases it is 1950–1990, and in some cases it is a slightly shorter period.) In all cases the data set includes the worst years of the Great Inflation. Take a look at columns 1 and 2 in the first half of table 4.1: how strong does the correlation look? Then take a look at columns 1 and 2 in the second half (the lower-inflation countries). Does the correlation look stronger or weaker? The correlation between money growth and inflation seems obvious for the thirty-nine high-inflation countries but much less obvious for the forty lower-inflation countries.

Let me draw your attention to seven facts illustrated by table 4.1. First, the quantity theory of money *seems* to work better for high-inflation countries than for low-inflation countries. Let's try to think about why that might be. Column 4 shows the discrepancy between money growth and inflation. If the simplest version of the QTM held true—that is, if the money demand curve never shifted—then prices would always change in proportion to the

TABLE 4.1 **Money growth, inflation, and real growth during the Great Inflation**

Country	(1) $\dfrac{\Delta P}{P}$	(2) $\dfrac{\Delta M}{M}$	(3) $\dfrac{\Delta Y}{Y}$	(4) $\dfrac{\Delta M}{M} - \dfrac{\Delta P}{P}$	(5) NGDP growth
Brazil	77.8	77.4	5.6	−0.4	83.4
Argentina	76.0	72.8	2.1	−3.2	78.1
Bolivia	48.0	49.0	3.3	1.0	51.3
Peru	47.6	49.7	3.0	2.1	50.6
Uruguay	43.1	42.4	1.5	−0.7	44.6
Chile	42.2	47.3	3.1	5.1	45.3
Yugoslavia	31.7	38.7	8.7	7.0	40.4
Zaire (Congo)	30.0	29.8	2.4	−0.2	32.4
Israel	29.4	31.0	6.7	1.6	36.1
Sierra Leone	21.5	20.7	3.1	−0.8	24.6
Turkey	20.1	22.9	5.9	2.8	26.0
Ghana	19.3	18.6	2.5	−0.7	21.8
Iceland	18.8	18.4	4.3	−0.4	23.1
Mexico	18.7	23.2	5.4	4.5	24.1
Colombia	13.9	18.5	4.7	4.6	18.6
South Korea	12.8	22.1	7.6	9.3	20.4
Paraguay	12.5	16.9	4.8	4.4	17.3
Sudan	12.0	16.3	2.3	4.3	14.3
Costa Rica	11.8	16.5	4.6	4.7	16.4
Ecuador	11.6	15.7	4.7	4.1	16.3
Jamaica	11.2	15.7	4.7	4.5	15.9
Nigeria	10.8	14.2	4.1	3.4	14.9
Portugal	9.9	11.5	4.7	1.6	14.6
Iran	9.9	18.5	4.7	8.6	14.6
The Gambia	9.8	11.5	3.2	1.7	13.0
Guyana	9.8	13.8	−0.4	4.0	9.4
Greece	9.5	14.9	4.7	5.4	14.2
Madagascar	9.5	8.8	1.5	−0.7	11.0
Spain	9.2	13.1	4.5	3.9	13.7
Senegal	8.7	12.2	1.1	3.5	9.8
Mauritius	8.6	12.7	3.9	4.1	12.5
Dominican Republic	8.6	13.2	4.7	4.6	13.3
Trinidad and Tobago	8.5	10.5	1.9	2.0	10.4
Egypt	8.0	12.0	4.1	4.0	12.1
Nepal	8.0	14.4	3.1	6.4	11.1
Venezuela	8.0	10.7	4.4	2.7	12.4
Philippines	7.8	11.3	4.8	3.5	12.6
Gabon	7.6	10.0	5.3	2.4	12.9
New Zealand	7.6	6.4	2.6	−1.2	10.2
El Salvador	7.6	8.1	3.3	0.5	10.9
South Africa	7.5	10.1	3.7	2.6	11.2
Cameroon	7.5	10.7	5.5	3.2	13.0
Ivory Coast	7.3	12.0	5.0	4.7	12.3
Italy	7.3	10.3	4.6	3.0	11.9
Ireland	7.2	7.9	3.3	0.7	10.5
India	7.2	10.7	4.2	3.5	11.4
Pakistan	6.8	10.7	4.7	3.9	11.5

continues

TABLE 4.1 *(continued)*

Country	(1) $\dfrac{\Delta P}{P}$	(2) $\dfrac{\Delta M}{M}$	(3) $\dfrac{\Delta Y}{Y}$	(4) $\dfrac{\Delta M}{M} - \dfrac{\Delta P}{P}$	(5) NGDP growth
Syria	6.7	15.0	5.3	8.3	12.0
Finland	6.7	8.6	4.2	1.9	10.9
Togo	6.6	13.8	4.4	7.2	11.0
United Kingdom	6.5	6.4	2.4	−0.1	8.9
Australia	6.4	8.5	3.9	2.1	10.3
France	6.2	7.0	4.1	0.8	10.3
Sweden	6.2	7.4	2.9	1.2	9.1
Denmark	6.1	7.7	3.0	1.6	9.1
Norway	6.1	6.4	3.8	0.3	9.9
Burkina Faso	5.9	10.1	3.6	4.2	9.5
Sri Lanka	5.9	10.6	5.0	4.7	10.9
Niger	5.8	9.9	3.2	4.1	9.0
Saudi Arabia	5.5	15.0	6.1	9.5	11.6
Morocco	5.5	11.1	3.9	5.6	9.4
Tunisia	5.5	11.0	6.1	5.5	11.6
Libya	5.4	25.0	5.7	19.6	11.1
Guatemala	5.4	9.1	3.9	3.7	9.3
Thailand	4.9	9.4	6.8	4.5	11.7
Honduras	4.9	9.5	3.6	4.6	8.5
Haiti	4.8	9.8	1.8	5.0	6.6
Japan	4.7	11.2	6.9	6.5	11.6
Iraq	4.7	14.1	6.6	9.4	11.3
Canada	4.6	8.1	4.2	3.5	8.8
Austria	4.5	7.1	3.9	2.6	8.4
Cyprus	4.5	10.5	5.2	6.0	9.7
Netherlands	4.2	6.4	3.7	2.2	7.9
United States	4.2	5.7	3.1	1.5	7.3
Belgium	4.1	4.0	3.3	−0.1	7.4
Malta	3.6	9.6	6.2	6.0	9.8
Singapore	3.6	10.8	8.1	7.2	11.7
Switzerland	3.2	4.6	3.1	1.4	6.3
West Germany	3.0	7.0	4.1	4.0	7.1

Note: The exact period under consideration differs from one country to another, depending on data availability. In most cases it is 1950–1990, and in some cases it is a slightly shorter period. In all cases the data set includes the worst years of the Great Inflation.
Source: Barro (1993).

money supply. In that case, column 4 would be just a bunch of zeros. But column 4 is not full of zeros: the money growth rate is not identical to the inflation rate. The next thing to focus on is the size of the discrepancy. In every case but one, the discrepancy in column 4 is a single digit, less than 10%. So, the second fact: in the very long run (say, forty years or more), the discrepancy between money growth and inflation is almost always less than 10% per year in absolute value. Third, let's look to see whether the discrep-

ancy is usually positive or negative: in the very long run, the money supply usually rises faster than the price level. There are a few cases, though,
in which prices rise faster than the money supply. Do you see any pattern
there? (This is a tough question.) And this brings us to fact 4: most of the
cases where prices rise faster than the money supply occur in high-inflation
countries. How about real GDP growth—notice any patterns? So the fifth
fact is that RGDP tends to rise over long periods of time. (Table 4.1 includes only one exception to this rule.) But there doesn't seem to be much
difference in RGDP growth rates for the high-inflation countries as compared to the low-inflation countries. That supports fact 6, the claim that
faster money growth doesn't lead to faster RGDP growth. And fact 7: how
fast does RGDP tend to rise? In the very long run, output tends to grow at
single-digit rates.

David Hume did not have the advantage of possessing this great data
set. He had to develop the QTM while sitting in an armchair and thinking about the problem logically. At best, he had a bit of crude evidence
that the flow of gold and silver from the Americas to Europe had led to
moderate inflation in the sixteenth century. Your data set is far better, so
you should be able to advance monetary theory far beyond Hume. But
Hume was pretty smart, and it wasn't easy to get ahead of him—it took
215 years.

Shifts in the Demand for Money

In the helicopter-drop thought experiment, we held the demand curve fixed.
People wanted to hold $200 in purchasing power. If you doubled the money
supply to $400 per person, people spent the excess cash until prices dou-
bled. When the price level doubled, their *real* purchasing power was back
at $200 (i.e., $400 divided by 2). In other words, as long as the demand
curve for money doesn't shift, the simple quantity theory of money holds
exactly true: price levels move proportionally to the money supply.

But our data set tells us that the QTM is not exactly true, and hence we
know that the demand for money does change. Column 4 in table 4.1, which
shows the discrepancy between money growth and inflation, also tells us
precisely how much the real demand for money changed over time. In
most countries real cash holdings rose modestly over time, which means
the real demand for money was increasing. But there were eleven negative
signs in column 4—that means there were eleven countries where real cash

holdings fell over long periods of time. If we rearrange the dynamic version of the equation of exchange, we can see that growth in real money
holdings (i.e., $\Delta M/M - \Delta P/P$) is positive when real GDP growth is greater
than the change in velocity:

$$\frac{\Delta M}{M} - \frac{\Delta P}{P} = \frac{\Delta Y}{Y} - \frac{\Delta V}{V}.$$

Let's illustrate this using Singapore as a specific example:

$$10.8\% - 3.6\% = 8.1\% - 0.9\%.$$

In Singapore, the money supply grew at a relatively fast 10.8%, and yet
inflation was only 3.6%. So real cash balances increased by 7.2% per year.
Why? In an accounting sense, the answer is simple. Real GDP grew much
faster than velocity, which implies that real money demand rose sharply. But
what does that *really* mean? How did Singaporeans behave in response
to the flood of new money? Why did they behave that way? Why did this
result in a much lower inflation rate than what would be predicted by the
simple version of the QTM?

In our helicopter-drop example, we assumed that people prefer to hold
enough real cash balances to do a week's worth of shopping. In that case, it's
clear that real cash balances might change for one of two reasons. Maybe
people prefer to hold larger or smaller cash balances as a share of expenditures. That is, perhaps they suddenly prefer to hold enough for two weeks'
worth of shopping. That would represent a change in V, from 52 to only
26. Or maybe they continue to prefer to hold just enough cash for a week's
worth of shopping, but the actual amount of stuff they buy increases, as
the country gets richer. If they buy more real stuff, that corresponds to
an increase in real GDP (Y). Let's simplify things for now by focusing ex-
clusively on changes in real GDP, which seemed to be the main factor in
Singapore.

There's an old saying that "inflation is too much money chasing too few
goods." Singapore did print lots of money, but it avoided high inflation by
also generating fast economic growth. Look at the equation of exchange
with the inflation rate isolated on the left side:

$$\frac{\Delta P}{P} = \frac{\Delta M}{M} + \frac{\Delta V}{V} - \frac{\Delta Y}{Y}.$$

Do you see something surprising? If not, take another look. Fast economic growth is actually deflationary. The real growth rate gets subtracted from the money and velocity growth. Thus, for any level of nominal spending, higher real growth means lower inflation. You've just learned something that even some PhD economists don't yet know (until they read this book)! *Fast economic growth is deflationary.*

As usual, David Hume was way ahead of us: "Suppose a nation removed into the *Pacific* ocean, without any foreign commerce, or any knowledge of navigation: Suppose, that this nation possesses always the same stock of coin, but is continually encreasing in its numbers and industry: It is evident, that the price of every commodity must gradually diminish in that kingdom; since it is the proportion between money and any species of goods, which fixes their mutual value."[2]

In Singapore, the money supply grew at a rate of 10.8% a year, and as if that weren't enough, each year Singaporean dollars got spent slightly faster than before—0.9% faster, to be exact. These changes led to a rise in total spending of 11.7% per year. That's growth in what economists call *aggregate demand.* But most of that growth was absorbed in spending on fast-rising real output. Singaporeans willingly held larger and larger real cash balances because they were getting richer and doing more shopping. Since real GDP was rising by 8.1% per year, only the extra 3.6% represented excess cash balances, which showed up as inflation. According to Hume's example, if Singapore had not increased the money supply, its price level would have decreased over time.[3] Indeed something like that happened in the US between 1865 and 1896, when real GDP increased faster than the money supply, leading to three decades of deflation.

OK, we might say—the fast-economic-growth-is-deflationary theory fits pretty well for Singapore, but how well does it work on average? It turns out that if we do a regression analysis where inflation is the dependent variable, then money growth shows up with a positive coefficient of close to 1—1.03, to be precise. That means that a 1% faster growth rate in the money supply is associated with, on average, a 1.03% rise in the inflation rate. The result is not significantly different from 1, which is the coefficient we would expect if the QTM were true.

In the same regression equation, the coefficient on real GDP growth is *negative* 1.065, again not significantly different from one. But in this case we don't really have any good theory predicting the exact relationship. Looking at the equation of exchange, you might expect higher real GDP growth to lead to lower inflation, if the money growth rate were held constant. But

would you expect a one-for-one reduction in inflation? That depends on
whether you think economic growth might increase or decrease velocity.

The evidence suggests that economic growth doesn't have much effect
on velocity and that each extra 1% real growth leads to roughly 1% less
inflation, holding money growth constant. This is why Singapore's inflation
rate was so far below its money growth rate. Inflation was held down by
fast real growth. And indeed economic growth also explains the third fact
from the earlier list—for most countries the money-supply growth rate is
higher than the inflation rate.

We can make the equation of exchange even simpler by focusing on
nominal GDP growth rather than looking at inflation and real growth
separately:

$$\frac{\Delta M}{M} + \frac{\Delta V}{V} = \frac{\Delta(PY)}{PY}.$$

That's pretty simple—the growth rate of the money supply plus the rate
of change in velocity equals the nominal GDP growth rate. In the original QTM that focused on money and inflation, we needed two assumptions for the theory to hold precisely true—both velocity and real GDP
had to be held constant. If we switch our focus to NGDP, we just need
one assumption—velocity is constant. If velocity is constant, then NGDP
moves exactly in proportion to changes in the money supply.

Unfortunately, velocity is not constant, and in recent years it has been
highly erratic in the US. That's an issue we'll address in the next two chapters. We'll see that the big international data set from table 4.1 contains
other clues that we haven't yet worked through. But we've already covered a lot of theory and evidence, so let's take stock of what we know so
far. What should we make of the quantity theory of money? Is it true? Is
it useful?

How True Is the Quantity Theory of Money?

As mentioned earlier, in the social sciences it's often more helpful to ask
whether a theory is useful than whether it's true. I opened the chapter
with five versions of the QTM: versions 3, 4, and 5 are useful, but not versions 1 and 2. This is because the change in the money supply is not always
equal to the change in the price level (contrary to version 1). These two

variables were strongly correlated during the Great Inflation, but even then the correlation was far weaker for the low-inflation countries, which included most developed countries. Even worse, the correlation in recent decades has been even weaker than during the Great Inflation. The same is true for money and NGDP (contrary to version 2)—the correlation was never perfect and is getting worse. So why do I like this Great Inflation example so much? Is it just boomer nostalgia?

In my view, the Great Inflation is like a lab experiment under extreme heat or extreme pressure: under such conditions we can identify properties not otherwise easily visible. In that period I see a lot of support for versions 3, 4, and 5 of the QTM. Looking at growth in the money supply does help us understand long-run inflation (in support of version 5). There is evidence that an X% increase in the money supply leads, in the long run, to prices and NGDP being X% higher than otherwise (in support of version 3). Yes, real GDP and velocity also change, but probably not (in the long run) in response to changes in the money supply. (The short run is different, as we'll see later.) And of course we don't see any cases of sustained long-run inflation without pretty high money growth rates (in support of version 4).

But what about the "correlation doesn't prove causation" argument? Why single out money? The answer is simple—money is not like other goods. The price of money is fixed at 1.0. The only way the value of money can change is if the price level changes. If lots of apples are produced, the price of apples in the marketplace can fall, restoring equilibrium. If lots of money is produced, the nominal price of money cannot fall. Instead, the only way that the value of money can fall is for the nominal price of other goods and services to go up. As we saw, gasoline prices aren't much different now than they were in the 1930s in terms of silver or gold, but gas is much more expensive now in dollar terms. Inflation is a *monetary phenomenon*.

So, both theory and evidence suggest that money growth is a necessary and sufficient condition for sustained periods of high inflation. But this leads to a more sophisticated argument against the QTM—the claim that although money growth may be essential to the inflation process, it's not really the root cause. Rather, the root cause is some other factor, and money growth is merely a symptom. The root cause most often cited is deficit spending.

Go back and look at the high-inflation countries in table 4.1. Maybe you wondered why Brazil and Argentina printed so much money. Were they unaware of the QTM? Clearly not: rather, these countries (or, more precisely, their governments) decided that inflation was the lesser of several evils, with the alternatives being either fiscal "austerity" or bankruptcy. Tax increases and spending cuts are unpopular, and bankruptcy can make it hard for countries to borrow in the future. Printing money to cover the budget deficit was viewed as the easy way out.

In the case of the Great Inflation of 1966–1981 in the US, one could argue that a root cause was presidents Johnson and Nixon twisting the arms of Fed chairmen to adopt an expansionary monetary policy, in the hope that it would provide a short-term boost to the real economy. Nonetheless, even if budget deficits or political arm twisting led central banks to print lots of money, money creation was *still* the proximate cause of the Great Inflation. We know from experience that budget deficits, by themselves, are not very inflationary. President Reagan dramatically expanded the deficit, yet inflation fell sharply during the 1980s owing to the tight money policies of Fed chair Paul Volcker. The same occurred under President Obama.

Many of the high-inflation developing countries shown in table 4.1 did not have particularly big budget deficits compared to the US deficit in 2009. The difference is that the US has always had good enough credit to borrow whatever it takes to finance its deficits, whereas many developing countries do not have credit ratings that are as good. As a result, they print money to cover their budget deficits.

In the end, it all comes down to money. Sustained periods of high inflation are almost always caused by rapid money growth. Even at lower inflation rates, monetary policy still determines the inflation (and NGDP growth) rates. The two growth rates might not be exactly the same, but a permanent X% increase in the money supply will always cause prices and NGDP to be roughly X% higher than otherwise in the long run.

Consider Roger, who makes $76,000 per year in 2019. The reason he makes $76,000 per year rather than $4,000 per year is that FDR took the US off the gold standard in 1933 and set in motion a new monetary policy that ultimately boosted the price level by a factor of 19. If he had not done so, and if the US were still on the old gold standard, Roger's income would be only about $4,000, but he'd still have the same buying power that his actual current $76,000 income gives him—because prices would also be proportionally lower.[4]

Unfortunately, the QTM also leaves a lot to be desired. It's not going to be a very useful tool for looking at short-run changes in the economy unless we can adequately explain changes in velocity, which have been quite dramatic in recent years. Explaining such changes is essential for allowing us to model nominal GDP growth. Then, once we complete a model of the nominal side of the economy, we'll look at how NGDP shocks have an impact on the real side—output and employment. Finally, we'll use these theoretical tools to examine monetary policy and explain how Federal Reserve policy errors caused the Great Recession. But first let's get a better hold of this velocity issue.

CHAPTER FIVE

Money at the Extremes

Hyperinflation and Deflation

In the previous chapter we used the equation of exchange to examine the relationship between money and prices. We saw that the inflation rate is affected by two factors: shifts in the supply of money and shifts in the demand for money. When the money demand curve is stable, the quantity theory of money holds true. Prices move in proportion to the money supply. When money demand changes, things get more complicated.

Changes in demand for real money balances can be further broken down into two components, real GDP growth and velocity of circulation:

$$\frac{\Delta M}{M} - \frac{\Delta P}{P} = \frac{\Delta Y}{Y} - \frac{\Delta V}{V}.$$

If we isolate inflation on to the left side of the equation, we get the following:

$$\frac{\Delta P}{P} = \frac{\Delta M}{M} - \left(\frac{\Delta Y}{Y} - \frac{\Delta V}{V}\right).$$

We've already seen that increases in real GDP growth tend to result in roughly one-for-one decreases in inflation, at least in the long run. So that just leaves one more variable to explain—velocity. So let's return to the data set from the previous chapter (table 4.1) and take another look at all the clues.

Hyperinflation and Money Demand

There's one clue we have not yet addressed: the tendency for money growth rates to exceed inflation in most countries. Why might that be the case? As a matter of arithmetic, money growth exceeds inflation any time that real GDP growth exceeds the change in velocity. If velocity did not change at all, then money growth would almost always exceed inflation, because every single country but one had positive real GDP growth, on average, over the sample period.

Unfortunately, there are eleven examples (out of seventy-nine) where money growth falls short of inflation. What might explain those eleven cases? One hint is that they tended to occur more often in the high-inflation cases. In seven of the thirteen countries with the highest inflation, money growth fell short of the inflation rate. Among the other sixty-six cases, only four saw money growth fall short of inflation.

In the eleven countries where money growth fell short of inflation, it must be the case that velocity increased, and by more than real GDP increased. So in those eleven exceptional countries, we saw a rapid increase in velocity. And why might that be? What led residents of places like Argentina to spend money much more rapidly in 1990 than they did in 1952?

Suppose you were living in Germany during the famous hyperinflation of 1923. How would that inflation have affected your demand for real cash balances? Think about the fact that during the peak of the hyperinflation, prices were rising at 20% *per day*. That means that the cash in your pockets was losing purchasing power at a rapid rate. I don't know about you, but I would have tried to spend my money quickly, before prices rose even further. During the worst of the hyperinflation, German workers were paid twice a day: they'd go shopping during their lunch break with their noontime pay and then again at the end of the workday.

Think of rising inflation as increasing the opportunity cost of holding cash. If that's the case, higher inflation can be expected to lead to lower demand for real cash balances. This often confuses people, because in *nominal* terms the Germans were holding lots of cash—billions of German marks. But the purchasing power of those cash balances was even less than the purchasing power that Germans held in normal times. So while an American during 1923 might have held enough cash for two weeks' worth of purchases, a German might have held enough for only one day's worth of purchases. And that low demand for money translated into a high velocity of circulation.[1]

To summarize, it seems sensible that people would spend money more quickly if that money were losing purchasing power at a rapid pace. And there is a strong positive correlation between the rate of inflation and the velocity of circulation. Velocity tends to be higher in countries with high inflation. But that's not quite what we observed in table 4.1. The data do not show whether velocity is high or low; they show whether it was *increasing* or *decreasing*. Thus, we'd expect negative signs in column 4 (where V is rising rapidly)—not in countries with high inflation, but in countries where inflation was much higher at the end of the period than at the beginning of the period. In many cases those are also countries with high average levels of inflation, but not always. That's why we see negative signs in column 4 for only seven out of the top thirteen inflation rates. Those seven are presumably the countries where inflation rates rose rapidly between 1950 and 1990. Indeed, inflation rose so rapidly that the rise in velocity (which boosts inflation) more than offset the rise in real GDP (which holds down inflation).

In other countries at the top of the table, the average rate of inflation was quite high, but probably not increasing over time. This idea can be confusing, because most people aren't used to distinguishing between changes in levels and changes in rates of change. In 1990 there was a poll asking people whether inflation was higher or lower than ten years earlier. Most people said it was higher, and this was taken to be an example of how the public is not well informed. In fact, inflation had fallen dramatically, from about 12% in 1980 to less than 5% in 1990. The public may have known this but conflated inflation with cost of living. While inflation ($\Delta P/P$) was much lower in 1990 than in 1980, the cost of living (P) was much higher in 1990 than in 1980. Countries with very high inflation combined with a rising demand for money (i.e., a positive number in column 4 of table 4.1) may have been similar to the US in the 1980s: places that had experienced a huge rise in the cost of living but at a slower rate of increase over time.

We now have a pretty good model of inflation, at least during the Great Inflation. The primary factor determining inflation is money growth. Other things being equal, an X% rise in the money supply will lead to an X% rise in the price level. The next step is to add in real GDP growth. Inflation will tend to fall short of the money growth rate by an amount roughly equal to the real GDP growth rate. And finally, if the inflation rate changes over time, velocity will tend to move in the same direction.

That means that an acceleration in the money supply growth rate will often cause inflation to rise by even more than the money supply, because velocity also tends to increase during these periods. The money supply rose rapidly during the German hyperinflation, but with velocity also increasing, the price level rose even faster.

Unfortunately, the model that does a pretty good job of explaining inflation during the Great Inflation ended up doing a pretty lousy job of explaining inflation during the Great Recession (or, for that matter, during the Great Depression of 1929–1941). Once again, unstable velocity was the culprit, but this time it was the opposite situation from the German hyperinflation—velocity slowed very sharply during both the Great Depression and the Great Recession. Thus, we need to take a closer look at the demand for money to figure out what happened in 2008–2009.

Interest Rates and Money Demand

When thinking about money demand and velocity, economists generally do not focus on how inflation affects the public's desire to hold cash. Rather, they use the *nominal interest rate* as the opportunity cost of holding cash. Because cash does not earn any interest, the opportunity cost of holding cash can be thought of as the interest forgone on alternative investments. If you hold $1,000 in cash and the interest rate on safe investments is 3%, then you are forgoing $30 per year in interest when you choose to hold cash.

Back in the early 1980s, I wrote my PhD dissertation on currency hoarding. I discovered that most currency is hoarded, which means it is held as a sort of "store of value" rather than as a medium of exchange. For instance, most currency in the US consists of $100 bills, held for reasons such as tax evasion.[2] Fortunately, that's not really a problem for the quantity theory of money, because even if cash is held as a store of value, people ultimately care about the purchasing power of cash balances.

Think about the decision made by someone hoarding cash who is hoping to evade taxes on income. If the income tax rate is 20% and the interest rate is 5%, then you'll make out better if you hoard cash for up to four years than if you pay taxes on the unreported income and invest the funds. Thus, the ratio of tax rates to interest rates represents the incentive to hoard cash. Higher interest rates mean less demand for cash, and lower interest rates mean greater demand for cash. I found a correlation between the ratio of tax rates to interest rates and the share of GDP held as currency.[3] High taxes and low interest rates, as during and after World War II, led to very large cash balances. Because tax rates don't change much from year to year, most economists focus on how interest rates have an impact on money demand.

Now let's see how interest rates affect the actual demand for money in the US economy. Currency is a good place to start, because it pays no interest. Thus, the opportunity cost of holding currency is simply the nominal interest rate. In figure 5.1, I use the yield on a three-month Treasury bill as the interest rate, because it is a nice, safe liquid asset that is a good substitute for cash. Notice that interest rates rose sharply between 1959 and 1981, and as a result, the demand for cash fell from 6% of GDP to just over 4% of GDP. Who wants to hold lots of zero-interest cash when you can earn 16% on T-bills?

When interest rates began falling after 1981, the cash-to-income ratio leveled off and then started rising again. Notice that cash holdings responded to lower interest rates with a delay (called a *time lag* by economists), because large cash hoards are costly to adjust. Try quickly accumulating or spending a suitcase full of a million dollars without attracting the unwanted attention of the government.

Former House Speaker Dennis Hastert went to prison for providing misleading statements regarding frequent withdrawals of $3,000 in cash from his own bank account, an activity viewed very suspiciously by the federal government. Those who are trying to avoid detection are better off accumulating or spending cash gradually. For instance, if you desire to hold larger cash balances, you might augment your holdings by setting aside a bit of unreported income each month. To reduce cash balances, a hoarder can gradually spend the money on goods and services.

At the end of 2008, something very unusual happened—the interest rate fell to roughly zero. Now, cash and T-bills were very close substitutes as investments. Because cash is more anonymous than bonds, and can be used to evade taxes, the demand for cash rose sharply as soon as rates hit zero. There was no longer any "opportunity cost" to holding cash (except the risk of theft, or the cost of renting a safe-deposit box). This meant that cash holders were no longer forgoing interest on alternative safe investments. As a result, the public's desire to hold cash soared much higher, from 5.5% of GDP in late 2008 to almost 9% today. Because cash hoarders respond with a lag, and (importantly) because foreign demand for US cash is still rising, this ratio may go even higher.

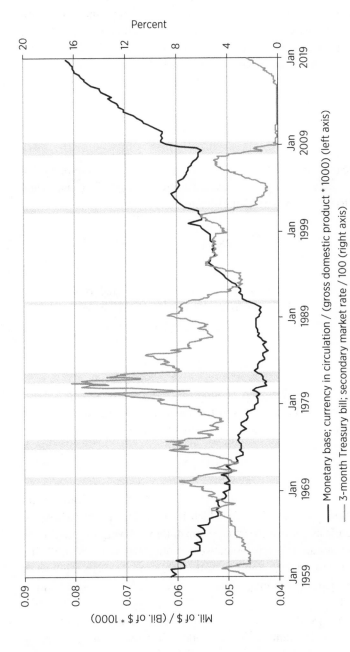

FIGURE 5.1. US interest rates and demand for cash, 1959–2018

Note: Gray bars indicate periods of recession.

Source: FRED, via Board of Governors of the Federal Reserve System (US), https://fred.stlouisfed.org/series/MBCURRCIR, https://fred.stlouisfed.org/series/TB3, https://fred.stlouisfed.org/series/GDP.

To summarize, the public's demand for cash seems to be affected by interest rates in exactly the way we might expect, although there are a few complications, such as the slow adjustment process and the fact that other variables such as income tax rates and foreign demand also have an impact on the demand for cash. Nonetheless, we have a pretty good model of money demand:

$$\frac{M}{P} = f(Y, i),$$

where the real demand for cash balances is positively related to real GDP (Y) and negatively related to the nominal interest rate (i). We can also link these ideas to the old equation of exchange:

$$\frac{M}{P} = f(y, i) = \frac{Y}{V}.$$

In addition, the ratio of cash to GDP (see figure 5.1) is equal to M ÷ (P × Y) (with M defined as cash), which is also the inverse of velocity:

$$\frac{M}{P \times Y} = \frac{1}{V}.$$

Over in Cambridge, England, economists preferred to use another version of the equation of exchange, which made it easier to see the role played by money demand. They replaced $1/V$ with the letter k:

$$M = k \times P \times Y.$$

To a mathematician, this is essentially the same as the American version of the equation (M × V = P × Y), which Irving Fisher preferred. We've just relabeled V as $1/k$. But to an economist, they are very different ways of thinking about the relationship between money and nominal GDP. The American version, M × V, emphasizes the role of money as a *medium of exchange*: the quantity of money times the speed at which it is spent equals nominal GDP.

Recall that gross domestic product equals gross domestic income. Total output and total income are just two sides of the same coin. Thus, in the Cambridge version of the equation, the focus is on money as a store of value, an asset in one's portfolio. The total quantity of money in the economy is the total gross domestic income times the share of income held as money. Thus, if V is 52, as in the earlier example, then k is 1/52, or just under 2% of income. In that case, the public would choose to hold roughly 2% of a year's income in the form of money. If the average person had an annual income of $52,000, this person would choose to hold $1,000 in the form of money (cash).

In my view, the Cambridge version is more intuitive. The Cambridge k really does reflect the share of income held as money, whereas V does not really represent the average number of times each dollar bill is spent in a year. For instance, money is spent at garage sales, but that transaction is not part of GDP. In addition, the k ratio naturally fits in with the concept of money demand. A higher k ratio means a higher demand for money, as a share of NGDP. In contrast, a higher velocity means a lower demand for money. The real demand for money can rise for one of two reasons— either real income (GDP) rises, or the share of income held as money (k) rises.

There is a great deal of evidence that changes in nominal interest rates affect the demand for money. The higher the interest rate, the lower the demand for money, as a share of GDP. That is, higher interest rates lead to a lower Cambridge k, because people hold a smaller share of their income in the form of cash. But where do these interest rates come from? Are they set by the Fed? This is a difficult problem, which we'll have to address in stages. The first stage involves distinguishing real from nominal interest rates.

The Fisher Equation and the Fisher Effect

We began this chapter by noticing that people spent money faster when inflation was very high. This meant that the demand to hold real cash balances fell as inflation rose. People don't want to hold lots of an asset that is rapidly losing value. Then we saw that nominal interest rates were a better indicator of the opportunity cost of holding money. In this section we'll link inflation and nominal interest rates. The key relationship is the Fisher equation, which states that the real interest rate (r) is equal to the nominal interest rate (i) minus the inflation rate ($\Delta P/P$):

$$r = i - \frac{\Delta P}{P}, \text{ or } i = r + \frac{\Delta P}{P}.$$

Just as in the cases of the equation of exchange and the Cambridge equation, a mathematician would view these two versions of the Fisher equation as essentially identical. Obviously we've just rearranged terms between the first version and the second version. And, as with those two earlier equations, an economist would interpret these two Fisher equations slightly differently, despite the fact that they are mathematically identical.

In the first version, we put the real interest rate (r) on the left side of the equation. In a sense, this makes the equation a definition of the real interest rate, just as the equation of exchange can be considered a definition of velocity. It shows us how to calculate the real rate of return on an investment. In contrast, the version with the nominal interest rate on the left side of the equation is most useful if we are thinking about what *determines* the nominal interest rate. The nominal interest rate has two components: the real rate and the inflation rate. If we frame things that way, we can try to explain changes in interest rates by separately explaining the factors that determine real interest rates and then the factors that determine inflation.

Earlier we saw that the equation of exchange is often confused with the quantity theory of money. The former is actually just an accounting relationship, whereas the latter is a causal relationship—a *theory*. The two get mixed up because the equation of exchange is often used to explain the QTM. Something very similar happens with the Fisher equation. Like the equation of exchange, the Fisher equation is simply an accounting relationship—a definition. Yet it also comes along with a theory, called the *Fisher effect*. The Fisher effect is the theory that an X% increase in the inflation rate (more specifically, the expected inflation rate) leads to an X% increase in the nominal interest rate.

To really understand this stuff, let's step back and consider what we are doing at a very basic level. The quantity theory of money is the most important of a nearly infinite number of similar theories, relating real variables, nominal variables, and the price level. Let's write down a generic version of the relationship and then use it to generate a set of similar, related theories. First, the accounting relationships:

change in nominal variable = change in real variable + inflation.

The left side of the equation might be the percentage change in the money supply ($\Delta M/M$) or the percentage change in the value of a one-year Treasury bill (i), or it might be the percentage annual pay increase your boss gives you. In each case there is an accompanying theory, which is based on the general concept of *money neutrality*. Money is neutral if changes in nominal variables have no impact on real variables. If money is neutral, then an increase in the money supply does not impact the public's real money demand—rather, it shows up as inflation. If money is neutral, then an increase in inflation does not affect the real interest rate—rather, it shows up as a one-for-one rise in nominal interest rates. And if money is neutral, then an increase in inflation has no impact on your real wage rate—rather, it gets passed along one-for-one as a nominal pay raise.

We've already seen that the quantity theory of money is not precisely true, at least in its simplest form. An X% rise in the money supply doesn't always lead to an X% rise in the price level. For similar reasons, none of the other theories relating real, nominal, and price-level variables are exactly true. The QTM, however, was shown to be useful in certain contexts, particularly for high-inflation countries. The same is true of all the other related theories—including some we have not even considered yet, such as *purchasing power parity*: they work best when countries experience high rates of inflation for a prolonged period of time.

The Fisher effect is most noticeable at high inflation rates, when it completely dominates changes in the real interest rate. Because real interest rates are usually fairly close to zero, a persistent inflation rate of 40% per year will lead to very high nominal interest rates—also close to 40% per year. The bigger the swings in inflation, the more dominant inflation becomes as a determinant of nominal interest rates. But when inflation is stable, as when a central bank targets it at 2%, then changes in nominal interest rates tend to reflect changes in the real interest rate, with fluctuations in inflation playing only a minor role. That has been the US experience since about 1991.

To better understand interest rates, let's consider an economy with no inflation and then add in inflation and see what happens. Figure 5.2 shows the loanable funds market. Let's say the supply of loanable funds is upward-sloping, as higher interest rates induce savers to supply more loanable funds to banks and bond issuers. Now consider demanders of loanable funds. They might want to build a new project or buy a house. The higher the cost of the loan, the lower the quantity demanded. In a world where no inflation is expected, the nominal interest rate would equal the real interest rate—3%, in figure 5.2.

Now let's assume that the expected rate of inflation rises to 4%, as it was in the late 1980s. In this case, savers will demand 4% higher nominal interest in order to be willing to supply the same quantity of funds, and

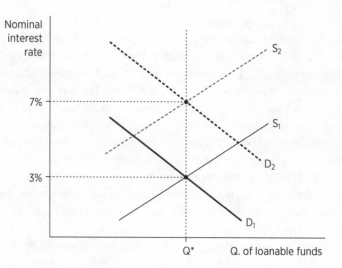

FIGURE 5.2. Loanable funds market

borrowers will be willing to pay an extra 4%, knowing that the inflation will reduce the real value of the dollars that they repay in the future. If money is neutral and does not affect real variables, then the nominal interest rate will rise to 7%.

Is this how things work in the real world? Not quite, because nominal interest is taxable in most countries. That means the real tax rate on investment income rises as inflation rises. Taxes on investment income drive a wedge between the interest paid by borrowers and the interest received by savers. Higher rates of inflation result in higher taxes on investment income, which leads to less saving and investment in the economy, thus creating a deadweight loss. Note that this is a long-run effect; later we'll see that in the short run a higher inflation rate can, under certain conditions, create a temporary boom in the economy.

To summarize, concepts such as the quantity theory of money, the Fisher effect, and monetary neutrality provide the basic structure for thinking about the long-run impact of changes in the money supply. This framework is especially useful when there are persistently high rates of inflation. As a result, these monetarist themes tend to become highly popular when high inflation is a problem, such as right after World War I and again during the period from 1966 to 1981.

Unfortunately, these concepts don't help much with some of the most interesting problems in monetary economics. For instance, during periods of deflation, the quantity theory of money generally does not predict well. When prices are falling, monetary policy has important effects on real variables, not just inflation.

The Great Recession was one of the periods where money growth and inflation rates diverged sharply, and this has resulted in the QTM falling out of favor. During the Great Recession, I and a few other economists developed a version of the quantity theory of money that could be applied to a zero-interest-rate environment such as that of 2009, when huge increases in the money supply failed to produce the inflation that traditional monetarists anticipated. In the next chapter we'll get into those ideas, which are often referred to as *market monetarism*.

CHAPTER SIX

It's (Almost) All about Expectations

W̲e started with a fairly simple version of the quantity theory of money. An increase in the money supply causes a proportional increase in the price level and NGDP, at least in the long run. Then we looked at velocity and saw that it depended on the opportunity cost of holding base money, which until 2008 was the nominal interest rate. If velocity changes, then QTM predictions may fail.

All of this has been known since the time of David Hume. Nonetheless, many people (especially monetarists) were caught off guard by the failure of quantitative easing (QE) to cause high inflation after 2009. I was fortunate to avoid predicting high inflation, perhaps because I happened to have a set of research interests that allowed me to anticipate the impact of very low interest rates. In particular, I had studied

- the currency injections of colonial America, enacted to finance wars against Native Americans
- the QE program of spring 1932, aimed at boosting a severely depressed economy
- the Japanese QE of 2001–2006, aimed at ending deflation.

In all three of these cases there was a very significant increase in the monetary base, and it failed to lead to higher inflation.

Temporary Currency Injections

A number of economists have argued that several big currency injections in colonial America were not inflationary because the money was "backed" by sufficient assets to redeem the currency notes in the future. Currency notes were treated as zero-interest bonds. These economists viewed this "backing theory" of money as an alternative to the quantity theory of money. Monetary injections, even printing paper money, was not inflationary if the money was backed by sufficient assets.[1]

I reached a different conclusion in a 1993 paper, arguing that the currency injections were not inflationary to the extent that they were viewed as *temporary*.[2] Indeed, I believe that all three of these episodes shared one common trait: the currency injections were widely viewed as temporary.

Recall the simple helicopter-drop thought experiment from chapter 3: Imagine that the money supply doubles overnight, and members of the public initially holds twice as much money as they wish to hold. It's fairly easy to show that the price level must double in order to restore equilibrium. Once prices double, equilibrium is restored and all individuals are content with their level of cash balances.

But consider a case where the monetary injection is viewed as temporary and is expected to be withdrawn after a year. Would prices still double, and then a year later fall back to the original equilibrium? That seems very unlikely, not because prices can't quickly double (they've done so in a number of different hyperinflation episodes), but because it's hard to imagine the price level *being expected to fall in half*, especially in just a year.

Recall that the price level is the value of money. Thus, if prices were expected to halve in one year, then the value of cash would be expected to double equally fast. That's a real rate of return of 100% in just twelve months! In fact, real rates of return on safe assets like cash rarely exceed 5% or so. If cash were really expected to offer such a high real rate of return, then demand for cash would rise sharply. But this would prevent the initial currency injection from being inflationary in the first place. Recall that rising demand for cash holds down prices.

It might be easier to envision this with a concrete example from the asset markets. Suppose you were a die-hard believer in the simple quantity theory of money. A temporary doubling of the money supply should cause prices to double (in your view) and then halve when the money is withdrawn later. If this is true, it should also apply to house prices, shouldn't it? So the prediction is that houses costing $200,000 will suddenly rise to $400,000, and then fall back to $200,000 a year later.

Once again, the initial (unexpected) doubling from $200,000 to $400,000 is quite possible, especially in hyperinflationary countries. But how can house prices be expected to fall back from $400,000 to $200,000 a year from today? If people thought a certain house would be worth $200,000 a year from now, why would they pay $400,000 for it today? The answer is simple: they would not. The prices of assets such as houses (or common stocks) are never expected to fall sharply in the near future, because if they were then they would *already* have fallen sharply. Rational people will not pay far more for a house than they expect it to be worth a year from now.

Five years after I wrote my paper on colonial currency, Paul Krugman wrote a far more important paper on Japan's liquidity trap. Whereas I was working in the monetarist tradition, Krugman used a much more sophisticated mathematical model in the New Keynesian tradition. But the results were basically the same: temporary currency injections are not likely to be inflationary.[3]

And how could it be otherwise? The simple house example is just common sense. Someone in finance could make the same argument about stock prices. A permanent doubling of the profit margin will make the price of a stock soar in value, perhaps two-fold. But if the doubling of profit margins is expected to last only one quarter, perhaps from, say, a windfall earned in litigation, then the price of the stock won't rise very much.

The insight that temporary currency injections are not inflationary may seem like common sense, but it pushes us into a strange new world, one in which we have to leave behind the comforting rules of thumb that we observed during the Great Inflation. No longer can we assume that 80% growth in the monetary base will lead to roughly 80% inflation. Now everything will depend not on the current money supply but on the expected future path of the money supply.

Economists sometimes refer to an "indeterminacy problem" in modern fiat money models. Once you bring expectations into the picture, it's very hard to model the value of money, or to explain why money has any value at all. Under the gold standard, we could always refer back to the underlying value of gold, which backed paper money. The value of gold itself reflected the basic laws of supply and demand. But what determines the value of fiat money?

It turns out that the value of money today depends very much on what people think it will be worth a year from now. But the value of money a year from now is closely linked to what people think it will be worth two years from now—and so on, to the end of time. Or perhaps to the end of money.

Do people believe that the government will somehow ensure that the value of money does not fall sharply? In the US, I believe that they do. Americans saw that when the French franc was discontinued in 2002, the

French people were given something of equal value. In that case it was just another fiat currency. But it seems plausible that if all fiat money came to an end, the government would redeem the currency notes with something else of value, such as bonds or gold.

I'm not going to worry about those philosophical problems—instead, I focus on factors that are much better understood, such as changes in the money supply, the opportunity cost of holding money (i.e., the nominal interest rate), and real output. Fortunately, those factors will give us all the tools we need to examine even difficult problems, such as the Great Recession.

Krugman's Expectations Trap

In an important and underrated 1998 paper, Paul Krugman looked at traditional models of the liquidity trap—that is, the case where nominal interest rates fall to zero. The traditional view was that money and T-bills become perfect substitutes at zero interest rates. So if the central bank buys T-bills with newly injected money, nothing should change, because it is just swapping one zero-interest asset for another.[4]

Krugman saw that this traditional view was wrong, once you accounted for expectations. Yes, the new money might be a perfect substitute for T-bills today, but this would not be true once nominal interest rates rose back above zero. At that point the hot-potato effect would take over, and prices would rise. Krugman showed that if this expected future price rise were well understood, then a monetary injection today would reduce long-term real interest rates by raising inflation expectations. Monetary stimulus could still be expansionary, even when interest rates were temporarily stuck at zero.[5]

Krugman's basic idea is that any policy expected to lead to higher prices in the future is also likely to lead to higher prices today.[6] Once again, a stock market analogy might be useful. If a company is expected to get approval from the Food and Drug Administration for a new drug in twenty-four months, that expectation will cause the stock price to rise today. When people found out that Disney expected to build a theme park in Orlando, the price of nearby land shot up immediately, even before the park was built. That's also true for the overall price level. If you think prices will be higher in the future, you are more likely to spend money today. That makes velocity go up and prices rise today.

But Krugman didn't just criticize the standard Keynesian theory of the liquidity trap; he replaced it with an alternative explanation for why monetary policy might be ineffective at zero interest rates. In this new theory, the problem is not that money and T-bills are perfect substitutes at zero interest rates—the real problem is that monetary injections that are expected to be temporary are likely to be ineffective. Krugman's 1998 paper was aimed at better understanding the situation in Japan, and in 2006 it received a striking confirmation when the Bank of Japan (BOJ) decided it didn't need any more monetary stimulus, so it sharply reduced the size of Japan's monetary base (fig. 6.1).[7]

Krugman saw that monetary injections at the zero bound were effective only to the extent that they were viewed as permanent. In that case, the current money supply didn't matter much at all. Or perhaps it would be more accurate to say that current monetary injections (QE) matter only to the extent that they lead to expectations of a larger future money supply. The key to successfully moving from deflation to inflation is having the central bank commit to a higher future money supply, even if it leads to higher inflation. Krugman once called this "promising to be irresponsible."[8] This is perhaps an injudicious phrase if you are trying to push conservative central bankers to become more aggressive. But as we'll see, Krugman's insight underlies some increasingly popular policy proposals for monetary stimulus in the zero-interest-rate environment.

Krugman suggested that what people were calling a "liquidity trap" was actually an "expectations trap."[9] If the BOJ was unable to create inflation, it was because it could not convince the Japanese people that it would be willing to allow higher future inflation, especially once interest rates rose above zero. Paradoxically, the very fact that BOJ officials were so highly respected made their job much harder (although it also made their job easier when trying to prevent inflation). Perhaps if the BOJ board had been replaced with central bankers from hyperinflation-prone Zimbabwe, then it would have had an easier time convincing the Japanese people that inflation was on the way.

Economists call this the *time inconsistency problem*, but in this case you might also call it the "curse of competence." The underlying problem occurs more often than you might expect. For instance, a student's parents might threaten to not pay for college if their child uses drugs but then later relent because they feel their threat has failed, and they would still prefer for their child to go to college, all things considered. A wealthy businessman in Colombia might loudly proclaim that he'd refuse to pay ransom if

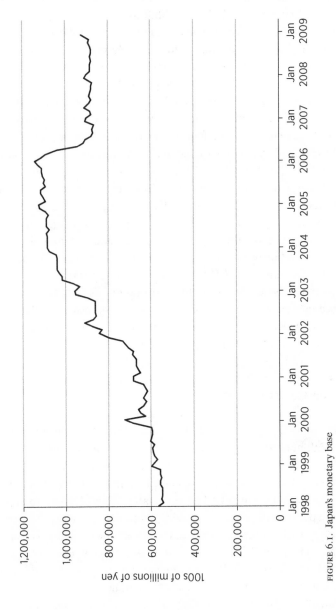

FIGURE 6.1. Japan's monetary base

Source: Bank of Japan, https://www.boj.or.jp/en/statistics/boj/other/mb/index.htm.

his child were kidnapped, and if he were believed, this might indeed help keep his children from being taken hostage. But if his pronouncement fails to deter the kidnapper, how will he react in the moment of truth? And what if the kidnapper can tell that he's bluffing?

After the 1970s, many countries reformed their central banks, with the goal of creating institutions that would credibly prevent high inflation. The central banks were made more independent of political pressure, and conservative hard-money types were appointed to lead the institutions. (Think of the coldhearted billionaire J. P. Getty, who rebuffed pleas to pay ransom to free his kidnapped grandson.) When these conservative policy makers found themselves needing to push inflation higher during the Great Recession, they had to struggle to change the public's perception of central bankers. The European Central Bank struggled more than most, precisely because it was created after the Great Inflation, and its mandate most strongly incorporated the anti-inflation views that held sway in the wake of that earlier policy failure.

Krugman's paper on the expectations trap assumed that the zero-interest-rate situation was temporary, which seemed reasonable at the time. But how long is temporary? It turns out that to be "permanent," a currency injection must last at least until the economy has exited the liquidity trap. Once interest rates rise above zero, the excess cash balances create inflation and, as Krugman emphasized, merely the expectation of future inflation will cause prices to start rising today.[10]

Interest on Reserves

Old-style monetarism received several more blows, which further weakened the link between the money supply and inflation. The first occurred in October 2008, when the Fed began paying interest on reserves (IOR) to commercial banks out of a misguided fear that high inflation would persist. The second occurred a few years later, when it began to appear that many countries might be facing near-permanent zero interest rates, if not slightly negative interest rates. Let's start with the interest on reserves.

Before 2008, the Fed paid no interest on base money (cash held by the public, and bank reserves). When interest rates were positive, the monetary base was almost entirely currency (including bank vault cash), with only about 2% of the total comprising bank reserves deposited at the Fed. Banks didn't want to hold lots of zero-interest excess reserves, because interest-bearing T-bills were just as useful a source of liquidity and offered a higher interest rate. After 2008, bank deposits at the Fed soared more than a hundredfold (fig. 6.2). Today, these bank deposits at the Fed account for more than half of the monetary base. Why?

For bank reserves to rise to such high levels, the opportunity cost of holding reserves must fall to close to zero. That can occur in one of two ways. In the 1930s, there was no interest on reserves, but market interest rates (on T-bills) fell to close to zero, so banks held lots of excess reserves. After 2008, bank reserve demand soared for two reasons: nominal rates fell to close to zero and the Fed began paying IOR.

At the end of 2015, the Fed began raising interest rates above zero. If the IOR had never been created, then the demand for bank reserves would have plunged sharply as soon as the Fed began raising rates. Without IOR, the Fed would be *unable* to raise interest rates without triggering inflation, unless it sharply reduced the amount of excess bank reserves in the economy. Banks simply don't want to hold trillions of dollars in zero-interest reserves if other safe assets like T-bills offer a higher yield.

In a world without IOR, bank reserves would have been cut back to very low levels before the Fed began raising rates in late 2015. But with IOR, the Fed can raise rates and avoid withdrawing the trillions in bank reserves injected in the three QE programs and still avoid high inflation. The IOR essentially "sterilizes" the excess reserves; it causes banks to continue holding on to excess reserves rather than pushing them out into the economy, where they will cause inflation.

Think of IOR as creating a permanent liquidity trap. Previously, bank reserves were close substitutes of T-bills only at zero interest rates; now bank reserves continue to be close substitutes at positive interest rates. This means that we should expect the correlation between the monetary base and the price level to be much weaker in the future than it was in the past. The quantity theory of money, which was already on the ropes after the early 1980s, will appear to be even less useful going forward.

Nonetheless, there will continue to be some correlation between monetary base and price level because currency continues to earn no interest. The currency portion of the base will continue to be strongly correlated with changes in the price level over the long run, at least when interest rates are positive. And it is still true that if you permanently double the monetary base, then, other things being equal, the price level will double in the long run.[11]

The second problem with monetarism is that there are indications that countries such as Japan and Switzerland may never exit the liquidity trap, or at least not for a period of many decades. If it ever became clear that

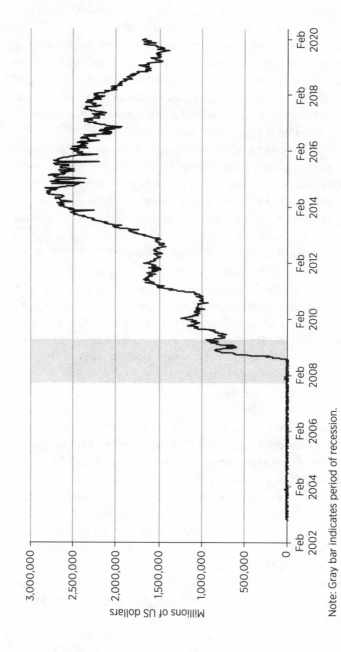

Note: Gray bar indicates period of recession.

FIGURE 6.2. Reserve balance at the Federal Reserve banks

Note: Gray bar indicates period of recession.
Source: FRED, via Board of Governors of the Federal Reserve System (US), https://fred.stlouisfed.org/series/WRBWFRBL.

interest rates on government bonds would never again rise above zero, then the monetary base and government debt would become almost perfect substitutes. In that case the relevant "money supply" would include both the base and the stock of zero-interest government debt.

While the US has never faced that sort of extreme liquidity trap, even during the Great Recession, both Japan and Switzerland have zero or even slightly negative yields on long-term government bonds. For monetary policy to be effective in a world of zero yields on long-term bonds, the central bank may have to purchase an asset that is not a close substitute for base money, such as equities or foreign bonds. The Bank of Japan did acquire substantial holdings of Japanese equities, and the Swiss National Bank accumulated large holdings of foreign bonds.

At first glance one might expect Switzerland to become a giant hedge fund, printing zero-interest money and using it to buy up foreign assets, thus creating a massive sovereign wealth fund. The already-wealthy Swiss could become even wealthier. However, the Swiss franc is very popular with outsiders precisely because investors know that the Swiss will not abuse franc holders by trying to cash in on the reputation of their currency. Fortunately, the near-zero yield on Swiss government bonds does not prevent the Swiss National Bank from stabilizing its price level. It buys and sells foreign assets to adjust the Swiss franc-euro exchange rate as needed to keep Switzerland from falling into a deep deflation.

It's not clear why the Japanese don't circumvent their liquidity trap by devaluing the yen to create inflation. One popular theory is that if they did so the US would accuse Japan of "currency manipulation" and impose retaliatory trade barriers. I'm not sure that's true, but clearly something is holding the Japanese back.

Expectations that Japanese inflation will remain quite low have led to a situation in which Japan's nominal interest rate is stuck near zero, and the demand for Japanese base money is extremely high. Before the Great Recession, the monetary base of a typical developed country was about 5% of GDP. Now (in 2019) the ratio is over 15% in the US, and Japan and Switzerland have monetary bases that are close to 100% of their GDPs.

How to Think about Monetary Theory in a Fiat Money World

We'll take another look at the widely misunderstood liquidity trap issue later, when we examine the role of monetary policy in the Great Recession.

For now let's summarize what we know about monetary policy and the price level, under a fiat money regime, from the first five chapters.

First, the circumstance that economists understand best is rapid and persistent money-supply growth rates, such as the US saw during the Great Inflation. In such a case, the long-run increase in the price level is roughly proportional to the long-run increase in the money supply. More importantly, the inflation is clearly *caused by* the persistent increases in the money supply. We know this because changes in the other two parts of the equation of exchange (real GDP growth and the average annual change in velocity) tend to be rather small during periods when nominal interest rates are above zero.

Second, rapid *acceleration* in the growth of the money supply (when interest rates are positive) adds only one minor complication. During the period of acceleration, the velocity of circulation also rises, because people and banks are less willing to hold base money that is losing value at a more rapid rate than before. We are still mostly in a QTM world, except that inflation outpaces money growth during the transition to high inflation (and vice versa when inflation declines).

Third, everything changes when increases in the money supply are temporary. New Keynesians like Paul Krugman emphasize that temporary currency injections are not very inflationary at the zero bound. I would go even further: temporary currency injections are *never* very inflationary, even if they begin when the economy is not at the zero bound. Again, no one wants to pay $400,000 today for a house that was worth $200,000 last week and will be worth $200,000 again after the currency injection is withdrawn. And that's true even if interest rates were 5% at the time of the currency injection.

But this raises a question: how do we get people to hold these large excess cash balances if the temporary doubling of the money supply occurs when interest rates are still positive? What prevents the normal hot-potato effect in that case? The answer is simple: if the injection is expected to be temporary, then short-term interest rates will immediately fall close to zero, which will motivate people and banks to hold on to the extra base money. Little or no inflation will occur as long as money demand rises along with the increased money supply. Therefore, it is misleading to argue that temporary currency injections are ineffective when they occur in a liquidity trap. Temporary currency injections are *never* effective, because if the economy is not already in a liquidity trap, then the temporary currency injection will create one.

Fourth, the quantity theory of money is generally least useful when interest rates are zero. But this is not because base money and T-bills are perfect substitutes at zero interest rates—rather, it is because a monetary injection that drives rates to zero is usually expected to be temporary. Consider these four cases:

1. A permanent doubling of the money supply at a time when interest rates are 5%
2. A permanent doubling of the money supply at a time when interest rates are 0%
3. A temporary doubling of the money supply at a time when interest rates are 5%
4. A temporary doubling of the money supply at a time when interest rates are 0%

If we focus on zero interest rates as the key issue, we will have assumed that monetary policy is ineffective in cases 2 and 4, where interest rates are zero. But that's not the case. In case 2, prices rise strongly because the injection is expected to produce lots of inflation once the economy is no longer at the zero bound. Instead, it is cases 3 and 4 in which monetary policy is ineffective. The only complication is that in case 3 the interest rate will immediately fall to zero after the currency injection.

Why Does Fiat Money Have Any Value?

Because the effect of today's monetary policy depends on the future path of policy, there is a basic *indeterminacy problem* embedded in any fiat money model of the economy. It's impossible to evaluate the impact of Fed policy in 2020 without knowing the inflation rate in 2021. But it's not possible to know the inflation rate in 2021 without knowing Fed policy in 2021 as well as the inflation rate in 2022, and so on. To evaluate the impact of current monetary policy, we need to know more than what the Fed is doing right now. Ignorance of this fact led to enormous confusion during the Great Recession, when the effect of monetary policy was widely misdiagnosed.

For example, suppose the public thought the Hong Kong dollar would collapse in the year 2047 (when Hong Kong is scheduled to lose its autonomy), leaving the money with zero value. If that were the expectation, then no one would want to hold Hong Kong dollars in 2046, knowing that the currency would soon be worthless. But that fact would make the Hong Kong dollar worthless in 2046. And that expectation would make the Hong Kong dollar worthless in 2045. Using backward induction, it's not obvious why fiat money has any value at all.

Economia não é pra mim.
& Economicia

There are many solutions to this dilemma. Perhaps fiat money has value because it can be used to pay taxes. Or because the risk of it becoming worthless is less than 1% in any given year, and it's useful enough for people to take that risk. As we saw with colonial currency, some claim that fiat currencies in low-inflation countries are implicitly "backed" by government debt.

My view is closely related to this backing theory. I believe that the public (perhaps subconsciously) assumes that if a government abolishes a currency, it will give money holders something of equal value in return. Thus, holders of French francs were given euros when the franc was abolished in 2002, and Hong Kong residents probably expect to receive equivalent Chinese yuan in 2047. If all currency is abolished, holders probably expect to receive something of equal value, such as T-bills or accounts at the central bank. You may not think that bumblebees should be able to fly, but they clearly do. You may not think that fiat money should have any value, but it clearly does.

In the end, I don't worry too much about explaining why currency has value, but I do worry about explaining how its value changes over time. And the indeterminacy problem makes it really difficult to do so. Because the value of a currency today depends heavily on what it is expected to be worth in the future, and because that future value depends on the future path of monetary policy, it's almost impossible to predict the impact of any single "concrete action" taken today by the central bank. An increase in the money supply or a change in IOR can have very different effects, depending on whether the change is expected to be temporary or permanent.

Nick Rowe, a well-known blogger on monetary issues, called people who failed to see this point "the people of the concrete steppes."[12] These are people obsessed with establishing the impact of a specific monetary policy by evaluating what concrete steps were taken to implement the policy. But these debates are completely sterile. "Does QE boost inflation?" doesn't even rise to the level of a question. Compared to what? Accompanied by what future policy? Consider the following two policy shocks:

1. The Bank of Japan suddenly doubles the monetary base, promising to remove all the extra money from circulation the moment inflation shows signs of exceeding 2%.

2. The Japanese government replaces the leadership of the BOJ with a team from Zimbabwe. This team indicates no change in the monetary base for the next year, but after that Japan will adopt a 500% inflation target and will buy up as

many assets from all over the world (with newly printed yen) as needed to hit that target. The salaries of these Zimbabwe officials will be directly linked to BOJ profits from printing yen. (These profits are called *seigniorage*.)

The first policy option looks inflationary to the "concrete steppes" people but would actually have almost no impact. The second policy option involves no short-term concrete steps at all, but could well push Japan into hyperinflation before a single new yen is printed. The mere expectation of this policy regime could easily cause the velocity of yen already in circulation to rise by a factor of 10, if not more.

The Market Test

Because fiat money models involve an indeterminacy problem, we need to find some solid ground to stand on. It does no good to say we have no idea what QE or IOR will do because the effect depends on future action. Policy makers need guidance. In my view, this solid ground can be found in only one place: the asset markets. We need to evaluate the stance of monetary policy by looking at the expected impact on the price level. (Later we'll see that the impact on expected nominal GDP growth is even more important.) And the most important expectations are those of investors who buy and sell assets. The broader public generally takes its lead from the asset market reaction.

One useful approach is to find inflation expectations embedded in existing asset markets, such as the spread between interest rates on conventional Treasury securities and the interest rate on Treasury Inflation-Protected Securities (TIPS). Because the interest rate on conventional Treasury bonds is a nominal interest rate, whereas the yield on TIPS is a real interest rate, the Fisher equation tells us that the gap should equal roughly the expected rate of inflation.

More specifically, the TIPS spread should provide a good estimate of expected inflation in the case where the two bonds are viewed as close substitutes, with *total* rates of return from each investment expected to be roughly equal. Thus, if conventional bonds yield 5% and TIPS give their holders 2% (real) plus the actual future inflation rate, then these two bonds would have equal total yields if inflation were 3%. If the two bonds were close substitutes, equally appealing to investors, then 3% would be the market's expected rate of inflation.

If the so-called TIPS spread does not accurately measure inflation expectations (because the two bonds are not perfect substitutes), then we
need to try to create alternative prediction markets to derive the consensus forecast of inflation and other key variables such as NGDP. More on
that later.

By the end of this book I hope to convince you to ignore what the
Fed is doing to the current money supply, or to its interest rate target,
and instead focus on market expectations of inflation, or—better yet—
NGDP growth. Monetary shocks will be represented by *changes in expected NGDP growth*. These monetary shocks may or may not be caused
by concrete actions taken right now by the central bank. If they are policy
mistakes, they may be errors of omission or errors of commission. More
importantly, it makes absolutely no difference which type of error they
are. For instance, we'll see that the Great Recession was triggered by a
tight money policy that looks like an error of omission if you focus on interest rates and an error of commission if you focus on the monetary base.

In the end, there is no such thing as the central bank "doing nothing,"
because there are a dozen different ways of evaluating what the central
bank is actually doing. Does it control the base? Interest on reserves?
Longer-term interest rates? Exchange rates? The broader M2 money supply? The price of gold? The expected inflation rate in TIPS markets? Doing nothing to the monetary base might mean doing something to interest
rates, and vice versa.

Nick Rowe likes to point out that it makes no sense to ask whether the
capitalist economy is "inherently" unstable.[13] The term *inherently* has no
meaning here. The answer depends entirely on what monetary regime
is lurking in the background. A capitalist economy might be stable with
NGDP level targeting and unstable on a gold standard. For similar reasons, it makes no sense to talk about a *fiscal multiplier* because the effect
of fiscal policy depends on what the monetary authority is doing at the
same time, and—as we've just seen—it's nonsensical to talk about central
banks "doing nothing."

Don't worry if you don't agree with the philosophical perspective Nick
Rowe and I have taken: nothing of substance depends on holding this view
of how to describe central bank policies. But this perspective does make
it easier to understand where we're going in the second half of the book.

This concludes the first part of the book, which has begun to explain monetary theory by focusing on monetary policy's impact on nominal variables

such as the price level and NGDP. But the most interesting monetary issues revolve around the effect of policy on real variables. Next we will look at money and business cycles, followed by money and interest rates; finally, we will end the theory half of the book with money and exchange rates. When we move into business cycles in part 2, we leave behind the world of monetary neutrality.

PART II

The Dance of the Dollar

CHAPTER SEVEN

The Great Depression
and the AS-AD Model

W hen I was young, I was greatly influenced by Milton Friedman and
Anna Schwartz's *A Monetary History of the United States*. Like
most readers, I was particularly interested in their analysis of the Great
Depression, and when I eventually became a college professor, my primary research interest was monetary policy and theory during the interwar period (1918–1939).

Friedman and Schwartz were leaders of the monetarist school of thought
and rivals to the more dominant Keynesian consensus. Before they wrote
Monetary History, the Great Depression was widely seen as an example
of the inherent instability of capitalism (a meaningless concept, as we just
saw). In this view, the financial system is especially prone to crisis and panic.
Between 1929 and 1933, a stock-market crash, a series of banking panics,
and a loss of confidence in the gold standard led to the hoarding of money
and a steep drop in aggregate demand (total spending). The result was
deflation and high unemployment. Monetary policy was seen as expansionary but largely ineffective for standard liquidity-trap reasons.

This is quite similar to today's consensus view of the Great Recession.
In 2007–2008 we had financial instability combined with a monetary policy that was seen as expansionary but largely ineffective. Today, most
economists reject the pre-1960 consensus view of the Great Depression.
Now, we need a similar reevaluation of the conventional narrative about
the Great Recession.

Friedman and Schwartz convinced many economists that Fed policy
was actually excessively contractionary during the Great Depression,
and that this policy failure largely explains the depth and severity of the

1929–1933 contraction. Many of today's economics textbooks provide something like Friedman and Schwartz's critique of Fed policy in their discussion of the Great Depression. Ben Bernanke is a big fan of their work, and he famously promised that the Fed would never again repeat the mistakes of the 1930s. At Friedman's ninetieth birthday celebration, Bernanke said, "Let me end my talk by abusing slightly my status as an official representative of the Federal Reserve. I would like to say to Milton and Anna: Regarding the Great Depression. You're right, we did it. We're very sorry. But thanks to you, we won't do it again."[1] On the other hand, it's fair to say that the Great Recession has led to some second thoughts about the Friedman and Schwartz story. Bernanke (who was Fed chair at the time) certainly doesn't believe that a tight money policy caused the Great Recession.[2]

Later I'll argue that the Fed did "do it again," fortunately with errors that were an order of magnitude less severe. But if Bernanke's Fed was unable to prevent the Great Recession, does that call into question Friedman's claim that the Fed could have prevented the Great Depression? Revisiting this issue will provide a useful vantage point from which to reexamine the Great Recession.

Monetary History Was Ahead of Its Time

My view of Milton Friedman doesn't neatly align either with that of his (Keynesian) critics or with that of his (monetarist) supporters. I see Friedman as the great theorist of fiat money, and yet the book he coauthored with Anna Schwartz describes an economy operating under three different versions of a gold standard. To see why this distinction matters, let's think about the Friedman and Schwartz explanation for the Great Contraction of 1929–1933, at its most basic level. In Friedman and Schwartz's view, the proximate cause of the Great Contraction was a roughly 50% plunge in M × V, which implies a 50% plunge in NGDP (P × Y). Put simply, by early 1933 Americans were, in aggregate, earning and spending only about half as much as they had been in 1929.

The proximate cause of this huge plunge in M × V (in Friedman and Schwartz's view) was a highly contractionary Fed policy, which caused (or allowed, depending on your perspective) the broader monetary aggregates (M1 and M2) to plunge by about 30%. (Falling velocity explains the rest.) Regardless of whether you view this as a Fed error of omission or of commission, Friedman and Schwartz argue that it was in the Fed's power to prevent it, and hence the Fed was to blame for the Great Depression. The fall in velocity was a side effect of the Depression, but the fall in M was the primary cause. As M × V fell sharply, both P and Y did as well.

We've already seen how money can affect prices, and in this chapter we'll begin exploring how it affects real output as well. Before doing so, however, let's see if we can better understand the changing fortune of Friedman's monetarism.

Between 1879 and 1933, the dollar was pegged to gold at $20.67 per ounce. From 1934 to 1968, the price of gold was $35 per ounce. During most of the period when the US was on the gold standard, the trend rate of inflation averaged close to zero, with a few periods of high inflation during the 1940s, as the price level adjusted to the 1934 devaluation of the dollar and to the ban on Americans owning gold. Nonetheless, when Friedman and Schwartz's book came out in 1963, the US was still loosely attached to gold, and it was by no means clear that the Fed had as much ability to control the money supply and price level as Friedman and Schwartz assumed in *Monetary History*.

The story Friedman and Schwartz told was in some ways more appropriate for a fiat money regime, in which the central bank has virtually unlimited ability to expand or contract the money supply. In a stroke of good fortune, *Monetary History* was published just five years before the price of gold began rising, and right on the eve of the Great Inflation. Even better, the dominant Keynesian view of the Great Depression did share one important area of agreement with Friedman and Schwartz: that the nearly 50% fall in M × V was the proximate cause of the Great Contraction. People often overlook this point because Keynesians preferred terminology such as "aggregate demand" over "M × V." But both sides saw the Depression as being caused by a spending shortfall.

Thus, to convince Keynesians of their thesis, Friedman and Schwartz didn't need to convince them that plunging M × V was the big problem, only that the Fed could have prevented M × V from falling with more responsible monetary policies. And in a sense it was even easier than that, because the Keynesian theory of inflation suggested that prices fall during depressions and rise during booms. Thus, if Friedman and Schwartz could convince the Keynesians that the Fed could have prevented deflation, or even created a bit of inflation, then, ipso facto, they would have demonstrated that erroneous monetary policy caused the Great Contraction. And what better time to convince economists that the Fed could have prevented deflation during the 1930s than during a period when the main problem was rapid inflation, a problem that (in the 1960s and 1970s) seemed much easier to create than to stop?

I imagine that when older Keynesians expressed skepticism that the Fed could have created 2% inflation in the 1930s, younger Keynesians shook their heads in disbelief. To see why, go back and look at table 4.1. Previously, I suggested that this international money and inflation data convinced lots of economists that different trend inflation rates could be chosen as items can be ordered off a menu: "Waiter, I think I'll order 4% inflation for this decade." As interest rates soared into the double digits, the notion of a liquidity trap seemed increasingly quaint. Another famous monetarist, Allan Meltzer, asked why, if Keynes was so worried about monetary policy ineffectiveness, he didn't just recommend a high enough inflation target so that nominal interest rates would never fall to zero.[3] Excellent question! In the wake of the Great Recession, many prominent macroeconomists asked exactly the same question of modern central banks.

To summarize, by the 1970s and the early 1980s, it seemed obvious that central banks could create inflation if they wished to do so. Whether the gold standard precluded that sort of policy in the 1930s was considered a question of interest to only antiquarians. Surely, preserving the gold standard was not worth risking a Great Depression, especially one that may have contributed to the rise of the Nazis.[4] The costs of the Great Depression seemed vastly greater than the costs of fiat money, even during the worst of the Great Inflation. Thus, a whole generation of younger Keynesians accepted much of Friedman and Schwartz's view of the Depression, and this led to a new hybrid view, dubbed "New Keynesianism," which combined monetarist ideas about the importance of money and Keynesian ideas about interest-rate targeting and stabilization policy.

By the 1990s, there was a rather broad consensus that the Fed needed to do something like inflation (or NGDP) targeting and that the failure to do so in the 1930s had been a hugely consequential mistake. After 2008, however, old-style Keynesianism came roaring back into intellectual fashion. Interest rates fell to zero and economists again began questioning the effectiveness of monetary stimulus. Fiscal stimulus came back in vogue. The global financial crisis revived theories of the inherent instability of capitalism. Revisionists such as Paul Krugman began to question the accuracy of Friedman and Schwartz's explanation of the Great Contraction.[5] Unfortunately, Friedman died in 2006 and could not defend his view that monetary policy is the key to the business cycle.

Ironically, I think Friedman and Schwartz's basic story better fits the

Great Recession, which Friedman never lived to see, than the Great Depression of the 1930s, which he and Schwartz were trying to explain. Now we do have the sort of pure fiat money regime that monetarism is best suited to explain. Unlike in the 1930s, central banks really did have unlimited ability to print money and prop up inflation in 2008.

In fairness, the Fed avoided the worst mistakes of the 1930s and also did much better than the European Central Bank. Monetary policy errors were certainly not the only cause of the Great Recession; the US also faced some structural problems, which slowed the recovery. Nonetheless, the Fed does bear most of the blame for the Great Recession. Later we'll see how a different Fed policy regime could have prevented anything worse than a mild recession in 2008–2009.

Aggregate Supply and Demand

Why should a 50% plunge in nominal GDP also lead to a sharp decline in real GDP? In other words, why didn't the tight money policy of 1929 merely reduce prices, leaving output unchanged? Why aren't changes in the money supply neutral? It turns out that this is the central problem in macroeconomics and also one of the most difficult to solve. Even today, there is no consensus about why money seems to be highly nonneutral in the short run and roughly neutral in the long run. The view that is (misleadingly) called *classical economics* predicts that printing money should just lead to higher prices, not greater real output. And the reverse should also be true: a reduction in the money supply should reduce prices, leaving real output unchanged.

Actually, even the classical economists knew that money was nonneutral in the short run. Here is David Hume:

> We must consider, that though the high price of commodities be a necessary consequence of the encrease of gold and silver, yet it follows not immediately upon that encrease; but some time is required before the money circulates through the whole state, and makes its effect be felt on all ranks of people. At first, no alteration is perceived; by degrees the price rises, first of one commodity, then of another; till the whole at last reaches a just proportion with the new quantity of specie [money] which is in the kingdom. In my opinion, it is only in this interval or intermediate situation, between the acquisition of money and rise of prices, that the encreasing quantity of gold and silver is favourable to industry.[6]

So money affects prices only in the long run, but during a transition period before prices have adjusted, changes in the money stock also affect real output. Most economists still look at things that way. In fact, Hume's short essay "Of Money" from 1752 is a stunning intellectual achievement, in many ways unsurpassed until the 1970s. Here's another example, discussing a decrease in the money stock, occurring just two pages after the previous one:

> A nation, whose money decreases, is actually, at that time, weaker and more miserable then another nation, which possesses no more money, but is on the encreasing hand. This will be easily accounted for, if we consider, that the alterations in the quantity of money, either on one side or the other, are not immediately attended with proportionable alterations in the price of commodities. There is always an interval before matters be adjusted to their new situation; and this interval is as pernicious to industry, when gold and silver are diminishing, as it is advantageous when these metals are encreasing.[7]

And perhaps even more pernicious: "The workman has not the same employment from the manufacturer and merchant; though he pays the same price for everything in the market. The farmer cannot dispose of his corn and cattle; though he must pay the same rent to his landlord. The poverty, the beggary, and sloth, which must ensue, are easily foreseen."[8] Hume is describing what the Great Depression looked like, and what caused it, back in 1752!

Hume also understood that economic growth is deflationary, ceteris paribus—a point still not understood by many modern economists: "It seems a maxim almost self-evident, that the prices of every thing depend on the proportion between commodities and money, and that any considerable alteration on either has the same effect, either of heightening or lowering the price. Encrease the commodities, they become cheaper; encrease the money, they rise in their value."[9] Recall the equation of exchange:

$$M \times V = P \times Y.$$

Hume is saying that an increase in M leads to higher prices, whereas an increase in Y (other things remaining equal) leads to lower prices. And he's right.

You might think that Hume was a simpleminded monetarist who didn't understand that velocity could also impact aggregate demand. Not so: "It is also evident, that the prices do not so much depend on the absolute quantity of commodities and that of money, which are in a nation, as on that of the commodities, which come or may come to market, and of the money which circulates. If the coin be locked up in chests, it is the same thing with regard to prices, as if it were annihilated."[10] Hume is saying that a fall in velocity is every bit as deflationary as a fall in the money supply. Thus, what really matters is not movements in M, but movements in M × V. And when M × V changes, it initially has an impact on both prices and output, but in the long run only prices are affected. This is also my basic view of monetary economics.

In the twentieth century, macroeconomics initially took a step backward with early Keynesianism. Not surprisingly, macroeconomics took another step backward after 2008, because the Great Recession was misdiagnosed in an almost identical fashion to the events of the 1930s, and for much the same reason. To the casual observer it looked as if capitalism were inherently unstable and monetary policy largely ineffective—two ideas that are central to old-style Keynesianism.

The early Keynesians thought that inflation was caused by a booming economy, whereas Hume had shown that booms are actually deflationary. Unlike Hume, early Keynesians mostly ignored the supply side in their models. They also assumed fixed prices in the short run, with output determined solely by demand shocks. You may have seen this in a "Keynesian cross" graph in a principles of economics textbook.

Later in the twentieth century, macroeconomists again caught up to Hume, with the development of the aggregate supply and demand (AS-AD) model, pictured in figure 7.1. At first glance, this looks like an ordinary diagram of supply and demand, albeit for the entire economy. In fact, it's completely unrelated to the supply-and-demand model of microeconomics, which applies to individual markets. In fact, this diagram should not even use the terms *supply* and *demand*. For instance, when the price of a single good rises, people shift to substitute goods. But when the overall price level rises in an AS-AD model, there are no substitute goods to shift to. That's because Y includes all goods.

The aggregate demand curve has nothing to do with the concept of demand as used in microeconomics. I wish the AD curve had instead been labeled "NS" for *nominal spending* or "NI" for *nominal income*. But that's not the world we live in.

Similarly, the AS curve is completely different from an individual-industry supply curve. For instance, in most industries the long-run supply

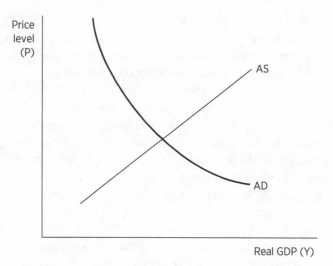

FIGURE 7.1. Aggregate supply-and-demand model

curve is almost perfectly elastic (flat), because rising prices draw in new firms, bringing prices back down in the long run. But at the aggregate level, the long-run supply curve is perfectly inelastic (vertical), because it reflects the productive capacity of the entire economy. Because resources are limited, printing money to boost aggregate demand serves only to increase prices in the long run, with output unaffected.

Demand Shocks in the Short and Long Run

In theory, the AS-AD model can be used to explain inflation, to explain long-run economic growth, or to explain business cycles. But the real purpose of the model was to explain business cycles—those other issues are better explained with alternative models. So let's focus on business cycles, especially those created by demand shocks (changes in M × V).

Let's start by looking at the short- and long-run impact of an expansionary monetary policy (or an increase in V): take a look at figure 7.2. After the money supply increases, people try to get rid of excess cash balances by spending them. Aggregate demand (nominal spending) increases, shifting to the right. Because some wages and prices are "sticky," or slow to adjust, some of the increased spending shows up as higher output, and only a portion shows up as higher prices (point B). This is the inflationary boom that leads many Keynesians to wrongly view any fast-growing economy as necessarily inflationary. As you can see, a boom that results from increased aggregate supply (holding M × V fixed) is actually deflationary. Higher inflation will occur only if the boom is caused by higher aggregate demand.

In the long run, all wages and prices adjust to the new reality after AD increases. At that point, the short-run AS curve has shifted back, and output returns to the *natural rate*, which is the long-run equilibrium once all wages and prices have had time to adjust (point C). In this long-run equilibrium, the price level has risen exactly in proportion to the increase in nominal spending. Think of the AS-AD model as illustrating Hume's intuition about money, velocity, prices, and output, in both the short run and the long run. Of course in the real world things are often complicated, with both AD and AS changing at the same time.

Figure 7.3 shows the situation during the early 1930s. At point A we are in macroeconomic equilibrium. Nominal GDP (the product of P and Y) was about $100 billion in 1929 and fell to roughly $49 billion in early 1933.[11] That 51% decline in nominal spending is reflected in the sharp decline in AD, which initially reduced both prices and output by roughly 30% (point B). At that point wages and prices should have adjusted downward,

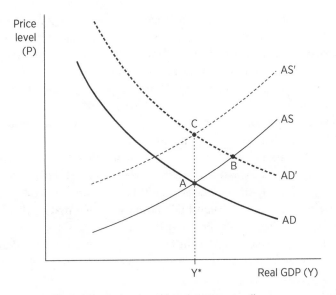

FIGURE 7.2. Model of the impact of an expansionary monetary policy

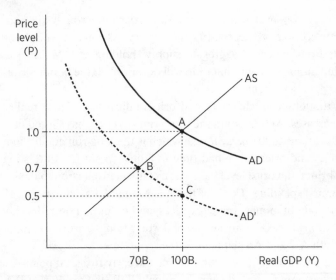

FIGURE 7.3. Model of the US situation during the early 1930s

and the US economy should have returned to equilibrium at point C, with prices at only about half the 1929 levels.[12] Before that long-run adjustment could occur, American voters became fed up with four years of deep depression and brought a new administration into power in March 1933.

Almost immediately, President Roosevelt began trying to boost AD, mostly by sharply devaluing the dollar. For the most part he succeeded: AD rose very rapidly between 1933 and 1934. Initially output also grew explosively, with monthly industrial production rising by an astounding 57% between March and July 1933, three times faster than at any other point in US history.

So why did the Great Depression drag on until 1941? Unfortunately, FDR could not leave well enough alone. He viewed deflation and falling wages as the cause of the Great Depression and therefore had Congress enact the (misnamed) National Industrial Recovery Act (NIRA) to boost wages and prices. Farmers and merchants were ordered to reduce output in order to boost prices. Then FDR began worrying that workers were falling behind inflation, and he decided to artificially boost wages through an emergency executive order. In late July 1933, firms were ordered to raise hourly wages by roughly 20% almost overnight, and the recovery immediately stalled.

Industrial production would not regain levels from July 1933 for another two years, after the NIRA program was ruled unconstitutional in

May 1935. The rapid recovery resumed but was repeatedly interrupted by counterproductive federal actions throughout the late 1930s. My research on the Great Depression helped me to better understand the Great Recession, especially when it got serious in late 2008.[13]

Never Reason from a Price Change

Roosevelt's entire NIRA program was based on a fallacy that I've dubbed "reasoning from a price change." Economics students, journalists, and even distinguished economists occasionally make the mistake of drawing implications from the change in a price. For example, they might see rising oil prices and predict that consumers will use less oil.

Many people erroneously assume that this sort of reasoning is based on the supply-and-demand model, but they are wrong. High prices are just as likely to be associated with rising consumption as with falling consumption—it all depends on the cause of the price increase. If oil prices rise because the Organization of the Petroleum-Exporting Countries, or OPEC, cuts back on production, then consumers will indeed consume less oil. This occurred in 1974. But if oil prices rise because of a booming global economy, then consumers will use more oil. This occurred in 2008.

Rather than reasoning from a price change, we want to first ask, "Are the higher prices caused by less supply or by more demand?" Later we'll see that the worst forms of reasoning from a price change occur with interest rates. Indeed, misinterpreting the implications of falling interest rates played a big role in *causing* the Great Recession. But first let's return our focus to the price of goods and labor, and think about what FDR was doing wrong.

Roosevelt noticed that prices and wages often rose during periods of prosperity and fell during periods of depression. This all makes sense—or at least seems to—at an individual level. Low prices lead companies to lose money and go bankrupt, and low wages make workers poorer, which reduces aggregate demand. Although this interpretation might *seem* to make sense, it's actually an example of reasoning from a price change. It's like a middle-class person noticing that wealthy people often have big swimming pools and expensive Italian sports cars, and wrongly assuming that purchasing these items will make someone richer.

Roosevelt's high-wage policy put the cart before the horse. What was needed was more aggregate demand to boost output, which would eventually lead to higher wages and higher living standards. But artificially raising hourly wages has the effect of reducing aggregate supply, discouraging companies from employing workers. As the aggregate supply curve shifts to the left, prices do indeed rise, but it's not the sort of inflation you get from a booming economy—it's the inflation that David Hume had in mind when he discussed the implications of reducing the number of commodities while holding the money supply constant.[14]

The Phillips Curve

The notion that inflation leads to prosperity was so deeply ingrained during the 1930s that it led to seemingly absurd policies, such as killing off lots of pigs to push meat prices higher and telling farmers not to plant wheat. A more subtle form of this fallacy developed in the 1960s, with the growing popularity of the so-called Phillips-curve model. This model was named after an empirical relationship discovered (actually rediscovered) by A. W. Phillips in 1958. (Irving Fisher illustrated the Phillips curve concept in his 1923 paper "The Business Cycle Largely a 'Dance of the Dollar.'")

Phillips showed that there had been a fairly strong negative correlation between the rate of wage inflation and the rate of unemployment in Great Britain during the previous hundred years. So FDR was right about one thing: rising wages really were associated with strong labor markets more often than not. But this does not imply that artificially pushing up the cost of labor will lead companies to want to hire more workers. If you don't agree, I encourage you go out and purchase a Ferrari and see if it makes you rich.

Phillips's research had a profound effect on economic thinking during the 1960s. Keep in mind that the leading policy makers in government are typically around fifty or sixty years old. In the 1960s, this generation would have come of age during the Great Depression, a time of high unemployment and periods of deflation. Because people tend to form their political views when relatively young, this generation was much more concerned about unemployment than inflation.[15] They decided to try to exploit the Phillips-curve relationship by adopting expansionary monetary and fiscal policies. There was a widespread assumption that Phillips's research had demonstrated the existence of a trade-off between inflation and unemployment, and that lower unemployment could be purchased at the cost of a bit more inflation. To their credit, this policy did work for a period of time (fig. 7.4).

Keynesian policy makers weren't completely oblivious to the "never

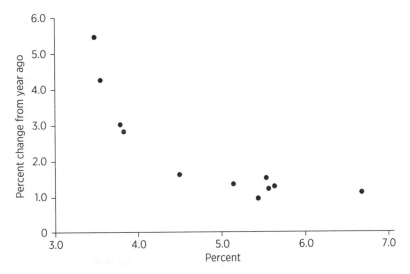

FIGURE 7.4. The relationship between inflation and unemployment during the 1960s

Source: FRED, via Bureau of Labor Statistics, https://fred.stlouisfed.org/series/CPIAUCSL, https://fred.stlouisfed.org/series/UNRATE.

reason from a price change" issue. Instead of relying on adverse supply-side policies such as the NIRA, the Keynesians of the 1960s promoted policies that would boost aggregate demand—that is, policies that would increase M × V at a faster rate than before. As an aside, contrary to the "guns and butter" story that you were probably taught in school, expansionary fiscal policy of the Vietnam War era was not a factor in the 1960s inflation. It was expansionary monetary policy that caused the inflationary boom of the 1960s. Budget deficits were pretty small during the 1960s, especially in real terms. Also recall that strong economic growth is actually deflationary, other things being equal.

Unfortunately, after 1969 it all fell apart, and we moved into the stagflation of the 1970s, with both higher unemployment and higher inflation. And the way this fell apart is one of the most interesting stories in all of macroeconomics. In other fields, such as physics, the discovery of new theories does not change the way the world works. This is not the case in economics. The discovery of the Phillips-curve relationship, as well as its subsequent impact on policy, created a situation in which the Phillips-curve model no longer worked. In the next chapter, we'll find out what was wrong with the original Phillips-curve model and how the discovery of its flaws led to a revolution in macroeconomics.

CHAPTER EIGHT

One Derivative beyond Hume

I t should have been obvious from the beginning that there was a problem with using the Phillips curve as a "structural" model of the economy, which means a model that is based on fundamental principles and that can be expected to continue providing accurate predictions when policy changes. But it wasn't obvious at the time, and I think we now know why. Economists in the 1960s had very little experience with a pure fiat money regime, at least in major developed economies. And the experiences they did have, such as the various postwar hyperinflations in Europe, were viewed as pathological cases—exceptions, not the rule.

Just as fish don't realize they are wet, economists never recognized that they had mostly lived under monetary regimes with commodity anchors. In 1968, an eighty-nine-year-old economist would have lived his or her entire life with the price of gold being either $20.67 per ounce or $35 per ounce, with the only major exception occurring during a nine-month period of transition in 1933–1934. That commodity anchor usually led to near-zero inflation expectations. Actual inflation was often very different from zero—sometimes positive and sometimes negative. But the *expected* rate of inflation was generally close to zero, or perhaps in the low single digits in the post–World War II period. As an analogy, the actual movement in a US stock market index, such as the S&P 500, on any given day is often quite substantial—say 50 or 100 basis points. But that's almost entirely unexpected; the expected daily move is probably just 1 or 2 basis points, which is its long-term upward trend.

Macroeconomic models, including the Austrian and Keynesian models (but not monetarism), reflected the gold standard much more than people realized. Keynes is often viewed as an opponent of the gold standard, but he was even more strongly opposed to a pure fiat money regime. In *A Treatise on Money* (1930), Keynes called an unmanaged gold standard "the worst of all conceivable systems (apart from the abuses of a *fiat* money which has lost all its anchors)."[1] Three years later, Keynes reiterated his support for a gold anchor for prices:

> At all stages of the post-war developments the concrete proposals which I have brought forward from time to time have been based on the use of gold as an international standard, whilst discarding it as a rigid national standard. The qualifications which I have added to this have been always the same, though the precise details have varied; namely (1) that the parities between national standards and gold should not be rigid, (2) that there should be a wider margin than in the past between the gold points, and (3) that if possible some international control should be formed with a view to regulating the commodity value of gold within certain limits.[2]

This is why Keynes never recommended a positive inflation target as a way of overcoming the liquidity trap. You can't have a positive inflation target without abandoning gold and moving toward a pure fiat money regime. Instead, Keynes favored a flexible gold standard, something not all that different from the Bretton Woods regime (1944–1971), which Keynes helped to develop.

The End of Gold and the Natural-Rate Hypothesis

In the late 1960s, Edmund Phelps and Milton Friedman developed the natural-rate hypothesis. They argued that what mattered was not whether inflation was high or low, but whether it was higher or lower than expected. Unemployment will be low when inflation is higher than expected, and it will be high when inflation is lower than expected. When expected inflation adjusts to actual inflation, the unemployment rate will move back to what Phelps and Friedman called the *natural rate*, which represents the rate of unemployment when wages and prices have adjusted to an economic shocks.[3] In the US, this rate is believed to fluctuate between about 3.5% and 6.5%.

Because inflation expectations were close to zero under the gold standard, any Phillips curve estimated during that period will show high unemployment when prices were falling and low unemployment when prices were rising. But suppose we try to manipulate the Phillips curve by artificially pushing inflation higher with an expansionary monetary policy. What happens next?

The Phillips-curve relationship might continue to hold for a few more years, because the initial increase in inflation was largely unanticipated. Because wages are slow to adjust, a sharp and unexpected rise in inflation will initially lead to more output, more jobs, and a lower unemployment rate. That describes the latter half of the 1960s. But this persistent inflation eventually caused problems, because the price of gold was pegged at $35 per ounce. As prices rose, investors saw that gold was a bargain and began demanding gold in exchange for dollars. On March 14, 1968, the US government stopped allowing foreign individuals to redeem dollars for gold. (Americans had been banned from holding gold bullion since 1933.) The free-market price of gold began rising above $35 per ounce in the international gold markets, and it hovered around $40 per ounce in the second half of the year.

In retrospect, more than two thousand years of human history ended with a whimper on March 14, 1968, when commodity money was effectively dead.[4] But initially, almost no one realized what had happened. That's partly because the US had been gradually edging away from the gold standard since 1933, so closing the window to foreign individuals didn't seem that big a deal. The dollar wasn't officially devalued until August 1971, when the window was also closed to foreign central banks. You might say that after the 1971 devaluation, instead of refusing to sell gold at $35 an ounce, the US began refusing to sell gold at $38.50 an ounce!

Because the importance of this transition was not recognized at the time, the economics profession was woefully unprepared to understand what was coming. Milton Friedman was probably best prepared, although perhaps for the wrong reason. Recall that Friedman and Anna Schwartz have been criticized for interpreting monetary policy during the 1930s as if the Fed had no important constraints on its ability to print money. Now they were in a world where this formerly dubious assumption was actually true. Inflation expectations began rising almost immediately—and Friedman (along with Edmund Phelps) recognized two key points, which the broader profession initially overlooked:

- He recognized that as the trend rate of inflation rose, inflation expectations also increased, causing the Phillips-curve relationship to break down.
- He recognized the importance of the Fisher effect. For years the profession had been mostly ignoring the distinction between real and nominal interest rates.

Low nominal rates were assumed to reflect easy money, and high nominal rates were assumed to reflect tight money. Once inflation expectations began rising, this assumption (dubious in the best of times) became spectacularly unreliable.

In 1968, President Johnson's (Keynesian) economic advisers talked him into a major tax increase in order to address the recent acceleration in inflation. The budget deficit, which was never particularly large during the 1960s, suddenly swung into surplus (fig. 8.1). If the Keynesian model were correct, this policy should have worked, stopping inflation. Instead, inflation continued to accelerate, because it was monetary policy, not wartime deficit spending, that was driving inflation.

Why didn't economists recognize that monetary policy was too expansionary? Keynesians judged the stance of monetary policy by looking at nominal interest rates, which were relatively high in the late 1960s. They assumed that the Fed had already adopted a contractionary monetary policy, and they were just waiting for the results of this combined fiscal and monetary "austerity." But those relatively high nominal interest rates merely reflected rising inflation expectations; real interest rates were far too low to restrain the overheated economy.

It wasn't until the 1980s that the economics profession as a whole figured out the problem with using nominal interest rates to measure the stance of monetary policy. It's odd that it took economists so long to catch up to Milton Friedman, as the Fisher effect (discussed in chapter 5) had been known for decades. But again, this shows how deeply engrained this form of "money illusion" was after more than two thousand years of commodity money regimes.

When inflation remained high in 1970 and 1971, President Nixon was encouraged to use wage and price controls. Today we know that wage and price controls don't work, and that should have been well understood even back in 1971. But Keynesians were so discouraged by the apparent failure of demand-side policies such as tax increases and higher nominal interest rates that they were willing to try almost anything in desperation.

President Nixon pressured his handpicked Fed chair (Arthur Burns) to juice the economy with easy money when Nixon was up for reelection in 1972. Wage and price controls temporarily held inflation down during this period, and the economy boomed. But there was a price to pay after the election—stagflation.

In late 1973, the OPEC oil embargo made things even worse, and there was a second oil shock after the Iranian Revolution of 1979. But just as

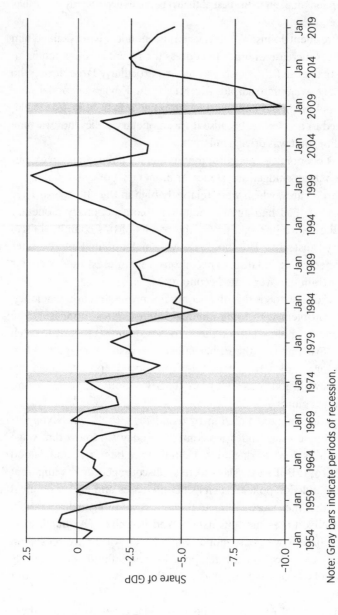

FIGURE 8.1. US federal budget surplus or deficit, 1954–2019

Note: Gray bars indicate periods of recession.

Note: Gray bars indicate periods of recession.

Source: FRED, via Federal Reserve Bank of St. Louis, https://fred.stlouisfed.org/series/FYFSGDA188S.

with the overhyped Vietnam War budget deficits, the history books got the oil shocks wrong. The two oil shocks played only a bit part in the Great Inflation of 1966–1981. Between 1972 and 1981, NGDP (i.e., M × V) rose at a rate of about 11% a year, which made high inflation almost inevitable, regardless of what had happened to oil prices. Real GDP rose at roughly 3%, which was a bit slower than during the previous decade, but not unusually slow for the US. Perhaps without the two oil shocks the US would have had something like 3.5% growth and 7.5% inflation, instead of the 3% growth and 8% inflation it actually had.[5]

President Carter appointed G. William Miller to be Fed chair in 1978, but as inflation soared ever higher in 1979, Carter pressured Miller to move over to secretary of the Treasury and appointed Paul Volcker to head the Fed. In the standard accounts of this period, Volcker was an inflation hawk who immediately jacked up interest rates and slew the inflation dragon. Or perhaps he switched from interest-rate targeting to monetary-supply targeting and slew the inflation dragon. Neither of these stories is quite right, although both contain a grain of truth.

Under Volcker, the Fed began to pay more attention to controlling money supply growth, and monetary tightening did cause interest rates to spike to nearly 20% in late 1979 and early 1980. The economy plunged into a short (six-month) recession in early 1980. But then something happened that is not a part of the official legend—Volcker eased monetary policy sharply in the second half of 1980. There was no good reason for this policy easing—inflation was still running in the double digits. Perhaps this was a favor to President Carter, who was in a difficult battle for re-election. Or perhaps Volcker overestimated how much monetary restraint had already been applied.

Even many economists don't know that Volcker presided over some of the most expansionary monetary policy in all of American history. In the fourth quarter of 1980 and the first quarter of 1981, NGDP growth soared to an annual rate of 19.2%. Long-term yields on Treasury bonds rose to record levels (nearly 15%) as investors lost faith in the ability of the US government to control inflation. This reversion to an easy-money policy in the second half of 1980 made Volcker's job that much harder in the spring of 1981, when he once again decided to tighten monetary policy, and this time for good. By that time Volcker had lost some credibility with the markets. It was Volcker's second tight-money policy that finally broke the back of double-digit inflation and established his credibility as a monetary hawk. Monthly inflation figures fell almost immediately after mid-1981, and inflation averaged only about 4% for the remainder of the 1980s (and has remained at roughly 2% since 1991).

The Rise and Fall of Monetarism

From 1968 to 1984, Milton Friedman won almost every battle but lost the war. He was right that the 1968 tax increases wouldn't slow inflation. He was right that wage and price controls were a mistake. He was right that the Fed's interest-rate targeting regime of the 1970s meant that there was nothing to anchor the price level. He was right that interest rates don't measure the stance of monetary policy. He was right that higher inflation would reduce unemployment only temporarily and that unemployment would go back up once inflation expectations caught up with reality. He was right that controlling money-supply growth provided an anchor for the price level and would allow the Fed to bring inflation under control. And he was right that expectations would eventually adjust to the new and lower inflation rate and that the high unemployment of 1982 would fall back toward the natural rate once wages and prices adjusted to this new reality.

This period should have been the crowning achievement of monetarism, a school of thought that had been on the fringes of the profession for decades. Instead, monetarism all but collapsed after the early 1980s, squeezed on one side by a resurgent "New" Keynesianism that stole many of its best ideas, and on the other by a set of "new classical" ideologies that began by building on monetarism but ended by abandoning its principles. My own views borrow from all three camps: I take what I think are their best ideas, discard the worst, and add a few of my own.

Monetarism was essentially a more sophisticated form of the crude quantity theory of money discussed in earlier chapters. Monetarists did understand that velocity could fluctuate somewhat, but they nonetheless favored a simple rule for money-supply growth rate, such as setting a target growth rate for M1 or M2 of perhaps 3% or 4% per year. The hope was that this would lead to stable prices and also moderate the business cycle. Friedman and Schwartz believed that their *Monetary History* demonstrated that most business cycles were caused by erratic growth in the money supply (M1 and M2).

In retrospect, monetarists should not have relied on the assumption of fairly stable velocity. Rather, they should have advocated targeting inflation or nominal GDP growth. So why didn't Friedman and the other monetarists see this at the time?

Friedman believed (with some justification) that much of the instability in velocity was ultimately due to unstable monetary policy. Thus, velocity fell sharply in the early 1930s because deflationary monetary policies encouraged the public to hoard money. Conversely, velocity tends to speed up sharply during hyperinflation. Friedman believed that if the money supply growth rate is kept stable then velocity will also be relatively stable.[6]

More importantly, Friedman was worried about the problem of *policy lags*. His historical research with Schwartz convinced him that the Fed was prone to act like a military general fighting the previous war. Policy appropriate for a boom was often not adopted until the country was already moving into the next recession, and vice versa. He saw three major policy lags: recognition of the business cycle, implementation of a new policy, and the policy's impact on the economy.

Because macroeconomic data often come out after a long delay and because it takes at least several observations to discern a new trend, economists often don't even recognize that the US is in a recession until it is well under way. To noneconomists, this must sound absolutely appalling. Not only are we unable to forecast recessions, we can't even "nowcast" them! During the past three recessions (prior to COVID-19), the consensus of professional economic forecasters didn't predict a recession until roughly six months after the downturn had begun.

So Friedman had good reason to worry about the recognition lag. Fortunately, the implementation lag is relatively short for monetary policy. The Fed meets every six weeks, and it can meet even more often during a crisis. Friedman's greatest concern was the impact lag, the delay between a change in monetary policy and its impact on output and prices. Friedman viewed this lag as being both long and variable, lasting for roughly six to eighteen months.

Because of all these policy lags, Friedman worried that central banks trying to steer the economy would end up destabilizing the business cycle through poorly timed actions. Consider the predicament of a novice sailor who is asked to steer a supertanker. The sailor turns the wheel and doesn't notice any immediate change in the enormous ship's direction. So the sailor likely turns the wheel even further, until the ship begins noticeably turning in the right direction. But this will likely lead to an overshoot, forcing the sailor to frantically swing the wheel back in the opposite direction to put the ship back on course.

You can imagine the ship's path tracing a sort of S-curve across the water—not too dissimilar from a business cycle shown on graph paper. In this metaphor, the wind and currents are like the economic shocks that move velocity up and down. Do you get a more stable path for the supertanker by holding the steering wheel at one setting or by trying to offset the impact of wind and waves?

Friedman's lags story is an appealing theory, and it certainly contains a grain of truth. It also seems to fit nicely with Friedman's laissez-faire instincts on economic policy more broadly.[7] But in the end Friedman appears to have been wrong. During the period after 1982, the Fed adopted the sort of discretionary policy that Friedman had warned would destabilize the economy, and for the next twenty-five years the economy did pretty well. By the end of his life (he died in 2006), Friedman had made peace with Fed chair Alan Greenspan's inflation-targeting approach.[8] Of course the economy did very poorly after 2007, but this was only partly due to the problem of policy lags.

Ironically, the very success of the New Keynesian policy regime of the 1980s and 1990s owed a great deal to several monetarist insights, including the need to be much more cognizant of the Fisher effect—that is, the tendency of rising inflation expectations to lead to higher nominal interest rates, with no change in real interest rates. Another important insight was the natural-rate hypothesis, which led the Fed to focus on stable inflation and smoothing out employment fluctuations, and to abandon any thought of trying to permanently reduce the rate of unemployment through permanently higher inflation rates.

It's interesting that both of these key insights, which contributed so much to improved monetary policy under the New Keynesian policy regime, came from a better appreciation of the implications of permanent changes in the long-run trend rate of inflation. Recall that this understanding was not possible until the world moved decisively beyond commodity money and central banks gained the ability to choose any rate of inflation almost as easily as a diner chooses an item off a menu. Friedman understood this better than other economists: "As I see it, we have advanced beyond Hume in two respects only; first, we now have a more secure grasp of the quantitative magnitudes involved; second, we have gone one derivative beyond Hume."[9] Friedman was basically saying that we have better data than in David Hume's day, and that we now understand not just the effects of one-time changes in the price level (which Hume fully understood) but also changes in the first derivative of the price level—that is, changes in the *rate of inflation*. And of course Fried-man was the economist most responsible for moving the profession "one derivative beyond Hume."

Friedman was right that the field of macroeconomics had made sur-prisingly little progress since 1752. And what little progress had been made was mostly due to Friedman, and also to Irving Fisher. Ironically, Friedman's comment occurred just as macroeconomics was about to go through a major revolution, pushing us more than just one derivative be-yond Hume.

Friedman's work had a major impact on my own market-monetarist worldview. Next we'll look at the twin theories of efficient markets and rational expectations, which compose the second pillar of market mon-etarism. As with "old" monetarism, these theories fall a bit short, eventu-ally requiring augmentation from the world of New Keynesian economics. Only then will we be able to put together the complete market-monetarist model and a convincing explanation of the Great Recession.

CHAPTER NINE

Rational Expectations and Efficient Markets

In Milton Friedman's model of the economy, the expected rate of inflation plays a central role. Not surprisingly, Friedman had a theory about
how the public formed expectations. He believed that inflation expectations were mostly adaptive—that is, that the public gradually updates its
forecast of future inflation on the basis of recent changes in the actual rate
of inflation.[1]

Imagine you are trying to forecast the outcome of the Super Bowl. Because football is such a complicated game, it's hard to evaluate the talent
of each team one player at a time. Instead, people evaluate football teams
based on their overall performance. Recent games are obviously more
meaningful than games that occurred many years ago. At the same time,
you wouldn't want to rely solely on the most recent game, which might not
reflect the team's actual talent. One approach would be to take a weighted
average of a team's performance over the past ten to twenty games, with
a heavier weight placed on the more recent games. This would be an example of what's called *adaptive expectations*.

Friedman believed that the public forecasts inflation by looking at actual inflation over the past few years, putting a higher weight on the more
recent past and a lower weight on the more distant past. For the forecast
to be unbiased, on average, the weights attached to past inflation rates
should add up to 1.

Let's assume that the public does use adaptive expectations to forecast
inflation. If the central bank adopts an expansionary monetary policy, increasing the rate of inflation, then the actual rate of inflation will rise above
the expected rate of inflation for a period of time. This would lead to a

period of relatively low unemployment, and this is essentially Friedman's explanation of the late 1960s.[2] Conversely, a falling inflation rate would push actual inflation below the expected level of inflation, leading to a temporary period of high unemployment. This is Friedman's explanation for the 1982 recession, which occurred as Volcker's tight money policy drove inflation from more than 10% down to about 4%.

Rational Expectations

The football analogy will help us understand one flaw with the adaptive expectations model. The optimal, or "rational," forecast of a football game would certainly take into account past performance by each team, but it would also include any other factors that might be relevant. These might include injuries to key players, home-field advantage, weather conditions, grass versus artificial turf, and whether each team's defense is well suited to contesting the opposing team's preferred strategy.

In the 1970s, the economist Robert Lucas argued that economic models should incorporate "rational expectations."[3] That is, models should assume that the public makes an optimal forecast of variables such as inflation on the basis of all publicly available information. The term *rational expectations* was unfortunate, and it has caused this modeling strategy to be widely misunderstood. Critics claimed that rational expectations proponents assumed that the public fully understood the highly complex mathematical models that were being published in academic economics journals. That assumption seems highly dubious, if not completely ludicrous. Fortunately, it's not what rational expectations actually means.

Some economists have argued that a more descriptive term for Lucas's idea is *consistent expectations*.[4] What rational-expectations models actually assumed is that if the true model of the economy claims that "the world is X," then the public also believes that "the world is X." Expectations are consistent with the model. To better understand why rational expectations make sense as a modeling strategy, imagine a model that doesn't feature rational expectations. In all non-rational-expectations models, where expectations play a role in economic outcomes, the modelers are basically assuming that if the model says that "the world is X," then the public believes that "the world is not X." If you're going to argue that the public doesn't believe your model, especially in some specific way, then you need a pretty good justification.

Lucas's rational expectations theory was well timed, because it seemed to provide a much more satisfying explanation for the natural-rate hypothesis than Friedman's adaptive-expectations model. Consider the pre-Friedman Phillips-curve model of the 1960s, which implicitly assumed that inflation expectations were stable at zero, or perhaps in the low single digits. If that dubious claim were actually true, then policy makers could permanently lower the unemployment rate through the sort of expansionary fiscal and monetary policies that pushed inflation up from about 1% in the early 1960s to about 5% in the late 1960s.

But that policy can be effective in the long run only if workers are naïve and don't understand what policy makers are doing. Friedman basically said that the workers would eventually catch on to the higher inflation, adjust their inflation expectations, and then start demanding greater pay increases. And this is exactly what happened. Once workers fully adjusted to the situation, unemployment (which had been unusually low in 1969) rose back to the natural rate of about 5% in the early 1970s. You can fool some of the people some of the time but not all of the people all of the time.

Lucas argued that Keynesians had implicitly assumed (in their models) that workers were very irrational, not adjusting their inflation expectations as economic policies changed. He also claimed that Friedman had exposed this flaw in the Keynesian model. But Lucas didn't stop there: he suggested that even Friedman had not gone far enough.[5] Adaptive expectations are certainly better than an expected rate of inflation that never changes, but even adaptive expectations fall short of complete rationality. Adaptive expectations are often pretty good, but not optimal.

Suppose the money-supply growth rate increases by 1% each year, from 3% to 4% to 5% to 6%, and so on. To make things simple, let's also assume that inflation gradually rises, as the quantity theory of money predicts. The old Keynesian model would implicitly assume that the public never changes its inflation expectations, which become increasingly out of line with reality. That's clearly wrong. Friedman's adaptive-expectations model predicts that the public will gradually increase its expected rate of inflation but will tend to always lag a bit behind actual inflation. Lucas would argue that the public does not make systematic errors, and thus even the adaptive expectations model is not good enough. If the money growth rate rose steadily, year after year, it seems implausible that the public would underforecast inflation every single year, for decades on end. Surely people would notice that inflation was rising over time and take that into account in their forecasts.

In practice, central banks don't tend to do crazy things like increasing inflation by 1% each year for decades on end. Thus, it's hard to know whether rational expectations lead to significantly different implications than adaptive expectations. The analogy I like is Newtonian physics, which was later superseded by Einstein's theory of relativity. It turns out that Newtonian physics gives pretty good forecasts for the sorts of speeds and masses that we observe on Earth. Subtle differences show up in only extreme cases and are mostly observed in the distant cosmos.

Similarly, quite often the best forecast of inflation is probably not too different from the prediction of adaptive expectations, especially if you add in temporary factors such as supply shocks to oil prices. In May 1997, however, we did observe a nice test of adaptive versus rational expectations, when the Labour government in the United Kingdom suddenly announced that the Bank of England would be made independent of the government. This occurred soon after a series of academic studies seemed to show that independent central banks free of government oversight and meddling do better at controlling inflation, with the German central bank considered exhibit A for the conjecture.

According to Friedman's adaptive-expectations theory, the mere announcement of an independent central bank should not have affected inflation expectations in the UK. After all, past inflation rates had not been affected. However, a study showed that the announcement of an independent Bank of England did seem to modestly lower inflation expectations, as the spread between the (nominal) interest rate on conventional bonds and the (real) interest rate on indexed bonds suddenly narrowed during the week of the announcement.[6]

This example is analogous to the famous 1919 experiment that occurred during a total eclipse of the sun, which showed that starlight was bent by the sun's gravitational field. This natural experiment demonstrated the advantage of Einstein's theory of relativity over traditional Newtonian physics. Similarly, the decision to make the Bank of England independent provided a rare case in which adaptive and rational expectations have clearly different implications.

To summarize, both adaptive and rational expectations have pretty similar implications in a wide range of settings. Any optimal forecast of inflation is likely to rely heavily on actual inflation rates in the recent past. In a few cases, however, the public will have additional information that is relevant to forecasting inflation, and in those cases, the rational expectations assumption seems to be superior. Lucas went one step further than this, showing that the rational expectations assumption was especially important when it came to *policy evaluation*.

The Lucas Critique

In 1976, Lucas published a paper entitled "Econometric Policy Evaluation: A Critique." Lucas argued that models lacking rational expectations would do especially poorly if used as a guide to policy formation. Once again, this is best understood in reference to the Phillips-curve debate, but it actually applies to many other areas, including temporary tax changes.

Think of a simple Phillips-curve model of unemployment, which was first developed during the gold standard regime:

$$U = Un - \frac{\text{inflation}}{2},$$

where Un is the natural rate of unemployment. In this model, unemployment is high when inflation is negative and low when inflation is positive. Inflation expectations play no role in the model, and people might have justified that exclusion by claiming, "Well, in theory inflation expectations might matter, but in practice they are close to zero, so we can ignore them." Indeed, John Maynard Keynes did have roughly this sort of dismissive attitude toward Irving Fisher's model of the distinction between real and nominal interest rates:

> Now, as against this, my contention is that the expectation of a change in price has *no* effect on the rate of interest, since it leaves unchanged the relative attractions of cash and loans. Are you denying this? Do you think that an expectation of higher prices in [the] future causes the rate of interest to rise?[7]

Keynes thought that (apart from unusual cases like hyperinflation), inflation expectations could be safely ignored because they were usually near zero, and hence real and nominal interest rates were quite similar.

Now let's assume that the true model of unemployment is more like Friedman's natural-rate hypothesis, in which expected inflation plays an important role:

$$U = Un - \frac{\text{inflation} - \text{expected inflation}}{2}.$$

Now the unemployment rate is low only when inflation is higher than expected, and vice versa. The simpler model that ignores expectations seems to imply that policy makers can manage a trade-off between inflation and unemployment. They might even rely on econometric models estimating the Phillips curve using one hundred years of data, all during a period when the price of gold is pegged. But those models would be dangerously incomplete, and the expected inflation rate would start to change as soon as actual inflation rose for any extended period of time.

Lucas saw a need for a more general model that would hold up under a wide range of policy changes. The beauty of Lucas's general model is that unlike Friedman's (special) model of adaptive expectations, it can apply to any type of policy regime. Any policy that tries to achieve some objective by consistently fooling the public is likely to break down at some point. Lucas's rational-expectations model offered a far more elegant solution to the Phillips-curve conundrum than Friedman's adaptive-expectations model, and this made it highly appealing to younger academics. Even younger Keynesian economists were attracted to this approach, because Friedman, Lucas, and other "Chicago school" economists had been right about the 1970s, whereas the older (often quite distinguished) Keynesians of Harvard and Massachusetts Institute of Technology had lagged well behind in figuring out what was wrong with the original Phillips-curve model.

To see the difference between adaptive and rational expectations, look at the more accurate later equation for predicting the unemployment rate. That equation would be one part of a bigger econometric model. If you use adaptive expectations, you'll add a second equation to the model to derive inflation expectations, and that equation would be a weighted average of past inflation rates. If you use a rational-expectations modeling strategy, your expected inflation variable will depend on a wide variety of variables, indeed on anything that the model suggests actually causes inflation.

Thus, if you had a very simple monetarist model of inflation, in which the actual inflation rate next year equals the money-supply growth rate this year, then the model would assume that the public forms inflation expectations the same way—that the public's expected inflation rate is equal to the actual money supply growth rate twelve months earlier. In practice you might want to add lots of other variables, such as labor-market conditions, fiscal policy, oil price shocks, and so on.

After Lucas, most of the sophisticated macroeconomic models featured rational expectations. This means that if you plugged in all the macroeconomic data and the model predicted 3% inflation in the year 2006, then the model would also assume that the public expected 3% inflation in 2006. That is, the model would assume that the public's forecasts would be consistent with the model. That's why economists such as Bennett McCallum suggested that the term should actually be *consistent expectations*, not *rational expectations*.

Economists are fully aware that this might be wrong. But this modeling strategy is appropriate, for one simple reason. If not 3%, then what? If your model predicts 3% inflation for 2006, then why would you assume that the public expects 4.7% inflation or 1.1% inflation in 2006? Or any number other than 3%? The public will clearly make many mistakes (as will the experts), but what basis do we have to claim that the public's errors are likely to be *systematic*? There is no obvious reason to believe that the rational-expectations forecast is not the *best guess* about what the public expects. If you can provide me with such a reason, I'm willing to listen.

From Rational Expectations to New Classical Economics

To understand what happened next, we need to know a bit about the ideology of macroeconomics. This digression into politics will be important later on when we try to understand what went wrong in 2008. During the past eighty years, various forms of Keynesianism have generally been thought of as somewhat left-of-center approaches. In contrast, monetarism and rational expectations are viewed more as ideas on the right. And yet there is no particular reason it had to be this way. One can imagine an alternative universe in which economists on the right call for tax cuts (fiscal stimulus) during recessions and those on the left prefer to rely on monetary policy to stabilize the economy.

Contrary to what many noneconomists are led to believe, macroeconomic disputes are not ideological in the normal sense of the word. It's almost never about the trade-off between equity and efficiency. There is no good evidence that one type of monetary policy favors the poor while another type favors the rich. Keynesian economics has no necessary relationship to progressive ideas such as a large or activist government. Keynesians simply believe that the budget deficit should be countercyclical, with deficits rising during recessions and falling during booms. Policy makers can accomplish that equally well with small government as with big government. Indeed, there have been plenty of Keynesian economists, such as Martin Feldstein and Gregory Mankiw, who favored small government. Back in the 1920s, the quantity theory of money was viewed as a left-wing idea; today it's associated with conservatives.

Having said all that, there still is clearly an ideological aspect to macroeconomic debates. But why? I believe that economists themselves have often misunderstood the implications of their models and have therefore favored certain policies for the wrong reason. For example, Milton Friedman once debated fixed versus floating exchange rates with Robert Mundell, an economist whose ideas contributed to the creation of the euro. Friedman (who held libertarian views) argued that fixed exchange rates were undesirable for the standard reason that any government price control is inefficient. However, Friedman favored money-supply targeting, and basic microeconomic theory holds that quantity controls are just as inefficient as price controls—just as interventionist. I happen to agree with Friedman that fixed exchange rates are usually a bad idea, but his argument was actually quite weak. In my view, Mundell clearly won the debate.

Another common trope is that liberals care more about unemployment while conservatives care more about inflation. Even if that were true, it wouldn't really have much bearing on modern macroeconomic debate. Conservatives do not believe that liberal (Keynesian) policies would lead to lower unemployment. The disagreements are technical, not ideological.

In one respect, I have a rather unusual vantage point from which to observe this ideological debate. I believe that wage and price stickiness is the central problem in macroeconomics and that demand shocks largely explain the business cycle. This is typically pegged as a left-of-center perspective. But in most other respects my views are right of center. I studied under Robert Lucas at the University of Chicago in the late 1970s, during the heyday of the rational-expectations revolution. I'm also a big fan of Milton Friedman's monetarist writings. I favor small government and a rules-based approach to monetary policy. I'm not a fan of Keynesian economics, nor do I favor fiscal stabilization policy. Take all this into account when considering the following comments.

When Lucas developed the rational-expectations theory in the 1970s, it seemed plausible that it would become Monetarism 2.0. One could imagine Friedman's theories with adaptive expectations replaced by rational expectations. I wish that had happened—I'm trying to make it happen. Instead, the rational-expectations revolution led to something called "new classical" economics, which drifted far away from traditional monetarism. Much (not all) of the new classical research, especially a branch known as real-business-cycle theory, largely dispensed with assumption of wage and price stickiness.[8] At first, new classical models of the business cycles relied on "monetary misperceptions." That is, a decrease in the money supply would lead to less nominal demand for each producer's goods. At first producers would wrongly assume that the real demand for their goods had fallen (not knowing the money supply had fallen), and they would respond by cutting output.

When the empirical evidence didn't seem to support the monetary misperceptions approach, many right-of-center researchers switched to real-business-cycle theories that relied on "technology shocks." Many of these new classical researchers tried to construct models with flexible prices in which aggregate demand shocks did not create business cycles. Indeed, by the 1980s and 1990s, sticky wage models featuring demand shocks were increasingly viewed as Keynesian, even though these ideas also played a key role in monetarist models. But among younger economists on the right, monetarism was considered passé by 1990.

The new classical movement made a crucial error, overestimating how badly Keynesianism had been discredited by the rational-expectations revolution. Lucas's critique did make the Keynesian models of the 1960s look out of date. It really was a smashing intellectual victory. But the new classical economists never presented any decisive evidence specifically against the sticky wage and price assumption, which underlay not just Keynesian economics but also monetarist economics and *actual classical economics* from David Hume all the way up through Irving Fisher.

Almost every prominent economist from Hume through to Fisher, Keynes, and Friedman believed that wages and prices were sticky in the short run, and hence that demand shocks had real effects on the economy. There's also a mountain of evidence in favor of that proposition. And yet the new classical models mostly abandoned that assumption, or at least no longer had demand shocks playing a central role in business cycles.

You can probably tell my bias, but given my high respect for Lucas, I hope I'm less biased than many other critics of real-business-cycle economics. I believe that Lucas and other new classical economists are wrong about wage and price stickiness and underestimate its role in the business cycle, but they are not *obviously wrong*. When doing traditional econometric studies, it's surprisingly hard to correctly "identify" monetary shocks to the economy and find evidence of those shocks playing a major role in the business cycle. Lucas himself was once a huge fan of Friedman and Schwartz's *Monetary History*, which showed how erratic Fed policy led to booms and busts, but he later became more skeptical when post–World War II studies using more sophisticated techniques had trouble finding much impact from monetary shocks. Later I'll explain why I think those studies are wrong.

In my view, wage and price stickiness is not a left-of-center assumption; in some ways it's just the opposite. Consider that Friedman and Schwartz's *Monetary History* was originally viewed as a right-leaning project. Friedman and Schwartz showed that the Great Depression did not happen because of the "inherent instability of capitalism"; rather, it was caused by inept Fed policy. The government was to blame for the Great Depression. Today, many of the most prominent defenders of *Monetary History* are on the left. When economists on the right deny that demand shocks are a problem because of sticky wages and prices, left-of-center economists often point to *Monetary History* to criticize this view.

Ironically, if Keynesians and monetarists are not right about the cause of the Great Depression, if it was not caused by demand shocks hitting an economy featuring sticky wages and prices, then capitalism really is in trouble. In that case, the left-of-center charge that capitalism is inherent unstable really *is* true.[9] The argument for national planning, or jobs programs like the Works Progress Administration during recessions, would be far stronger. However, if (as I believe) wage and price stickiness is the problem, then stable monetary policy can make the world safe for free market capitalism.

Earlier I argued that Milton Friedman won most of his battles but lost the war because he opted for a money-supply rule. Perhaps he thought such a rule represented a more "free market" approach than discretionary monetary policy. If so, he was wrong. Free markets do not arbitrarily set constant growth rates for the quantity of any good in question, any more than they set fixed prices. Indeed, it is not clear how any given government-determined monetary policy setting could be viewed as "more free market" than any other. Similarly, Lucas and his followers won the battle over how to model expectations and also how to think about optimal policy rules, but they lost the war because they put too little weight on the importance of demand shocks in economies featuring wage and price stickiness. So who won?

One could argue that liberals always win in the end, because liberalism is the name given to the winning ideology, whatever it is. If prohibition is in style, then prohibition is considered a liberal view. If it's out of style, then opposition to prohibition is regarded as liberal. The same is true of free trade, free speech, price controls, government ownership of industry, and a host of other issues.

In macroeconomics *Keynesian* is the analogy to *liberal* in the world of politics. *Keynesian* is the name given to the winning ideas. Keynesians adopted many of Friedman's key insights, including the importance of the Fisher effect, the superiority of monetary policy over fiscal policy, and the natural-rate hypothesis. Then, in the late 1970s, they began absorbing Lucas's best ideas (rational expectations and systematic policy rules) and discarding the weakest (the view that wage and price stickiness are not big problems). Economists like John Taylor and Stanley Fischer built rational-expectations models with sticky wages and prices. Unlike in Lucas's models, in these "New Keynesian" rational-expectations models, monetary policy could still play a useful role in stabilizing the economy.

In the end, the New Keynesians won. Their approach to macroeconomics is the only one taken seriously at the highest levels of policy making, especially at central banks. But again, it's not quite the ideological victory that you might assume. New Keynesians such as Taylor, Feldstein, and Mankiw are probably just as far to the right of center as Lucas is. Even more surprisingly, the big ideological debates over theoretical modeling issues didn't spill over into the policy realm, at least not during the period from 1983 to 2008. During that twenty-five-year period, both New Keynesians and new classical economists seemed pretty happy with Fed policy. There was increasingly broad support for something close to a 2% inflation target, even though the two groups had radically different views about why such a policy was desirable. But things were going well, so both sides were happy to claim credit.

It is not surprising that this policy consensus could not survive the crisis of 2008, which exposed deep divisions between these two schools of thought. Suddenly, brilliant economists on either side of the divide could not believe the absolutely moronic things being said on the other side. Both sides missed the boat in 2008, but to understand how market monetarism differs from these other schools of thought, we need to add one more feature—the market.

Efficient Markets and the Road Not Taken

If the multiverse is real, then I suspect that in most alternative universes the rational-expectations revolution led in a different direction. Instead of deemphasizing wage and price stickiness and moving toward the real-business-cycle approach, economists should have fixed the problems with Milton Friedman's monetarism by adding *efficient markets* to the model. After all, there are eerie similarities between Lucas's rational-expectations model and Eugene Fama's efficient market hypothesis (EMH), starting with the fact that both were developed at the University of Chicago at roughly the same time.

In the rational-expectations model, the public is assumed to make the optimal forecast of inflation, given all publicly available knowledge. In the EMH, asset prices are assumed to reflect optimal forecast of future cash flows, given all publicly available information. Over the course of my career, I've become increasingly convinced that the EMH can and should play a much greater role in macroeconomics. Here are four ways that the EMH could improve on Friedman's monetarism.

First, in my research on the Great Depression, I found that Friedman and Schwartz had misidentified a number of monetary shocks. Fed decisions that they viewed as highly significant turned out to have had little impact on either the asset markets or the broader economy. Monetary shocks that they missed often had a major impact on asset prices. Their key error was underestimating the importance of the international gold market—an importance that was keenly understood by stock-market participants.

Second, because Friedman and Schwartz misidentified monetary shocks, they had trouble linking monetary policy changes to broader changes in the macroeconomy (prices and output). This led them to rely too much on the idea that monetary policy had an impact on the economy with "long and variable lags." The problem with that view is that although money might affect goods prices and output with a lag, it seems very implausible that it would affect asset prices with a lag. Thus, suppose that tight money in 1928 caused output in the US to move sharply lower in late 1929. In that case, stock prices should have crashed in 1928 in anticipation of the depression that would eventually result from the tight money.

I found that during the 1930s, asset prices (stocks and commodities) were highly correlated with broader economic data (inflation and industrial production). Either monetary policy was affecting both with a lag or it wasn't affecting either of them with a lag. Because the EMH doesn't allow for policy to affect asset prices with long lags, it seems more likely that both were being affected almost immediately. I believe that there are no long and variable lags between monetary policy and the broader economy. When monetary shocks are correctly identified, they affect the economy quite quickly.

Third, this conjecture was most strongly confirmed when I looked at exactly those monetary shocks that were most easily identified, such as the decision to devalue the dollar in April 1933. In those cases, one could see an almost immediate reaction in both prices and output. Monthly industrial production and wholesale price indices soared immediately after the devaluation, and news of the dollar's depreciation had an immediate and powerful effect on asset prices.

Fourth, Friedman advocated a fixed money-supply growth rate of perhaps 3% or 4% per year. But the EMH suggests that the optimal monetary policy is the one that the market thinks is most likely to lead to on-target growth in the policy goal variables. For simplicity's sake, let's assume that the goal is 2% inflation. Then, according to the EMH, the Fed should set monetary policy at a level at which the market expects 2% inflation. This might mean a stable money-supply growth rate if the market agrees that the monetarist model is the true model of the economy. More likely, the money supply growth rate would move around in a way the market thinks is needed to offset changes in money demand.

There are several possible ways to measure market expectations of inflation. One option is to create a CPI futures market. Another is to look at TIPS spreads, which provide a rough indication of investors' expectations of inflation. Whichever way is chosen, this approach eliminates the need for big economic models of the economy, which try to predict how policy will have an impact on prices and or output. There are hundreds of such econometric models, and we have no idea which one is right. Actually, we know that each and every one is wrong, because the economy is far too complex to be accurately described by any simple set of equations. New classical economists were rightly contemptuous of early Keynesian attempts to model the economy, but while their models avoided some of the worst mistakes of 1960s Keynesianism, they were never able to produce any sort of alternative that was useful for policy purposes.

These are some of the ways that the rational expectations–EMH revolution affected my worldview, and it's where I would have expected other economists to focus. The Fed should target market expectations of the goal variable, which might be inflation or nominal GDP growth. Set policy levers at a position where the market expects policy to succeed. Instead, the economics profession almost completely ignored the implications of the EMH for macroeconomic theory and policy. When the Great

Recession hit, many right-of-center economists were predicting that quantitative easing would lead to high inflation, even as the asset markets predicted exactly the opposite.[10] If even Chicago-school economists won't take the EMH seriously, who will? The answer is market monetarists.

To summarize, both Friedman's monetarism and Lucas's rational-expectations theory made great contributions to modern macroeconomics. Friedman's and Lucas's best ideas underlie much of my own worldview and were also adopted by New Keynesian economists. But each school of thought had a fatal flaw, which allowed the alternative New Keynesian school to dominate the highest reaches of academia and policy making. So why didn't I become a New Keynesian? In the next three chapters we'll look at how mainstream economists (including New Keynesians) all too often fall into the trap of "reasoning from a price change."

我

Nossa, odeio este programa

一二三四五
六
七
八
九
十

PART III

Never Reason from a Price Change

1. What can we learn from the financial crisis that we didn't know before 2008, is it still relevant today?

2. Why are interest rates one of the least useful metrics for measuring monetary policy?

3. EMH, market bubbles, bitcoin, company arguments

The Musical-Chairs Model

Thus far this book has focused on the topic of inflation. We've examined how changes in the supply and demand for money impact the price level, and the way that unanticipated changes in the price level can have an impact on unemployment. Now I'm about to tell you that inflation doesn't matter, and that we should actually be focusing on nominal GDP.

So why did I waste all your time with changes in the price level, if it is nominal GDP that really matters? Why didn't I start with NGDP? After all, it turns out that the theories we've discussed actually work *better* for NGDP growth than for inflation. For instance, the quantity theory of money works better when applied to NGDP rather than to the price level. As for the Phillips curve, an unanticipated fall in inflation often leads to an increase in unemployment, but an unanticipated fall in NGDP growth is *even more likely* to do so.

In some ways the basics of macroeconomics are easier to explain using a familiar concept like inflation rather than the less familiar NGDP. It is easier to trace the development of macroeconomics by focusing on inflation because that's what most other economists have focused on. In addition, the inverse of the price level is a more intuitive and natural definition of the "value of money" than the inverse of NGDP, even though later on we'll see that the latter definition is more *useful*. But don't worry: almost all the key ideas that relate to inflation carry over to NGDP growth.

Unfortunately, inflation also has some important flaws, and so it's time to move on to a better nominal aggregate—NGDP. In this chapter I'll show you how the price level and NGDP relate to each other and why NGDP is the more useful nominal aggregate. We'll conclude with what I call the musical-chairs model, which helps to explain the Great Recession.

What Is the AS-AD Model Actually Telling Us?

The Great Depression gave birth to the model of aggregate supply and demand, which is probably the best way to visualize how economists think about the business cycle. Unfortunately, this model is widely misunderstood, to some extent even by economists. Recall that, despite the name, it actually has nothing to do with the supply and demand model used in microeconomics to analyze individual markets. Many basic errors in macroeconomics come from treating the AS-AD model as if it were like an ordinary supply-and-demand model.

There are many ways of modeling the aggregate demand curve, and unfortunately economics textbooks often use a needlessly complicated approach that not one student in a hundred actually understands. A much simpler approach is to treat each specific AD curve as a given level of nominal GDP. Because nominal GDP is equal to $P \times Y$, and because those variables are each represented on an axis of AS-AD graph, the AD curve then becomes a rectangular hyperbola—a line along which the product of P and Y is a constant. Thus, we have one AD curve for $10 trillion in total spending, another for $15 trillion, and a third for $20 trillion (fig. 10.1). As the public spends more, the AD curve shifts outward, and as the public spends less, the AD curve shifts inward. Because $M \times V$ equals $P \times Y$, all increases in AD are caused by an increase in the money supply, a higher velocity, or some combination of the two.

The long-run AS curve is roughly vertical, because nominal shocks are assumed to not have real effects in the long run. Thus, printing lots of money won't make a country richer in the long run; it will merely result in higher prices (fig. 10.2).

If figure 10.2 were the end of the story, there would be absolutely no point in even creating an AS-AD model. More specifically, let's think about three issues that could be evaluated with an AS-AD model: long-run real GDP growth, long-run inflation, and the business cycle. Figure 10.2 is simply not a very interesting model. Yes, it can show long-run inflation. You can also use it to show long-run real GDP growth, by shifting the long-run AS (LRAS) line to the right. But those are pretty trivial results that could be more easily derived with other models. Instead, the AS-AD model was basically created to explain business cycles such as the Great Depression. And to use it for that, we need to add a short-run AS curve (SRAS), as in figure 10.3.

The SRAS curve is the key to understanding the entire AS-AD model. It is what makes the model *interesting*. Why is the SRAS curve drawn with an upward-sloping line? Unlike in microeconomics, this is not something

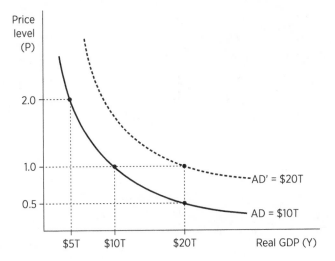

FIGURE 10.1. Two aggregate demand curves

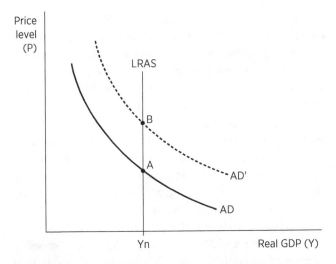

FIGURE 10.2. Effect of an increasing money supply over the long run

that economists would have expected on the basis of what we know about how people behave. Indeed, we would have expected the SRAS curve to be vertical. Rather, we draw an upward-sloping SRAS curve because in the real world short-run aggregate supply seems to be upward-sloping.

Once it was understood that nominal shocks had real effects in the short run, economists began to look for explanations for the upward slope

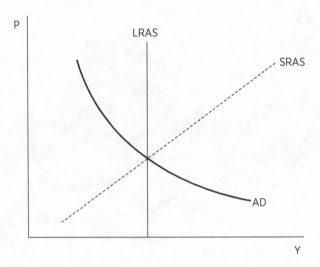

FIGURE 10.3. Aggregate supply and demand model

of the SRAS curve. By far the most common explanation is the "sticky wage and price" assumption, or the idea that wages and prices respond slowly to changes in nominal spending. And this means that changes in nominal spending don't just have an impact on prices (as basic economic principles might lead you to expect); they also have an impact on real output, at least for a period of time.

Sometimes people refer to complete wage and price flexibility combined with a vertical AS curve as the "classical model." That's because a vertical AS curve is grounded in basic economic ideas that have been well understood for centuries. But in another sense this does a disservice to actual classical economists. As we've already seen, even David Hume understood all the basic ideas underlying the sticky price AS-AD model.

To understand why the AS-AD model using NGDP shocks is better than Phillips-curve models that rely on inflation, we need to take a brief digression and examine a common fallacy in economics.

Never Reason from a Price Change

For thirty years I taught introductory economics to both undergrads and MBA students. After covering supply and demand, I liked to pose the following question, to see how much they had learned:

Suppose you are interested in testing the theory of supply and demand. You go out to observe the number of people who attend movies when the price is $6, and also when the price is $10. You find that, on average, there are 40 patrons in the movie theater when the price is $6 and 120 patrons when the price is $10. Is this result consistent with the laws of supply and demand? Explain.

The make-believe field-test data are diagrammed in figure 10.4.

More often than not, after I posed this question, there was complete silence. Occasionally one student would know the answer. The correct answer is that this finding is completely consistent with the laws of supply and demand, as would be any other pair of equilibrium points. But most students don't see this. Why not?

To make it easier to see, I point out that the $6 price might occur in the afternoon, when demand is low, and the $10 price in the evening, when demand is high. Some students will object that I haven't "held other things equal." But that's a nonsensical response, because we are comparing two different equilibrium points, and if P and Q have changed, then obviously other things could not possible have been equal. Any change in price and quantity requires a shift in supply or a shift in demand, or both.

Here is the real problem. When looking at these two data points, students subconsciously try to align them along a single demand curve, as in figure 10.5. That is, it looked as if the field study of movie theaters had

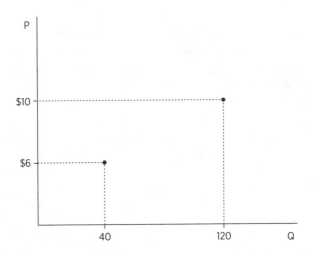

FIGURE 10.4. The movie-theater model

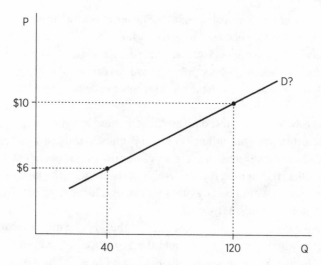

FIGURE 10.5. The wrong way to think about two data points

discovered an upward-sloping demand curve. In fact, the two points lie along a given supply curve, and it's the demand curve that has shifted. Not only is my example not some sort of weird puzzle or paradox; it is as straightforward an application of the theory of supply and demand as you can imagine.

Even most high school students know that if a storm wipes out 90% of the orange crop in Florida, then the price of oranges will rise. That's an example where the supply curve shifts, and equilibrium moves along a given demand curve. Students who are confused by the movie-theater question are probably implicitly assuming that price changes are caused by supply shifts, and that we should move along a given demand curve. If the price is higher (they incorrectly reason), we can expect consumers to buy less. But that's not at all the prediction of the supply-and-demand model! Whether consumers end up buying more or less depends entirely on whether the price change was caused by a shift in supply or a shift in demand.

During the 1970s, the world experienced two big shocks to oil prices. In 1973–1974, and again in 1979–1980, the global supply curve for oil shifted to the left, owing to political factors in the Middle East. In both cases, oil prices soared and oil consumption declined. From 2006 to mid-2008, there was another period of soaring oil prices. But this time oil consumption did not fall—it kept rising. Pundits wrote articles implying that rising oil consumption "despite" higher prices was somehow in violation of the laws of supply and demand, which is nonsense.

The 2006–2008 oil-price shock was different from the two 1970s examples. In the latter period, there was soaring global demand for oil, partly because of rapid growth in developing countries such as China. Because it's difficult to quickly ramp up oil production (fracking was still in its early stages back then), the soaring global demand for oil caused prices to shoot up, until the global recession became intense in the latter half of 2008.

The bottom line is that one should never say, "The price of X is rising (or falling) and therefore we can expect the equilibrium quantity of X to fall (or rise)." I call this misuse of the basic supply-and-demand model "reasoning from a price change," and that phrase seemed to catch on with some bloggers and journalists after 2009. I've used this phrase as the title of Part 3 of the book because this misuse of supply and demand theory underlies many of the problems with modern macroeconomics.

This chapter focuses on the mistake people make when reasoning from a *price-level* change. The next chapter looks at an even more serious error, reasoning from an *interest-rate* change. And in chapter 12 we'll look at how reasoning from an *exchange-rate* change leads to unnecessary discord between countries. In a previous book I argued that reasoning from a price change was the primary underlying cause of the Great Depression,[1] and here we'll see that it also played a major role in causing the Great Recession.

To be clear, other economists are aware of this issue—it is an implication of the basic supply-and-demand model, after all. Indeed, this fallacy closely relates to an issue that economists call the *identification problem*, which captures how hard it is to identify the shapes of supply and demand curves merely by observing the equilibrium price and quantity points that we see in the real world.

Economists like to joke about how the public confuses equilibrium points with either supply or (more commonly) demand. You might have seen a time-series graph with data from 2020 to 2050 on the horizontal axis and an upward-sloping line showing forecasts of "oil demand." Economists find this funny, because it could just as well be called "oil supply." These graphs are actually showing the equilibrium quantity of oil. Another silly example occurs when the news media reports that "stock prices plunged sharply today, as a selling wave hit Wall Street," even though it would be just as accurate to say that "stock prices fell sharply as a buying wave hit Wall Street." After all, each day the number of shares sold is exactly equal to the number of shares purchased.

Economists, however, have no reason to be smug. I have occasionally made this mistake, as have some much better and more distinguished economists. Consider this example, which quotes Nobel laureate Robert Shiller, who teaches at Yale:

> Real interest rates have turned negative in many countries, as inflation remains quiescent and economies overseas struggle.
>
> Yet, these negative rates haven't done much to inspire investment, and Nobel laureate economist Robert Shiller is perplexed as to why.
>
> "If I can borrow at a negative interest rate, I ought to be able to do something with that," he tells U.K. magazine *MoneyWeek*. "The government should be borrowing, it would seem, heavily and investing in anything that yields a positive return."
>
> But, "that isn't happening anywhere," Shiller notes. "No country has that. . . . Even the corporate sector, you might think, would be investing at a very high pitch. They're not, so something is amiss."
>
> And what is that?
>
> "I don't have a complete story of why it is. It's a puzzle of our time," he maintains.[2]

In fact, there is no mystery here at all. There is nothing at all surprising about low levels of investment coinciding with low interest rates—*it's the norm.*

Shiller is actually making two mistakes here. One is reasoning from a price change. Sometimes that's not a big problem, as when background information makes it obvious which curve has shifted, and when that information is implicit in the analysis being offered. But in this case Shiller is also wrong about the historical record. Investment is usually low during periods when interest rates are low and high during periods when interest rates are high. The reason is quite simple: the investment schedule (which you can think of as the demand for credit) is more unstable than the saving schedule (which you can think of as the supply of credit). During a typical recession, interest rates are low and investment is low. During booms, high levels of investment usually coincide with higher interest rates. So not only is it not "a puzzle of our time," it's no puzzle at all. It's simply Supply and Demand 101.

I am picking on Shiller, but one can find similar examples from many other top economists. Indeed, the problem is far worse in macroeconomics—the topic of this book—than in microeconomics, where good economists can usually quickly zero in on whether we are dealing with supply shifts or demand shifts. Most microeconomists are smart enough to know that rising oil output need not be associated with higher oil prices, but many macroeconomists do expect increases in aggregate output and employment to be associated with rising wage and price pressures.

The Phillips Curve as Reasoning from a Price Change

Earlier I pointed out that the AS-AD model is nothing like the simple supply-and-demand model from microeconomics. The two models do have one similarity, however: both are susceptible to reasoning from a price change. Indeed, the entire Phillips-curve theory of the business cycle might be viewed as nothing more than reasoning from a price change. Recall that the Phillips curve predicts that higher inflation will be associated with lower levels of unemployment. That implies that high inflation should occur during booms, when output is also high. That might be true, but only if the economy is being buffeted by demand shocks and moving along a relatively stable SRAS curve, as shown in figure 10.6.

During the transition between points a and c, prices are rising at the same time that output is above its natural rate and that fact implies that unemployment is likely below its natural rate. In contrast, if there are supply shocks, then higher inflation rates might be associated with lower output and by implication more unemployment, as we saw in 1974 and 1980 (fig. 10.7).

But monetary policy is supposed to *prevent* demand shocks. Thus, the Phillips curve is a useful forecasting model only to the extent that monetary policy is incompetent—that is, when aggregate demand is unstable. That makes it rather odd that recent Fed chairs have relied on Phillips-curve models when forecasting inflation. In fairness, modern Keynesian economists understand the problem of supply shocks, but attempts to incorporate these shocks into Phillips-curve models remain only partly successful, and the model continues to give false alarms on inflation.

In fact, the original Phillips-curve model works only under certain highly restrictive conditions: demand shocks must be far more important than supply shocks, the expected rate of inflation must be stable, and the

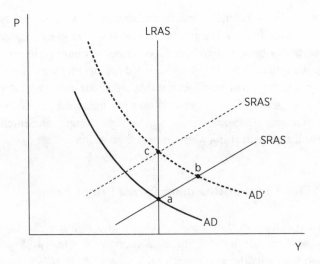

FIGURE 10.6. Short- and long-run impact of increasing aggregate demand

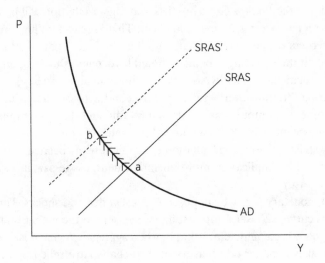

FIGURE 10.7. Short-run impact of falling aggregate supply

natural rate of unemployment must be fairly stable. During the period studied by Phillips, all three conditions were often reasonably well satis-fied. During the period since the Phillips curve was discovered, none of the three conditions has been satisfied. The US has been hit by a number of major supply shocks, especially during the 1970s. In the period after

1982, supply shocks became less important, but the Fed also reduced the volatility of aggregate demand. Even worse, the expected rate of inflation was unstable during the period from the 1960s to the 1980s. And finally, the natural rate of unemployment rose during the 1970s and 1980s, and then fell during the 1990s and the decade after 2000. As a result, there has been almost no correlation between inflation and unemployment for the US since 1984, as shown in figure 10.8.

In contrast, during the period since 1983, Hong Kong has met most of the conditions required to generate a downward-sloping Phillips curve: It has had a stable natural rate of unemployment, owing to laissez-faire policies. It has had a stable expected rate of inflation, owing to the combination of an exchange rate fixed to the dollar and a fairly stable expected inflation rate in the US. It has had a very unstable actual rate of inflation, owing to large swings in its real exchange rate, especially during major economic crises such as that of 1997–1998. Because Hong Kong continues to meet the conditions required for a stable Phillips curve, the correlation between its inflation and unemployment is still relatively high, as shown in figure 10.9.

Many Keynesian economists are fans of Phillips-curve models. Most conservative economists are more skeptical. The truth is that the Phillips curve is a very ad hoc model. It works well when all the necessary conditions are

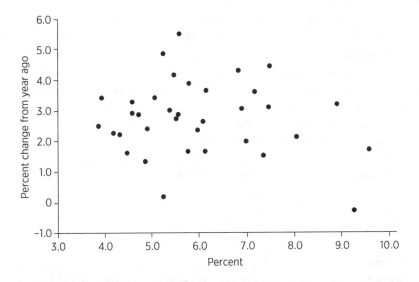

FIGURE 10.8. The Phillips curve after 1984

Source: FRED, via Bureau of Labor Statistics, https://fred.stlouisfed.org/series/CPIAUCSL, https://fred.stlou isfed.org/series/UNRATE.

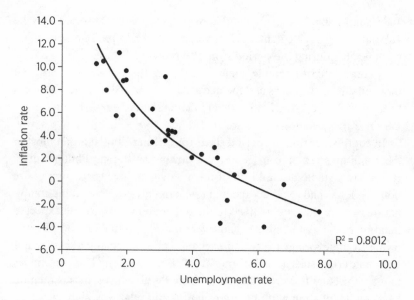

FIGURE 10.9. Hong Kong Phillips curve, 1982–2014

Source: Trading Economics, https://tradingeconomics.com/hong-kong/unemployment-rate, https://tradingeconomics.com/hong-kong/inflation-cpi?continent=europe.

met, and not otherwise. I count myself as a skeptic—not because there is no validity to the model, but because we have better options.

The biggest problem with Phillips-curve thinking is that it treats the inflation rate as an indicator of nominal shocks. Thus, a high inflation rate is viewed as an indicator of strong aggregate demand, and low inflation implies weak demand. My view is that, rather than using inflation as an indicator of aggregate demand, we should use *aggregate demand* as an indicator of aggregate demand. And nominal GDP, which measures total spending, is basically what people mean by aggregate demand. In the 1980s, I made the intellectual journey from being an economist obsessed with inflation to being one obsessed with NGDP.

The Phillips Curve and Real-Wage Cyclicality

My earliest research (during the 1980s) focused on the interwar period, from 1919 to 1939. I noticed that the sharp economic contractions of 1920–1921, 1929–1933, and 1937–1938 were associated with falling prices and rising real wages.[3] This seemed to support the "sticky wages" theory of the business cycle, which has been around for hundreds of years. The basic idea was that a combination of falling prices and sticky nominal wages caused the real wage to rise sharply during these three periods. And these high real wages caused firms to lay off workers, which in turn led to falling output and mass unemployment.

If the sticky-wages theory is correct, then real wages should be *countercyclical*, rising during recessions and falling during booms. Indeed, in a sense this theory views countercyclical wages as the *cause* of the business cycle. During periods of falling prices, such as 1929–1933, real wages increased. As a result, firms could no longer profitably employ workers at the same nominal wages. During these deflationary episodes, workers were laid off and unemployment rose sharply.

It's worth noting that both liberals and conservatives often misinterpret the sticky-wages model of the business cycle. Conservatives often see labor as the problem—workers are too stubborn to accept the pay cuts required to hold their jobs, even as their cost of living declines. Some liberals see sticky-wage models as "blaming the victim" and prefer alternative theories, such as the sticky-price model.

Both sides are wrong. It makes no more sense to blame workers for mass unemployment than it would to blame gravity for airplane crashes. Sticky wages are simply part of our world, and no individual has the power to do anything about the problem.[4] Even if a single worker is willing to take the necessary pay cut, the worker's firm will still shut down the plant if other workers are not willing to do so. The company won't keep an expensive factory open in order to employ a single worker, no matter how low that individual's wage demands. This is what economists call the *fallacy of composition*, the false belief that what is true at the aggregate level is also true at the individual level.

But there is an even-more-basic reason to reject the view that workers should be blamed for sticky wages. The same problem occurs in the bond markets, *indeed to a far greater extent than in the labor market*. That's right, the "masters of the universe" in the New York bond market exhibit even worse money illusion than the average worker. The vast majority of bonds and other loan contracts are not indexed to inflation, which means that unexpected deflation raises the real burden of repaying these loans. And this isn't just a few years of nominal stickiness (as in labor markets): nominal bonds can have maturities of thirty years or more. Wage, price, and nominal debt stickiness are features of the world we live in, features that monetary policy makers must take into account when setting policy. Some conservative economists seem reluctant to confront that fact.

During the 1980s, I began to discover research that called into question the validity of sticky-wage models of the business cycle.[5] These studies typically looked at more recent (post–World War II) data and found little evidence of countercyclical real wages. Some even found procyclical real wages, especially during the 1970s. Given the strongly countercyclical real wages that I had observed during the interwar period, these studies puzzled me.

I quickly discovered that the cyclicality of real wages depended on the type of shock that was hitting the economy. When there was an adverse demand shock, price inflation fell more quickly than wage inflation, and real wages tended to rise—just as the sticky-wage model predicted. When there was an adverse supply shock, inflation rose more sharply than nominal wages, and real wages fell. But the adverse supply shocks also increased unemployment—which meant that real wages were falling just as output was declining. This was inconsistent with the standard interpretation of the sticky-wage model, which predicted countercyclical real wages.

My colleague Stephen Silver and I did some empirical research on this question.[6] We labeled years when inflation and unemployment moved in opposite directions (as predicted by the Phillips curve) "demand-shock years." Years when inflation and unemployment moved in the same direction (e.g., 1974, 1980) we labeled "supply-shock years." We found that real wages were strongly procyclical during supply-shock years and countercyclical during demand-shock years. Thus, the simple sticky-wage model seems to fit the data pretty well when the economy is affected by demand shocks, but not so well when the economy is buffeted by supply shocks.

This research led me to become increasingly distrustful of the price level as an indicator of nominal shocks. The meaning of a rise in prices caused by a drop in aggregate supply is far different from that of a rise in prices caused by an increase in aggregate demand. When AD rises, there is an increase in nominal GDP. It is the rising aggregate demand that is expansionary, not rising prices. Again, never reason from a price change. When prices rise, you don't know which curve has shifted. But if NGDP rises, you do know that AD has increased.

From the Price Level to Nominal GDP

The research on real-wage cyclicality led me to rethink my entire approach to macroeconomics. I began to see NGDP as the key nominal indicator and inflation as an almost useless appendage. Once you start seeing the world this way, you begin to discover more and more reasons to favor NGDP over the price level. Eventually I discovered that economist George Selgin had already developed many of these ideas.[7] But before we delve into them, let's examine why most economists think inflation is more important than NGDP growth.

Most economists see the NGDP growth rate as the sum of two very different variables: real GDP growth and inflation. These are the variables that are important to the average macroeconomist. Growth determines employment and living standards, whereas inflation imposes various "costs" on the economy. But what are the costs of inflation?

Surprisingly, economists don't worry about the thing that 99% of the public worry about when they hear the term *inflation*: an increased "cost of living." Economists interpret inflation through the "circular flow diagram," which tells us that higher prices correlate with higher incomes, and thus inflation doesn't directly make the public as a whole poorer, at least in any simple cost-of-living sense. Instead, economists worry about these more subtle costs:

1. *Excess taxation of capital from higher inflation rates.* As inflation rises, the nominal return on capital increases, and because tax systems are typically not indexed, people end up paying higher taxes on interest, dividends, and capital gains than they would otherwise. This reduces saving and investment and makes the economy poorer. I view this as inflation's most serious cost, by far.
2. *"Shoe leather" costs.* This refers to the fact that inflation is like a tax on cash balances. So when inflation is high, people will economize on cash by going to the ATM more often and holding smaller cash balances at any given point. Money is no different from anything else—taxes on money are inefficient because they lead to smaller holdings of real cash balances. The only efficient taxes are those that fall on things of which we want less produced, such as pollution.
3. *Menu costs.* The prices on menus and in catalogs must be changed more frequently when inflation is higher.
4. *Borrower-lender redistribution.* When inflation is higher than expected, wealth gets transferred from lenders to borrowers. When inflation is lower than expected, wealth is redistributed from borrowers to lenders. If inflation is far below expectations, it can trigger a financial crisis.

In three of these four cases, including the highly important taxation-of-capital problem, NGDP is actually a better proxy for the welfare costs of inflation than inflation itself. And menu costs is pretty much a wash.

The first two inflation costs reflect the fact that higher inflation tends to lead to higher nominal interest rates. This is true, but in many cases NGDP growth is actually better correlated with nominal interest rates than is inflation itself. The nominal interest rate has two components: a real interest rate and an inflation rate. Because the real interest rate is correlated with the real GDP growth rate, and because obviously inflation is 100% correlated with itself, the NGDP growth rate is actually pretty strongly correlated with the nominal interest rate. Thus, in an economy with 2% inflation and 3% real GDP growth, you might expect a nominal interest rate of roughly 5%, consisting of a 3% real interest rate and 2% more of expected inflation.[8]

If you are worried about either excess taxation of capital or shoe-leather costs, then you are actually worried about excessively high nominal returns on capital. And the best way to control nominal returns on capital is to stabilize NGDP growth, not inflation.

Regarding menu costs, you might think that controlling inflation would be the best way to avoid the menu costs of having to change prices. However, the government's various price indices do not measure the average change in prices on menus; they measure price changes *adjusted for changes in quality*. And there are other problems as well. If oil prices soar much higher than other prices, then an inflation target would force price cuts for products that are not oil. In contrast, under NGDP targeting the total expenditure on oil would rise by less than the price of oil, and that means you wouldn't need to reduce other, non-oil prices quite as sharply. Also, NGDP targeting is likely to result in less need to renegotiate nominal wage contracts, which is also an important menu cost. None of this means that NGDP is better with regard to menu costs—just that the relative advantages of inflation and NGDP are unclear.

Finally, NGDP stability does a better job of balancing the interests of lenders and borrowers than does inflation stability, so that each absorbs roughly equal risk. George Selgin has argued that, although it's true that unexpectedly higher inflation makes it easier for borrowers to repay loans, the exact same claim can be made for unexpectedly higher real GDP growth. In contrast, NGDP represents total income in the economy. You can think of NGDP as the total resources available to people, businesses, and governments for repaying their nominal debts. It is nominal income that determines ability to repay debts, not the inflation rate. Recent studies by Evan Koenig and Kevin Sheedy have confirmed Selgin's insight.[9] If you stabilize NGDP growth, then you will reduce the frequency of debt crises, which tend to be triggered by sharp declines in NGDP.

So NGDP growth is much more than just the sum of real growth and inflation—it's "the real thing." It's the single most important variable in all of macroeconomics. It's the variable that drives the business cycle—especially unemployment—as well as the occasional periods of financial distress. It better measures the welfare costs of inflation than does inflation itself. And yet the field of macroeconomics does not even have a word for this concept. Ideally, we'd use the terms *inflation* and *deflation*, but they are already taken. Thus, we are forced to fall back on the ungainly terms *rising nominal GDP* and *falling nominal GDP*.

You might wonder why we don't just say *GDP* instead of *nominal GDP*. After all, when people talk about the interest rate or the price of their home or their annual salary, they don't typically say "the nominal interest rate" or "my nominal house price" or "my nominal salary." Unfortunately, macroeconomists have made *real* GDP the default whenever they simply say "GDP." Also note that (correctly measured) GDP is exactly equal to GDI—gross domestic income. So in a perfect world we'd just refer to rising income and falling income. It would be much easier to explain to the public that the Fed favors a steady 4% growth in national income than to explain that it favors a 4% growth in NGDP. But alas, that's not the world we live in. Even in their choice of terminology, economists have subtly denigrated the single most important variable in all of macroeconomics.

Sticky Wages and the Musical-Chairs Model

The sticky-wage model can be improved by replacing the price level with NGDP. Thus, the real wage is no longer the ratio of wages and the price level (W/P): now we focus on the wage-to-NGDP ratio, which is the average nominal hourly wage relative to total nominal GDP. Figure 10.10 compares the wage-to-NGDP ratio to the unemployment rate during the Great Recession. The unemployment rate rose from about 4.5% in 2007 to a peak of 10.0% in October 2009. Why did unemployment rise so sharply during this period, and why did the labor market later recover from this shock?

The other line represents the ratio of nominal hourly wages to NGDP (per capita). Because hourly wage growth tends to be pretty stable over time (owing to sticky wages), almost all the variation in this variable is produced by fluctuations in NGDP per capita, the denominator of the wage-to-NGDP ratio. Indeed, it's actually mostly just owing to NGDP,

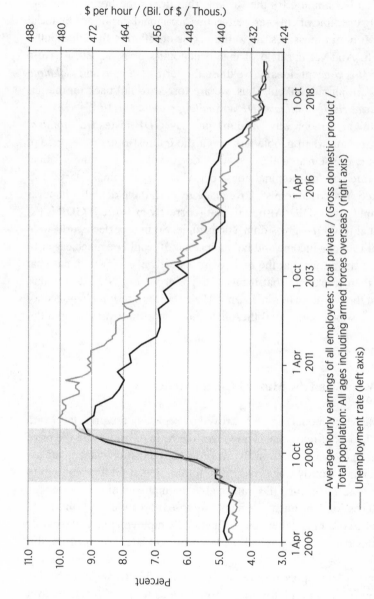

FIGURE 10.10. The unemployment rate and wages-to-NGDP per capita

Note: Gray bar indicates period of recession.

Source: FRED via Bureau of Labor Statistics, https://fred.stlouisfed.org/series/UNRATE, https://fred.stlouisfed.org/series/CES0500000003.

because population growth is also very stable from year to year. The huge surge in the wage-to-NGDP ratio during 2008–2009 occurred as NGDP growth fell by more than 8%—from its usual 5% trend (before the Great Recession) to below –3%. Because NGDP is in the denominator of the wage-to-NGDP ratio, this plunge in NGDP growth made the ratio soar much higher, and that boosted unemployment as well.

In the years after the recession, NGDP started growing at about 4% per year. Wage growth slowed modestly, from roughly 3.5% before the recession to 2% afterward. This allowed the labor market to gradually recover, although with faster NGDP growth (or slower wage growth) the recovery would have been quicker.

In my view, macroeconomists tend to produce excessively complex models of the business cycle. The underlying forces can be modeled pretty simply. Monetary policy drives NGDP growth (M × V), and NGDP drives employment. I like to use the musical-chairs metaphor for this process. Recall how in the game of musical chairs, every time the music stops, a few chairs are removed from the game. Because there are fewer chairs, some of the players are inevitably forced to sit on the floor.

By analogy, NGDP represents the funds that businesses have to pay their workers. If NGDP growth slows unexpectedly, fewer workers can be employed at the nominal hourly wage specified in contracts that were previously negotiated under expectations of a higher NGDP. Firms cut back on employment and the unemployment rate rises. For a recovery, you need some combination of faster NGDP growth and more moderate wage demands. Inflation is a fifth wheel; it adds nothing useful to the model.

If we had known all along that macroeconomic models would be based on NGDP rather than inflation, then NGDP would have been put on the vertical axis of the AS-AD model. And because what matters is not whether NGDP growth is high or low, but rather (just as with the Phillips curve) whether it is higher or lower than expected, we could further simplify the model by putting *unexpected* NGDP growth on the vertical axis. This simple and elegant graph (fig. 10.11) is sometimes called the Lucas supply curve.

Note that Yn in figure 10.11 is the natural rate of output, which is the long-run equilibrium once nominal wages have adjusted to an unexpected change in NGDP. Even better, we could replace real GDP with total hours worked on the horizontal axis. After all, if you are dropping inflation from your model, why not drop real GDP as well? Nominal GDP

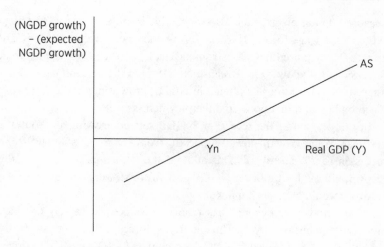

FIGURE 10.11. The Lucas supply curve

shocks cause hours worked to fluctuate above and below the natural rate of employment.

The result is a very simple model, but one that is not susceptible to "never reason from a price change" flaws, as are more traditional Phillips-curve-type models. This is the framework I'll use to analyze the Great Recession in the second half of this book.

What Is Monetary Policy?

If you follow the news, then you can't help but notice that monetary policy is one of the most widely discussed topics in all of economics. The media is full of pundits pontificating on whether money is too easy or too tight. Most economists have an opinion on the subject, as do many reporters, businesspeople, and politicians. But here's something you might not know: it is not at all clear what monetary policy *is*. Even many economists don't know what it is, and—what's worse—they don't know that they don't know.

Given the way terms like *easy money* and *tight money* are thrown around, you might assume that these terms have a well-defined meaning—maybe not in the popular usage, but at least among PhD-credentialed monetary economists. This is not the case. As we will see, most of the commonly cited definitions are extremely misleading, if not useless, and the most useful definitions are accepted by only a very few.

Interest rates are probably the single most commonly cited metric for determining the stance of monetary policy; they are also one of the least useful metrics. In the popular media, and even among many economists, high interest rates represent tight money and low rates are taken as evidence of easy money.

This definition is extremely misleading. It is so misleading that a new school of thought has recently arisen with the exact opposite view. The "Neo-Fisherians" claim that low interest rates represent tight money and high interest rates represent easy money. I hope it's obvious that this is a deeply embarrassing state of affairs. Imagine if physicists who belonged to one school of thought claimed that gravity attracted two objects while physicists who belonged to another school of thought claimed that gravity repelled any two objects.

The term *Neo-Fisherian* is a reference to the Fisher effect—that is, the tendency of higher rates of expected inflation to be associated with higher nominal interest rates. It turns out that the Fisher effect is merely one of four ways in which monetary policy affects interest rates. The complex interaction of money and inflation largely explains the confusion over terms like *easy* and *tight* money. I used to joke to my students that if someone asked them, "Does an expansionary monetary policy raise or lower interest rates?" they should simply answer yes.

The first thing we need to do is figure out just how monetary policy affects interest rates. Only then will we be able to even begin to answer to the question, What is monetary policy? This question does not have a clear, unambiguous answer—it merely has answers that are more or less useful. Because I'm a pragmatist, later I'll argue for what I regard to be the most useful definition of the *stance* of monetary policy.

Money and Interest Rates in a World with Flexible Prices

There are at least four major ways in which money can affect interest rates: via the liquidity effect, the price-level effect, the income effect, and the Fisher effect. That's pretty complicated! So let's make things easier by starting with an assumption of complete price flexibility. Here you might object, "Don't waste my time with unrealistic models of the world." But I'm not wasting your time—prices really are flexible in the long run. So we are going to start by looking at the way money affects interest rates in the long run (the price-level effect and the Fisher effect); then we'll look at the additional short-run effects.

To examine the price-level effect, let's review the money supply and demand diagram from chapter 3 (fig. 11.1). Recall that if prices were flexible then a doubling of the money supply would cause the price level to also double, because the value of money would fall in half. What does this thought experiment look like using a diagram where nominal interest rates are on the vertical axis (fig. 11.2)? For simplicity's sake, we'll continue to assume that money equals cash and also that cash pays no interest. In this case, the nominal interest rate is the opportunity cost of holding cash, and thus the demand for money (cash) slopes downward and to the right. But notice that demand slopes downward for a completely different reason in figure 11.2 than in figure 11.1. Now it's all about the *opportunity cost* of holding cash. When you hold cash, you forgo holding an alternative

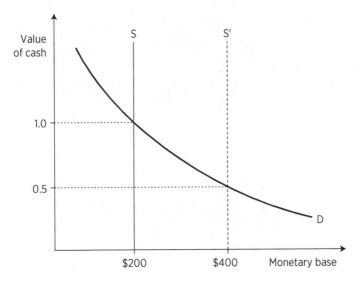

FIGURE II.I. Supply and demand for fiat money

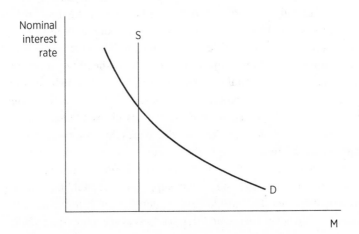

FIGURE II.2. Supply and demand for money as a function of interest rates

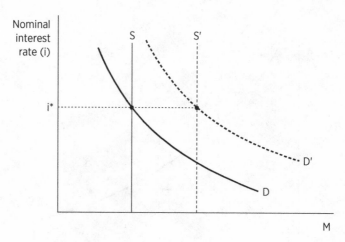

FIGURE 11.3. Impact of an increase in money with flexible prices

asset that could earn the nominal interest rate. (One assumption that does not change is that the supply of money is a vertical line set by the Fed.)

If we were to double the money supply, you might think that interest rates should fall. And it looks like that's what's happening in figure 11.2, but only at first glance. If prices truly were flexible, then a doubling of the money supply should also cause an immediate doubling of the money demand (fig. 11.3). That's because prices would now be twice as high as they were before the money was injected (per the price-flexibility assumption), and therefore people would prefer to carry twice as much cash at any given interest rate. The demand curve would shift right exactly as much as the supply curve shifted right. Interest rates would be unchanged.

Do we know this is true? Yes, we do. That's because there is one sort of change in the money supply that occurs with complete price flexibility: currency reforms. When the Mexican government replaces 1,000 old pesos with one new peso, the money supply immediately falls by 99.9%. Normally a fall like that would cause a depression. But during currency reforms, all the wage, price, and debt contracts are immediately adjusted by the same factor as the change in the money supply. With complete price flexibility, there is no change in interest rates.

When there are smaller changes in the money supply, prices are somewhat sticky in the short run, and later we'll see that this means that money does affect interest rates in the real world. But we've already learned one important fact: a one-time change in the money supply does not have any long-run effect on interest rates. Once all wages and prices have fully adjusted, interest rates return to their original level.

If only things were so simple. We must deal with two complications: sticky prices and changes in the growth rate of the money supply. Let's start with the money growth rate and keep assuming flexible prices for the moment. According to the quantity theory of money, a one-time increase in the money supply results in a proportional increase in prices (and nominal GDP), but no higher inflation from that point forward. But what if the growth rate of the money supply permanently increases? In that case the growth rate of prices will also increase—in other words, we would experience a higher rate of inflation. Once this inflation is anticipated, it feeds through to higher nominal interest rates.

This is the Fisher effect, and it is what causes Neo-Fisherians to suggest that easier money will be associated with higher nominal interest rates. More money growth means higher inflation, which causes lenders to demand a higher nominal interest rate. Just as importantly, the higher expected inflation makes borrowers willing to pay a higher interest rate.

The Fisher effect largely explains why interest rates increased during the 1960s and 1970s. Beginning in the 1960s, the Fed sharply accelerated the rate at which it was creating money (fig. 11.4). The growth rate of the monetary base rose from about 1% during the 1950s to about 8% in the 1970s. The inflation rate (the GDP deflator) also rose sharply. Note, however, that the two do not always move together. In this case, high inflation was caused by changes in the growth rate of the supply of money. Later we'll see that shifts in the *demand* for money were the dominant factor explaining the drop in inflation during the Great Recession.

As shown in figure 11.5, the increased inflation eventually pushed inflation expectations higher, and nominal interest rates (T-bill yield) rose as well. The takeaway here is that an increase in the money supply *can* cause higher inflation and higher nominal interest rates, not that it always does cause higher interest rates.

To summarize, in a flexible price model a one-time change in the money supply has no impact on interest rates. In contrast, a permanent increase in the money-supply growth rate can cause a permanent increase in the inflation rate, and hence a permanent increase in the nominal interest rates.

We are halfway through the model—we have covered the price level and Fisher effects. Now we need to examine how money affects interest rates in a sticky-price model. This will result in two additional effects: the liquidity effect and the income effect.

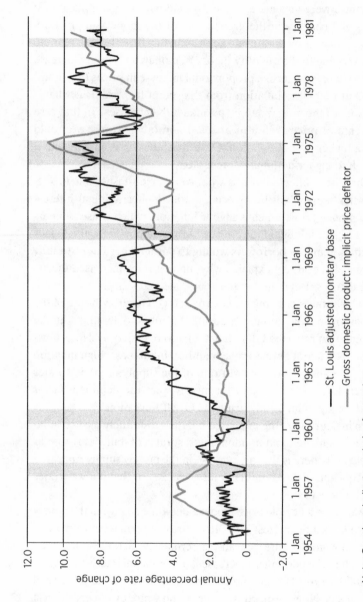

Note: Gray bars indicate periods of recession.

— St. Louis adjusted monetary base
— Gross domestic product: implicit price deflator

FIGURE 11.4. Changes in the US monetary base and the inflation rate, 1954–1980

Note: Gray bars indicate periods of recession.

Source: FRED via Federal Reserve Bank of St. Louis & U.S. Bureau of Economic Analysis, https://fred.stlouisfed.org/series/AMBNS, https://fred.stlouisfed.org/series /GDPDEF

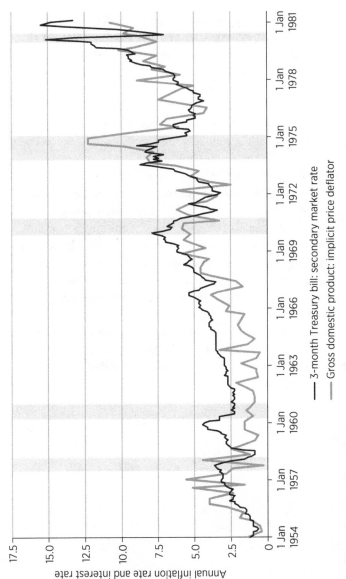

FIGURE 11.5. Changes in the US inflation rate and the nominal interest rate, 1954–1981

Note: Gray bars indicate periods of recession.

Source: FRED via Board of Governors of the Federal Reserve System (US) and US Bureau of Economic Analysis, https://fred.stlouisfed.org/series/TB3MS, https://fred.stlouisfed.org/series/A006RD3Q086SBEA.

Money and Interest Rates in a World with Sticky Prices

Let's return to the familiar model of money supply and demand, with the value of money on the vertical axis (fig. 11.6). What if we double the money supply, and because of sticky prices there is no instantaneous increase in the price level? In that case we'd be at point b, which is not at equilibrium. My friends in the market-monetarist community call this *disequilibrium*. In a sense they are right: it looks as if people are holding more money than they wish to hold. But are people actually forced to hold more cash than they wish to hold? No, and neither are banks forced to hold more reserves than they wish to hold.

So what makes people willing to hold more base money than they "need" at this price level? The answer is simple: the nominal interest rate, which is the opportunity cost of holding cash, immediately plunges after the new base money is injected. It falls so low that people are now willing to hold more "liquidity"—that is, larger real cash balances. Figure 11.7 shows this so-called liquidity effect, and it's the *only* effect of money on interest rates that many people are aware of. This is basically what the media are talking about when they discuss "monetary policy," even though it's only one of four effects.

The lower nominal interest rates mean you *shift* the demand curve to point b on the supply-and-demand diagram in figure 11.6 (with the value of money—1/P—on the vertical axis) while you move *along* the demand

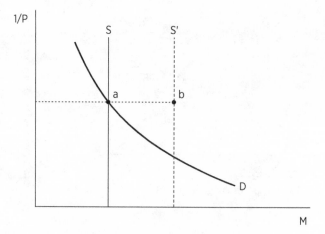

FIGURE 11.6. The short-run impact of an increase in money with sticky prices

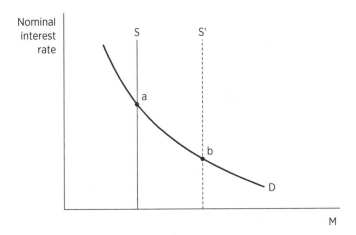

FIGURE 11.7. The impact of an increase in money with sticky prices

curve to point b for the supply and demand diagram in figure 11.7 (with interest rates on the vertical axis). This short-run equilibrium occurs at the points labeled "b" in the two graphs of figure 11.8.

In the very long run, the price level doubles and the demand for money on the interest-rate graph (the second graph in figure 11.8) shifts to the right. This brings interest rates back to their original level (point c). On the price-level diagram (the first graph in figure 11.8), the demand curve shifts back once interest rates have returned to their original level, and the value of money falls in half (point c) as prices double.

At point c, we have returned to the example from the beginning of this chapter, which showed that in a world of flexible prices an increase in the money supply has no effect on interest rates, and prices rise in proportion to the increase in the money supply. In a sticky-price world, point c becomes the long-run result, because prices that are sticky in the short run become flexible in the long run.

Whenever you hear the news media talking about the Fed raising or lowering interest rates, the reporters are assuming that the change in interest rates reflects the liquidity effect. Before 2008 these adjustments were almost always done by changes in the supply of base money. So when reporters said, "The Fed cut interest rates by a quarter point today," what they really meant is that the Fed voted to instruct its New York branch to inject base money until the market interest rate on interbank loans (the federal funds rate) fell by 0.25%.

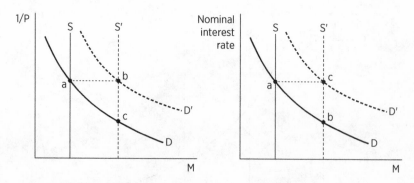

FIGURE 11.8. Two ways of modeling an increase in the money supply

You might think that talking about interest rates rather than money supply is an innocuous shortcut. It is not. As we will see later, this shortcut caused great misunderstanding during the Great Recession, because people (and even economists) wrongly assumed that the changes in interest rates that they were observing were evidence of an easy money policy by the Fed. The Fed can move interest rates via the liquidity effect, but rates can also move for numerous other reasons.

Unfortunately, things have become somewhat more complicated since 2008, because the Fed has adopted new and needlessly complicated policy tools. From the beginning, the Fed has had some ability to influence the demand for base money by adjusting reserve requirements. But now the Fed has much more control over the demand for base money because it can influence demand by paying more or less interest on bank reserves. This policy of adjusting the IOR also produces a liquidity effect, but it looks different on the two graphs in figure 11.8. The basic principles discussed in this chapter don't change, however. The liquidity effect remains a short-term effect that occurs because of sticky prices, and it fades away over time as the price level adjusts to the new money supply (or demand).

There is one final effect to consider—the income effect. In previous chapters we saw that because wages and prices are sticky, a change in the money supply has an effect on real GDP—that is, real income. Because the demand for credit is very sensitive to the business cycle, a monetary policy that creates a boom or a recession can dramatically impact interest rates, even if inflation expectations stay close to 2%.

Consider a tight money policy such as that of 1929–1933. That policy drove the US economy into a deep depression. As a result, firms had little need to borrow money to expand their facilities. Far fewer people borrowed money to buy a home or an automobile. Because of the sharp decline in the demand for credit, interest rates fell sharply.

There's some dispute about whether the decline was just in nominal interest rates or in real interest rates as well. After all, prices fell sharply during the early 1930s. In my view, however, the deflation of 1929–1933 was mostly unanticipated, and thus even the real interest rate was low during the early 1930s. Most certainly this was true after 1933, when prices began rising but nominal interest rates stayed close to zero.[1] Of course, we saw a similar phenomenon during the Great Recession, when both real and nominal interest rates were at very low levels, even during the recovery.

The Future Is Right Now

During periods of high and volatile inflation, the Fisher effect has the biggest impact on interest rates. During periods of low and stable inflation (e.g., the period since 1990), the income effect is the most important. The liquidity and price-level effects are the least important. Imagine there were no income or Fisher effects after a one-time change in the money supply. What would the path of interest rates look like if there were a sudden and unexpected 10% boost in the monetary base? It would look something like figure 11.9.

Notice how interest rates immediately fall in response to the monetary injection, and then gradually increase back to the original level. Thus, any given change in interest rates is equally likely to reflect the liquidity and price level effects. They are equally important. Rates might be falling

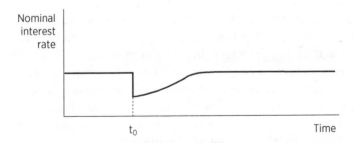

FIGURE 11.9. Time path of interest rates after a one-time increase in money

owing to a current easy money policy, or they might be rising owing to the long-run effect of an earlier easy money policy. However, the liquidity and price-level effects are actually the two weakest effects. When you add the income and Fisher effects, we end up with a situation in which the overwhelming majority of changes in interest rates do not reflect "Fed policy," at least not in the way that most people think of that term (i.e., the liquidity effect).

To the news media, a cut in the federal-funds target is an easy money policy, whereas an increase in interest rates is a tight money policy. The media treat all changes in interest rates as if they reflect the liquidity effect. If I'm right that this is a basic error, then how could so many people have become confused on this point? I see two mistakes being made, both of which are very subtle mistakes—easy cognitive illusions to which one might fall prey.

The first mistake is to confuse the phrase *in the short run* with *right now* and *in the long run* with *later*. I used to make this mistake myself until Robert Lucas opened my eyes. Right now, right this minute, we are seeing interest rates respond *in the long run* to actions the Fed took months or years ago. Never wave away long-run effects as things we don't need to worry about just because they will occur out there in the future. The famous John Maynard Keynes once remarked that "in the long run we are all dead," and many Keynesians put too little weight on long-run effects.[2]

You have probably also noticed that the excessive focus on the liquidity effect is an example of reasoning from a price change. A fall in the nominal interest rate *might* indicate an easier monetary policy, as so many people assume. But more likely the "price of credit" is falling because of other factors, such as falling inflation or declining real output. It is never OK to draw any sort of conclusion from a rise or fall in interest rates, unless you know *why* interest rates have changed.

There's another reason people overemphasize the liquidity effect. Because the Fed targets the short-term interest rate, there is a sense in which that rate is under the control of monetary policy makers. And because it seems as if the Fed can effortlessly move rates up and down according to its whims, it's hard for people to shake the idea that when they see interest rates change they are seeing Fed policy in action—more specifically, that they are seeing the liquidity effect in action. Especially because it is true that on any given day a Fed rate cut is an easier money policy than a Fed rate increase. So what's wrong with treating interest rates as an indicator of monetary policy?

The problem here is that people forget about the Fed's deeper objectives. Although the Fed may target interest rates on a day-to-day basis, at a deeper level it is targeting inflation and employment. Consider the following example. The European Central Bank (ECB) tightened monetary policy in July 2008 by raising its interest-rate target. So far the conventional view is correct. But suppose that this tight money policy was a mistake, which drove the eurozone into a deep recession with falling inflation. We've already seen that the long-term effect of a tight money policy can actually be lower income, lower inflation, and thus lower nominal interest rates.

And *this* is where the confusion occurs. When those lower eurozone interest rates finally materialized (in late 2008), almost nobody treated them as the long-run effect of the July decision to tighten policy. Instead, they were viewed as new short-term steps by the ECB, an easing of monetary policy. Actually, in late 2008 the ECB was merely going along with market forces, which were driving interest rates much lower in anticipation of a deep recession. Market interest rates fell even before the ECB moved in late 2008, in anticipation of ECB rate cuts.

I suppose you could still argue that the ECB was cutting rates, after all, and it didn't have to reduce its interest-rate target in late 2008, did it? I'd say that for all practical purposes, it did have to cut rates, because the ECB has a mandate to keep inflation close to 2%. If a central bank is going to target inflation and if it makes a mistake that temporarily drives inflation below its target, then it must cut interest rates to avoid going even further off course.

We'll later see that the entire Great Recession makes far more sense if you think of the falling interest rates of late 2008 not as an easy money policy but as the *long-run effect of an earlier tight money policy*. It might be easier to comprehend this in a couple of time-series graphs. In figure 11.10 we see the short- and long-term effects of a tight money policy: notice how rates initially rise owing to the liquidity effect, and then later decline with the other three effects. If inflation ends up permanently lower, then nominal interest rates will also move to a permanently lower path. Everything reverses when we look at the short- and long-term effects of an easy money policy (fig. 11.11).

Note that the initial move in interest rates—the liquidity effect—is the one that the news media focuses on. But when you observe movements in interest rates in the real world, perhaps 10% of the time you are observing the liquidity effect, and 90% of the time you are observing the price-level, income, and Fisher effects.

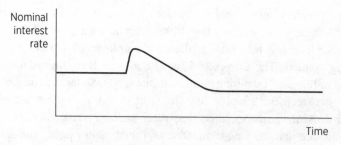

FIGURE 11.10. Short- and long-term effects of a tight-money policy

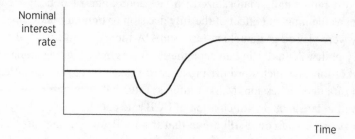

FIGURE 11.11. Short- and long-term effects of an easy-money policy

If It's Not Interest Rates, What *Is* Monetary Policy?

Because I'm making some pretty unconventional claims about the stance of monetary policy, I'd like to back them up with quotations from more well-known economists. Let's start with Milton Friedman:

> Low interest rates are generally a sign that money has been tight, as in Japan; high interest rates, that money has been easy. . . .
>
> After the U.S. experience during the Great Depression, and after inflation and rising interest rates in the 1970s and disinflation and falling interest rates in the 1980s, I thought the fallacy of identifying tight money with high interest rates and easy money with low interest rates was dead. Apparently, old fallacies never die.[3]

Notice that Friedman says that low rates indicate that money "has been" tight—he is implying that it became tight at some point in the past. He's not a Neo-Fisherian; in fact, he agrees with the conventional wisdom that a tight money policy will initially raise interest rates via the liquidity effect (as do I). Rather, Friedman is telling us that most of the interest-rate movements that we observe reflect longer-term factors, such as the Fisher effect. Also note his dismay at the fact that (as of 1997) so many people still had not learned the basic lesson that tight money and easy money don't equate to high and low interest rates. Friedman passed away in 2006, but things are no better today—this issue is still widely misunderstood.

Friedman preferred to define monetary policy in terms of the broader money supply, such as M1 or M2, which includes various types of bank deposits. But in the early 1980s the velocity of circulation became increasingly unstable, and the profession moved away from the monetarist view that the money supply measured the stance of monetary policy.

Recall the three key lessons from Frederic Mishkin's textbook that I quoted back in the introduction:

- "It is dangerous always to associate the easing or the tightening of monetary policy with a fall or a rise in short-term nominal interest rates."
- "Other asset prices besides those on short-term debt instruments contain important information about the stance of monetary policy because they are important elements in various monetary policy transmission mechanisms."
- "Monetary policy can be highly effective in reviving a weak economy even if short-term rates are already near zero."[4]

For decades I taught these ideas to my students, naïvely assuming that other economists also believed them to be true. Why did I assume that? Partly because these statements *are* true, and partly because Mishkin's book was the number-one best seller among monetary economics textbooks. Mishkin served on the Fed's Board of Governors until 2008, and his textbook was considered the standard in universities across the country.

Then in late 2008 I discovered that almost no one else believed this stuff. It is not even clear whether Mishkin believes it anymore. The term *highly* has been removed from the third point in the most recent editions of his textbook,[5] perhaps under pressure from instructors. You can see why this set of views was so controversial. As I pointed out in the introduction, if we take these ideas seriously, then the clear implication is that the Fed adopted a tight money policy that triggered sharp declines in almost all asset markets, and that the zero bound on interest rates in no way prevented the Fed from adopting a much more expansionary monetary policy. I believed that in late 2008, and I still believe that. But almost no one shares this view, which is based on once-mainstream assumptions.

Thus far, we've considered three possible indicators of monetary policy: interest rates, the money supply, and "other market indicators." In my view, the first two are highly flawed. Ben Bernanke shares this view— here's Bernanke in 2003, the year he first joined the Fed:

> The imperfect reliability of money growth as an indicator of monetary policy is unfortunate, because we don't really have anything satisfactory to replace it. As emphasized by Friedman . . . nominal interest rates are not good indicators of the stance of policy. . . . The real short-term interest rate . . . is also imperfect. . . .
>
> Ultimately, it appears, one can check to see if an economy has a stable monetary background only by looking at macroeconomic indicators such as nominal GDP growth and inflation.[6]

So Bernanke finds that the money supply is inadequate as an indicator of monetary policy and that interest rates are no better. Even the real interest rate is imperfect, because a tight money policy can drive an economy into depression, and this reduces real interest rates over time. Thus, falling real interest rates are not an indicator of easy money. In the end, Bernanke points to two possible indicators: inflation and NGDP growth.

By now you have probably guessed that I prefer NGDP growth, because inflation suffers from the "reasoning from a price change" problem. A rising inflation rate might indicate easy money, if it's due to rising aggregate demand. But it might equally well reflect an adverse supply shock. For the moment let's accept Bernanke's dual criteria for judging the stance of policy—inflation and NGDP growth. Under this assumption, how would we characterize monetary policy during the first five years of the Great Recession? The average inflation rate was 1.37%, and the average NGDP growth rate was 2.23%. If we average those two numbers, we get 1.80%, which happens to be the lowest rate over a five-year period since Herbert Hoover was president in the early 1930s.

Think about just how ironic that fact is. Ben Bernanke was a distinguished scholar of the Great Depression, and his account of the failures of monetary policy during the early 1930s is pretty similar to my own view. He blamed the Fed for conducting an excessively tight policy that led to falling prices and falling NGDP. By the late 1990s, Bernanke was criticizing Japan for its inadequate monetary stimulus at a time when Japanese interest rates were stuck at zero. And yet he presided over some of the tightest money since the Great Depression, *using his very own criterion.*

Just as it's no longer clear that Frederic Mishkin believes monetary policy is "highly effective" when interest rates are zero, it's no longer obvious that Bernanke believes that inflation and NGDP growth are the proper way to measure the stance of monetary policy. I still favor using nominal GDP growth, but once Bernanke became Fed chair he repeatedly suggested that the Fed was providing a very "accommodative" monetary policy, and thus was assisting the recovery from the Great Recession.[7] And yet I see no basis at all for Bernanke to have made that claim. He certainly could not have been pointing to the low interest rates or the program of quantitative easing to expand the monetary base, because he had already correctly noted that these indicators were much inferior to inflation and NGDP growth. And he had criticized the Japanese central bank when it pointed to low interest rates as evidence that it was conducting an expansionary monetary policy. Here's Bernanke in 1999:

> The argument that current monetary policy in Japan is in fact quite accommodative rests largely on the observation that interest rates are at a very low level. I do hope that readers who have gotten this far will be sufficiently familiar with monetary history not to take seriously any such claim based on the level of the *nominal* interest rate. One need only recall that nominal interest rates remained close to zero in many countries throughout the Great Depression, a period of massive monetary contraction and deflationary pressure. In short, low nominal interest rates may just as well be a sign of expected deflation and monetary tightness as of monetary ease.[8]

In the end, there is no objective method for determining the stance of monetary policy. An observer is free to look at interest rates, the money supply, the price level, the price of foreign exchange (i.e., exchange rates), the price of gold, the price of zinc, or a thousand other indicators. Because I'm a pragmatist, I believe it's best to pick the most useful definition. For me, that would be a definition that gets at the question of whether policy is too easy or too tight *to hit the central bank's target.*

Under the Fed's dual mandate, which combines low inflation and high employment, NGDP growth might be the single best indicator of the stance of monetary policy. When NGDP growth is high, the Fed is usually exceeding its target, and monetary policy could be said to be excessively expansionary. If NGDP growth is too low to meet the Fed's dual mandate, then policy could be viewed as excessively contractionary. Thus, it probably makes no sense to talk about *easy* or *tight* money in an absolute sense, but only in reference to the central bank's target. Is money too easy or too tight to hit the target? That's the question that we should focus on.

We also need to recall that monetary policy is forward-looking. Nothing can be done about past inflation or past NGDP growth; the goal should be to set policy at a position that is expected to lead to on-target inflation and NGDP growth going forward. In that case, perhaps the best measure of the stance of monetary policy is not NGDP growth in the recent past, but the *expected rate of NGDP growth* going forward. I've helped to set up an NGDP prediction market, partly for this very reason—to provide a real-time indicator of the current stance of monetary policy. I believe that if a more liquid version of this market had been in place in 2008, it would have given the Fed a clear signal that Fed policy was too tight to hit its targets for inflation and employment.

If my analysis of Fed policy sounds highly critical of Bernanke, keep in mind that Bernanke's Fed did far better than the ECB, and also that Bernanke was working hard to do even more, against strong internal opposition within the Fed. Needless to say, the Fed under Bernanke handled a major banking crisis far better than did the Federal Reserve in the 1930s. Nonetheless, the Fed erred in allowing NGDP expectations to fall so sharply during 2008.

Nominal GDP will play a central role in the remainder of this book. NGDP growth is the best indicator of the stance of monetary policy, and it is also the best variable for the Fed to target. Unstable NGDP growth leads to business cycles and financial crises. There is a pressing need to create more accurate tools for forecasting NGDP growth, such as a highly liquid NGDP futures market.

We've now covered all the tools required to understand the Great Recession in the US. But the recession was a global event, and hence an international perspective will help to shed light on its underlying causes. The final theory chapter examines another case of reasoning from a price change, this time involving the price of foreign currencies—exchange rates.

CHAPTER TWELVE

Nominal and Real Exchange Rates

We've seen that real and nominal GDP are radically different concepts, but they become strangely entangled in the short run owing to wage and price stickiness. The same is true of exchange rates. Unfortunately, most people tend to confuse nominal exchange rates (the ones you see listed in airport kiosks) and real exchange rates (the ones that matter for international trade and investment flows).

There are four key nominal variables in macroeconomics: the price level, NGDP, nominal interest rates, and nominal exchange rates. Any analysis of these four variables begins with one of the three basic classical models of money: the quantity theory of money (for the price level and NGDP), the Fisher effect (for nominal interest rates), or purchasing power parity (for nominal exchange rates). We've seen that the quantity theory of money can explain inflation best when real money demand is stable, and it can explain NGDP best when velocity is stable. Similarly, the Fisher effect can explain nominal interest rates best when real interest rates are stable. Now we will see that purchasing power parity (PPP) can explain nominal exchange rates best when the real exchange rate is stable.

In practice, none of the three classical theories is precisely true, because real money demand, real interest rates, and real exchange rates change over time. As a general rule, all three theories work pretty well when inflation rates are extremely high, because in those cases inflation dominates other (real) changes in money demand, real interest rates, or real exchange rates.

In this chapter we'll learn what PPP does and does not tell us about nominal exchange rates. Then we'll look at how monetary shocks affect real and nominal exchange rates. Finally, we'll develop a more complete theory of real exchange rates, and see why accusations of "currency manipulation" should be viewed with a great deal of skepticism.

Bruh

What's the Point of Purchasing Power Parity?

Purchasing power parity is based on a very simple concept—the law of
one price. If goods are freely traded and transport costs are negligible,
then the price (net of tax) of any particular good should be the same any-
where in the world. Consider the following example. Two neighboring
countries both produce oil. In one of the countries, oil reserves are vast
and the cost of production is low. In its neighbor, reserves are tiny and
the cost of production is high. In which country will oil prices be higher?

Surprisingly, as long as PPP holds true, the price of oil should be
roughly the same in both countries. As an analogy, consider two nearby
lakes, one of which is fed by a large river while the other is not. If the
two lakes are connected by a free-flowing channel of water (as with Lake
Michigan and Lake Huron), then their surface levels should be identical,
despite the fact that one lake is not being fed by a river. Alternatively, if
the two lakes are separated by a physical barrier (as with Lakes Erie and
Ontario, separated by Niagara Falls), then their water levels may be quite
different. Similarly, relative prices depend on local supply and demand
factors only if some sort of barrier prevents arbitrage from equalizing
prices in two markets.

If PPP held for all goods, then prices would be the same everywhere in
the world. Tourists would not find some countries to be a bargain while
others are expensive. In that case, all *real* exchange rates would be exactly
one. The real exchange rate is simply the ratio of prices in the home country to prices in the foreign country, when expressed in the same currency.
Thus, if prices in Switzerland are 50% higher than in the US, on average,
then the real exchange rate for the Swiss franc (in terms of US dollars)
would be 1.5.

We can also apply this concept to inflation differentials. If PPP holds,
then the rate of appreciation for a currency should be the foreign inflation
rate minus the domestic inflation rate:

rate of appreciation of domestic currency =
foreign inflation – domestic inflation.

Thus, if the US had 3% inflation and Switzerland had 1% inflation, then the
Swiss franc (domestic currency in this case) should appreciate by roughly
2% per year. The dollar would be expected to depreciate by 2% per year.

Anyone with even a passing familiarity with exchange rates and inflation differentials knows that PPP does not hold true—not even close. For
instance, since the euro was created in 1999, the value of the euro (against
the US dollar) has fluctuated between roughly $0.85 and $1.65. That's a
huge range, especially given that the inflation rate in the eurozone has
been pretty similar to the inflation rate in the US. If PPP were true, then
the euro-to-US-dollar exchange rate would have stayed pretty stable.

So if PPP doesn't hold true, why do we spend so much time studying the
concept? Why is it so important? Let's return to the concept of the value
of money. Here are three plausible ways of defining the purchasing power
of money: in terms of the quantity of goods and services that can be purchased (e.g., CPI, GDP deflator), in terms of the share of output that can
be purchased with a dollar (NGDP), or in terms of the quantity of foreign
exchange (exchange rates). So exchange rates are obviously a monetary
phenomenon—they are literally the "price of money," or at least one version of that concept. And we have already seen that other monetary theories
such as the quantity theory of money are very useful, despite often failing
to hold true in certain specific situations. Thus, even though the massive increase in the monetary base after 2008 did not result in anything close to a
proportional increase in prices or NGDP, the quantity theory of money remains the essential starting point for monetary analysis. Similarly, PPP is the
benchmark at which we'd be wise to begin any analysis of exchange rates.

Recall that the quantity theory of money worked best for high-inflation
countries, as shown in figure 12.1. That's because in the long run, the real
demand for money tends to change by less that 10% per year. That means
that if money growth rises to 30%, 40%, or 50% per year for many decades,
then it will tend to show up in higher rates of inflation, not in a higher real
demand for money.

The same is true for PPP. Real exchange rates do fluctuate quite a bit
from one year to the next, but over the long run the annual change in the
real exchange rates tends to be, on average, in the single digits. Thus, if
the inflation differential rises to 30%, 40%, or 50% per year for many
decades, this will show up primarily in rapid depreciation of the currency,
not a higher real exchange rate. Figure 12.2 shows the strong correlation between inflation differentials and currency depreciation for high-
inflation countries. If PPP held exactly true, then all points would lie
along the forty-five-degree line.

Of course the same is true for interest rates. Real interest rates do fluctuate over time, but they usually remain in the single digits. Therefore, very

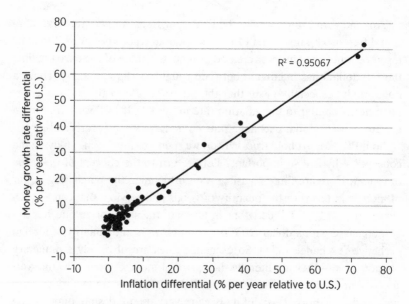

FIGURE 12.1. Inflation rates and money growth rates, 1975–2005

Source: Worth Publishers, International Economics, Feenstra/Taylor.

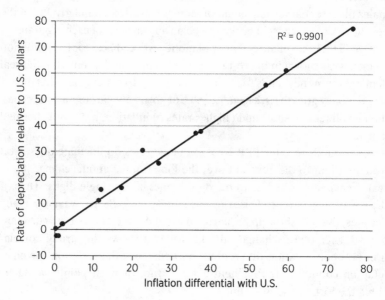

FIGURE 12.2. Currency depreciation and inflation rates, 1975–2005

Source: Worth Publishers, International Economics, Feenstra/Taylor, p. 26 of 98.

high inflation rates generally lead to very high nominal interest rates. To summarize, if a country adopts a policy of increasing its money supply by 50% per year for many decades, then the result will be an inflation rate of roughly 50%, nominal interest rates of roughly 50%, and a roughly 50% annual increase in the price of foreign currencies (where the other country has near-zero inflation). That means rapid depreciation in the domestic currency.

Does this mean that the concept of PPP has no implications for low-inflation countries? Not at all. Inflation differentials are always exerting pressure on exchange rates, even when PPP does not hold true. For instance, the exchange rate for the Japanese yen is not much different from what it was twenty years ago, despite the fact that the US averages close to 2% inflation, whereas Japan has had near-zero inflation. This means that the real exchange rate for the Japanese yen has fallen sharply over the past two decades, by roughly 2% per year. This makes the PPP theory look bad. But if Japan had had similar inflation to that of the US, that real depreciation would have occurred through a depreciation in the nominal exchange rate. Instead, Japan has had much lower inflation than the US, which has allowed a necessary depreciation in the real exchange rate to occur without any major change in the nominal rate.[1]

Purchasing power parity tends to work best for goods that can be easily arbitraged, such as commodities. Unfortunately, though, for the proponents of PPP, commodities make up a far smaller share of our economy than they did a hundred years ago, when the theory was first developed. One area in which arbitrage still does work pretty well is in the financial markets. Because it is easy to move funds among countries with open capital markets, the expected rate of return on safe assets is pretty similar in most developed countries. This leads to the financial market equivalent of PPP, called the interest parity condition:

expected appreciation of domestic currency = foreign interest rate
– domestic interest rate.

Thus, if interest rates are 3% in the US and 1% in Switzerland, then the Swiss franc will be expected to appreciate at 2% per year. In that case, the expected return on investments in the US and Switzerland would be identical (in terms of US dollars), at 3%. Or you might say the rates of return are identical in terms of Swiss francs, at 1%. Interest parity does not hold perfectly, because domestic and foreign assets are not perfect substitutes, but it holds far more precisely than PPP.

Monetary Shocks and Dornbusch Overshooting

Recall the Venn diagram from chapter 1 that illustrated the relationship between the real and nominal side of macroeconomics (reproduced in figure 12.3). On left side are long-run growth issues, determined by supply-side factors. On the right side is the concept of money neutrality, because nominal shocks have no long-run real effects on the economy. And in the middle is the interaction of nominal and real variables, caused by wage and price stickiness.

The same sort of dichotomy occurs with real and nominal exchange rates. Thus far, we've looked at how monetary policy influences relative inflation rates, and hence nominal exchange rates, in the long run. Now let's consider the short-run impact of monetary shocks in a world where wages and prices are sticky. It turns out that this case is surprisingly tricky, because monetary policy produces three seemingly incompatible effects: Monetary stimulus leads to lower interest rates in the short run (liquidity effect), lower interest rates lead to an expected appreciation of the currency (interest parity condition), and monetary stimulus leads to currency depreciation (quantity theory of money + PPP). Can all three of these be true? Surprisingly, yes. In 1976, the economist Rudi Dornbusch worked out the implications of wage and price stickiness for exchange rates in his famous "overshooting model."[2] Instead of just giving you the reason, let me provide a hint and see if you can solve the puzzle on your own.

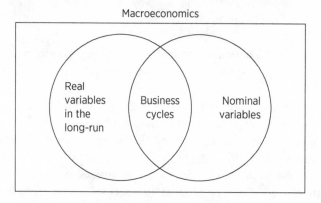

FIGURE 12.3. Components of macroeconomics

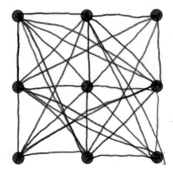

FIGURE 12.4. Nine dots and four lines puzzle

Here's the hint: You're given a grid with nine dots, arrayed in three rows of three dots each (fig. 12.4). Now try to connect all nine dots by drawing four straight lines one after the other, without taking your pen off the paper between lines. (You'll need to think outside the box to solve this puzzle.)

Dornbusch's model has several components:

- Money is neutral in the long run. Thus, an unexpected, exogenous, and permanent 10% increase in the money supply should cause the price level and the price of foreign exchange to rise by 10% in the long run. Of course a 10% rise in the price of foreign exchange means a comparable depreciation of the domestic currency in the long run.
- Because wages and prices are sticky in the short run, a sudden monetary injection will not immediately raise prices by the same proportion; instead, nominal interest rates will decline in the short run.
- Because of the interest-parity condition, a lower nominal interest rate implies that the domestic currency is expected to appreciate over time. (For simplicity's sake, assume that domestic and foreign interest rates were equal before the monetary shock.)

Do you have the solution yet? First let's examine figure 12.5 for the solution to the problem of nine dots and four lines. Notice how you need to go outside the box to get a solution. The same basic idea is true of monetary policy and exchange rates.

Dornbusch showed that if the exchange rate is expected to depreciate by 10% in the long run relative to the preshock level, but is also expected

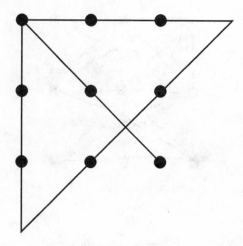

FIGURE 12.5. Solution to the nine dots and four lines puzzle

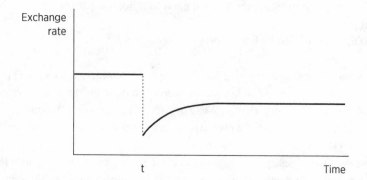

FIGURE 12.6. Dornbusch's overshooting model

to *appreciate* after the monetary shock lowers interest rates, then the immediate impact of a 10% monetary injection is for the exchange rate to fall by more than 10%—that is, to "overshoot" its long-run equilibrium.[3] Thus, it might immediately depreciate by 15% or 20% before rising over time, ending up only 10% lower than it was before (fig. 12.6). In the long run, the price of goods will rise by 10% and the exchange rate will end up with a depreciation of 10%.

On the day of an unexpected monetary shock, the overall price level is almost unchanged, owing to price stickiness. PPP does not hold in the short run, because the nominal exchange rate depreciates sharply despite no change in the relative price levels. Indeed, it immediately depreciates by more than 10% in this example. This means that monetary stimulus can cause both real and nominal exchange rates to depreciate in the short run. A good example occurred on March 18, 2009, the day the Fed announced the first major quantitative easing program. Right after the announcement, the US dollar depreciated by $.06 (more than 4%) against the euro, an unusually large movement for a single day. Because the US and eurozone price levels show very little change on a single day, this nominal depreciation was accompanied by an almost identical real depreciation of the dollar against the euro.

To summarize, monetary policy can have both a short-run and a long-run impact on nominal exchange rates. The standard model predicts that money is neutral in the long run but impacts real interest rates, real output, and real exchange rates in the short run. In contrast, real variables can have a long-run impact on real exchange rates. When we get to the currency manipulation debate, we will see that these distinctions are important as we try to sort out the differing perspectives on the effect of changes in exchange rates.

Never Reason from an Exchange Rate Change

We've already seen that many pundits make the mistake of reasoning from a price change or from an interest-rate change. Unfortunately, the same sort of mistake occurs with changes in exchange rates. People often talk confidently about the effect of changes in the exchange rate on the trade balance and fall victim to reasoning from a price change.

I cannot emphasize enough that any discussion of the impact of exchange rates is *utterly meaningless* without evidence about why the exchange rate is changing. For instance, an exchange rate might appreciate because of strong growth in export industries, perhaps triggered by a major oil discovery. In that case a stronger exchange rate will be associated with increased exports. Alternatively, an exchange rate might appreciate owing to a tighter money policy, as happened with the Swiss franc in January 2015. In that case the stronger exchange rate is likely to be associated with decreased exports.

Just as it is meaningless to talk about the effect of inflation or higher interest rates without any context, exchange rates by themselves have no effect on the economy; they are affected by deeper forces, which have an impact on exchange rates but also on lots of other variables.

It's useful to divide exchange rate changes into two categories. Nominal exchange rates might change for either of the following two reasons: a difference in inflation rates between two countries (PPP in action) or a change in the real exchange rate. We've already discussed how monetary policy can lead to persistent changes in nominal exchange rates, reflecting the quantity theory of money and PPP. Here we'll focus more on real exchange rates, which are what most people are (overly) concerned about.

There is enormous misunderstanding about the causes and consequences of changes in exchange rates. As far back as the 1700s, David Hume wrote about the "jealousy of trade"—that is, the fear that foreign exports would steal business away from domestic firms. Today, many economists worry about "currency manipulation" taking place in countries such as China, which they see as contributing to current account deficits. In the remainder of this chapter I'll try to peel back some of these issues and expose a few of the many fallacies that surround exchange rates.

It's Not a Zero-Sum Game

One often hears complaints that a currency is being "manipulated" (or held down) to give a country an "advantage" in international trade. I use scare quotes because it's not clear whether countries are advantaged or disadvantaged by a weaker currency. During the global Great Inflation of the 1960s–1980s, lots of developing countries depreciated their currencies in order to boost exports. In most cases, countries that tried to depreciate their way to prosperity merely ended up with more inflation (because of PPP), and the real exchange rate went back to its long-run equilibrium. Once it became clear to countries that they couldn't depreciate their way to prosperity, central banks around the world mostly gave up on this strategy and adopted inflation targeting.

People used to cite the fixed exchange rate between the Chinese yuan and the US dollar as evidence of currency manipulation. This is a rather odd claim, because during the 1980s and 1990s the Europeans set up a fixed-exchange-rate regime with the express purpose of preventing currency manipulation. Members of the European Union worried that countries might depreciate their currencies to gain an advantage in international trade, and they tried to avoid that problem by setting up the

European Monetary System, which fixed exchange rates. So which is it? Are fixed or flexible exchange rates "manipulated"?

As with many economic misconceptions, there is a grain of truth in the argument that central banks can manipulate exchange rates. As we saw with Dornbusch overshooting, an expansionary monetary policy can cause exchange rates to depreciate sharply in the short run. And because wages and prices are sticky in the short run, even the real exchange rate will depreciate when there is an unexpected move to a more expansionary monetary policy.

But even in the short run, it's not clear that currency depreciation has the effect that many assume. Countries often depreciate their currencies during a recession as a way of creating jobs. This does make exports more competitive, which might tend to boost a country's current account balance (say, from deficit to surplus). But critics forget that this sort of monetary policy does not just produce a *substitution effect* toward domestic goods—there is also an *income effect*, as real GDP rises in response to the monetary stimulus.[4]

After the dollar was sharply depreciated in April 1933, the trade surplus actually became smaller, not larger. That's because while the cheaper currency made US exports more competitive, the easier money also boosted output sharply, sucking in imports. Whenever real GDP rises strongly, imports tend to rise as consumers buy more goods and firms buy more inputs into the production process. Thus, the dollar depreciation did not turn out to be a "beggar thy neighbor" policy—it did not contribute to trade deficits in foreign countries. Something similar happened after the August 1971 devaluation of the dollar: once again the US economy boomed and the US current account did not "improve." Instead, the US imported even more goods.

The positive correlation between international stock returns also casts doubt on the argument that currency manipulation is a problem. If currency manipulation actually hurt trading partners, then you might have expected European stock indices to have fallen after the March 18, 2009, quantitative easing announcement in the US, which raised the price of euros by $.06. In fact, European stock indices actually opened higher on the following day. Indeed, one often observes worldwide stock rallies in response to major monetary policy stimulus in one country—even at the zero bound. Here is a typical headline, from December 2, 2015: "Global Stocks Slammed by ECB; Euro Jumps Most since 2009."[5]

The European Central Bank could be said to have "manipulated" the euro higher and the dollar, yen, and pound lower. If manipulation had been

at work here, the ECB's action would have been contractionary for Europe and expansionary for the rest of the world. Yet stocks declined even in non-European markets. Why? The only plausible interpretation of these global stock-market reactions is that the income effect (less exports from the US, Japan, and the UK owing to weaker global growth) dominates the substitution effect (more net exports owing to depreciation in the dollar, yen, and British pound). International economics is not a zero-sum game. Contractionary actions that make the world poorer tend to hurt all countries, even if they seem to improve a given country's "competitiveness."

To summarize, monetary stimulus has no long-term effect on the real exchange rate. It merely leads to higher inflation, which offsets any advantage exporters derive from a weaker exchange rate. In the short run, monetary stimulus might depreciate the real exchange rate (owing to sticky prices), but the substitution effect of people switching toward domestic goods is roughly offset by the income effect as growth draws in more imports. Monetary policy has little impact on the current account balance.

And even if monetary stimulus did have the short-run effect of boosting a country's current account balance, the effect would be temporary. So this sort of "manipulation" cannot explain the sort of persistent current account surpluses that we tend to see in East Asia and northern Europe. That doesn't mean that currency manipulation doesn't occur, just that if we are going to explain the sort of persistent imbalances that pundits worry about, we need to look beyond monetary policy.

All Currencies Are Manipulated

People often overlook the fact that all currencies are "manipulated." Indeed, it is the job of central banks to manipulate their domestic currency in such a way as to achieve their policy objectives. Let's take the example of Japan. Assume the Japanese adopt a 2% inflation target and need a more expansionary monetary policy to achieve this policy goal. One option is to depreciate the yen by an amount large enough to push inflation up to 2%. Another option is to do enough quantitative easing to achieve 2% inflation. These are essentially identical policies. Suppose the yen needed to fall to 140 yen per US dollar to achieve Japan's 2% inflation target. Then if Japanese policy makers instead chose to use quantitative easing, they'd have to buy enough assets to depreciate the yen to 140 per dollar in order to achieve their inflation target.

During the first few years after 2000, Japan received a barrage of criticism from the US. The US Department of the Treasury, as well as many pundits and politicians, attacked Japan for allegedly adopting a weak yen policy. In contrast, academic economists like Ben Bernanke accused Japan of adopting an *excessively strong* yen policy, pointing to the falling price level. Interestingly, very few people seemed to notice the conflict between these two arguments, probably because they reflected radically different policy goals, models, and even language. The Treasury thought of exchange rates in terms of trade, whereas academics looked at exchange rates in terms of aggregate demand and inflation (or deflation, in Japan's case). Academics focused on the nominal exchange rate while the Treasury focused on the real exchange rate.

Japan experienced a nearly two-decade period of deflation, from 1994 to 2013. A number of prominent academics, including Lars Svensson and Bennett McCallum, suggested that Japan could use currency depreciation as a method of reflating the economy.[6] Svensson even called this a "foolproof" approach, because (unlike with interest rates) there is no zero lower bound on exchange rates.[7] So why has Japan had so much trouble exiting from deflation if currency depreciation is such a foolproof method? To answer this question, we'll need to take a closer look at what actually happened in Japan.

The long Japanese deflation is one of the most widely misunderstood problems in macroeconomics. Media accounts often suggest that the Bank of Japan tried very hard to prevent this deflation but failed because of the zero-interest-rate bound problem. But even as far back as 2004, Bernanke and his coauthors Vincent Reinhart and Brian Sack saw that the story was much more complex:

> An important recent example of a conditional commitment is the zero interest-rate policy of the Bank of Japan. The BOJ reduced the call rate to a level "as low as possible"—to zero, for all practical purposes—in February 1999. In April 1999 then-Governor of the BOJ Masaru Hayami announced that the BOJ would keep the policy rate at zero "until deflationary concerns are dispelled," clearly indicating that the policy commitment was conditional. However, in a case of what might be called commitment *interruptus*, the BOJ then raised the call rate to 25 basis points in August 2000. In February 2001, following a subsequent weakening in economic conditions, the rate increase was partly retracted.[8]

Bernanke and his coauthors did not know it at the time, but Japan would repeat this "mistake" again in 2006, raising interest rates just as inflation rose above zero. One policy tightening might be viewed as a mistake; two such episodes surely reflect a conscious policy choice. Japan had an official policy of stable prices, which policy makers seemed to interpret as zero inflation. The BOJ tightened policy each time inflation rose to zero. That's consistent with a central bank that views zero inflation as a ceiling, not a floor.

When Japan returned to deflation in the first few years after 2000, the BOJ switched to QE as a method of propping up the price level. This involved the purchase of both Japanese government bonds and US dollar assets such as Treasury bonds. By 2004 the purchase of dollar assets had become highly controversial. In 2010, John Taylor wrote a blog post recalling his actions as a Treasury official in 2003–2004.[9] Taylor made several points. First, he noted that while the Treasury usually objected to Japan depreciating the yen, he was willing to cut Japan some slack in 2003. Second, he explained that even he had objected when the Japanese policy of buying foreign assets with newly created yen became particularly aggressive in early 2004:

> But the dollar did not weaken and on March 5 the Japanese had purchased $11.2 billion dollars that day which made the dollar appreciate rather than depreciate as one would expect. They were not simply smoothing the market, they were working against it. Zembei [Mizoguchi, the vice minister of Japan's Ministry of Finance,] had told me that they were going to do more intervention before they did less, but this was simply excessive. He was working against market fundamentals. I called him over the weekend to complain that this type of intervention was completely unwarranted and I was as forceful as a friend and ally could be. Zembei acknowledged that they were still intervening heavily now, but the March 5 dollar buy was part of the exit plan. I argued that the exit period had gone on long enough.[10]

Notice that Taylor cites improving data out of Japan, which led him to suggest that there is no further need for this sort of extraordinary intervention. Even so, why would the US object? Isn't it the BOJ's job to determine when the Japanese economy is overheating? Especially given that, in retrospect, we now know that Taylor was wrong: Japan had still not achieved a durable exit from its deflationary trap.

At the time of Taylor's complaints to the Japanese, the US was still recovering from the 2001 recession. The Fed had cut rates to 1%, but the rate of job creation remained more sluggish than during previous recoveries. The Treasury's view was that currency depreciation in Japan would worsen the current account deficit in the US and hence was a threat to the US economy. A week later Japan ended its currency intervention program. Japanese officials may have feared retaliation from the US, perhaps recalling the various trade barriers enacted during the 1980s, when the Japanese "threat" first became a major political issue.

To summarize, there seem to be two factors contributing to the long period of mild deflation in Japan. First, BOJ officials were excessively cautious in their various monetary stimulus programs, often ending the stimulus before Japan had achieved a durable exit from deflation. In addition, Japan seemed reluctant to push currency depreciation too far, perhaps out of fear of retaliation from the US. Back in 2001, Paul Krugman offered a very similar diagnosis of the situation, citing excessive caution at the BOJ and pressure from the US Treasury:

> The real tragedy right now is that however innovative and open-minded [Prime Minister] Koizumi may be, he will fail unless other important players—mainly the Bank of Japan, but also the U.S. Treasury Department—are prepared to learn from Andrew Mellon's mistake. And all the evidence is that they are not. The head of the Bank of Japan insists that the country's continuing slump is the result of inadequate reform—that is, insufficient purging of the rottenness. And although the details are in dispute, the U.S. Treasury secretary, Paul O'Neill, appears to have warned Japan not to let the yen weaken too much.
>
> Poor Japan. It is the victim of those who refuse to learn from the past, and thereby condemn others to repeat it.[11]

In my view, complaints about currency manipulation by central banks are mostly without merit. First, in the long run monetary stimulus merely leads to inflation, with no long-lasting impact on real exchange rates. Second, the short-run effect of currency manipulation involves both a substitution effect and an income effect, which largely offset each other. Finally, accusations of currency manipulation are often made against countries with monetary policies that are already too contractionary to achieve their policy targets. In other words, countries accused of having "undervalued" currencies often in fact have overvalued currencies.

Nonmonetary Currency Manipulation

Some quite distinguished economists are aware of everything I've said thus far but still worry about currency manipulation.[12] These more sophisticated concerns tend to revolve around nonmonetary factors influencing real exchange rates. I'll explain these arguments and then indicate why I view them as unpersuasive.

At the most comprehensive level, international trade is always balanced. Foreign countries don't simply give cars to the US; they want something in return. In practice, when people talk about the "current account deficit" (about 2.4% of GDP in 2019) they are referring to trade in goods and services. The flip side of the US current account deficit is the capital account surplus, which is also about 2.4% of GDP. Think of the US importing Hondas and BMWs and then exporting stocks and bonds to Germany and Japan in payment for those cars. The current account for the US is in deficit, but overall trade in goods, services, and assets is balanced, because US exports of financial assets offset US imports of goods. One must always give something up in exchange for getting something.

Many people assume that the current account deficit drives the capital flows, but more likely the reverse is true. Because America as a whole invests more than it saves, it draws in foreign saving. This means that if the US imports $500 billion more than it exports, there is a net inflow of $500 billion in foreign saving to pay for those imports. In that case, US domestic investment is $500 billion more than US domestic saving:

$$\text{domestic investment} = \text{domestic saving} + \text{CA deficit}$$
$$(\text{i.e., foreign saving}).$$

As a general rule, high-saving countries tend to run current account surpluses and low-saving countries tend to run current account deficits. More importantly, the causation probably goes from the capital account to the current account. Thus, we don't draw in foreign saving because we have a current account deficit; rather, we have a current account deficit because we draw in foreign saving. When foreigners are particularly interested in putting their savings into the US—such as during the tech boom of the late 1990s and the housing boom of 2004–2006), the inflow of foreign money pushes up the dollar, and the US current account deficit gets larger.

Some people are deceived by the famous national-income accounting equation:[13]

$$\text{GDP} = \text{consumption} + \text{investment} + \text{gov't output} + (\text{exports} - \text{imports}).$$

They see how a current account deficit appears as a negative in the equation and wrongly assume a causal relationship. But if imports are $500 billion larger than exports, then it's equally true that investment is $500 billion larger than domestic saving. Current account deficits have no direct impact on GDP. Imported goods show up with a negative sign in (exports – imports), but as an equal positive in consumption plus investment. Indeed, if imports did reduce GDP, then the Fed would simply expand the money supply enough to offset any negative effect.

So what, then, is the sophisticated argument regarding currency manipulation? Why did some prominent economists complain about an undervalued Chinese yuan or about Germany's large current account surplus? There are actually two sophisticated arguments, one general and one specific to the zero bound. First, the general: Some worry that current account surpluses boost global savings rates, reducing aggregate demand. When not at the zero bound, the contractionary effect of increased saving can easily be offset by expansionary moves at other central banks. But John Maynard Keynes (as well as modern Keynesians such as Paul Krugman) worried that central banks would be unable to offset the effect of more saving when the economy is at the zero bound. Keynesians see a sort of "paradox of thrift," in which global attempts to save more are self-defeating. Rather than boosting global saving, this depresses global aggregate demand and output, exporting austerity around the world.

Second, the specific argument: others worry that current account deficits could create problems for specific sectors of the economy, even when overall aggregate demand is not an issue in the US. A study by the economists David Autor, David Dorn, and Gordon Hanson suggested that rising Chinese exports during 1990–2007 resulted in significant job losses in US regions with lots of manufacturing, especially in areas that compete with Chinese products.[14] Notice that this study covered a period when the overall US economy was doing fine and the Fed was ensuring an adequate level of overall employment despite a large increase in the current account deficit for the US. Nonmanufacturing sectors such as services and construction were absorbing workers who lost jobs in manufacturing.

These more sophisticated arguments against currency manipulation focus on the role of savings rates and current account surpluses. The overall argument isn't really about exchange rates at all, though: it's actually an argument for the existence of "saving manipulation." For instance, Germany has the world's largest current account surplus, but it doesn't even have a currency of its own to manipulate. Even so, Germany's high savings rate can depress its real exchange rate.

If Germany saves more than it invests, it needs to run a current account surplus. But what is the mechanism enabling that to actually occur? If Germany shares a currency with eighteen other eurozone members, what causes the exchange rate to move to a level that creates Germany's large surplus?

Here we need to recall the difference between the nominal and the real exchange rate. Although Germany doesn't have control over the nominal exchange rate (except indirectly through its influence at the ECB), it can reduce its real exchange rate by reducing its domestic price level. The high German savings rate put downward pressure on the German price level (and wages) during the first and second decades of the twenty-first century, depreciating the real exchange rate for the German portion of the eurozone. This process continued until German industry became so competitive that the German current account surplus became large enough to accommodate the German public's desire to move large amounts of private saving into foreign economies.

To most people, high savings rates seem completely unrelated to the issue of currency manipulation, even though saving manipulation is actually the only coherent way of thinking about the concept. Instead, currency manipulation is seen as a government activity, a nefarious attempt to artificially boost exports by depressing the exchange rates. So how are these two concepts related?

Let's imagine that a country understands that any gains from monetary stimulus will be ephemeral. Its policy makers have seen Latin American countries repeatedly depreciate their currencies, with nothing to show for it in the long run except inflation. Suppose this country wants to create a permanent current account surplus. How could it do so? The answer is simple: discourage domestic investment and encourage domestic saving. And because very few countries wish to discourage domestic investment (which is the engine of growth), they opt to boost domestic saving.

But what sort of government policies can boost domestic savings rates? It turns out that there are many such policies—far more than many people realize. The most straightforward approach would be to boost government saving, which means running budget surpluses. In fact, very few countries have the discipline to do this persistently, but those that succeed (think of Norway and Singapore, with their huge sovereign-wealth funds) do in fact tend to run extremely large current account surpluses. Or the government might try to boost private saving by switching from an income tax to a consumption tax, or by taxing earnings from investments at a relatively low rate.

As a practical matter, there is one type of government saving that gets most of the criticism: the purchase of foreign assets. Thus, during the decade after 2000, the Chinese government gradually accumulated more than $3 trillion in international reserves, including large quantities of US Treasury bonds. Many other East Asian countries did something similar. This was not necessarily motivated by any desire on these countries' part to artificially depreciate their currencies; rather, it was at least in part a precautionary move so that the government would have adequate reserves should there be another period of turmoil similar to the East Asian crisis of 1997–1998.

Nonetheless, politicians in the West often accused countries that accumulated massive reserve hoards (e.g., China) of currency manipulation. Interestingly, these accusations were less frequently made against countries like Norway, Singapore, and Switzerland, even though these countries had much larger current account surpluses as a share of GDP, and even though these surpluses were also likely linked to pro-saving government policies. A country is especially likely to get blamed if its pro-saving policies consist of accumulating foreign exchange reserves. If currency manipulation as it is usually defined (buying foreign exchange) were banned by international treaty, then countries could achieve roughly the same effects by running budget surpluses.

Everything You Know about Currency Manipulation Is Wrong

Let me conclude with a few comments about poorly understood aspects of currency manipulation:

- There's not much evidence linking current account imbalances with unemployment. Countries with deficits (especially in the English-speaking world) typically have lower unemployment than the eurozone, which runs large surpluses.
- During Japan's long period of deflation, it was frequently accused of having an "undervalued currency" because it ran large trade surpluses, even though in nominal terms its currency was clearly overvalued. It is possible to have a nominal exchange rate that is overvalued at the same time that the real exchange rate is undervalued.
- The US current account deficit is smaller than it was thirty-three years ago as a share of GDP. Thus, the US trade imbalance has not contributed to deindustrialization since 1987.
- The US current account deficit tends to be at its largest when unemployment rates are lowest.

- Criticism of currency manipulation makes sense only if such criticism is understood as criticism of saving manipulation. In my view, however, even the more sophisticated critics of countries running current account surpluses gloss over the difficulty of defining what sorts of saving manipulation are OK and what sorts are unacceptable, or fail to explain why some countries are targeted and not others.

- People often complain about China's fixed-exchange-rate policy. Yet if currency manipulation means anything, it surely has nothing to do with the question of whether a country has a system of fixed or floating exchange rates. China could have just as easily run large current account surpluses with a flexible exchange rate policy. Chinese current account surpluses were caused not by manipulating the dollar-yuan exchange rate but by high Chinese savings rates.

- Germany was just as able to manipulate its real exchange rate after it had adopted the euro as when it still had its own currency (the deutschemark).

- China's decision to stop revaluing its currency in late 2008 helped support Chinese nominal GDP growth, and the resulting rapid economic growth during 2009 helped prevent the global economy from falling into depression (i.e., the income effect seemed to outweigh the substitution effect). Nonetheless, China was criticized for this move.

- Current account imbalances between countries are not "problems," any more than a current account imbalance between Texas and California is a problem. However, the factors that cause current account imbalances in places such as Greece may well constitute a problem—especially if they reflect excessive borrowing.

- Countries running persistent current account deficits are widely viewed as "debtor nations." For countries such as Greece, this label is certainly accurate. But current account deficits do not actually measure the net increase in indebtedness. Consider the case of Australia, which has run persistent current account deficits for many decades. If Australia buys cars from Asia and pays for them with bonds, then its net indebtedness has increased. But suppose instead that Australia has swapped condos on the Gold Coast for new cars from Asia. That transaction will show up as a "trade imbalance," but only because the condos are arbitrarily viewed as a capital export, not a goods export. Yet there is no accumulation of debt for Australia, and the construction of the condos creates jobs for Australians. Even more bizarrely, the US export of a mobile home to Asia shows up as a goods export, whereas the sale of a brand-new Los Angeles home to a Chinese buyer is not viewed as a goods export.

Obviously there is much more that could be said about exchange rates. My hope is that this chapter has given you a sense of just how unreliable most of the media analysis is on this topic. For instance, there is too little awareness about the distinction between nominal and real exchange rates. Monetary policy involves nominal exchange rate manipulation in the short and long run but real exchange rate manipulation only in the short run. Yet many of the trade imbalances that people complain about are long-run issues, not cyclical issues.

People also overlook that it is real exchange rate manipulation that matters for trade, that real exchange rate manipulation is actually saving manipulation, and that some types of saving manipulation are highly controversial while other types that have almost identical effects escape criticism.

Even the more "sophisticated" arguments against currency manipulation (discussed above) are highly questionable. Later we'll see that the zero bound does not prevent central banks from offsetting the impact of trade on aggregate demand, and the sort of sectoral impacts that Autor, Dorn, and Hanson identified are exactly what we want from international trade—creative destruction.[15] The world would be a better place if nations focused on putting their own houses in order rather than blaming other countries for problems caused by their own flawed monetary and saving policies.

PART IV

How to Think about Macroeconomics

CHAPTER THIRTEEN

The Path to Market Monetarism

In late 2008 and early 2009, I was one of a very few economists arguing that a tight money policy by the Fed had caused (or at least greatly worsened) the Great Recession.[1] It will be useful to retrace my steps to show you how I reached this heterodox view.

Looking back on things, I suspect that I benefited from having done research in three specific areas: the use of futures market prices as a guide to monetary policy, the role of monetary policy in the Great Depression, and problem of the liquidity trap in Japan. I'm not the only person to have researched those topics, but when the recession began, I was probably the only person to have devoted substantial time to researching *all three* areas. In this chapter I'll show how this unique set of research interests allowed me to see what many others missed—that an excessively tight monetary policy created the Great Recession.

The New Monetary Economics of the 1980s

I studied economics at the University of Wisconsin between 1973 and 1977. Then between 1977 and 1980 I was in the PhD economics program at the University of Chicago. That decade saw a big battle between two radically different approaches to monetary economics. Keynesians at Wisconsin used an interest-rate-oriented approach to monetary policy, according to which the *rental cost of money* (i.e., the nominal interest rate) was the key indicator of the stance of monetary policy. Their principal rivals were the Chicago monetarists, who used the *quantity of money* as their indicator of the stance of monetary policy. At the time I was much more sympathetic to the monetarists, who were steadily gaining ground because the problem of stagflation seemed to discredit the traditional Keynesian model.

The monetarist victory was quite short-lived, however, because the quantity of money also came to be seen as an increasingly unreliable indicator of monetary policy when velocity became unstable. Another group (including, but not limited to, supply-siders) began promoting a third view of monetary policy, according to which the *price of money* became the key indicator of the stance of monetary policy. During the 1980s, I gradually moved away from traditional monetarism and toward this price-of-money approach.

As with the rental-cost and quantity-of-money approaches, there are many different ways of measuring the price of money. The Nobel laureate Robert Mundell focused on the price of money in terms of foreign exchange. Another group of supply-siders led by economist Arthur Laffer focused on the price of money in terms of gold, or in some cases in terms of a "basket" of commodities.

Unfortunately, a stable price of money in terms of either foreign exchange or commodities does not necessarily produce a stable macroeconomic environment. The real exchange rate may fluctuate for a variety of reasons. If the nominal exchange rate is not allowed to adjust, then all the adjustment must occur through changes in the price level, which can destabilize the economy. Later we'll see that this is one of the two big flaws with the euro.

The same problem occurs with a commodity standard. The real value of gold or even of a basket of commodities can change over time. Any currency pegged to gold would see its purchasing power fluctuate with changes in the real value of gold. Imagine if Switzerland had adopted the gold standard in 2001, when the price of gold in US dollars was below $300. By 2011, soaring demand for gold in emerging economies such as China and India had pushed the price of gold to US$1,800 per ounce. If Switzerland had been on the gold standard, then the value of the Swiss franc would have soared along with the price of gold, causing the franc to appreciate more than sixfold against currencies such as the dollar.

For goods for which the US dollar price remained stable, the price in gold-backed Swiss francs would have fallen to roughly one-sixth of its original level between 2001 and 2011. If the Swiss franc had been exchanged at 2.40 to the dollar in 2001, it would have been exchanged at only about 0.40 to the dollar in 2011. Imagine a ton of steel that cost US$100 in 2001 (i.e., 240 Swiss francs) and $120 in 2011. In terms of Swiss francs, the price of steel would have fallen by roughly 80%, from 240 to 48, as the Swiss franc appreciated sixfold. This would have plunged Switzerland into a deep deflationary depression.

The central problem in monetary policy is that the variables that a central bank can easily control on a day-to-day basis, such as the fed-funds rate, the monetary base, and the price of gold, do not reliably correlate with the things we really care about, such as the CPI, unemployment, and nominal GDP. As I thought about this issue, it occurred to me that we need to stabilize the price of the entity that most closely correlates with our goal variable.

Around the same time that I came to this conclusion, a consumer price index futures contract began trading in New York. I was aware of the efficient-market hypothesis, which had been developed at the University of Chicago. Because financial markets aggregate lots of individual forecasts into an efficient market forecast, it seemed plausible that the price of a CPI futures contract would be better correlated with next year's CPI then would any of the traditional levers of monetary policy, such as interest rates, the money supply, or the price of gold.

I wrote this idea up as a paper that incorporated ideas such as decentralized knowledge of prices and the wisdom of crowds and presented it at the American Economic Association meetings in 1987. By the time the paper was published in 1989, I favored nominal GDP targeting rather than inflation targeting, so the paper advocated a policy regime in which the central bank would stabilize the price of nominal GDP futures contracts.[2]

The basic idea is that the central bank sets its policy instrument (interest rates or the monetary base) at a position where the consensus view of futures market traders is that nominal GDP will grow at precisely the rate desired by policy makers. If traders expect excessively fast nominal GDP growth, then they will buy NGDP futures contracts from the central bank. This represents an open-market sale and will tend to automatically reduce the money supply. The process will continue until NGDP growth expectations are equal to the target rate. If traders expect excessively slow NGDP growth, then they will sell NGDP futures contracts to the central bank, and this will automatically tend to increase the money supply.

I still think this is an excellent policy option, although I currently favor a modified version (examined in chapter 21) that addresses some of the criticisms levied against this proposal. Back in the late 1980s, I thought I might have been the first to propose this sort of policy, and perhaps I was the first to make that specific proposal. But I discovered that there was already a school of thought referred to as "new monetary economics," and that the basic idea of using market forces to direct monetary policy was already being developed by Earl Thompson, Robert Hall, David Glasner, and Robert Hetzel.[3]

Why Wouldn't You Target the Forecast?

In the early 2000s, Lars Svensson (who was then a colleague of Ben Bernanke and Paul Krugman at Princeton) advocated a policy of "targeting the forecast."[4] This meant that the central bank should always set its policy at a position that led its economic forecasting team to expect on-target inflation (or NGDP growth). Thus, if the bank's target is 2% inflation, it makes no sense for it to set interest rates at a position where its own forecasting team is predicting 1% inflation or 3% inflation. If you want 2% inflation and you are not predicting 2% inflation to occur within a year or two, then you need to adjust the policy instrument.

Consider a nautical analogy. You are on a cruise ship headed from Paris to New York City. One day you meet the captain on deck and ask how soon the ship will arrive in New York. The captain informs you that he expects to reach Boston in forty-eight hours. You exclaim, "I thought this was a cruise to New York!" The captain replies, "Yes, but due to wind and current we've been pushed off course and we now expect to dock in Boston rather than New York." I don't know about you, but I would ask the captain why the steering wheel wasn't adjusted to offset the effect of wind and currents, so that the city the captain expected to reach was the same as the city he hoped to reach. That is, the *predicted* destination should be the same as the *target* destination.

This may seem like common sense, and in the world of ocean liners I am fairly confident that it is how things are done. But this is *not* how central banks operate. There are times, such as late 2008, when monetary levers are set at a position where central banks expect to fail to hit their target. This is especially true at the zero-rate bound, but the problem was already occurring in the US by October 2008, months before the US reached near-zero interest rates (in mid-December).

Lars Svensson wanted central banks to target their own internal forecast of inflation or NGDP. In contrast, my NGDP futures targeting proposal envisioned having central banks target the *market* forecast. In retrospect, I believe that my work on targeting the market forecast allowed me to see what was going wrong with monetary policy before most of the rest of the profession. Consider the Federal Open Market Committee meeting that occurred on September 16, 2008, just two days after Lehman Brothers failed. The Fed statement indicated that its target interest rate would remain at 2%. It justified this lack of action by pointing to roughly equal risks of recession and high inflation. There certainly was a risk of recession—indeed, the US had already been in recession for nine months by this time.

But the bigger problem was the Fed's fear of inflation. Not only was there not a risk of high inflation, by September 2008 the risk was that there would be excessively *low* inflation going forward. On the day of the meeting, the TIPS spread on five-year Treasury bonds was only 1.23%, implying an expected inflation rate well below the Fed's 2% target. The markets were suggesting that a more expansionary monetary policy would allow inflation to get closer to the 2% target and also make the recession milder—a win-win situation.

It is true that TIPS spreads can be distorted during periods of market turmoil, when there is a flight to safety. In such a case the less liquid indexed Treasury bonds might earn a higher expected return than the more easily traded conventional Treasury bonds. This may reduce the TIPS spread to a level below the public's expected inflation rate. However, this would hardly count as a reason not to ease monetary policy, because this sort of market turmoil would clearly indicate an asymmetric risk, in which the danger of deep recession is much higher than the danger of high inflation. If every asset class other than Treasury bonds is plunging in value in a rush for safety, including even relatively safe Treasury inflation-indexed bonds, then it is a pretty safe bet that inflation is not the number-one risk.

Because I was one of the few economists who looked at monetary policy from the perspective of targeting the market forecast, I saw that money was much too tight in September 2008. For the first time in my career I felt completely out of step with the rest of the profession. At the time, economic blogging was catching on, and I decided that blogging would be the most effective method of injecting my ideas into the policy debate.

The Great Depression

Most of my research career has been devoted to studying the Great Depression. I've had a long fascination with monetary history, perhaps sparked by my childhood interest in coin collecting. As a teenager, I was particularly fascinated by the account of the Great Depression in Milton Friedman and Anna Schwartz's *A Monetary History of the United States*. What interested me the most was the beauty and elegance of monetary theory—especially how it allowed one to see the world in a radically different way.

By the time I began my own Depression research in the 1980s, Friedman and Schwartz's *Monetary History* had already been around for more than two decades. Some researchers criticized its authors for overlooking the constraints imposed on monetary policy makers by the international gold standard. Barry Eichengreen used the metaphor "golden fetters" in the title of his influential 1992 book on the Great Depression, which focused on how the gold standard constrained the central banks of the interwar period.[5]

I published a number of academic papers on the role of the international gold standard in the Great Depression, as well as on the effect of various New Deal interventions into the labor market. Not all of this research is directly relevant to the Great Recession of 2007–2009, because US monetary policy is no longer constrained by a link to gold. But several of my findings did prove valuable when the economy plunged into a deep slump in 2008. Here are some examples:

- What matter most are shocks that affect the *expected future path of policy*.
- There is a strong correlation between monetary policy, asset prices, and industrial production.
- The price approach to monetary policy is more useful than either the (Keynesian) interest-rate approach or the (monetarist) quantity-of-money approach.
- The Great Depression was almost universally misdiagnosed during the 1930s, 1940s, and 1950s in a way that is almost identical to how I believe the Great Recession has been (and currently is) misdiagnosed.

This research led me to read a great deal of material from older news publications such as the *Commercial and Financial Chronicle*, the *Wall Street Journal*, and *The Economist*. I spent one year reading (on microfilm) key political and financial news stories in almost the entire set of *New York Times* issues from 1929 through 1938. I was especially fascinated by data showing the way that asset prices did or did not respond to the policy shocks that others thought were important, as well as to the policy shocks that seemed important to me.[6]

I quickly discovered that asset prices did not respond to many of the Fed policy decisions in the way that one might expect on the basis of Friedman and Schwartz's account of what went wrong during the Great Depression. That doesn't mean that Friedman and Schwartz were entirely wrong; I do accept their basic argument that excessively tight Fed policy played a major role in causing the Great Contraction of 1929–1933 and the double dip in 1937–1938. Rather, I characterize that tight money policy differently, focusing more on gold standard decisions and less on day-to-day decisions involving monetary policy tools such as open-market operations, discount rate changes, and reserve requirements.

Asset-market participants in the Depression era seemed particularly interested in policy decisions that were likely to change the *future path of policy*. A good example occurred in April 1933, when President Roosevelt began depreciating the dollar against gold. This action had little immediate impact on traditional policy indicators such as interest rates or the money supply. However, the increase in the price of gold had a dramatic effect on the expected future path of monetary policy. Raising the price of gold from $20.67 per ounce to $35 per ounce had the effect of raising the expected future money supply and price level. Indeed, this effect was so strong that the US experienced significant inflation during 1933–1934. Despite 25% unemployment, the wholesale price index soared by roughly 20% in just twelve months.

Sometime around 2005, I began corresponding with Gauti Eggertsson, who was working with Michael Woodford at Princeton. Eggertsson saw that my empirical research supported some of the (New Keynesian) theoretical work he was doing with Woodford, which showed that the current setting of monetary policy is far less important than the expected future path of policy. This research would prove very influential during the Great Recession, especially once the US hit the zero-interest bound and was perceived as no longer having the ability to use conventional policy.[7]

My work on the Depression allowed me to better understand why President Hoover's quantitative easing was not very effective. Owing to gold-standard constraints, the QE program of 1932 was not expected to persist for an extended period of time. As we saw in chapter 6, temporary monetary injections simply aren't very effective. In contrast, FDR's policy of dollar devaluation was highly effective at boosting prices, because the increased price of gold provided a credible signal that monetary policy would be more expansionary in the coming years and decades. And in the case of the dollar depreciation, there wasn't even an immediate boost in the money supply—no QE. It was all done through the expectations channel—what some skeptics deride as the "expectations fairy."

Friedman and Schwartz's research led them to conclude that there are long and variable lags between changes in monetary policy and changes in the economy. There are certainly some lags, especially for sticky prices. But on the whole I believe they were mistaken on this point, and I think

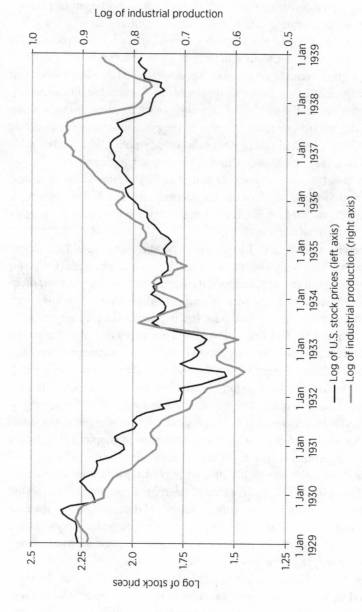

FIGURE 13.1 US stock prices and industrial production, 1929–1938

I know why. Because Friedman and Schwartz had relied on the money supply as an indicator of the stance of monetary policy, they often ended up observing monetary "shocks" that did not seem to have an immediate impact on the economy. For instance, they claimed that the Fed tightened monetary policy beginning in 1928, but the economy kept booming right into the summer of 1929.

In my view, Friedman and Schwartz's reliance on the money supply led them to misidentify a number of important monetary shocks. (Keynesians made a similar error, by relying too much on interest rates as an indicator of the stance of monetary policy.) As a result, today the overwhelming consensus among economists is that monetary policy shocks affect the economy with long and variable lags.

In my Depression research, I noticed that industrial production, which is measured monthly, was highly correlated with asset prices (fig. 13.1). Recall my discovery that monetary policy was also highly correlated with asset prices during the 1930s. This suggests that monetary policy was highly correlated with both asset prices and industrial production—something that should not have been true if there are long and variable lags between monetary policy and output, which is the standard view. After all, monetary policy clearly does not affect asset prices with a lag.

I also noticed that the more distinct and easily identifiable the monetary shock was, the more obvious it was that there were no long and variable lags. The sharp monetary tightening of 1920–1921 and 1929–1930 depressed the economy almost immediately, whereas the extremely powerful stimulus provided by dollar devaluation almost immediately led to the fastest economic growth in all of American history. Industrial production surged by 57% between March and July 1933, yet there was little change in the money supply or interest rates. Instead, there was a radical change in expectations about the future stance of monetary policy. Indeed, it might make more sense to talk about long and variable *leads*, because expectations of future monetary easing can cause prices and output to rise today.

Why the History of Economic Thought Is Important

As I learned more about the Great Depression, I also became more interested in the history of economic thought. I discovered that economists such as Irving Fisher, Gustav Cassel, and especially Ralph Hawtrey had anticipated many of the ideas in my book on the Great Depression. As a result, I now have a radically different view of how to teach macroeconomics than most of my colleagues do. I believe that PhD programs in macroeconomics should be one-third economic history, one-third history of economic thought, and one-third modern macroeconomic theory. During the Great Recession we saw well-known economists "discovering" perspectives that had been widely understood during the period between the two world wars but since forgotten.

Because I knew about 1930s proposals for negative interest on money, I was one of the first to publish such a proposal.[8] Because I knew that President Hoover's QE program had failed because of gold-standard constraints (not because there was a liquidity trap), I understood that the same policy could be more effective under a fiat money regime. (Although even under such a regime it would not be effective if it were temporary.) Because I was aware of the Fed's mistaken decision to raise reserve requirements in 1936–1937, I was able to recognize the tragic mistake the Fed made in October 2008 when it began paying interest on bank reserves—a policy every bit as contractionary as raising reserve requirements.[9] Very few other economists criticized the Fed's decision at the time.

By reading the history of economic thought, I discovered that the price-of-money approach was quite popular during the interwar period. Economists such as Irving Fisher and George Warren recommended adjusting the price of gold each month to counteract changes in the price level. As long as there were just two plausible monetary policy indicators—the Keynesians' interest rate and the monetarists' money supply—it was possible to see the dispute as a battle that one side would eventually win. But with three possibilities on the table, it became ever more obvious that the entire concept of the stance of monetary policy was arbitrary. This freed me up to focus on the important question—which indicator is the most useful? At times it might be interest rates, at other times the money supply, and at still other times the price of gold (or foreign exchange). But there was one constant: changes in NGDP almost always provided a useful indicator. Very rapid NGDP growth meant money was too easy, and falling NGDP meant money was too tight.

During 2008–2013, reading the current news was a lot like reading the news media of the 1930s, with one key difference. As I read news from the earlier period, I was able to second-guess contemporaneous interpretations with the twenty-twenty hindsight of knowing how history had played out, as well as how improvements in economic theory have allowed us to better understand the role of expectations. To take an obvious example from outside the field of economics, it wasn't hard for me to second-guess a *New York Times* story from 1930 that reported something to this effect: experts agree that Herr Hitler will be forced to moderate his policies as he gets closer to power.

In the field of economics during the 1930s, there was a continual tendency to underplay the importance of monetary policy. At the time, very few people thought that tight money was worsening the Great Depression (although a few perceptive economists such as Cassel and Hawtrey did understand this fact).[10] Most didn't even think that money was tight at all, because interest rates had fallen to a very low level and QE programs had been adopted. Does this sound familiar? By 2003, even Bernanke famously admitted that the Fed had caused the Great Depression.[11] One of my goals for this book is to lead people to reevaluate the role of the Fed in the Great Recession, just as Friedman and Schwartz led people to reevaluate its role in the Great Depression.

If the public during the 1930s did not blame the central bank for the Depression, what did people think was causing it? The answer is simple: financial turmoil. Stock market crashes, bank failures, exchange rate crises, debt defaults. Does this sound familiar? In fact, with the possible exception of the 1929 stock-market crash, these problems were mostly caused by the Great Depression itself. And even the 1929 crash was partly in anticipation of a deep slump that was already under way.[12] But even if the crash was an entirely exogenous shock, it likely had very little impact on the economy. A stock-market crash of almost identical size occurred in October 1987, and the broader economy did not suffer from even a tiny ripple—the Reagan boom continued for several more years. *Stock-market crashes do not cause recessions.*[13]

I was also able to use my findings about the causes of the Great Depression as a way to reevaluate Keynesian economic theory. In one paper I argued that the Keynesian model was essentially a gold-standard model. At no time in Keynes's career did he ever envision a policy such as a 4% inflation target, even though setting a suitably high inflation target is an easy way to avoid liquidity traps, and this would completely eliminate the need for fiscal stimulus—*even in the Keynesian model*. This blind spot reflected the fact that Keynes never favored a monetary regime that was not at least loosely attached to gold.

Indeed, Keynes once called a pure (unconstrained) fiat money regime, the sort of regime that all countries use today, the very worst possible monetary system—even worse than a rigid gold standard (a policy he also opposed).[14] Instead, as I noted in chapter 8, Keynes favored something closer to the Bretton Woods regime: a system with a commodity anchor but with more room for adjustment during emergencies. A fixed price of gold, however, prevents central banks from targeting inflation.

The true radicals during the 1930s were people like Fisher, who was more supportive of FDR's dollar depreciation policy than Keynes was. Similarly, during the Great Recession, the small group of market monetarists was more aggressive in pushing for monetary stimulus than most (but not all) Keynesians. Indeed, many Keynesians thought the Fed was doing a pretty good job and shifted their focus to fiscal stimulus.

The Japanese Liquidity Trap

The more I studied Keynes's work, the more I concluded that his famous *General Theory of Employment, Interest and Money* was based on two key errors of interpretation. First, Keynes wrongly assumed that President Hoover's 1932 QE program failed because the US was in a liquidity trap with near-zero interest rates, whereas the actual problem was the constraints of the international gold standard. Second, Keynes wrongly assumed that the long-drawn-out recovery from the Great Depression reflected the fact that capitalist economies were subject to getting stuck in a permanent equilibrium of high unemployment owing to a lack of aggregate demand, whereas the actual problem was FDR's misguided labor market policies, which reduced aggregate supply.

But there was one problem with this analysis: if the real problem in the 1930s was the gold-standard constraint, then liquidity traps should not be a problem under a fiat money regime. And yet during the 1990s Japan got stuck at the zero bound, something I never would have expected in a non-gold-standard country. Naturally, I became interested in figuring out what was going on in Japan. I began examining the views of other researchers on Japan. The consensus view of people such as Paul Krugman, Ben Bernanke, Lars Svensson, Bennett McCallum, Allan Meltzer, and many others was that the problem in Japan was not the liquidity trap, but an excessively contractionary policy stance by the Bank of Japan. Attitudes among American economists ranged from condescension to exasperation. Needless to say, when the Fed faced the same set of issues in 2009, the attitude of the economics community changed dramatically. Bernanke later told reporters that he regretted his harsh criticism of the BOJ.[15] As head of the Federal Reserve, Bernanke found things to be much more difficult than he had imagined as an academic.

But what exactly did economists discover in the period after 2008 that led the profession to reevaluate the Japanese case? I believe that the Fed made the same mistakes as the BOJ. After all, the BOJ had used ultra-low interest rates as well as QE, and yet Japan remained mired in deflation until it finally adopted a 2% inflation target in 2013. The Fed had the option of raising its inflation target (something Bernanke recommended that the BOJ do) and decided to stand pat. We didn't learn that central banks were impotent at the zero bound; we learned that they were conservative institutions, reluctant to adopt the proposals of academics like Ben Bernanke.

Many economists have only a superficial understanding of the long Japanese deflation. During almost the entire period, Japan did not have a 2% inflation target. Its actual target was rather vague (stable prices) but was understood to be close to zero. And the actual inflation rate was very close to zero, so Japan came quite close to hitting its implicit inflation target. More importantly, the BOJ *acted as if* it were hitting its inflation target. In both 2000 and 2006 the BOJ raised rates to prevent inflation from rising above zero. Most Western economists assumed that the BOJ had tried to push Japan out of deflation and failed and that this showed how hard it is to boost inflation when stuck at zero rates. But this is not at all what happened. The BOJ tightened policy in 2000 and 2006 because it was quite happy with 0% inflation.

I would go even further and argue that Japan did a better job hitting its inflation target than almost any other country in all of world history. Japan's CPI was 96.1 in January 1993 and 95.9 in January 2013. I know of no more impressive example of price stability over a period of two decades, at least not under a fiat money regime (fig. 13.2).[16]

In chapter 6, we saw how Paul Krugman's famous 1998 paper explained why temporary currency injections have little or no effect on the price level.[17] This paper turned out to be remarkably prescient, because Japan unwound a good share of its 2001–2003 QE program in 2006. The Japanese public had willingly held all this extra base money, assuming that the BOJ would never let it create any inflation. And in 2006 their assumptions were confirmed when the BOJ sharply reduced the monetary base (and raised interest rates) just at the point when it saw evidence that inflation would soon rise above zero (fig. 13.3).

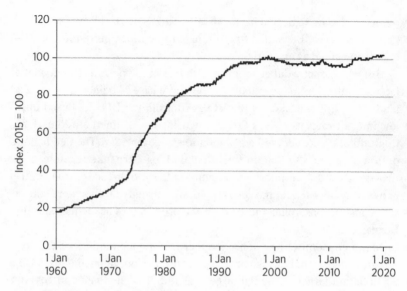

FIGURE 13.2. Japanese CPI, 1960–2019

Source: FRED via Organization for Economic Co-operation and Development, https://fred.stlouisfed.org/series
/JPNCPIALLMINMEI.

My specific research interests have allowed me to develop a pretty good
understanding of not just the role of money in the Great Depression but
also the way that contemporaneous observers misdiagnosed the crisis—a
theme I'll return to repeatedly in subsequent chapters. My research on
using asset prices as a guide to monetary policy pushed me to pay close
attention to factors such as TIPS spreads during the financial crisis. As
we saw in the introduction, the asset markets were clearly signaling that
money was too tight during late 2008. My research on the Japanese liquidity trap helped me to avoid falling prey to the mistaken belief that
monetary policy is ineffective at the zero bound.

   In the remaining chapters I'll develop a narrative of the Great Recession. Not only do I believe that the events leading up to the Great Recession have been misdiagnosed—I also intend to show that this misdiagnosis played a big role in *causing* the recession. We will start with the famous
housing bubble of 2001–2006, which probably wasn't a bubble at all.

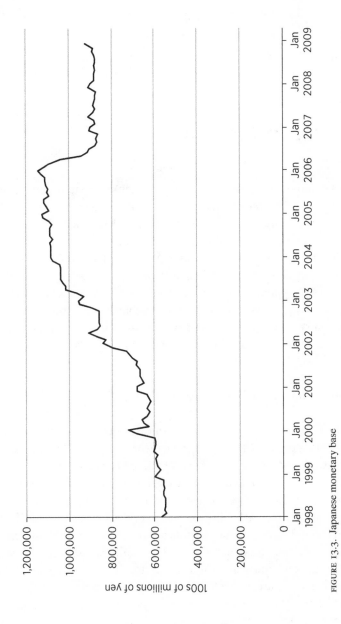

FIGURE 13.3. Japanese monetary base

Source: Bank of Japan, https://www.boj.or.jp/en/statistics/boj/other/mb/index.htm/.

CHAPTER FOURTEEN

I See Dead Patterns

Market monetarists like myself have a tough time convincing people that the Great Recession was caused by a tight money policy implemented by the Fed and other major central banks. To begin with, most people don't think recessions are caused by tight money. Even worse, most of those who do view the Fed as a villain in past recessions don't believe that money was tight during 2008. And finally, most people see an obvious alternative theory: a bout of irrational exuberance—perhaps combined with poor government policy—led to a housing bubble that later burst, depressing the economy and triggering a financial crisis. I'm going to try to convince you that this standard view is almost entirely wrong.

Was There Actually a Housing Price Bubble?

Let's start with the housing "bubble" because it came before the banking crisis and recession. I don't believe bubble theories are a *useful* way of looking at the world. More precisely, I don't believe bubbles exist.

The term *bubble* can be defined in several different ways. To some, it is merely a surge in asset prices that is followed by a crash. Because it is patently obvious that market prices often gyrate wildly, let's use the more common and potentially more useful definition: a bubble occurs when an asset price has *clearly* become overvalued in relation to fundamentals such as future cash flows and is likely to fall back to a more reasonable level at some point in the future. It would be quite useful to be able to reliably identify asset price bubbles, because we could then avoid overvalued investments (or profit from them through short selling). But is this possible?

American home prices rose sharply between 2000 and 2006, and then they fell just as sharply after 2006. By 2010, that pattern looked to most people like a classic asset-price bubble—almost like a morality play. Think of the myth of Icarus, who flew too close to the sun before plunging to his death. I'm going to use many different arguments against this view, but my job will be easier if we start by revisiting figure I.6 from the introduction, which shows real housing prices during 1999–2014 in six English-speaking countries.

Real housing prices in the US rose strongly between 2000 and 2006, and then they lost most of those gains by late 2011. Home prices followed a similar pattern in Ireland. To most people, this looks like a classic asset-price bubble. But we are interested in a more important question—were housing prices *obviously* overvalued in 2005 and 2006? That proposition now seems far more dubious.

Britain, Canada, Australia, and New Zealand all experienced major housing-price booms during the first few years after 2000, quite similar to what the US experienced. If it was "obvious" that American homes were overvalued in 2006 and that their prices would decline in the future, then why was the same not equally obvious of these four countries? But while these countries saw home prices briefly dip during the global recession of 2008–2009 (which is to be expected), as of 2019 real housing prices are slightly above 2006 levels in Britain, and well above 2006 levels in Australia, Canada, and New Zealand.[1] A few other countries (e.g., Spain) experienced an American-style boom and bust, but most did not.

A potential homebuyer who refrained from buying in 2006 would have benefited in the US but would have lost money in numerous other countries where real prices are now above 2006 levels. And even within the US, the bubble theory has spotty evidence. There was no boom in home prices in many heartland states where it is easy to build new homes, such as Texas. And in many coastal cities in California and the Northeast, home prices have fully recovered from the crash. Nationally, real home prices are rising briskly and are now much closer to the peak levels of 2006 than to the trough of 2012, as shown in figure 14.1.

Any appraisal of the right value of an asset is always provisional. Markets are forward-looking, and prices are subject to change as new information becomes available. Thus, what looks like an asset bubble might later seem entirely rational in the light of new information. The tech-heavy NASDAQ fell from just over 5,000 at its peak in 2000 to under 1,200 in 2002. From the vantage point of 2002, the 5,000 level looked like an obvious bubble. But now that the Nasdaq has since risen well above 13,000, that judgment seems less conclusive. One could argue that it is the

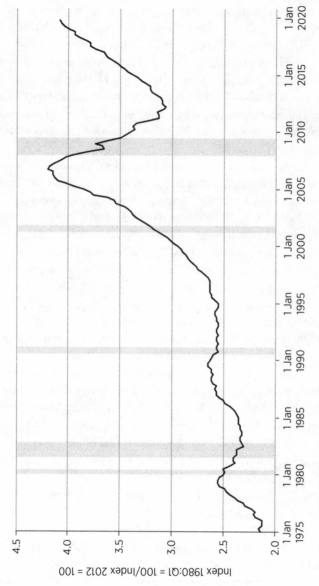

FIGURE 14.1. US real housing prices, 1974–2019

Note: Gray bars indicate periods of recession.

Source: FRED via US Federal Housing Finance Agency, https://fred.stlouisfed.org/series/USSTHPI.

Nasdaq's 2002 level that now looks more "irrational"—too low, in this case. Back in 2002, almost everyone agreed that in 2000 there had been excessive optimism about the future prospects of internet firms such as Amazon. From the vantage point of today, the extreme optimism of the tech boom in the late 1990s looks considerably less irrational.

On the basis of what we know today, is it possible to explain the boom, bust, and partial recovery in housing prices? Perhaps not perfectly, but I do think it can be mostly explained with "fundamentals." Let's start with the boom period, which I see as having been driven by at least four factors: a secular decline in real interest rates, which actually began in the 1980s; a stable economy during the so-called Great Moderation of 1984–2007 and a perception that the stability would persist into the future; a perception that immigration would accelerate over time, especially into Sunbelt cities (partly because President George W. Bush was promoting an immigration reform plan that would have effectively boosted the already-high rates of immigration, especially from Latin America); and the growing problem of "NIMBYism," or local authorities imposing increasingly restrictive zoning rules on new construction. Public policy also favored homeownership through a variety of channels. These included, among others, implied public support for Fannie Mae and Freddie Mac, a perception that big banks were too big to fail, Federal Deposit Insurance Corporation insurance for smaller deposits, tax deductibility of mortgage interest and property taxes, and regulatory pressure on banks to lend to lower-income groups. However, most of these policies did not change dramatically between 2000 and 2006, so their effect on the sharp price run-up is unclear.

Low interest rates are probably the most important driver of higher asset prices in recent decades. Other things being equal, the lower the real interest rate, the higher the value of assets that provide a given flow of cash or services over time. So that's one factor in the housing boom. However, we also need to avoid reasoning from a price change—asset prices often fall during recessions, when interest rates are low. Thus, low interest rates must also be considered in tandem with the flow of housing services over time. Was it rational for homebuyers in the first few years after 2000 to expect a high dollar value from future housing services?

Kevin Erdmann, who has studied this issue extensively, found little evidence of excessive home building during the so-called housing bubble.[2] US housing construction was a bit above two million units per year during the bubble, which is comparable to the rates observed during earlier expansions

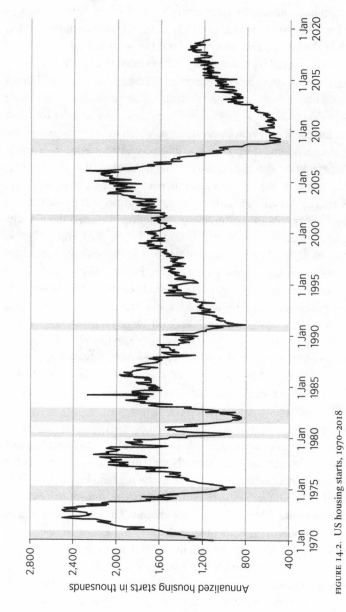

FIGURE 14.2. US housing starts, 1970–2018

Note: Gray bars indicate periods of recession.

Source: FRED via US Census Bureau, https://fred.stlouisfed.org/series/HOUST.

(which did not end in severe crises). What actually stands out is the low level of construction since 2008, shown in figure 14.2.

If there had been excessive construction during the "bubble," then one might have expected falling rents. But the rental cost of housing has actually trended upward fairly strongly in the US, both during and after the housing boom. Except for a brief period around 2010–2011, rents have trended upward at 3% to 4% per year, faster than the overall CPI. Erdmann's research suggests that home prices during the boom period were mostly rational, on the basis of a combination of relatively low real interest rates and expectations of fast-rising rents. Erdmann developed this theory during the housing bust, and the subsequent recovery in home prices has provided support for his hypothesis.

In my view, persistently low interest rates imply a "new normal" of higher asset prices relative to cash flows—not just for houses, but also for stocks, bonds, and many other assets. But in that case, how can we explain the post-2006 crash in home prices?

Despite the widespread view that home prices were excessive in 2006 and that the subsequent crash represented a return to normal, it is actually the crash that is more difficult to explain than the "bubble." The initial trigger might have been the combination of a switch in immigration policy in 2006 (away from President Bush's amnesty plan and toward tighter border controls) and a mild tightening of lending standards at banks. But the bigger factor was surely the severe recession that began in December 2007, as well as the much tighter lending standards imposed during and after the banking crisis. The recovery in house prices since 2011 is presumably attributable to a combination of economic recovery and the unexpected persistence of low real interest rates—factors that also help to explain the strong rise in stock prices during this period.

Are Bubbles a Cognitive Illusion?

My skepticism about bubbles puts me in the minority. Most people believe that asset price bubbles are obviously a feature of the world we live in. Why is it so hard to convince people that markets are efficient and that asset values reflect rational expectations about the present value of future rents, dividends, and so forth? First, the theory goes against common sense—lots of asset price changes seem puzzling when they occur. Furthermore, like other social science models, the efficient-market hypothesis is not precisely true. Even an EMH proponent like myself finds it hard to explain why stock investors would rationally value the aggregate value of US stocks on the evening of October 19, 1987, at a level roughly 20% lower than it was valued at just one day earlier. Markets do some peculiar things.

But even if the theory is not perfect, I view the efficient market hypothesis as being far more useful than various bubble theories, as well as other theories of market "anomalies." Even if there are occasional anomalies, most people vastly overrate their prevalence and underrate how difficult they are to identify. Simply put, bubble theories aren't useful. Consider the following reasons people might see bubbles where they don't actually exist: excessive pattern recognition, data mining and misuse of statistical significance, confirmation bias, underestimating the "wisdom of crowds," belief in a "normal price," and puritan morality tales. Human brains seem hardwired to notice patterns, probably because this ability confers survival advantages in a complex and unpredictable natural world. Excessive use of this facility, however, leads to superstition, as when an athlete notices that he has often done well when wearing his "lucky socks."

Like everyone else, I am subject to excessive pattern recognition. When I look at a chart of stock prices, I notice bull markets and bear markets in which stocks seem to have strong upward or downward momentum. So I'm not unsympathetic to people who suffer from cognitive bias. In fact, studies show that stock prices seem to follow a random walk. This means that on any given day there is a roughly fifty-fifty chance that prices will rise or fall. And the direction that stocks move on any given day is mostly uncorrelated with what happened the day before. You may think you notice patterns in the stock market data, but they are "dead patterns," unlikely to repeat in the future.

Let's look at this from a different angle. You can generate what statisticians call a *random walk* by repeatedly flipping a coin and graphing the results with a line that goes up one point for each head and down one point for each tail. Occasionally there will be an imbalance—perhaps you get sixteen heads out of twenty flips. On those occasions, the line will seem to have upward momentum, like a bull market. At other times you might randomly get fifteen tails out of twenty flips—which looks like a bear market, even to me. But we know that actually there is no momentum for a series of coin flips; each result is independent of the previous flip.

Financial economists generally consider belief in lucky socks to be a foolish superstition, but many demonstrate something remarkably similar when they search for market anomalies. An anomaly is nothing more than an unusual market pattern, which supposedly can be used to predict future movements in asset prices. For instance, one published study claimed that stocks in New York do worse on rainy days than on sunny days, perhaps because traders are depressed by gloomy weather.[3] The chance was less than one in twenty that the pattern this researcher found had been generated randomly. This sort of finding is sometimes claimed to be "statistically significant." But it is not: these studies typically misuse the concept of significance testing.

In a truly scientific field, a researcher would first publish a study suggesting a possible market anomaly and explaining why he or she believed that anomaly was likely to occur, and then another researcher would collect data to test that theory. Unfortunately, this is not how things are done. I'm going to try to explain what's wrong with much of economics, and indeed many of the social and physical sciences, with a gambling analogy. Consider two possible tests of red-black bias on roulette wheels in Las Vegas:

- A researcher studies the ownership of Las Vegas casinos and discovers a link with organized crime in one of the establishments—say, Lucky 7. She suspects that Lucky 7's roulette wheel is rigged and is being used to launder illicit money. To test this hypothesis, she studies whether the ball lands on a red number more or less frequently than it lands on a black number.
- A researcher goes to thirty-seven different casinos in Vegas and collects data on the frequency of reds and blacks at the roulette table. He finds that the greatest discrepancy occurred at the Venetian, where red was somewhat more common than black. Indeed, the chance of this imbalance occurring randomly is less than one in twenty. He writes a report suggesting that the roulette wheel at the Venetian has been rigged and favors those who bet on red.

I hope you see the problem here. If you look at thirty-seven casinos, then it's likely that at least one will show an unusual pattern, even one so unusual that it occurs only once every twenty observations. And that's true *even if there are no actual anomalies* and all casinos are completely honest in their practices. This sort of search for statistically significant patterns is called *data mining* or p-*hacking* and is a big problem in economics and in many other sciences. Because of this problem, you should be highly skeptical of media reports about various economic relationships, as well as of studies in many other areas such as nutrition, environmental health risks, and social psychology.

A group studying this problem recently proposed increasing the standard test from $p = .05$, which means a finding is considered statistically significant if the chance of it occurring randomly is less than one in twenty, to $p = .005$, which means that only findings that would occur randomly once in two hundred observations are considered significant. As we will see, however, simply adjusting the threshold of statistical significance may not be enough.

One problem is that even many scientists underestimate just how often unusual events occur. Here are a couple of examples from my own experience. In 1991, I entered a casino for the first time in my life. I sat down next to a friend who was good at blackjack, and he coached me on how to play my hands. I won the first twelve hands that I played. Given that the house wins more often than not, that's obviously an extremely unlikely event. Here's another. I grew up in the Midwest and moved to the Boston metro area. In 1991 I bought a house on a little cul-de-sac in Newton, Massachusetts, called Hunnewell Circle. A decade later my cousin started doing genealogy research and discovered that our ancestor had been the third resident of Newton, settling there in 1637. Where did this ancestor live? On an acre of land that much later become Hunnewell Circle. What are the odds of that, in a metro area that has nearly five million residents?

During our long lives we experience millions of events. Some of these are very unusual—one-in-a-million-type events. We notice those and ignore lots of other less interesting events. Scientists who study highly complex fields (e.g., economics, sociology, psychology, medicine, biology, nutrition) have no trouble finding lots of statistically significant relationships and publishing their reports. But unless there is a good theoretical justification for a relationship, it typically does not hold up when someone tries to replicate the study. All that these scientists have done is discover some interesting coincidences—like the athlete's lucky socks.

In addition to putting excessive weight on unusual coincidences, people also suffer from confirmation bias. They remember the times they correctly predicted that bubbles would pop and forget all their false predictions. People in the US who, back in 2006, predicted the housing crash tend to have vivid memories of that accurate prediction. People in Britain, Canada, Australia, and New Zealand who wrongly predicted housing crashes have mostly tended to forget their false predictions.

But it gets even worse. People often wrongly recall their predictions, believing that they accurately predicted a bubble that in fact they failed to predict. One of my favorite examples is from 2010, when *The Economist* magazine seemed to suggest that it had made accurate predictions regarding the housing bubbles: "A bubble is an unsustainable increase in prices relative to underlying fundamentals. These fundamentals are more or less observable; those who called the housing bubble did so based on historically anomalous increases in the ratio of home prices to rents and incomes. And many people did correctly identify the bubble years before it imploded, including writers at *The Economist* who were worrying about rapid home price increases while the American economy was still limping out of the 2001 recession."[4] This claim linked to an image of an advertisement for the magazine that had run in its September 11, 2003, print edition: "A SURVEY in *The Economist* in May predicted that house prices would fall by 10% in America over the next four years, and by 20–30% in Australia, Britain, Ireland, the Netherlands and Spain. Prices have since continued to rise, so have we changed our mind?" The irony here (and ironies just don't get any richer) is that this prediction was wrong. And not just slightly off, but monumentally wrong.

Consider the following analogy. Thomas Malthus and Paul Ehrlich are often (falsely) credited with predicting a "population explosion." Actually, they (wrongly) predicted the opposite—that the "limits of growth" would prevent Earth's population from rising to 7.5 billion. Similarly, *The Economist* was not predicting that a housing bubble would occur between 2003 and 2007; it was predicting that a housing bubble *would not occur*. It was predicting that house prices would fall sharply over the next four years. People who acted on this advice lost lots of money. And yet *The Economist* (my favorite magazine) was so proud of this false prediction that it used it in advertisements.

One might argue that *The Economist* didn't get the timing right, but surely it correctly noted some very real excesses in the housing market. Actually, no. Even if we relax the test and take away the four-year prediction window, the prediction was still wrong. Only Ireland saw home prices drop 30% below 2003 levels, and then only for a brief period eight years after the prediction. In the other four countries, prices have either risen slightly or moved sharply higher, as shown in figure 14.3. And this is using data from *The Economist*.

This sort of confirmation bias shows itself all the time. One frequently sees people cite Dean Baker's 2003 prediction of a housing bubble or Robert Shiller's 1996 claim that the stock market exhibited "irrational exuberance."[5] We are supposed to believe that these predictions came true, when in fact from the perspective of 2020, house prices in 2003 and stock prices in 1996 do not look particularly high at all. Those were not bad years to buy houses or stocks. How many people recall Shiller's 2011 suggestion that US stocks were overvalued?

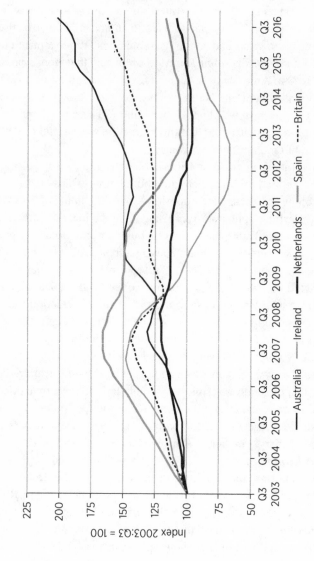

FIGURE 14.3. Housing prices in five countries, 2003–2016

Source: The Economist via OECD; ONS; Reserve Bank of New Zealand; Standard & Poor's; Teranet—National Bank, https://infographics.econo
mist.com/2017/HPI/index.html.

Perhaps we are also receptive to bubble theories because many of us do not have confidence in the "rationality" of our fellow human beings. When I used to ask my students to raise their hands if they thought advertisers manipulated consumers into buying stuff they didn't need, most hands shot up in the air. When I then asked if the students themselves were manipulated by advertisers into buying stuff they didn't need, far fewer hands were raised. It is no surprise that people are receptive to claims that a sort of mania can seize the public, leading to irrational increases in asset prices.

At the individual level, people often do exhibit a lack of good judgment. I certainly have. But in a market what matters is not the forecasts of individuals; rather, it is the "wisdom of the crowd." And predictions that aggregate the views of thousands of individuals are often remarkably accurate. Furthermore, even if a mob of foolish investors is pushing prices too far in one direction, the "smart money" can bet in the other direction.

Admittedly, it is not easy to short illiquid assets such as single-family homes. However, it is easy to short all sorts of other assets that would almost certainly fall sharply in value if house prices plunged by 30%. John Paulson earned more than $1 billion in 2008 by doing precisely that: shorting assets that would do poorly in a housing crash. However, Warren Buffett and many other savvy Wall Street investors lost a great deal of money in 2008—because it is really, really hard to predict asset-market crashes.

People are also led astray by the persistent belief that there is a sort of "normal price" to which markets should eventually revert. Bubbles are then viewed as "abnormal" phenomena, as a mania that will eventually end. But if asset prices follow a random walk, we cannot assume that prices will eventually return to normal. This concept of a normal price also explains why there is such strong opposition to "price gouging," even though price gouging is actually good for consumers, because it leads to a more efficient distribution of scarce resources during an emergency.

Perhaps the most powerful source of belief in bubbles is our intuition about life in general. There are all sorts of areas of life that really do exhibit bubble-like symptoms. Think of a wild night at a party with lots of heavy drinking. What comes next? An unpleasant morning sobering up after the previous night's excesses. This sort of thinking can lead to an instinctive puritanism, according to which a recession is seen as the price to be paid for the previous excesses. For instance, one strand of Austrian economics blamed the Great Recession on the Fed's allegedly "easy money" policy in the years after 2000. This supposedly led to an excessive boom in housing, called *malinvestment*. After the bubble burst, unemployment

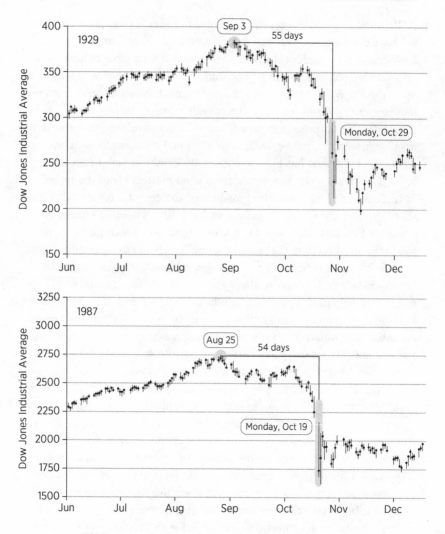

FIGURE 14.4. The Dow Jones Industrial Average in 1929 and 1987

Source: Blog post by JP Koning, "Fama vs. Shiller on the 1987 Stock Market Crash," http://jpkoning.blogspot.com
/2013/10/fama-vs-shiller-on-1987-stock-market.html.

soared as workers lost jobs in housing and related industries. But do the
data support this claim?

Let's start with the claim that asset price crashes can cause recessions.
Is it true? It might seem that way; after all, didn't the famous 1929 stock-
market crash trigger the Great Depression? Actually, no—the Great Depression was triggered by a tight money policy that sharply reduced nomi-

nal GDP. How do we know this to be the case? Because in 1987 we had an almost-perfect test of this hypothesis, shown in figure 14.4. As I explained in chapter 13, in 1987 there was a stock-market boom and bust of almost exactly the same size as in 1929, and not only was there no depression, there wasn't even a tiny slowdown in the economy. The US continued booming in 1988 and 1989. The difference is, of course, monetary policy, which kept NGDP growing strongly during the late 1980s.

The Real Problem Was Nominal

Earlier we saw that housing construction was above average during the housing boom but not unusually high relative to other expansions. But even if the boom was not particularly excessive, in terms of either construction or home prices, the crash in both was undeniably severe. And housing slumps are fairly common during recessions, including the Great Depression.[6] Was this housing crash a plausible cause of the Great Recession? Let's take another look at the numbers we examined in the introduction to this book. Table 14.1 shows housing starts, housing completions, and the unemployment rate from the peak of the housing boom to the peak in the unemployment rate.

From the average of starts and completions, we can get a sense of ongoing construction rates. Notice that housing construction declined by more than 50% between January 2006 and April 2008. But the unemployment rate barely budged, rising a statistically insignificant 0.3 percentage points. How was the economy able to remain at close to "full employment" despite one of the biggest housing crashes in American history? The answer is simple: other sectors of the economy were doing well. Commercial construction remained strong, as did manufacturing, exports, and services.

This is how an economy is supposed to work. If one sector of the economy needs to shrink, then resources such as labor and capital should be reallocated to other sectors of the economy. This process didn't work perfectly after the tech sector was overbuilt in 2000, but it worked considerably

TABLE 14.1 **US housing statistics versus unemployment rate**

Month and year	Starts	Completions	Average	Unemployment rate
January 2006	2,273,000	2,036,000	2,154,500	4.7%
April 2008	1,013,000	1,022,000	1,017,500	5.0%
October 2009	534,000	746,000	640,000	10.0%

Source: Federal Reserve Economic Data.

better than it did in 2008–2009. The Fed did enough to keep nominal GDP growing, and resources moved from tech into other sectors such as housing and services. Unemployment rose, but only to a peak of 6.3% in the recession of 2001 and slow recovery, which meant the recession was relatively mild. With an appropriate monetary policy, something similar might have occurred after the housing sector collapsed.

Instead, something very strange happened. After April 2008, almost all sectors of the economy began tanking. By the summer of 2008, NGDP was declining and the unemployment rate began rising rapidly—peaking at 10% in October 2009. In some ways even this understates the carnage, because millions of discouraged workers left the labor force and stopped searching for work. Not surprisingly, housing construction continued to decline, but this secondary slump was actually milder than the January 2006 to April 2008 housing crash. More importantly, it was *endogenous*, a reaction to the weak economy and tighter lending standards imposed by a banking system under stress.

Almost everyone assumes the real problem during 2008 was a real shock to the economy caused by a collapsing housing sector and the subsequent banking crisis. That's the "common sense" view. The evidence, however, strongly suggests that the real problem was nominal—falling NGDP led to declining output all across the economy, surging unemployment, and falling incomes. This also worsened the housing crash and caused it to spread to other sectors that had held up well until 2008, such as commercial construction. As a result of the decline in NGDP, a severe banking crisis developed in late 2008. But even this banking crisis was a symptom of the Great Recession, not a cause.[7] The cause was a contractionary monetary policy that depressed NGDP.

. An analogy can help illuminate this counterintuitive argument. Think of someone whose common cold turns into pneumonia. To an untrained observer, this might look like a mild cold turning into a bad cold. In fact, colds are caused by viruses and pneumonia is usually caused by a bacterial infection. If you don't understand this fact, then you won't know how to treat the illness. A cold can be treated with aspirin, whereas a bacterial infection needs to be treated with antibiotics.

By October 2008, the Fed finally understood that the economy was sliding into recession, but even then policy makers misdiagnosed the underlying problem. The Fed initially assumed that the "real problem" was banking distress. It then tried to fix banking without boosting NGDP. That's one reason the Fed did not cut interest rates in the first meeting after Lehman Brothers failed. In fact, the real problem was falling NGDP, and the Fed's bank-rescue policies were completely ineffective at boosting the overall economy. The Fed was bailing water out of the boat before plugging the leak. Only in March 2009 did the Fed belatedly recognize that the real problem was declining nominal spending and begin to move more aggressively on the monetary policy front. By then it was too late to prevent a severe recession.

To its credit, the Fed did much better than it had under similar circumstances in the 1930s, and also much better than the European Central Bank. But even so, the Fed's policy errors were the proximate cause of the Great Recession. Why was Fed policy so far off course? There was no nefarious plot to create a recession in order to advance some agenda. Instead, there was an almost-perfect storm of bad luck and bad decisions, most of which would have caused only minor problems under normal conditions. These errors included the following:

- too much focus on inflation and too little focus on NGDP growth
- adherence to growth rate targeting rather than level targeting
- too much focus on previous data and too little focus on market forecasts of the future path of the economy
- an unwillingness to "target the forecast"
- unfamiliarity with operating at the zero-interest-rate bound, including an unwillingness to adopt a "whatever it takes" approach
- misreading the current stance of monetary policy—putting too much weight on the level of interest rates
- taking a "wait and see" approach to monetary experiments instead of immediately recognizing the market verdict on their likely effectiveness
- overestimating the length of monetary policy "lags"
- assuming that the real problem was real (i.e., banking and housing)
- relying on faulty measures of inflation

In the remaining chapters these errors will be discussed in much more detail. We will see that not only are most analyses of the Great Recession full of cognitive illusions; in a very real sense these cognitive illusions can be said to have *caused* the recession. But before we get to that I'd like to explain how I prefer to think about ambiguous concepts such as bubbles.

Is the Bubble Theory True?

Most people like to differentiate between subjective belief and objective truth. I'm a bit skeptical of this distinction, and nowhere more so than in the case of bubbles. What does it actually mean to say that the Nasdaq was a bubble when it hit 5,000 in March 2000? Is that some sort of objective fact about the universe? Or is it a subjective description, like saying the Matterhorn is a beautiful mountain? How would we test the hypothesis that bubbles exist?

In my view, debates about bubbles are focusing on the wrong question. It will never be possible to prove that *any given asset-price boom* was or was not a bubble. That's because it's almost impossible to distinguish between the hypothesis that the public had a rational belief that later turned out to be false and the hypothesis that the public had a belief that was obviously irrational, even at the time.

Thus, I encourage people to spend less time thinking about whether bubble theories are true and more time thinking about whether they are *useful*. For me, the bubble theory is useful only if we view it as contradicting the efficient-market hypothesis, not merely as a big up and down in asset prices. Thus, my support of the EMH is an implicit rejection of the usefulness of bubble theories. So why do I regard the EMH as being more useful than theories of market irrationality?

There are three areas where the EMH is useful to me: as an investor, as an academic, and as a voter. In each case, bubble theories have real-world implications that are different from those of the EMH. For instance, consider investing. My belief in the EMH leads me to invest in index funds and to avoid wasting money on paying experts who claim to be able to beat market averages. If I believed in the existence of bubbles, I'd invest in mutual funds that specialized in selling short bubble assets and buying "negative bubbles"—that is, assets that are obviously priced irrationally low.

As an academic, the EMH has been very useful to me. I used this theory in my research on the Great Depression and found that asset markets often responded immediately to new information about public policy, which affected the expected rate of growth in NGDP. On the other hand, I found bubble theories to be almost useless in my research.

Now let's put on our voter hats. Should I vote for politicians who favor appointing regulators to prevent bubbles? After all, doesn't history show that stronger regulations would have prevented the subprime fiasco? Actually, no. One can look at the subprime fiasco from a theoretical perspective or from an empirical perspective, but what one cannot do is compare an *ideal* regulatory scheme to *actual* banking practices. It would be nice if we could go back in time and promulgate a regulation banning subprime mortgages in 2004. But if the regulators of 2004 had seen the future, the bankers would also have known what was coming and would never had made the riskier loans in the first place.

The anti-EMH argument for regulation is implicitly based on the view that bankers are irrational and make lots of foolish loans. Regulators are considered rational, able to have seen that these loans were too risky. In this view, the regulators are astute forecasters who can protect bankers from hurting themselves. At a theoretical level this seems highly unlikely. Why would modestly paid government regulators have a better understanding of which loans are likely to default than highly paid bankers who have an incentive to be successful?

More importantly, what happened in practice? What position did the "regulators" take in this crisis? First, we need to recall that regulators are embedded in a complex political system and (like bankers) respond to incentives. We need to consider the watchmen, those who watch the watchmen, and those who watch those who watch the watchmen. In other words, the president, Congress, the Fed, the media, and academics. How many of these people warned us about the subprime crisis? Many different levels of our political system were actually encouraging banks to behave even more recklessly than they did.

Real-world bankers did not see the subprime crash coming, and hence they lost lots of money. Real-world regulators did not see the subprime fiasco coming, and hence they issued regulations encouraging *more* mortgage lending, not less. This is not to say that the subprime crisis does not point to the need for tighter regulation. Rather, any regulation that comes out of this crisis should be justified on grounds other than market inefficiency—say, on grounds of mitigating moral hazard—unless you can convince me that future regulators will be able to predict markets better than future financiers.

This is a good time to trot out my favorite philosopher, Richard Rorty. In one of his books, Rorty quoted an old pragmatist maxim: "That which has no practical implications, has no philosophical implications."[8] I would reword that slightly for the current discussion: "That which has no practical implications has no implications for economic theory." Bubble theories are simply not useful—they don't help me as an investor, as an academic, or as a public policy maker. There may be asset-price movements that feel like bubbles, but unless that "feeling" has useful implications, it doesn't make a scientific statement about the world.

When I started blogging in February 2009, the comment sections in my blog were bombarded with all sorts of arguments against my defense of the EMH:

- The August 1987 (pre-crash) stock market seemed obviously too high.
- NASDAQ was obviously excessive when it hit 5000 in March 2000.
- Housing prices in 2006 were obviously way too high.
- Hedge funds and college endowments purportedly outperformed index funds.
- China was a bubble that was about to burst.
- The fact that Bitcoin soared from $2 to $30 and then fell back to $12 showed it to be a bubble.

None of those arguments look very strong today. The pre-crash stock market in August 1987 no longer looks excessive. The Nasdaq may have been much too high in 2000, but now that it has been well above 13,000 the claim no longer looks so obvious. American house prices are recovering strongly and home prices never really crashed in lots of other markets with similar characteristics. Hedge funds have not done well recently, as evidenced by the famous bet Warren Buffet won in 2017. The same is true of many college endowments. China did not collapse, as many bears predicted. And Bitcoin obviously rose far above the "bubble" price of $30. The test of a theory is how it performs "out of sample," or after it has been made, not how it applies to previous data. Patterns are easy to find.

In my blogging I have used these points to push back against what I see as cognitive illusions in this area. At the same time, I know that this is a losing battle. People are almost hardwired to see bubbles, and it's likely that by the time you read this book at least one of the markets mentioned already will have the sort of price movement that looks to most people like a bubble bursting. Indeed, you might say I was lucky to be blogging my pro-EMH views over the past ten years, which have not been kind to bubble theories, and not during 2000–2008, when my defense of the EMH would have looked almost laughably implausible.

That's why I keep going back to the criterion of usefulness. It is pointless to analyze an unusual asset-price movement in isolation. Unusual things happen all the time. To be judged useful, a bubble model needs to provide systematic evidence that is useful to you as an academic, investor, or voter. And that's where bubble theories fall short.

I implore people to work hard to avoid confirmation bias. Yes, if you keep calling "bubble" in a highly volatile market, eventually you'll see a price plunge. That's what volatile markets do. But it's not useful to call Bitcoin a bubble at $30 if it soars in price for years and then in the year 2022 its price plunges from $20,000 to $1,000. Focus less on what things look like and more on figuring out which theoretical concepts are actually useful.

CHAPTER FIFTEEN

Good Economists Don't Forecast, They Infer Market Forecasts

During the evening rush hour on August 1, 2007, a major eight-lane bridge in Minneapolis suddenly collapsed, killing 13 people and injuring 145. Although highway engineers often warn governments about the substandard condition of infrastructure, this bridge was certainly not expected to completely fail during 2007.

Should we have expected highway engineers to predict this bridge failure? I'd say no. The point of highway engineering is not to predict bridge collapses; it's to prevent bridge collapses. Surely if engineers had known this bridge was about to collapse, emergency repairs would have been done quickly. Even if Minnesota were a bit short of funds, resources earmarked for other projects would have been diverted to strengthening the I-35 bridge.

In this chapter I make a similar argument about the economics profession. We should not ask economists to predict recessions—we should ask them to prevent recessions. If we could predict them, then we could prevent them. Here's James Hamilton, a noted business cycle expert: "You could argue that if the Fed is doing its job properly, any recession should have been impossible to predict ahead of time."[1] Strictly speaking, Hamilton's observation applies only to recessions caused by demand shocks, but in practice supply shocks are also pretty unpredictable.

Most recessions occur precisely because policy makers are unable to predict them. Indeed, to say that economists are not good at predicting recessions is an understatement. Economists are extraordinarily bad at predicting recessions. The past three recessions were not predicted by a consensus of economists until the recession had been under way for many months. That's right, not only can economists not predict the future; they cannot even predict the present—they often can't even predict the recent past. In July 2008, economists were not able to "predict" that the economy had been in recession in January 2008![2]

I ran across Hamilton's observation in early 2008 while working on a paper arguing that economists would never again be able to forecast recessions. I had assumed that the Fed was following Lars Svensson's criterion of "targeting the forecast"—that is, that it always set monetary policy in such a way that the forecast equals the policy target. In plain English, I thought that the Fed set monetary policy at a position where it expected to succeed, to hit its target. And because the Fed presumably doesn't target recessions, it shouldn't be able to forecast them either.

Little did I know that events would discredit my hypothesis within a few months. Not because economists successfully forecast the coming recession (once again, the consensus didn't forecast a recession until months after it had begun), but because the Fed seemed to stop following Svensson's "target the forecast" criterion. By late 2008, nominal GDP growth forecasts for 2009 were far below what the Fed would have liked to see, and yet the Fed seemed strangely passive. This is the situation that radicalized me, that turned me into an advocate of monetary policy reform.

Hasn't this sort of policy fatalism always been true of recessions? No. In the New Keynesian era (1984–2007), the few recessions the US did have were almost over before the consensus of economic forecasters even realized they had begun. Once economists recognized that a recession was under way, there was an expectation that gradual recovery would occur over the following twelve months. Late 2008 was different—it was obvious that nominal spending in 2009 would be much lower than the Fed wished to see. And that's not just my view; in late 2008, Ben Bernanke began asking for assistance from fiscal policy makers.

It turns out that economic forecasting provides a key to understanding the cause of recessions, both of those that can be forecast and of those that cannot. Thus, we need to take a much closer look at the paradoxical world of forecasting. I am going to argue that the only recessions that we ought to be able to forecast are those that *we want to occur*.

When Should We Have a Recession?

One reason the business cycle is so difficult to forecast is that recessions can be prevented even after they have begun. That may seem like an on-

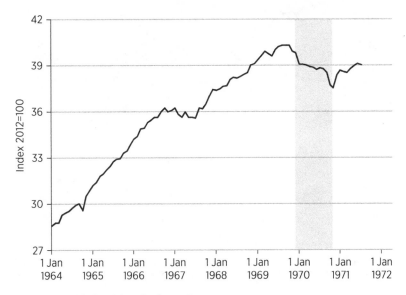

FIGURE 15.1. US industrial production, 1964–1971

Note: Gray bars indicate periods of recession.

Source: FRED via Board of Governors of the Federal Reserve System (US), https://fred.stlouisfed.org/series/INDPRO

tological impossibility, but it's true. A recession is defined as a sustained decline in output and employment. Minor declines don't count. Thus, if policy makers from 2009 could have gone back in a time machine to June 2008, they might have enacted some aggressive monetary stimulus to juice the economy. Not only might this have prevented the economy from being in recession in June 2008; it might even have prevented the economy from being in recession in January 2008. After all, January 2008 was considered a recession period only after a severe decline in output occurred in late 2008. At that point, January 2008 was no longer seen as just a minor dip in an otherwise expanding economy, but as the early stages of a recession that is now dated as having started in December 2007.

Let me illustrate the concept by comparing 1967 and 2008. In 1967, the Fed prevented a recession that had already begun. As a result, the history books show no recession in 1967. Output did not decline for a period sustained enough to constitute a recession. Figure 15.1 shows industrial production during the late 1960s: it declined by almost 1.9% between October 1966 and July 1967. But that's much less than the nearly 8% decline observed during the 1970 recession, which was itself fairly mild. The US had no recession in 1967 because the Fed sensed a slowdown and eased

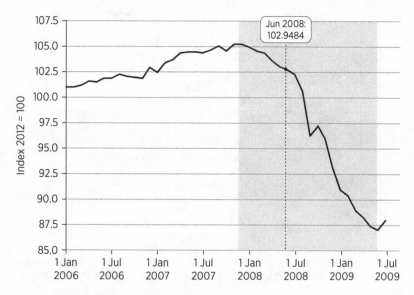

FIGURE 15.2. US industrial production, 2006–2009

Note: Gray bars indicate periods of recession.

Source: FRED via Board of Governors of the Federal Reserve System (US), https://fred.stlouisfed.org/series /INDPRO.

policy in the spring of 1967. Because of this action, unemployment merely nudged up from 3.6% in November 1966 to 4.0% in October 1967, before renewing its long decline.

Now let's look at industrial production during late 2007 and early 2008, shown in figure 15.2. After peaking in November 2007, industrial production fell by only 2.2% over the next seven months, which is similar to what happened in 1966–1967. After June 2008, output fell sharply, and by June 2009 it was more than 17.3% below pre-recession levels, indicating an unusually deep recession.

Unlike in 1967, the Fed decided not to ease monetary policy in the middle of 2008, despite growing signs of recession. Indeed policy was actually tightened sharply, as the fed-funds target was held at 2% from April to October despite a rapidly falling natural rate of interest. If the Fed had eased aggressively in June 2008, then it might have entirely prevented a recession that technically began in December 2007. The decline in output from late 2007 to June 2008 was simply too small to constitute a recession. Yes, the National Bureau of Economic Research eventually declared that the Great Recession began in December 2007, but there would have been no recession to set a date for in the first place if industrial production had risen in the second half of 2008, as it did in the second half of 1967. Later I'll argue that the post–Lehman Brothers crisis might also have been milder—even that Lehman might not have failed—if stimulus had been applied in mid-2008.

Ironically, the Fed made the wrong call in both 1967 and 2008. In 1967 the Fed should have allowed a (very mild) recession to occur in order to prevent the Great Inflation of 1966–1981 from occurring. That inflation did far more damage than would have a rise in unemployment to, say, 5% in late 1967. Indeed, a mild recession in 1967 might have made the 1970 recession unnecessary. In contrast, the Fed should have prevented the 2008 recession.

Why did the Fed get both calls wrong? In 1967, the Fed was thrown off course by Keynesian ideas that had taken over the profession. The Johnson administration promised fiscal austerity (tax increases) to hold down inflation and pressured the Fed to ease monetary policy. The tax increases did not occur until 1968, and the monetary stimulus led to higher inflation. At the time, many economists had a simplistic view of the Phillips curve, assuming a permanent trade-off between inflation and unemployment. Consider the following statement by Paul Samuelson, who during the 1960s and 1970s was the world's most respected Keynesian economist: "Today's inflation is chronic. Its roots are deep in the very nature of the welfare state. [Establishment of price stability through monetary policy would require] abolishing the humane society [and would] reimpose inequality and suffering not tolerated under democracy. A fascist political state would be required to impose such a regime and preserve it. Short of a military junta that imprisons trade union activists and terrorizes intellectuals, this solution to inflation is unrealistic—and, to most of us, undesirable."[3] Just a few years later this view of the world had been completely discredited as a result of the monetarist counterrevolution—but in the 1960s it was still a widely held opinion among the Keynesians who dominated the economics profession.

In 1968, President Johnson did finally enact a major tax increase, but it failed to slow inflation because inflation is determined by monetary policy, not fiscal policy. The Fed eased policy in 1968 to offset the tax increase, and inflation rose still higher in 1969 and 1970. Fiscal policy was far weaker than the Keynesians assumed.

The Fed's other mistake was to focus on inflation rather than nominal GDP growth. Inflation reflects both supply-side and demand-side factors,

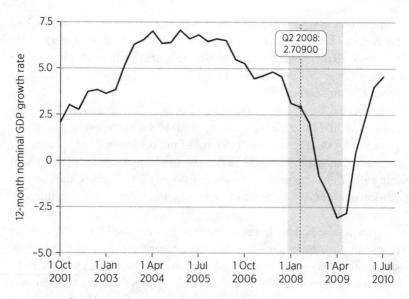

FIGURE 15.3. Growth rate of US nominal GDP, 2002–2010

Note: Gray bar indicates periods of recession.

Source: FRED via US Bureau of Economic Analysis, https://fred.stlouisfed.org/series/GDP.

and thus it is a poor guide to monetary policy. In contrast, NGDP growth reflects only demand-side influences; it essentially measures nominal aggregate demand. When NGDP growth is excessive (say, well above 5%), then money is too easy. When NGDP growth is low (say, well below 5%), then money is too tight. During the twentieth century, real GDP growth averaged about 3%, and thus 5% NGDP growth would deliver, on average, roughly 2% inflation.

Even at the low point of the second quarter of 1967, twelve-month NGDP growth was running at over 5.4%. There was no reason at all for the Fed to ease monetary policy. By the third quarter of 1968, twelve-month NGDP growth had soared to 9.9%—the Great Inflation of 1966–1981 was under way. Now look at figure 15.3, which shows NGDP growth in early 2008. In the second quarter of 2008, the twelve-month NGDP growth rate was only 2.7%. Admittedly, these data were not yet available to Fed officials in June 2008, but even the first quarter data showed only a 3.05% NGDP growth rate—far below trend.

So why did the Fed (passively) tighten policy in mid-2008 by keeping rates at 2% as the natural rate of interest plunged sharply lower? In a word—*inflation*. While monetary policy determines long-run inflation, short-run fluctuations in the CPI often reflect real factors such as energy price spikes. An economic boom in developing countries such as China pushed global oil prices to a peak of $146 per barrel in mid-2008. In the US, twelve-month PCE inflation (i.e., inflation as measured by the personal consumption expenditures price index) rose to a peak of 4.2% in July 2008, far above the Fed's 2% target. (CPI inflation reached 5.5%.) Even though the Fed was aware that oil prices were distorting the data, monetary policy makers were so frightened of losing credibility on inflation that they allowed monetary policy to tighten sharply.

The Fed should have focused on NGDP growth, which was falling to dangerously low levels. As long as NGDP growth was kept at a modest level, any rise in inflation attributable to soaring oil prices would have been transitory. Indeed, by the end of 2008, the twelve-month PCE inflation rate had plunged to below 0.4%, far below the Fed's target. So, one of the many causes of the Great Recession was the focus on inflation when the Fed should have been focusing on NGDP growth. This mistake is now so obvious that it goes a long way toward explaining the rapid increase in support for NGDP targeting. My fellow market monetarist (and blogger) Nick Rowe has indicated that this is one reason he converted from favoring inflation targeting to NGDP targeting—the latter seemed a much better policy indicator during the Great Recession.[4]

It turns out, however, that this mistake alone is not enough to explain the Great Recession. Many Fed officials understood the arguments I have made here, and in June 2008 they believed that NGDP would gradually pick up over time.[5] They certainly did not anticipate the 3% decline that actually occurred between the second quarter of 2008 and the second quarter of 2009, which was about 8% below the long-term trend at the time. Thus misdiagnosing the 2008 oil-price shock was not the only problem in 2008, and we need to explore some of those other reasons for the Fed's policy failure.

What Would It Have Taken to Prevent the 2008 Recession?

Over the past decade, I have continually run into one objection to my explanation of the Great Recession. Even if the real problem was a lack of nominal spending, and even if monetary policy should have been more expansionary, it doesn't seem plausible that some minor tweaks to policy during 2008 would have been strong enough to prevent the onrushing disaster, as a major financial crisis plunged the economy deep into recession. After all, the Fed did cut rates almost to zero in December 2008, and there were also major expansions of the monetary base (quantitative easing). And yet these steps seemed to have little effect. So my critics ask me, "Just how much would the Fed have had to do to prevent the Great Recession? And would that extraordinary level of stimulus have been plausible during mid-2008, a period of high inflation and a weak dollar?"

How much would the Fed have had to do? My response is, "Much less than it actually did do." That may at first sound paradoxical, just one more example of the "through the looking glass" world of monetary economics, where nothing is as it seems. Let me first try to prompt the intuition for this claim with an analogy. People who are very shy often struggle in social settings such as parties, and hence do very little socializing. So imagine how much harder it would be for a shy person to do a *lot* of socializing than a little. In fact, it is my experience that just the opposite is true. Socializing is much easier when you do it often and lose your inhibitions.

Among all the developed countries, Australia was the one with that sort of devil-may-care attitude, and it breezed through the Great Recession with only minor problems. And yet from a conventional point of view, the Aussies did the *least aggressive* monetary stimulus. Unlike most other developed countries, they did not cut interest rates to zero. Nor did they do any QE; their monetary base remained small, at only 4% of GDP. Yet by the Bernanke criterion for monetary policy (inflation and NGDP growth), Australia had the most *expansionary* policy of the major developed economies.

Ironically, it's precisely because the Reserve Bank of Australia's policy was credible and effective that policy makers had to do so little. Because Australia had rapid NGDP growth, the natural rate of interest stayed well above zero. (Recall that NGDP growth and nominal interest rates are strongly correlated.) And because interest rates stayed well above zero, Australian commercial banks had no incentive to hold massive quantities of excess reserves—they could do better holding alternative assets with a positive yield. Unlike in most countries, the hot-potato effect never stopped working in Australia.

Perhaps people who do well at parties are a bit lucky—born with genes that make them more outgoing. Australia (often nicknamed the "lucky country") might also have benefited from a bit of luck. Lots of people point to Australia's commodity exports—but that's not really an explanation. Reliance on commodities makes an economy *more unstable*, and

TABLE 15.1 **Annualized nominal GDP growth rates**

Region	Q2 1996–Q2 2006	Q2 2006–Q2 2013
Australia	6.6%	6.3%
United States	5.5%	2.8%
Eurozone	4.0%	1.7%

Source: Federal Reserve Economic Data.

yet Australia has not had a recession since 1991 (excluding the COVID-19 slump), despite a housing "bubble" that makes the one in the US seem modest, and despite wild swings in global commodity prices. No, the real secret sauce in Australia was sound monetary policy, which kept NGDP growing at a satisfactory rate.

Before 2006, Australian NGDP growth was about 6.6%, versus about 5.5% in the US and 4.0% in the eurozone. Australia's higher rate of NGDP growth was due to a couple of unrelated factors, such as a slightly higher inflation target (about 2.5% in Australia, vs. 2.0% in the US and below 2.0% in the eurozone) and also faster real GDP growth owing to very high rates of immigration.[6] The high trend rate of NGDP growth allowed interest rates to stay well above zero. But there was also another factor: during the global financial crisis, Australia's monetary policy looked more like "level targeting" than did policy in either the US or the eurozone.

Look at the growth rates in NGDP from 2006 to 2013, shown in table 15.1. The growth rate in Australia was not as stable as these figures make it seem, because the Australian economy grew above trend in 2007–2008 and then growth slowed sharply in 2009. But over the period as a whole, Australia maintained pretty steady growth. That is, its growth returned to the trend line when there was a temporary deviation. In contrast, the US and the eurozone saw sharp declines in 2008–2009 and no return to the previous trend line.

Thus, one of the major causes of the Great Recession was a lack of level targeting, a refusal to return to the previous trend line. Instead, the world's major central banks let bygones be bygones and started a new and much lower trend line at the bottom of the Great Recession. And here's what most people miss: the failure to recover to the previous trend line did not merely create a slow recovery; anticipation of the policy helped to make the initial contraction far worse than necessary.

Level targeting is especially essential when monetary policy has difficulty getting "traction," say, because of financial turmoil or the zero-bound problem. Level targeting allows the central bank to promise to bring nominal spending back on target in a couple of years, and this helps to boost nominal spending today. Indeed, a central theme of modern macroeconomic theory is that current levels of aggregate demand depend heavily on the expected future path of demand, just as modern finance predicts that the current level of a company's stock price is strongly affected by changes in its future expected value. Because nominal spending is the sum of price inflation and real growth, I'd like to provide the intuition behind level targeting with two examples, one involving prices and one involving output.

Here's the first example. Suppose that Saudi Arabia wants to stabilize the price of oil at $65 per barrel so adjusts its oil output to achieve that goal. Then Saudi Arabia faces a sudden problem: its oil industry has to shut down for two months owing to a computer virus. What's the best way for the Saudis to keep prices close to their $65 target during this two-month period when they lack the ability to take any "concrete steps" to stabilize oil prices? It turns out that the answer is easy—commit to push prices back to $65 per barrel once production is restored. If this policy is credible, prices may not rise much above $65, even in the short run when Saudi production is immobilized. Instead, once prices hit $66 or $67 per barrel, speculators will begin selling off inventory, anticipating that they will be able to buy back the oil at $65 per barrel once Saudi output is restored.

In general, a credible promise to peg future prices also tends to keep current prices more stable. But what about real output?

Here's the second example. The Chicago Spire was going to be by far the tallest and most impressive building in the United States, soaring two thousand feet above the Chicago lakefront. But the project was canceled when the economy was hit by a severe recession in 2008. When major projects are undertaken, investors are very concerned about the future market for the good or service that will be produced. If the Fed promises to quickly bring nominal spending back to the pre-2008 trend line, then investors will be more likely to stick with a costly project than they will be if they expect a long and painful recession. Developers are aware of the famous case of the Empire State Building, which was completed in 1931 and dubbed the "Empty State Building" during the Great Depression. People financing the Chicago Spire presumably did not want to repeat that mistake, and today the site is just a big hole in the ground.

I'm not the only economist to see the advantages of NGDP-level targeting; Michael Woodford is one of the world's leading theoretical macroeconomists, and he endorsed the idea in 2012.[7] More recently, Ben Bernanke endorsed level targeting of prices. Level targeting would make policy far more effective during a liquidity trap by raising the expected rate of future inflation when prices fell in the short run and thus lowering the real interest rate. So why haven't central banks moved in the direction of level targeting? There are two factors holding them back, one technical and one political.

The technical concern is what happens when inflation or NGDP move significantly above or below the target path. Wouldn't any attempt to bring the economy back to the trend line require an aggressive policy that might prove destabilizing? Under level targeting of prices, a 5% inflation rate one year might require a −1% rate the next, to keep prices close to a target path rising at 2% per year. The same objection applies to NGDP level targeting.

Assume NGDP were targeted along a +4% per year path. Then a temporary period of 6% NGDP growth would not lead to higher wage demands, because workers would anticipate a more contractionary policy in the near future. Rather, hourly wages would remain fairly stable, and there would be a temporary surge in profits. When NGDP growth slowed, profits would decline back to normal. The reason earlier periods of disinflation were so costly is that workers had come to expect sustained periods of very high inflation, and this was factored into labor contracts. Sharp declines in inflation were unanticipated. That would not be the case under level targeting.

There is also a political reason the Fed is reluctant to engage in level targeting: it would make it abundantly clear that the Fed is responsible for the path of nominal spending. Just to be clear, the Fed *is* responsible for the path of nominal spending under any conceivable fiat money regime. But the public (and even Congress) doesn't understand this. Most people see the Fed as just one part of the policy-making process, which makes occasional "gestures" to try to "solve economic problems." In fact, just as a ship captain is paid to steer a ship, not "solve ship problems," the Fed's mandate calls for steering the nominal economy. But as long as the public doesn't understand this, the Fed doesn't get blamed for big mistakes like the Great Depression, the Great Inflation, and the Great Recession. Indeed, at the time, the Fed was not blamed for any of those three disasters. During 2008 and 2009 the Fed was seen as making some fairly aggressive gestures, and if it fell short—well, it was time for other parts of the government to pitch in.

Under level targeting it would be much clearer that the Fed is responsible for the path of nominal spending. Several consecutive years of under- or overshooting would put the spotlight on the Fed in a way that the same situation does not under growth-rate targeting. It's one thing for inflation to be 1.4% when the target is 2.0%, and quite another for the price level to be 600 basis points below a 2% inflation trend line since 2008.

Regime Change in Fall 2008

Business-cycle forecasting offers a lens through which we can better understand what went wrong in 2008. Here it will be useful to think of recessions being caused by forecasts of recessions. Yes, I know that that sounds kind of weird, but in a sense it is true.

I've continually emphasized the importance of expectations: what matters is not the current stance of monetary policy, but the expected future path of policy. I've also argued (along with Ben Bernanke) that NGDP growth is a good way of visualizing the current stance of monetary policy. Thus, a decline in future expected NGDP is a tightening of monetary policy. Falling expectations of future NGDP growth then tend to reduce *current* NGDP, as consumers and businesspeople react rationally to a more pessimistic economic environment. This is probably the phenomenon that led Keynes to discuss the role of "animal spirits" in the business community.[8]

The mere expectation of a severe recession next year can help to push the economy into a recession *right now*. And that also implies that a good way to prevent recessions right now is to make credible promises to push NGDP back up to target any time there is a temporary dip in spending. We can't expect the central bank to always stabilize NGDP, because even short policy lags make this goal almost impossible. What we can expect is that central banks will always stabilize *expected future NGDP*, at a level that is consistent with the Fed's dual mandate.[9]

In 2008, I worked on a research project aimed at showing that recessions were unforecastable, because if they could be forecasted, then the Fed would do what it takes to prevent them. If this were true, then not only should small recessions be unforecastable, but even the dramatic intensification of a recession (as occurred in late 2008) should be unforecastable, because the Fed would especially like to prevent recessions from getting much worse.

Unfortunately for my theory, after Lehman Brothers failed in the fall of 2008, it became obvious to me that the US was entering a severe recession. And yet the US wasn't even at the zero bound, which means that the Fed clearly was not doing all it could to prevent this severe recession, even from the perspective of conventional policies such as cutting rates—and of course the Fed also has lots of unconventional tools like QE.

This made no sense to me, so I tried to figure out what was going on by talking to other economists. Wasn't money obviously too tight, or was I going crazy? At about this time I visited Harvard and had some useful conversations with some well-known macroeconomists: a new classical economist and a New Keynesian economist. The new classical economist thought the real problem was real, and that faster NGDP growth would merely lead to higher inflation. The recession (in his view) was not caused by a lack of nominal spending.

The New Keynesian economist had views closer to my own, agreeing with me that a demand-side recession was developing. I asked something to this effect: "Doesn't the Fed see what's going on here?" His response was something to this effect: "Oh, they see the problem, they just don't know what to do about it."

And that was the turning point for me. I'd spend my entire professional career assuming that the Fed *did* know what to do in this sort of situation—that policy makers did know how to avoid repeating the mistakes of the Great Depression. Bernanke had written a paper in 1999 telling the Japanese what to do in similar circumstances. Lars Svensson had a paper on "foolproof" ways to escape the liquidity trap.[10] The New Keynesian professor's response to my question seemed incredible, but subsequent events show that he was correct: the Fed really did not know what to do. But why not? Wasn't a more expansionary monetary policy appropriate at that time?

Recall that Svensson emphasized that the central bank must always target the forecast, setting policy at a position where aggregate demand is expected to be on target over the following few years. If aggregate demand is expected to be below target (as was obviously the case in the fall of 2008), then the stance of monetary policy is too contractionary.

As forecasts of 2009 and 2010 NGDP fell steadily below the 5% trend line, I kept wondering what was going on at the Fed. Its job is not to change its (nominal) forecast; its job is to *change its policy instrument until the forecast equals the goal*—targeting the forecast, to use Svensson's terminology. Or, to put it even more simply, its job is to set policy at a position where it expects to succeed, to hit its target, not where it expects to fail.

If the Fed had been stuck at the zero bound, then this policy failure might have been a bit more understandable (though equally inexcusable), but during 2008 the US economy was not even at the zero bound. In October 2008 the Fed introduced a policy of paying interest on bank reserves, with the express intention of keeping interest rates from falling to the zero bound. Lots of people believe the Fed was artificially depressing interest rates during this period, whereas it was actually *artificially propping them up*—keeping them far above the (fast-falling) natural rate of interest. This policy failure then depressed the economy (and inflation), causing the natural interest rate to fall even more sharply.

The Fed's failure to target the forecast in late 2008 can be viewed as a *regime change*. A regime change is when there is a fundamentally different approach to policy, not just an adjustment of policy within a given framework. Other examples of regime changes include leaving the gold standard, ending the Bretton Woods fixed-exchange-rate system, and adopting inflation targeting after the Great Inflation. The 2008 regime change was very destructive, causing a crash in all sorts of asset values, as well as greatly intensifying the financial crisis. But the real problem began a bit earlier. Even before the Fed stopped targeting the forecast, it was relying on the wrong forecast.

On September 16, 2008, two days after Lehman Brothers failed, the Fed met to discuss monetary policy. In the end, the Fed decided not to adjust its fed-funds target, which had been set at 2% since April. When you ask people about late 2008, they will often say something to the effect of "Wasn't the Fed doing all it could?" This perception is wildly inaccurate, and yet even many economists believe it to be the case. In fact, the Fed was not even close to doing all it could. A policy of stable interest rates in the midst of an asset-market crash is effectively a tightening of monetary policy. The Fed should have and could have done much more in late 2008.

So why didn't the Fed move aggressively at the September 16 meeting? To Bernanke's credit, in his memoir he says the Fed did err, and should have eased policy in September 2008. Am I just engaging in Monday-morning quarterbacking, relying on macroeconomic data that the Fed did not yet have in September 2008? Not really. Even at the time, market forecasts indicated that money was too tight; unfortunately the Fed was looking at the wrong indicators.

As I noted earlier, on September 16, the very day of the Fed's meeting, the TIPS market showed an expected inflation rate of only 1.23% per year for the following five years, down sharply from earlier in the summer. That's far below the Fed's target, and—even worse—this bond price spread is based on CPI inflation, which tends to run a bit above the PCE inflation targeted by the Fed. And yet the Fed announcement coming out of the meeting cited equal risks of inflation and recession, and by that the policy makers meant that they feared *high* inflation.

The Fed failed to move aggressively in September 2008 because it expected inflation to run well above target for the coming few years, whereas in fact the actual inflation rate was far below target between 2008 and 2013 (1.31% for the CPI)—roughly as markets predicted. That doesn't mean that markets are always right—sometimes Fed forecasts are more accurate. But market forecasts are probably the best we have, and in this case ignoring the market contributed to a major policy error.

One way to think of market monetarism is that it combines the old-style monetarism of Milton Friedman with the theories of rational expectations and efficient markets of Robert Lucas and Eugene Fama. The older monetarists favored a steady growth rate in one of the monetary aggregates (usually M1 or M2), whereas market monetarists tend to prefer setting monetary policy at a position where *the market* expects on-target growth in M × V, which is of course nominal GDP.

I don't want to overstate the importance of the September 2008 meeting. Even if the Fed had cut the fed funds target by 0.25% or 0.5%, the US might still have experienced a deep recession in 2009. Rather, I want to emphasize this as part of a broader failure, a policy regime that was not well suited to dealing with a combination of financial crisis and low nominal interest rates. The key mistakes were the failure to do level targeting, that is, no promise to return NGDP to the pre-2008 trend line; too much reliance on internal Fed forecasts and not enough on market forecasts; and a failure to do *whatever it takes* to target the forecast, to set policy at a position where future levels of nominal spending are expected to be at the level the Fed would like to see.

A combination of level targeting and targeting the market forecast would have greatly reduced the severity of the Great Recession. In my view, the unemployment rate would have peaked at closer to 6%, not the 10% that was actually reached in late 2009. The financial crisis would also have been much milder, because confidence that NGDP would soon return to trend would have helped to support asset prices, which would in turn have boosted the balance sheets of highly leveraged firms such as Lehman.

In the next chapter we'll dig deeper into the policy failure of 2008 and after. It turns out that the Fed, and the broader economics profession, seriously misread the stance of monetary policy. To sort all this out, we need to revisit the question of how monetary policy affects interest rates. Once again, I lucked out by having an academic interest in a topic that happened to shed light on what was going wrong in 2008—the relationship between monetary policy and interest rates.

CHAPTER SIXTEEN

The Secret History of Monetary Policy

If you follow the financial news, you might assume that you have a pretty good impression of the ebb and flow of monetary policy. There are alternating periods of easy money and tight money. But chapter 11 showed that monetary policy is not so easy to recognize. I'll try to show that there are actually two histories of monetary policy: the one almost everyone thinks they see, which is widely reported in the press, and a secret history that is far more revealing but known to only a tiny group of cognoscenti. You are about to join that select group.

Interpreting Market Responses to Fed Announcements

The twenty-first century came in with a bang. Here's the *New York Times* describing the stock market on January 3, 2001: "The Dow Jones industrial average ended the day up 299.60 points, or 2.8 percent, while the Standard & Poor's 500-stock index rose 5 percent. But the wildest ride was once again on the Nasdaq composite index—which rocketed up 324.83 points, or 14.2 percent, its strongest one-day gain ever."[1] As shown in table 16.1, long-term bond yields also rose dramatically, which is not all that unusual on a day when stock prices soared.

What is unusual is that the trigger for both of these events was the same: a sudden and unexpected decision by the Fed to slash the fed funds target from 6.5% to 6.0%. Notice that while long-term bond yields were rising, short-term interest rates fell, as the Fed eased monetary policy. Let's consider why each rate changed as it did:

TABLE 16.1 **Long-term bond yields on January 4, 2001**

	Yesterday	Previous day	Year ago
Discount rate	5.75	6.00	4.50
Federal funds	6.38	6.67	5.41
3-month T-bills	5.48	5.70	5.26
6-month T-bills	5.17	5.36	5.47
10-year TIPS	3.64	3.59	4.34
10-year T-note	5.16	4.91	6.59
30-year T-bond	5.49	5.34	6.62

Source: "The Markets; Key Rates," *New York Times*, January 4, 2001.

- The fall in the fed funds and T-bill rates reflected the liquidity effect of easier money.
- The small increase in the yield on ten-year inflation-indexed notes (i.e., the real interest rate) reflects the income effect—as easier money led to expectations of faster real economic growth.
- The big increase in the (nominal) yields on ten- and thirty-year bonds reflected both the income effect (a higher real interest rate) and the Fisher effect (higher inflation expectations). Indeed, on ten-year Treasuries, the real interest rates rose by 5 basis points, inflation expectations rose by 20 basis points, and thus the nominal interest rate rose by 25 basis points (from 4.91% to 5.16%).

How do we know that the Fed announcement of January 3, 2001, caused all these extraordinarily large and sudden changes in assets prices? Here is a *New York Times* article that accompanied the bond data:

> Deciding not to wait until their scheduled meeting on Jan. 30–31, the Federal Reserve cut interest rates aggressively, reducing the federal funds rate half a percentage point, to 6 percent. The Fed also lowered the discount rate, the interest rate it charges on loans to banks, by one-quarter point, to 5.75 percent.
>
> The moves were just what depressed stock investors needed to get back into a buying mode. Shares had drifted all morning. Then, a little after 1 p.m., the Fed made its surprise announcement. Despair over the ill effects that the nation's economic slowdown was having on corporate earnings gave way to euphoria that Mr. Greenspan would once more save the day.[2]

When stocks are drifting along and then rocket upward just seconds after a Fed announcement, showing spectacular gains in a very short period of time, the only plausible explanation is that the Fed announcement in some way caused the market moves. But if you want more rigorous evidence to back up this claim, a 1997 study by the economists Michael Fleming and Eli Remolona showed that if an entire year's worth of data in the bond market is sliced up into five-minute segments, almost all the biggest price changes occur during the five minutes immediately after key economic data announcements by the federal government.[3]

A more interesting question is why the markets moved this way on January 3, 2001. In a story in the January 4 *Wall Street Journal*, the reporter was at a total loss about why a sudden announcement that the Fed was *cutting* interest rates by more than expected would cause longer-term interest rates to *rise* sharply.[4] In fairness to the reporter, short- and long-term interest rates usually move in the same direction after Fed announcements, because there are relatively few cases when a Fed announcement significantly changes the expected rate of growth or inflation. In most cases the liquidity effect dominates. But not this time.

I'm not certain what made the January 3 announcement so distinctive, but I was grateful for an example that I could use to teach my students about the liquidity, income, and Fisher effects. One cause might have been the fact that the US was teetering on the edge of a recession at the time, so markets were especially sensitive to changes in monetary policy that might dramatically affect the future path of the economy. In contrast, most Fed announcements are more boring, occurring during a period when either recession or expansion is well established.

Fed Policy at the Onset of the Great Recession

Then it happened all over again. The 2008 global financial crisis first reached the attention of policy makers in August 2007, when risk spreads suddenly widened sharply. On September 18, 2007, the Fed responded with an unexpectedly large rate cut, from 5.25% to 4.75%. Just as in January 2001, it was the first rate cut of what would eventually become a roughly 500-basis-point decline, as the economy slid into recession. And, as in 2001, it occurred just a few months before the recession began and triggered a dramatic rally on Wall Street, as reported in the next day's *New York Times*:

> The reaction in stock markets was ecstatic: the Dow Jones industrial average jumped 200 points almost instantly and ended the day up 335 points, or 2.51 percent, at 13,739.39.

The move was the Fed's first rate reduction of any kind in four years, the steepest in nearly five years and its most abrupt reversal of course since January 2001, when policy makers sharply cut rates at an unscheduled emergency meeting just before the last recession.[5]

As in 2001, the markets responded in a very unusual fashion: short-term interest rates fell (the liquidity effect) while longer-term rates increased (the income and expected inflation effects). When bond prices continued to fall on September 19, Reuters pointed to inflation fears: "U.S. Treasury debt prices slid on Wednesday as the Federal Reserve's aggressive rate cut fanned inflation worries, hurting longer-dated bonds, and boosted demand for riskier assets such as stocks."[6]

Just as the January 2001 rate cut was seen as reducing the risk of recession after the tech bubble burst, the September 2007 rate cut was regarded as doing the same after the housing bubble burst. Here's the *Wall Street Journal*: "Yesterday's news spurred hopes that the Fed may be able to keep the economy out of recession, despite the worsening housing troubles, and that it will create enough renewed confidence to get financial markets going again."[7]

Of course we now know that the Fed failed to keep the economy out of recession on both occasions. But in 2001 it almost succeeded; the country experienced a quite mild recession, during which unemployment peaked at 6.3%. The Fed could have produced the same result after the housing bubble burst with suitable monetary policy.

Many people wrongly believe that easy money boosts stock prices because a given future cash flow has more value at a lower level of interest rates. That's very misleading, as the January 2001 and September 2007 market responses show. In both cases, longer-term interest rates (which are the rates that matter when discounting future cash flows) actually rose. Thus, the dramatic rallies in stock prices occurred despite rising interest rates. In fact, easier money boosts stocks (if at all) only to the extent that it leads to expectations of faster economic growth.

The Fed Triggers the Great Recession

Then the same pattern occurred again—in reverse. December 11, 2007, saw the most interesting market reaction to a Fed announcement that I've ever seen. The National Bureau of Economic Research dated December

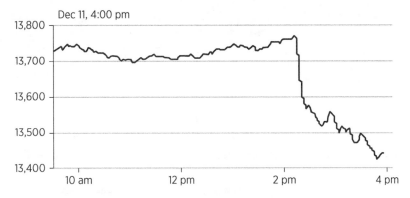

FIGURE 16.1. The Dow Jones Industrial Index on December 11, 2007

2007 as the beginning of the Great Recession, but it might as well have picked 2:15 p.m. EST on December 11, 2007. That's when the Fed announced a disappointingly small rate cut (0.25%, from 4.50% to 4.25%). I could write a whole book on this decision, because it has vast implications for monetary theory. But let's start with some basic data.

Figure 16.1 shows the stock market's reaction to the Fed's announcement. The Dow Jones Industrial Average immediately plunged by almost 1.5%, and ended the day almost 2.5% below the preannouncement level. The efficient-market hypothesis says that the immediate reaction is what counts, although there is often a delayed reaction as investors look past the headline interest-rate announcement and digest the Fed's full report, which can provide hints about the future path of policy. So let's say the announcement reduced the Dow by somewhere between 1.5% and 2.5%. The S&P 500 is a more accurate index, and it fell even more sharply than the Dow. Thus, a 1.8% to 2.8% decline is a good ballpark estimate of the impact of the announcement on US stock prices. Let's pick 2% for the S&P 500—a conservative figure.

In fact, this decline in stock prices grossly understates the impact of the December 2007 monetary shock, because before the announcement, the fed-funds futures market showed a 58% probability of a 0.25% rate cut and a 42% probability of a 0.5% rate cut. Thus, the dramatic market reaction occurred despite the fact that the actual announcement was considered the more likely outcome. A 0.5% rate cut would have likely produced an even larger move in stock prices, but in the opposite direction. If we assume that as of 2:15 p.m. on December 11 the expected return on

stocks over the following hour was near zero, then a 0.5% rate cut would
have been expected to boost stock prices by roughly

$$\frac{0.58}{0.42} \times 2\% = 2.76\%.$$

That means stocks were valued nearly 5% lower with a 4.25% fed-funds
target than they would have been with a 4.00% fed-funds target. That's a
huge difference for what most people (wrongly) consider a minor policy
adjustment.

But even this understates the impact of the Fed announcement, because stocks usually respond almost as strongly in foreign markets. (Later
we'll look at the reasons why.) If global stock-market capitalization was
about $50 trillion, then a 4% decline in global equity prices is about
$2 trillion.

Fed officials sat in a room on December 11, 2007, unsure about whether
to cut rates by 0.25% or 0.5%. It was a close call. In the end they opted for
0.25%, and this decision immediately left global wealth roughly $2 trillion
lower than if they had opted for the 50-basis-point cut. That's not just paper wealth. Markets are efficient, and tight money can destroy real wealth
by unemploying millions of productive workers and trillions of dollars in
physical capital.

As with the January 2001 and September 2007 announcements, the December 11 Fed announcement produced a powerful income and Fisher
effect. What made this decision so unusual was that these longer-term effects dominated the liquidity effect *at even three-month maturities*, as shown
in table 16.2.

We normally think of the income and Fisher effects as having a long-
run impact on interest rates, and thus mostly affecting the longer maturities. When tight money leads to a fear of recession, short-term rates rise
(the liquidity effect) and long-term rates fall. Sometimes the yield curve
will actually "invert," and longer rates will fall below the level of short-
term rates. This is a pretty good forecasting tool (albeit not quite as good
as its proponents assume—remember the dead patterns).

I recall struggling to explain the December 2007 announcement to my
students. Is it really possible that a 4.25% yield was expected to produce
lower interest rates, on average, over the following three months than a
4.00% fed-funds target? The income and Fisher effects would need to
kick in really, really fast for that to occur—faster than I've ever seen.

TABLE 16.2 **US Treasury bond yields, December 10–11, 2007**

Maturity	December 10 closing yield	December 11 closing yield
3-month	3.05%	2.94%
6-month	3.31%	3.17%
2-year	3.17%	2.94%
3-year	3.19%	2.99%
10-year	4.15%	3.98%

Source: Federal Reserve Economic Data.

And yet that's exactly what happened. Immediately after the Fed made its decision, asset markets started declining sharply. Investors became worried that the economy would enter a recession. The Fed became so worried that it took a very unusual step. Instead of waiting for their next scheduled meeting, it held an emergency meeting in early January 2008 and cut the fed funds target by a huge 0.75%. Then another 0.5% cut was announced at the next regularly scheduled meeting in late January. Once Fed officials realized how badly they'd blown it in December 2007, how far behind the curve they had fallen, they added a total of 125 basis points in rate cuts, as a sort of "make-up call."

This was Ben Bernanke's finest hour, and the rate cuts helped to stave off a severe recession for another six months. Real GDP rose in the second quarter of 2008, and a severe recession was still avoidable as late as midyear.

What lessons can we draw from all this? First, the business cycle has a powerful impact on interest rates, and (unless the Fed wants to allow a deep depression or high inflation) the Fed must follow along with changes in the natural rate of interest. Second, a monetary policy error can lead to economic changes that impact the natural rate of interest. Thus, a tight money decision can depress the economy, reducing the natural rate of interest and eventually reducing the actual rate of interest once the Fed catches on to what's happening to the economy. The bottom line is that interest rates are not a good indicator of what the Fed is doing. If the Fed had done the larger 0.5% rate cut in December, asset prices would have soared, and interest rates would have actually been *higher* in late January than they were with the smaller 0.25% cut.

Admittedly, the December 2007 example was an outlier—the liquidity effect usually dominates after Fed decisions. But that's only in the short run. When interest rates decline over a period of several years, their decline mostly reflects changes in expected real economic growth, expected

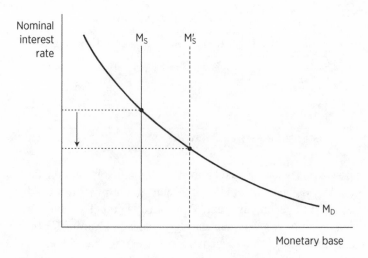

FIGURE 16.2. Conventional explanation of Federal Reserve policy, August 2007–May 2008

inflation, or both. Over longer periods of time, interest rates move lower on tight money and higher on easy money. When money is extremely easy, as in the 1970s, interest rates move much higher.

In a general sense, most good economists are aware that nominal interest rates don't just reflect the liquidity effect and thus can be misleading indicators of the stance of monetary policy. But while they understand that there can be problems in interpreting the implications of lower rates, many economists still overrate the extent to which interest rates measure the stance of monetary policy.

A good way to demonstrate this confusion is to ask an economist to illustrate Fed policy from August 2007 to May 2008. During this period, the fed-funds target fell from 5.25% to 2.00%. Economists who focus on interest rates as an indicator of the stance of monetary policy might illustrate the Fed's moves with a graph like the one shown in figure 16.2. Most economists would argue that the Fed adopted an expansionary policy during this period to boost aggregate demand, which was declining because of the housing bust. Unfortunately, the headwinds were too strong and the economy went into recession despite the Fed's best efforts.

This conventional narrative is incorrect. The monetary base did not increase between August 2007 and May 2008. In fact, just the opposite happened: the base had been trending upward for many years, and the growth in the monetary base came to a complete halt during that nine-month period. The Fed didn't cut interest rates by printing money; it stopped print-ing money and rates fell because there was a decline in money demand. Interest rates fell in late 2007 and early 2008, but expansionary monetary policy played no role in that decline. Instead, money demand shifted to the left.

Economists are taught that you should never reason from a price change, but that's a very difficult habit to shake. The ideas in this chapter (liquid-ity, income, and Fisher effects) are not difficult; we teach them to under-graduate students. But even top economists often fall into the trap of equating falling interest rates with easier money and rising interest rates with tighter money.

The secret history of monetary policy in 2007–2008 shows a Fed en-gaged in increasingly contractionary monetary policy. The Fed was not a firefighter that tried and failed to prevent recession; it was an arsonist that caused the Great Recession with tight money. Most economists probably disagree with this claim, and they'd deny that a tight money policy existed at all during 2007–2008. But their arguments are unpersuasive. Let's go over these arguments one at a time.

Are There Any Good Reasons to Deny That Money Was Tight in 2008?

When I suggest that money was tight at the onset of the Great Recession, economists often react with bewilderment. Wasn't the Fed "doing all it could" with a policy of easy money? Isn't that obvious? But when I ask these people to provide evidence, to explain what they mean by easy money, the responses are all over the map. Let's look at six plausible definitions of easy money:

1. Low nominal interest rates (vulgar Keynesian)
2. Low real interest rates (sophisticated Keynesian)
3. A fast-rising monetary base (crude monetarist)
4. Interest rates below the natural rate (New Keynesian)
5. Rising asset prices (Frederic Mishkin)
6. High inflation and NGDP growth (Ben Bernanke)

We can dismiss the first definition fairly easily. After all, interest rates are never higher than they are during hyperinflation, and I don't know of anyone who believes that hyperinflation is "tight money." Interest rates are never lower than during persistent deflation. Surely a deflationary monetary policy is not "expansionary."

When I point out the uselessness of nominal interest rates as a policy indicator, some economists suggest that the real interest rate is a good measure of the stance of monetary policy. But it suffers from the same flaws as nominal interest rates. Just as low nominal interest rates may represent deflationary expectations rather than easy money, low real interest rates may reflect falling output.

But let's suppose for a moment that real interest rates were a good indicator. Our best measure of real interest rates is the yield on TIPS, which represent both the ex ante expected real rate and the ex post actual real rate of return. Between July and early December 2008 we saw one of the sharpest increases in real interest rates ever recorded. The real yield on ten-year TIPS soared from 0.57% in July 2008 to 4.18% in late November, as shown in figure 16.3.

When I point to the sharp increase in real interest rates in the second half of 2008, just when the economy was tanking, a common reaction is, "Oh, I didn't know that." If economists really believe that the real interest rate is the right indicator, why weren't they paying attention to what it was doing in late 2008? How can economists not have noticed that real interest rates were soaring as the economy crashed?

Some people suggest that these yields were distorted by a flight to quality, which caused a rise in the price of the ultra-liquid conventional Treasury bonds and a fall in the prices of all other assets, including the less-liquid indexed bonds. (Recall that price moves inversely to yield.) But this is looking at the situation backward. In an absolute sense the TIPS were still quite safe and quite liquid. Banks had the option of earning a substantial return on TIPS, with no default risk, and thus the opportunity cost of money lent out to riskier private borrowers was rising fast. Pointing to the fact that things are so bad that the only asset people want to hold is conventional Treasuries is hardly evidence of easy money. Unfortunately, the economics profession puts too much weight on conventional Treasury yields as a policy indicator and too little on all other asset prices.

One of the strangest arguments for easy money is made by those who point to the fast-rising monetary base under the quantitative easing programs. Before 2008, few economists thought the monetary base was a good indicator of the stance of monetary policy. Even monetarists like Milton Friedman thought it was highly flawed. Most monetarist economists

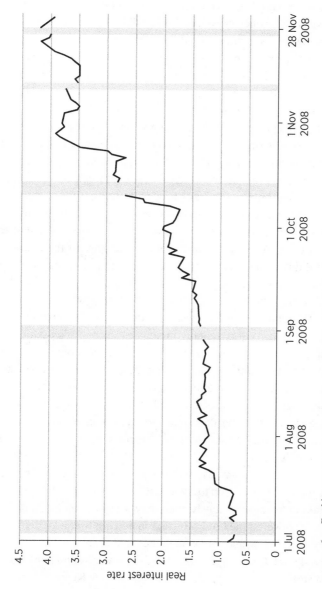

FIGURE 16.3. Real interest rates on 10-year Treasury bonds, July–December 2008

Note: Gray bars indicate non–trading days.

Source: FRED via Dow Jones & Company, https://fred.stlouisfed.org/series/DTP10J14.

preferred the broader monetary aggregates, but even those were largely abandoned after the early 1980s, when velocity became unstable. Then suddenly in 2008–2009 people started pointing to the monetary base as an indicator of the stance of monetary policy. The Fed did QE in the spring of 1932, and I don't know of any economists who regard that policy as easy money.

But again, let's suppose that the monetary base really were the right indicator. In that case, the Fed triggered the Great Recession by bringing growth in the base to a screeching halt between August 2007 and May 2008. And yet just as with the soaring real interest rates of late 2008, I find few economists who were paying attention to this slowdown in base growth. Where were the articles written in late 2007 and early 2008 complaining that the lack of growth in base money would tip the economy into recession?

Because people paid no attention to the base (before the QE program), a widely held view developed that the Great Recession was triggered by a fall in velocity. People holding this view often try to distinguish between errors of omission and errors of commission. They'll say that the Fed might have not moved aggressively enough to prevent the recession, but the Fed didn't actually cause it. Instead, in their view, the recession was triggered by falling velocity.

But that's false. The entire slowdown in NGDP growth in late 2007 and early 2008, in an accounting sense, was due to slowing growth in the monetary base; velocity was actually increasing during this period. The Fed was using "concrete steps" to directly push the economy into recession, and the private sector was valiantly fighting back by boosting velocity. Think about how far that reality is from the perception of the average educated observer at the time, or even today.

Just to be clear, I'd argue that tight money was to blame regardless of whether the base was increasing or decreasing in early 2008. As did almost all economists before 2008, I think the base is a poor indicator of the stance of monetary policy. My point is that those who claim the base is the right indicator often don't pay attention to what it is telling us. If they were taking the base seriously, then they'd be arguing that a decline in base growth triggered the Great Recession and a subsequent decline in velocity made it much worse. But who makes that claim?

Let's consider the three respectable definitions of easy and tight money, all of which support my interpretation of events. New Keynesian models suggest that what really matters is not the real or the nominal interest rate, but the market interest rate relative to the (unobservable) natural rate of interest, which is the interest rate consistent with a stable macroeconomy. Figure 16.4 shows an estimate of the natural rate of interest in recent years, measured in real terms.[8]

Beginning in 2007, the natural interest rate fell well below the actual market interest rate and stayed below it for many years. That means that money was much too tight. In later years this might have been partly attributable to the zero-bound problem, as the natural rate fell below zero. But that was no excuse in 2007 and 2008, when the actual interest rate had not yet hit the zero bound. It was tight money that caused the Great Recession, using the New Keynesian criterion.

I taught monetary economics for decades using a textbook by Frederic Mishkin, which was the top-selling text for such courses. Mishkin suggested that because nominal interest rates were not a good indicator of the stance of monetary policy, we should look to "other asset prices" instead.[9] Indeed, virtually every other asset price was screaming "tight money" in late 2008. We've already seen real interest rates; now let's look at commodity prices and the stock market (fig. 16.5) and the foreign exchange value of the dollar (fig. 16.6). Notice that both stock and commodity prices plunged sharply in late 2008, consistent with tight money.

Figure 16.6 is especially interesting, because in the vast majority of cases a country's currency plunges in value during a financial crisis. Think about the fact that as the US was experiencing its worst financial crisis since the early 1930s, the value of the dollar was soaring in the foreign exchange market. I can recall only a few similar examples, including the US in 1931–1932, Japan in the early 1990s, and Argentina in 1998–2001, and in each case the anomalous moves in exchange rates are now viewed as representing an inappropriately contractionary monetary policy. Eventually, late 2008 will be seen the same way.

Everywhere you looked in late 2008 the same story appeared. House prices in parts of the US that had avoided the original subprime crash (e.g., Texas) began falling. Commercial real estate prices had held up well until the second half of 2008 and then began falling. Inflation expectations embedded in TIPS prices began falling sharply in the second half of 2008. Other than (ultra-safe) conventional Treasury bonds, it is difficult to find a single asset that did not do poorly once NGDP started falling.

In chapter 11, I argued in favor of Bernanke's criteria for evaluating monetary policy—inflation and especially NGDP growth. These are closest to the goals of monetary policy, and hence they provide an indication of whether money is easy or tight *relative to the stance required to hit the Fed's targets*. And as we've already seen, money in the second half of 2008

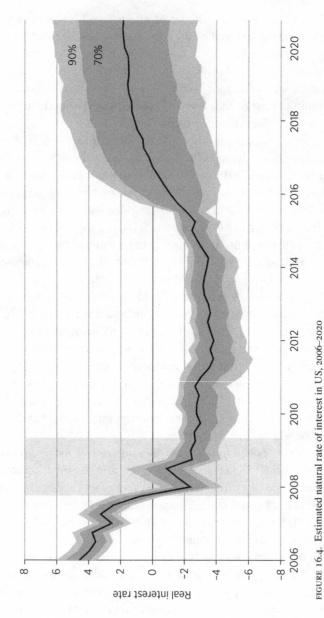

FIGURE 16.4. Estimated natural rate of interest in US, 2006–2020

Source: Vasco Curdia, "Why So Slow? A Gradual Return for Interest Rates," Federal Reserve Bank of San Francisco, October 12, 2015, https://www.frbsf.org/economic-research/publications/economic-letter/2015/october/gradual-return-to-normal-natural-rate-of-interest/.

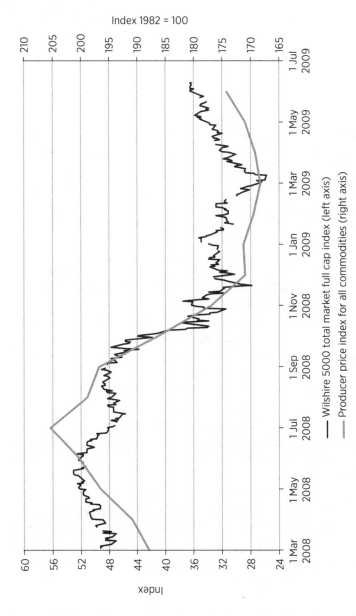

Index 1982 = 100

— Wilshire 5000 total market full cap index (left axis)
— Producer price index for all commodities (right axis)

FIGURE 16.5. US commodity and stock market prices, 2008–2009

Source: FRED via Wilshire Associates and Bureau of Labor Statistics https://fred.stlouisfed.org/series/PPIACO, https://fred.stlouisfed.org/series/WILL5000INDFC.

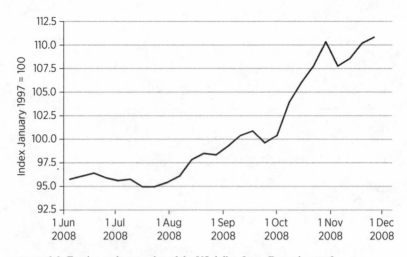

FIGURE 16.6. Foreign exchange value of the US dollar, June–December 2008

Source: FRED via Board of Governors of the Federal Reserve System (US), https://fred.stlouisfed.org/series /TWEXB.

was extremely tight according to this criterion, with the slowest five-year growth in NGDP since the early 1930s.

To summarize, there is a yawning chasm between the various criteria that sophisticated economists use to evaluate the stance of monetary policy and the perception in the popular news media. Whereas most people think they saw an expansionary monetary policy in 2008 that lacked enough firepower to offset a severe financial crisis, the evidence suggests that monetary policy was quite contractionary and very likely helped cause both the financial crisis and the Great Recession.

That's not to say that monetary policy was the only problem during this period. The early stages of the financial crisis in August 2007 predate the period of tight money. Even with appropriate monetary policy there might have been a mild recession in 2008. And if there had not been a recession, substantial inflation would have been associated with a modest decline in living standards. But the NGDP did not have to fall by 3% between mid-2008 and mid-2009 (8% below trend). This fall led to 10% unemployment, a far more severe financial crisis, and a larger-than-necessary loss in housing wealth.

In the next chapter we'll continue to work our way through the list of cognitive errors laid out in chapter 14. Fortunately, an excellent outline of the next chapter already exists, written by Ben Bernanke. In a 1999 paper entitled "Japanese Monetary Policy: A Case of Self-Induced Paralysis?," Bernanke brilliantly dissected the policy mistakes of the Bank of Japan, as it failed to stop deflation from taking hold. Much of his analysis shows an eerie similarity to the critique of Fed policy contained in this book, and because of that, I've borrowed his title for chapter 17.

PART V

The Great Recession

CHAPTER SEVENTEEN

Fed Policy in 2008

A Case of Self-Induced Paralysis?

I was quite pleased when Ben Bernanke was nominated to become chair of the Fed back in 2006. Bernanke's academic work included studies of the Great Depression that reached conclusions similar to those of my own work. We both focused on the deflationary impact of the interwar gold standard, as well as the problem of sticky nominal wages. Bernanke had also been critical of the passivity shown by the Bank of Japan in the face of years of mild deflation. He seemed an ideal choice to lead the Fed.

Once I began blogging, I became very critical of Fed policy. However, I've never been as negative about Bernanke as have some critics with similar policy views. The challenges of governance are very different from the challenges of academia, and it's easy to draw up optimal plans on a blackboard when you don't have a powerful, entrenched Fed staff, hawkish regional Fed presidents, and congressional committees breathing down your neck. I continue to believe that at the margin Bernanke was a positive force in policy making during his tenure at the Fed, so please take the criticisms in this chapter in that spirit.

Bernanke's 1999 Critique of the Bank of Japan

In early 2010, my fellow market monetarist Marcus Nunes sent me an eleven-year-old paper by Ben Bernanke that contained a remarkable number of similarities to various points I had made in my first year of blogging. The difference, of course, was that Bernanke was criticizing BOJ passivity at the zero bound, whereas I was criticizing Fed passivity at the zero bound. Here are some of the points Bernanke made back in 1999:

With respect to the issue of inflation targets and BOJ credibility, I do not see how credibility can be harmed by straightforward and honest dialogue of policy-makers with the public. In stating an inflation target of, say, 3–4%, the BOJ would be giving the public information about its objectives, and hence the direction in which it will attempt to move the economy. (And, as I will argue, the Bank does have tools to move the economy.)

Nonstandard open-market operations with a fiscal component, even if legal, would be correctly viewed as an end run around the authority of the legislature, and so are better left in the realm of theoretical curiosities.

... The yen has undergone a nominal appreciation since 1991, a strange outcome for a country in deep recession. Even more disturbing is the very strong appreciation that has occurred since 1998Q3, from about 145 yen/dollar in August 1998 to 102 yen/dollar in December 1999, as the Japanese economy has fallen back into recession. Since interest rates on yen assets are very low, this appreciation suggests that speculators are anticipating even greater rates of deflation and yen appreciation in the future.[1]

All I would add here is that the strong appreciation in the dollar during late 2008 was an equally "strange outcome for a country in deep recession."

Bernanke also mocked the view that a central bank could run out of ammunition:

To rebut this [pessimistic] view, one can apply a *reductio ad absurdum* argument, based on my earlier observation that money issuance must affect prices, else printing money will create infinite purchasing power. Suppose the Bank of Japan prints yen and uses them to acquire foreign assets. If the yen did not depreciate as a result, and if there were no reciprocal demand for Japanese goods or assets (which would drive up domestic prices), what in principle would prevent the BOJ from acquiring infinite quantities of foreign assets, leaving foreigners nothing to hold but idle yen balances? Obviously this will not happen in equilibrium.[2]

Then Bernanke argued that the real problem was nominal—that is, an aggregate demand shortfall:

I tend to agree with the conventional wisdom that attributes much of Japan's current dilemma to exceptionally poor monetary policy-making over the past fifteen years. ... If the Japanese monetary policy after 1985 had focused on stabilizing aggregate demand and inflation, rather than being distracted by the exchange rate or asset prices, the results would have been much better.

I do not deny that important structural problems, in the financial system and elsewhere, are helping to constrain Japanese growth. But I also believe that there is compelling evidence that the Japanese economy is also suffering today from an aggregate demand deficiency. *If monetary policy could deliver increased nominal spending*, some of the difficult structural problems that Japan faces would no longer seem so difficult.[3]

Not only is demand the core problem, more demand would actually reduce the severity of Japan's financial problems:

Again the picture is consistent with an economy in which nominal aggregate demand is growing too slowly for the patient's health. It is remarkable, for example, that nominal GDP grew by less than 1% per annum in 1993, 1994, and 1995, and actually declined by more than two percentage points in 1998.[4]

Bernanke then rejected the view that the low level of interest rates implied that Japanese monetary policy was expansionary:

The argument that current monetary policy in Japan is in fact quite accommodative rests largely on the observation that interest rates are at a very low level. *I do hope that readers who have gotten this far will be sufficiently familiar with monetary history not to take seriously any such claim based on the level of the nominal interest rate.* One need only recall that nominal interest rates remained close to zero in many countries throughout the Great Depression, a period of massive monetary contraction and deflationary pressure. In short, low nominal interest rates may just as well be a sign of expected deflation and monetary tightness as of monetary ease.....

My second response to the real-interest-rate argument is to note that today's real interest rate may not be a sufficient statistic for the cumulative effects of tight monetary policy on the economy.[5]

And then he suggested looking at inflation rather than interest rates:

One might want to consider indicators other than the current real interest rate—*for example, the cumulative gap between the actual and the expected price level*—in assessing the effects of monetary policy.[6]

Bernanke insisted that even if there were a liquidity trap, monetary policy could still boost nominal spending:

It is true that current monetary conditions in Japan limit the effectiveness of standard open-market operations. However, as I will argue in the remainder of the paper, liquidity trap or no, monetary policy retains considerable power to expand nominal aggregate demand. Our diagnosis of what ails the Japanese economy implies that these actions could do a great deal to end the ten-year slump.[7]

The paper concludes with a forceful call for a more expansionary monetary policy:

Japan is not in a Great Depression by any means, but its economy has operated below potential for nearly a decade. Nor is it by any means clear that recovery is imminent. Policy options exist that could greatly reduce these losses. Why isn't more happening? To this outsider, at least, Japanese monetary policy seems paralyzed, with a paralysis that is largely self-induced. Most striking is the apparent unwillingness of the monetary authorities to experiment, to try anything that isn't absolutely guaranteed to work. Perhaps it's time for some Rooseveltian resolve in Japan.[8]

The best way for the Fed to have shown "Rooseveltian resolve" in 2008–2009 would have been to set a more aggressive policy target, perhaps by adopting the sort of level targeting that Bernanke recommended to the Japanese. Alas, it never happened. Nor was there any significant outside pressure on the Fed to do more. Indeed, much of the criticism of the Fed during this period was from people complaining that policy was *too expansionary*. There were warnings that Fed policies such as quantitative easing would lead to high inflation. These complaints led a few astute pundits to recall a famous remark by Ralph Hawtrey, when similar misguided concerns were being expressed during the (deflationary) Great Depression: "Fantastic fears of inflation were expressed. That was to cry Fire, Fire in Noah's Flood."[9] Indeed.

Bernanke's 2003 Suggestions for Boosting Inflation in Japan

By 2003, Bernanke had joined the Board of Governors of the Federal Reserve. Soon after, he delivered a speech with three suggestions for dealing with the zero-bound problem:

First, . . . [r]ather than proposing the more familiar inflation target, I will suggest that the BOJ consider adopting a price-level target, which would imply a

period of reflation to offset the effects on prices of the recent period of deflation. Second, I would like to consider . . . the relationship between the condition of the Bank of Japan's balance sheet and its ability to undertake more
aggressive monetary policies. Although, in principle, balance-sheet consider-
ations should not seriously constrain central bank policies, in practice they do.
However . . . relatively simple measures that would eliminate this constraint are
available. Finally, and most important, I will consider one possible strategy for
ending the deflation in Japan: explicit, though temporary, cooperation between
the monetary and the fiscal authorities.[10]

In 2006, Bernanke was appointed chair of the Federal Reserve. During
the Great Recession, Bernanke did call for fiscal and monetary cooperation, but the actual fiscal stimulus provided was not very effective. However, the Fed did not take Bernanke's advice on either level targeting or
the Fed balance sheet. Instead, it continued to engage in inflation-rate targeting, even though the theoretical literature is quite clear that price-level
targeting is more effective at the zero bound. And it continued to worry
about the Fed's balance sheet, which Bernanke quite rightly pointed out
is a phony problem. This worry, in fact, contributed to the premature end
of each of the three QE programs.

I suppose one could argue that people have a right to change their
minds, and that joining the Fed might have given Bernanke a deeper understanding of the limits of monetary policy. If so, he lost this "deeper
understanding" soon after leaving the Fed: in 2017 he came out with a
proposal that price-level targeting be adopted during periods when the
economy is at the zero bound. This is not identical to what he discussed
earlier, but it provides almost all the gains from a permanent regime of
level targeting because the only real need for level targeting occurs at the
zero bound.

The point of all this is not to pick on Bernanke. He faced extraordinary opposition to monetary stimulus, both within and outside the Fed.
Transcripts clearly show that Bernanke worked hard to nudge the Fed's
hawkish members in a more accommodating direction. All one has to do
is compare the Fed to the European Central Bank under Jean-Claude
Trichet to see how things could have been far worse with a less enlightened
leader than Bernanke. Rather, the point of this exercise is to show that the
Fed possessed all the tools that were needed for a far more expansionary
monetary policy during 2008–2013, yet it failed to fully utilize those tools.

Although the Fed did better than the ECB, an even more aggressive
policy would have done a better job of achieving the Fed's inflation and

employment targets. So why didn't it do more? One factor was concern over balance-sheet risk. A highly expansionary policy could have led to higher inflation, and thus higher nominal interest rates. This would have depressed the price of the Fed's vast holdings of bonds purchased with the QE program.

This fear was unwarranted. In a budgetary sense, the Fed is part of the federal government. Its large profits are mostly turned over to the Treasury (after being used to cover the Fed's operating expenses). Because the Fed's T-bond assets are the Treasury's liability, any change in the value of its bond portfolio is a wash for the consolidated federal government balance sheet. Back in 2003, Bernanke clearly understood that this was a phony issue:

> Moreover, the budgetary implications of this proposal would be essentially zero, since any increase in interest payments to the BOJ by the MOF arising from the bond conversion would be offset by an almost equal increase in the BOJ's payouts to the national treasury. The budgetary neutrality of the proposal is of course a consequence of the fact that, as a matter of arithmetic, any capital gains or losses in the value of government securities held by the BOJ are precisely offset by opposite changes in the net worth of the issuer of those securities, the government treasury.[11]

The actual balance-sheet problem is political: the fear among Fed officials that they might have to report to Congress that the Fed is technically insolvent.

While Bernanke points out that reflation could help to improve the labor market and reduce unemployment, his most forceful arguments in the 2003 speech involved another benefit—reducing financial distress:

> One benefit of reflation would be to ease some of the intense pressure on debtors and on the financial system more generally. Since the early 1990s, borrowers in Japan have repeatedly found themselves squeezed by disinflation or deflation, which has required them to pay their debts in yen of greater value than they had expected. Borrower distress has affected the functioning of the whole economy, for example by weakening the banking system and depressing investment spending.[12]

This is correct, and indeed contractionary monetary policy presumably also contributed to the 2008 US financial crisis, when NGDP growth fell

to the lowest rate since 1949. But neither Bernanke nor any other prominent American economist drew that connection. For some reason, it was
easy for American economists to see how tight money in faraway Japan
had worsened that country's financial situation but much harder to recognize that mechanism in the US, when the tight money was implemented
by highly respected economists and represented something close to the
consensus view of elite American macroeconomists.

This is part of a much deeper problem in modern macroeconomics: the
tendency to view elite institutions as being close to infallible, and then to
let that assumption distort the construction of models of causality. Perhaps the most egregious example of this occurred after the zero-bound
period ended in 2015. In 2017, former Fed governor Jeremy Stein argued
that the below-2% level of inflation may have reflected an inability of the
Fed to raise inflation to the target, despite the fact that by 2017 the Fed
was repeatedly raising interest rates with the avowed goal of reducing inflation![13] This is like a car buyer complaining to the dealer, "My new car
has trouble accelerating to sixty miles per hour, despite repeated taps on
the brake."

Why did so many prominent economists question the Fed's ability to
boost inflation during a period when the Fed was explicitly trying to restrain inflation? My only explanation is that this fatalism occurred out of
a sense of exaggerated confidence in the ability of central bankers. If they
failed, the task must be impossible.

Why Did the Fed Stop Targeting the Forecast?

In order to be effective, monetary policy must consistently "target the
forecast." Policy needs to be set at a position where the central bank's
forecasts for the goal variables (e.g., inflation, NGDP) are equal to the
policy goal. During the so-called Great Moderation, policy generally
adhered pretty closely to this criterion.[14] At some point in late 2008 it
stopped doing so and became complacent, fatalistic, defeatist. Policy was
set at a position where the Fed itself understood that the US was likely to
undershoot its inflation and employment targets.

One way to visualize an efficient policy regime is to imagine how policy
makers would feel about surprise moves in aggregate demand. Under an
efficient policy regime, unexpected increases or decreases in aggregate
demand would be equally unwelcome. NGDP is expected to grow at a

target rate, and any shortfall or overshoot would be viewed as destabilizing for the economy.

From late 2008 until at least 2014 (and probably longer), the Fed was
basically hoping that NGDP would grow faster than it forecast. Faster-
than-expected growth in nominal spending was treated as "good news,"
and slower-than-expected growth in nominal spending was treated as bad
news. This state of affairs lasted so long that people began to view it as
normal, especially because it is basically the way incumbent politicians
who are worried about the next election view things even when the economy is operating normally and extra spending is not actually desirable.

The idea of targeting the forecast is so obviously logical that many
people cannot even envision any other approach to policy. Why would a
central bank ever set its policy levers at a position where it expected to
fail to hit its target? That makes no sense. Indeed, targeting the forecast
is so consistent with common sense that when it became obvious that aggregate demand was below the level the Fed wished to see, people simply
assumed that the Fed was out of ammunition. Many people assumed that
this was also Bernanke's view, even though throughout the Great Recession Bernanke consistently denied that the Fed was out of ammunition.
The Fed made it very clear that it could have done more to boost aggregate demand, but like Melville's Bartleby the scrivener, it simply choose
not to. But why not?

As the period of high unemployment and low inflation dragged on, reporters finally began asking more pointed questions. Why wasn't the Fed
doing more? Bernanke referred to ill-defined "costs and risks" of doing
more QE. Based on both his academic writings and the transcripts of Fed
meetings (released after a five-year lag), it is pretty clear that Bernanke
actually thought these costs and risks were overstated, at least in a technical sense.

That's not to say his perspective did not change at all after becoming
Fed chair. Obviously it's easier for an academic like me to say that the
Fed's balance sheet is a nonissue, and even that Fed bankruptcy would be
unimportant, than it would be for someone who would have to explain to
congressional committees why the Fed needed to be recapitalized. Bernanke was receiving pressure from all sides, and he clearly did not see QE
as the sort of infinitely powerful tool for boosting nominal spending that
an academic like me might claim it to be.

To summarize, once it became clear that there was a shortfall in aggregate demand, the Fed understood what needed to be done. And Bernanke

certainly knew what had to be done, since his critique of BOJ policy in the late 1990s and the decade following is quite similar to my critique of Fed policy during the Great Recession. The real problem was political. Unlimited QE exposed the Fed to balance sheet risks, or, more accurately, to the perception of risk—and in politics it is perceptions that matter. A switch to level targeting might have led to doubts about Fed credibility. The Fed had worked hard to convince the markets and the broader public that it would keep inflation close to 2%, whereas level targeting of prices might have required a period of catch-up inflation, running well above 2% for several years.

There is one other tool that might have been used—negative interest on reserves. Unfortunately, when the Fed did finally get around to adopting a program of interest on reserves, it set the rate on the wrong side of zero—that is, it set a positive rate. This may have been the single biggest mistake of 2008, and it deserves a chapter of its own.

CHAPTER EIGHTEEN

A Confession of Contractionary Effect

In 2006, the Fed was able to convince Congress to allow it to pay interest on bank reserves, beginning in 2011. Then in early October 2008, right during the worst of the financial panic, the Fed asked Congress to move up the starting date of the program, to authorize immediate payment of interest on reserves.

In retrospect, it seems unlikely that members of Congress understood what they were approving or why the Fed wanted this authority in the midst of a financial crisis. Most average people would defer to experts at the Federal Reserve in the middle of a financial crisis, especially over an arcane technical issue like interest on bank reserves. And when it comes to monetary theory, members of Congress are clearly average people.

The Stanford economist Robert Hall is most certainly not an average person when it comes to monetary theory, and (in an essay coauthored with Susan Woodward) he saw right through the Fed's policy request: "Oddly, [Bernanke] explained the new policy of paying 1 percent interest on reserves as a way of elevating short-term rates up to the Fed's target level of 1 percent. This amounts to a confession of the contractionary effect of the reserve interest policy."[1] That's right, the policy of paying interest on reserves, which was instituted during a period of sharply falling prices, sharply falling output, plunging stock prices, rising unemployment, and severe financial distress, was a *contractionary monetary policy*. Who says so? Actually, the Fed said so. The Fed's own explanation pointed to the contractionary intent of the policy—its sole purpose was to keep interest rates from falling. Indeed, when the policy was first implemented, the target interest rate was still 1.5%.[2]

This raises all sorts of questions: Why would the Fed do something so seemingly counterproductive? Why did the broader economics profession mostly ignore this policy error? Why didn't the Fed institute a negative interest rate on reserves? How did this policy affect asset prices? Why did the Fed double down on an interest-rate-oriented policy regime just when that sort of regime was failing? It turns out that IOR provides several keys to understanding the Great Recession, and also illustrates the usefulness of the market-monetarist approach to economics.

Yes, the Intent Was Contractionary

There is a surprisingly simple answer to the puzzle of why the Fed started paying IOR on October 8, 2008. Recall that on September 16, 2008, the Federal Open Market Committee had met two days after Lehman Brothers failed and decided to keep the fed funds target fixed at 2%. Furthermore, we know why the committee refused to ease policy: the minutes of the meeting noted that the Fed perceived a risk of both recession and high inflation. The committee viewed these risks as being roughly balanced (despite market indicators suggesting quite low inflation going forward, as noted earlier), and thus decided to stand pat.

Over the following few weeks a global banking crisis developed increasing momentum, and there were emergency meetings involving the Fed, the Treasury, and top congressional officials. This was the period of an initially failed but ultimately successful attempt to get the Troubled Asset Relief Program "bailout" through Congress. This was also when the global banking system started freezing up and the stock market began a dramatic decline. In response to the financial crisis, the Fed injected lots of liquidity into the banking system, sharply increasing the monetary base.

Until 2008, the Fed paid no interest on base money (cash plus bank reserves). Under that traditional system, an injection of new base money generally led to lower short-term interest rates in the short run. Without interest on reserves, the massive injection of liquidity during the crisis would have immediately pushed interest rates down to zero. That would actually have been very good, but at the time the Fed perceived lower rates to be a bad outcome. It still feared high inflation.

A cynic might say that the Fed used IOR so that it could rescue Wall Street without rescuing Main Street. The adoption of interest on reserves allowed the Fed to inject enough liquidity into the economy to rescue big banks without depressing interest rates and boosting aggregate demand for the goods and services produced out in the real economy. I'm not that cynical; I believe the Fed was well intentioned. Nonetheless, that is essentially what it was trying to do—provide liquidity to fix a collapsing financial system without boosting aggregate demand and inflation.

At this point there are two ways of thinking about the IOR experiment. Defenders of interest on reserves claim that IOR was not the real problem; the real problem was that money was too tight because the Fed set its fed funds target too high. I do understand that defense of IOR, and it does exhibit a sort of logic. But in the end I don't fully agree. I still regard IOR as a serious mistake, for two reasons. First, the Fed was quite determined to provide massive liquidity during the banking crisis. It began doing so even before IOR was authorized. It would have done so even if Congress had not moved up the authorization of IOR to October 2008. The only difference would have been that without IOR the liquidity injections would inevitably have eased monetary policy, which would clearly have been beneficial. There is, though, a second, more subtle problem with IOR. It represents one more step moving monetary economics away from a focus on the supply and demand for base money and toward a focus on interest rates. And the focus on interest rates is something close to the original sin of modern macroeconomics. It leads to a widespread problem of misdiagnosis, as economists wrongly assume that low rates mean easy money, and hence that the Fed could not possibly be causing the Great Recession. It also led to interest rate targeting, which is a policy lever that freezes up at zero rates, just when policy makers most need an effective tool.

Supporters of IOR sometimes point to the interest rate focus of policy as an advantage of interest on reserves. They develop theoretical models of an economy with no money. They say that IOR makes the quantity of money almost irrelevant. That's not quite true: money is still neutral in the long run, even with IOR.[3] But it is true that changes in the supply of money are much less informative when you are operating under a regime of paying interest on reserves.

I see these perceived advantages as actually being disadvantages. Monetary policy works best when the quantity theory of money underpinnings are most visible. Money needs to be kept front and center, and interest rates relegated to the background.

Why Did Economists Miss the Problem?

Today, the adoption of IOR in October 2008 looks like a huge mistake, an unforced error. So why weren't economists more critical?

A few of them were critical. And it is interesting that most of those who noticed the problem tended to use a monetarist approach to analyzing monetary policy. David Beckworth, one of the original market monetarists, wrote a blog post in late 2008 pointing to the similarity between interest on reserves and the Fed's famous decision to double reserve requirements during 1936–1937, which contributed to a double-dip recession in 1937–1938.[4] This earlier policy was well documented by Milton Friedman and Anna Schwartz in their book *A Monetary History of the United States*, and it is perhaps the most famous example of the Fed using reserve requirements as a tool of monetary policy. Both policies had the effect of increasing the demand for base money, which is clearly a contractionary action.

So now there have been two major examples of the Fed using monetary policy to sharply boost the demand for base money. Monetarists view both policies as serious mistakes. Even Keynesians agree that the 1937 reserve requirement decision was a big mistake, but for some reason many dismiss the importance of the Fed instituting IOR in October 2008. By December 2008, the rate of IOR was cut to 0.25%. Many economists that I spoke with wondered how a measly 0.25% could be all that important, forgetting that the infamous 1937 reserve requirement increase also boosted rates by only about 0.25%, and also forgetting that interest rates are a very poor indicator of the stance of monetary policy. Even a tiny change in interest rates can tip policy from a highly expansionary stance to a highly contractionary stance.

Ironically, a policy of IOR would have actually made a lot of sense in late 2008, as long as the interest rate had been set at a negative level.

During the latter part of 2008 I was trying to get newspapers to publish my views on monetary policy, with no success. I was able to get a couple of short papers published in the *Economists' Voice* in January and March 2009.[5] In both articles I mentioned that a negative IOR would be a better option. This was also the subject of my very first blog post (after the introductory post).[6] Today the decision to pay a positive rate of IOR in 2008 is widely recognized as a mistake, so it is interesting that market monetarists seem to have been among the first to notice the problem.

Over time, I started to receive pushback on the idea of negative IOR. Some critics suggested that I knew very little about banking (which is true) and that the idea would never work. I was told that serious central bankers would never consider such a wacky idea. Several columns in the *Financial Times* even insisted that a policy of negative IOR would be contractionary.

This is not a mistake that a monetarist would be likely to make, because negative IOR clearly reduces the demand for base money, which would be expansionary. But most people don't look at monetary issues from a monetarist perspective; they use a finance perspective. Most pundits think in terms of credit, not the supply and demand for money. In this finance-oriented view, if the policy of negative IOR reduces credit, it would be contractionary.

By 2016, negative IOR was a reality in many of the most important developed economies, including the eurozone, Switzerland, Denmark, Sweden, and Japan. When countries adopted negative IOR, the markets reacted to the news as if the policy were indeed expansionary, just as the monetarists had predicted. For instance, an unexpectedly sharp decline in IOR, into negative territory, generally caused currencies to depreciate in the foreign exchange market—a sign of expansionary impact.

That's not to say that the policies were highly effective; we've already seen that interest rates are not a particularly reliable tool of monetary policy. But the direction of the effect is clear: if you tax something, you reduce the demand for the thing being taxed. And less demand for base money is expansionary for nominal spending.

It's also important to recognize that the adoption of negative IOR does not make the zero-lower-bound problem go away; it merely reduces it to a lower level—the point at which bank reserves start getting converted into cash. We don't know exactly where that "effective lower bound" is, but 0.75% seems to be about the furthest negative that central banks have been willing to push nominal interest rates.[7]

Central banks aiming for negative rates are helped by governments' increasingly hostile stance toward the use of cash. Merely withdrawing $3,000 at a time in a series of "structured" transactions is considered illegal in the US, because it may be evidence of an attempt to evade the $10,000 threshold at which banks must report cash transactions. Arresting someone for withdrawing $3,000 several times in a row is analogous to the police pulling someone over for driving at precisely the speed limit, and accusing the person of obeying the law to avoid being pulled over for speeding (and perhaps having the car searched for drugs). In this anti-cash climate, large institutions do not wish to stuff billions of dollars in currency into safe deposit boxes, and hence they are forced to accept negative returns on funds temporarily parked in safe assets such as German government bonds.

This does not mean that there is no effective lower bound on nominal interest rates. It seems unlikely that people would be willing to accept

−3% interest for any sustained period of time. Thus, the focus of policy should continue to be in other areas, such as quantitative easing, the adoption of a nominal GDP level target, or even a higher inflation target, as a way of reducing the demand for base money.

How Contractionary Was the Policy of Interest on Reserves?

In 2010, I came across a very interesting article by *Forbes* writer Louis Woodhill, discussing the stock market reaction to the adoption of interest on reserves:

> At the time of the Fed's IOR announcement, the S&P 500 was down by a total of 12.18% from its pre-Lehman close, 15 trading days earlier. However, the day that the Fed announced IOR, the S&P 500 fell by 3.85%, and it was down by a total of 17.22% three days later.
>
> On October 22, 2008, the Fed announced that it would increase the interest rate that it paid on reserves. The S&P 500 fell by 6.10% that day, and it was down by a total of 11.11% three days later. On November 5, 2008, the Fed announced another increase in the IOR interest rate. The S&P 500 fell by 5.27% that day, and it was down by a total of 8.60% three days later.[8]

At first glance that's pretty impressive. During the Great Recession, the rate of interest on reserves was increased exactly three times. On each of those three occasions, stock prices fell sharply soon after the announcement, and they fell even more sharply over the following three days. In fact, the majority of the major bear market of late 2008 occurred over those three four-day windows, a total of twelve trading days.

This market reaction also fits my theory that the policy was a contractionary mistake by the Fed. Nonetheless, we also need to recall the message of chapter 14 ("I See Dead Patterns"), which is that people tend to spot correlations that are not actually there. More specifically, it is not clear why we should look at a four-day window. The efficient-market hypothesis suggests that the market reaction should be immediate.

I suppose you could tell a story in which IOR was an unfamiliar concept and it took markets a while to catch on. Maybe they didn't respond to the actual announcement of each rate change but to the perception that banks were increasing their demand for reserves in response to the policy. As much as I'd like to accept that hypothesis, I cannot quite do so. It seems too much like cherry-picking data to fit a preconceived idea.

Yet the immediate response to the Fed announcement is also sugges-
tive. Single-day declines of 3.85%, 6.10%, and 5.27% are unusually large.
If stocks fell by 15% because of three misguided increases in IOR, that by
itself would be a really big deal. So how seriously can we take the first-day
responses to these news events?

One reason to be cautious is that while a 5% single-day move in the
S&P 500 is quite unusual, it was not all that atypical in late 2008, when
the market was much more volatile than usual. So perhaps these three declines are not all that significant. On the other hand, we've already seen
that stocks often move sharply in response to major monetary policy announcements, and there are other examples from late 2008 when monetary policy clearly moved markets. For instance, stocks soared by 5.14%
on December 16, 2008, when the Fed slashed its interest rate target from
1% to a range of 0%–0.25%. And here's the *New York Times* on October 13, 2008:

> On Monday, for the first time this October, the Dow Jones industrial average
> ended the day higher than it began. Nine hundred and thirty-six points higher,
> to be exact, making for the biggest single-day percentage gain in 75 years.
>
> The surge came as governments and central banks around the world
> mounted an aggressive, coordinated campaign to unlock the global flow of
> credit, an effort that investors said they had been waiting for.[9]

Consider also this *New York Times* story from October 28, 2008:

> Wall Street indexes staged a rally Tuesday afternoon as expectations of a fed-
> eral interest rate cut helped lure investors back into the market, despite new
> signs that the broader economy continued to weaken.
>
> On a day when a consumer confidence report that showed Americans were
> more pessimistic about the economy in October than at anytime in 41 years, the
> Dow Jones industrial average rose 889.35 points, or 10.8 percent, to 9,065.12,
> closing above 9,000 for the first time in a week.
>
> The broader Standard & Poor's 500-stock index was 10.79 percent or
> 91.59 points higher, and the technology-heavy Nasdaq was up 9.53 percent or
> 143.57 points.
>
> Shares in Europe also finished higher. The Dow Jones Euro Stoxx 50 index,
> a barometer of euro zone blue chips, rose 3.8 percent, while the FTSE 100 in-
> dex in London gained 1.9 percent. The CAC 40 in Paris rose 1.5 percent.
>
> And the DAX in Frankfurt was 11.2 percent higher.[10]

The 10.79% rise in the S&P 500 was one of the largest single-day increases in history.

It didn't take a PhD to see the connection between monetary policy and financial markets during late 2008. I recall watching CNBC on November 6, 2008, and seeing Jim Cramer go into one of his famous rants. He noted that markets had rallied on an aggressive 1.5% rate cut by the Bank of England but then were severely disappointed by the lack of follow-though shortly after by the European Central Bank, which cut rates by only 0.5%. Cramer was often teased for his famous rant from 2007 (which spread far and wide on YouTube), when he railed against the cluelessness of the Fed in the face of a growing banking crisis.[11] But in retrospect Cramer was right both times and the world's top central banks were wrong.

Note that the November 6, 2008, decline after the ECB failed to act occurred during one of Louis Woodhill's four-day windows—further reason to be careful when attributing market changes to specific monetary announcements. However, an overly dismissive attitude toward these correlations is also inappropriate, because we often observe huge market moves within *seconds* of important monetary policy announcements. There is little doubt that monetary policy is an important factor in high-frequency stock-market moves, especially during periods of distress.

Memories of a Murdered Economy

An interesting aspect of the Great Recession is how widely misremembered it is. Even elite economists often have a very distorted recollection of what happened in the second half of 2008. Many do not know that the dollar appreciated strongly in the foreign exchange market or that real interest rates rose dramatically. But the most popular misconception is that the Fed was doing all it could but unfortunately simply ran out of ammunition. This view is doubly wrong.

Even if interest rates had been zero, the Fed would not have been out of ammunition. In 2015, Switzerland pushed interest rates down to −0.75%, a full 100 basis points below the lowest level set by the Fed during the crisis. And even if you take negative IOR off the table, rates never even got close to the zero bound until the second half of December 2008. The Fed adopted a tight money policy in 2008 and took explicit steps to prevent policy from easing. The three increases in IOR during late 2008 are hardly indicative of a central bank that was "doing all it could."

People also misremember the timing of the financial crisis. In the minds of many, the financial crisis was an "external shock" that caused a recession, which then led the Fed to ease monetary policy. In fact, a tight money policy by the Fed triggered the Great Recession, and the decline in NGDP dramatically worsened the financial crisis. Asset prices crashed when it became clear to the markets that the Fed would not do what was necessary to restore NGDP growth to a healthy level. This was obvious to market monetarists, and to a few perceptive stock-market observers such as Jim Cramer, but to almost no one else.

This interpretation of events raises an important question: why was the Great Recession global? In the next chapter we'll see that the international nature of the Great Recession provides additional support for the market-monetarist explanation.

CHAPTER NINETEEN

Schadenfreude on the *Titanic*

From the 1990s until shortly after 2000, there was a feeling of trium-phalism in the US. We had won the Cold War with the Soviet Union, and the "Washington Consensus" of free-market economics reigned supreme. The US was outperforming Europe by a wide variety of metrics and American high-tech firms were dominating innovative new industries. At international meetings, American policy makers often lectured other countries on their need to emulate the US economic system. And so there was some schadenfreude in Europe and elsewhere when what was seen as a US housing "bubble" burst, and America's banking system was shown to have engaged in some wildly excessive risk taking.

Five years later the tables were turned. The eurozone was much worse off than the US, and some Fed policy makers took a bit of satisfaction from the fact that the European Central Bank's policy regime was pretty clearly shown to be inferior to the Fed's approach under Ben Bernanke. Just a few years earlier, some ECB officials had been critical of Bernanke's aggressive policy of quantitative easing. By 2015, the formerly conservative ECB was pushed to adopt policies much more radical than anything attempted by Bernanke's Fed, such as negative interest on reserves.

What explains the global nature of the Great Recession? As we will see, the global recession that began in 2008 is almost impossible to make sense of if it is viewed as a nonmonetary event. To understand why, we'll need to examine a few key stylized facts.

Why Was the Recession So Much Worse in Europe?

According to the standard view, the Great Recession was caused by the collapse of the US housing bubble and the subsequent banking crisis. But if this had been the case, then we could have expected the recession to be much milder in places such as Europe, where a relatively small share of the economy is represented by exports to the US. Even adding in the financial channel—lots of European banks had bought subprime bonds—it's not at all clear why ECB monetary policy could not have offset the impact of the US crisis on eurozone GDP. In early 2008, it was well understood that eurozone banks were going to take significant losses from US mortgage investments, but most experts did not expect a European recession. So what changed after early 2008?[1]

Figure 19.1 shows the path of real GDP in the US and the eurozone between the first quarter of 2008 and the end of 2014. Notice that the eurozone did worse than the US during the second and third quarters of 2008—that is, the period right before Lehman Brothers failed. In the popular imagination, the Lehman event was the shock that caused the global banking system to freeze up, plunging the eurozone into recession. In fact, the eurozone was already in recession during the middle of 2008—indeed, it was deeper in recession than the US.

After the spring of 2009, the US real GDP began recovering at just over 2% per year, as did the eurozone. However the eurozone plunged into a double-dip recession in mid-2011, which lasted for two years. Thus, in the end, the so-called Great Recession in the US was actually far milder than the recession in Europe, even accounting for the fact that the trend rate of growth is slightly higher in the US than in Europe. If the US had a severe recession, then the eurozone had something more like an outright depression.

When it first became apparent that the housing and banking crisis might push the US into recession, it was widely expected that although other countries might be affected, the secondary effects overseas would be much milder than in the US. And in some countries such as Canada, Britain, and Australia that was the case, at least in terms of employment. So why was the recession so severe in the eurozone?

We need to break that question down into two parts. First, what was the proximate cause of the European Great Recession? And second, what were the policy errors that produced those recessionary forces?

Let's start with the proximate cause, weak nominal GDP growth (fig. 19.2). Once again, we see a divergence between the US and the eurozone, beginning gradually in mid-2008, and then getting worse over time. Even in America, the more than 3% fall in NGDP during the Great Recession was the biggest decline in more than fifty years. But in the eurozone the fall in NGDP was even bigger, indicating even tighter money.

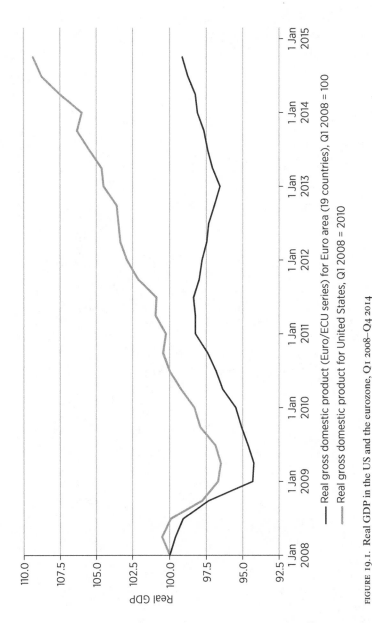

FIGURE 19.1. Real GDP in the US and the eurozone, Q1 2008–Q4 2014

—— Real gross domestic product (Euro/ECU series) for Euro area (19 countries), Q1 2008 = 100

—— Real gross domestic product for United States, Q1 2008 = 2010

Source: FRED via Eurostat and US Bureau of Economic Analysis https://fred.stlouisfed.org/series/GDPC1, https://fred.stlouisfed.org/series/CLVMEURSCA B1GQEA19#0.

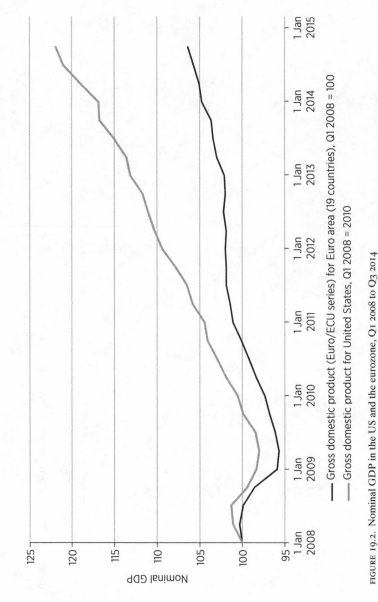

FIGURE 19.2. Nominal GDP in the US and the eurozone, Q1 2008 to Q3 2014

Source: FRED via Eurostat and U.S. Bureau of Economic Analysis, https://fred.stlouisfed.org/series/EUNNGDP, https://fred.stlouisfed.org/series/GDP.

During the recovery period, the US saw relatively stable NGDP growth, running at about 4% per year. Europe did almost as well from 2009 to early 2011, but then saw NGDP level off for two years. Because prices continued to edge higher, real GDP actually declined during Europe's double-dip recession. Interestingly, the parts of Europe that are not in the eurozone generally did not experience a double-dip recession, even those that had experienced severe banking problems.

In earlier chapters I discussed the blind spot of the economics profession regarding the Great Recession. While standard macroeconomic theory, circa 2007, clearly points to tight money being the culprit for the recession, the conventional wisdom has focused on other issues. When we switch over to the eurozone, things get far, far stranger. None of the usual excuses made for the failures of monetary policy in the US apply to the eurozone. And yet even in the case of the eurozone depression, there is a real reluctance to blame tight money. Why?

Consider two excuses commonly offered to exonerate the Fed from guilt for producing the worst performance of NGDP growth since the 1930s: (1) It was errors of omission—there were no contractionary "concrete steps" taken; (2) the Fed ran out of ammunition because it was at the zero bound. While I don't believe these two excuses explain even the Fed's behavior, they certainly do not apply to the ECB. The ECB took explicit steps to tighten money in July 2008, right before the severe slump of late 2008, and again in April and June 2011, right before the double-dip recession in the second half of 2011. At no time during this entire period was the ECB facing a zero-bound problem. And even when it did finally face the zero bound a few years later, it showed no hesitation about cutting rates to levels below zero. With a bit of hyperbole, here is how I tried to metaphorically shake the profession by the shoulders in 2014:

> [The standard view] completely ignores the fact that the 2008–09 NGDP plunge in Europe began earlier than in the US and was actually deeper (a bit over 4% vs. a bit over 3% in the US).
>
> But it's even worse; the Eurozone was already in recession in July 2008, and Eurozone interest rates were relatively high, and then the ECB *raised them further*. How is tight money not the cause of the subsequent NGDP collapse? . . . I get that people are skeptical of my argument when the US was at the zero bound. But the ECB wasn't even close to the zero bound in 2008. I get that people don't like NGDP growth as an indicator of monetary policy, and want "concrete steppes." Well the ECB raised rates in 2008. The ECB is standing

over the body with a revolver in its hand. The body has a bullet wound. The revolver is still smoking. And still most economists don't believe it. "My goodness, a central bank would never cause a recession, that only happened in the bad old days, the 1930s."

For God's sake, what more evidence do people need?

And then three years later *they do it again*. Rates were already above the zero bound in early 2011, and then the ECB raised them again. Twice. The ECB is now a serial killer. They had marched down the hall to another office, and shot another worker. Again they are caught with a gun in their hand. Still smoking.

Meanwhile the economics profession is like Inspector Clouseau, looking for ways that fiscal contraction could have cause the second dip, even though the US did much more austerity after 2011 than the Eurozone. Real GDP in the Eurozone is now lower than in 2007, and we are to believe this is due to a 2006 housing bubble in the US, and turmoil in the Ukraine? If the situation in Europe were not so tragic this would be comical.[2]

More seriously, a 2017 study by David Beckworth provides abundant empirical evidence that favors the monetary explanation of the eurozone double-dip recession over alternative theories based on debt problems and fiscal austerity. It is especially noteworthy that monetary tightening preceded economic slowdowns both in the core countries of northern Europe and in the more fragile economies along the Mediterranean.[3]

Why Did the European Central Bank Create a Double-Dip Recession?

In retrospect, it seems almost inevitable that the eurozone would have had a more severe recession than the US, but only if you believe that the recession was fundamentally a problem of monetary policy. That's because the eurozone had several fundamental weaknesses, which made it even more susceptible to monetary policy errors than the US. These include a single mandate for low inflation; an asymmetrical inflation target of "close to but less than 2%"; a currency zone with multiple countries, each having large sovereign debts; and a technocratic elite with an even weaker understanding of the importance of aggregate demand shocks than was the case with policy makers in the US. The euro project represented a compromise between European federalists and skeptical Germans. A single currency seemed to make a lot of sense from the perspective of the Maastricht single market project, but the Germans worried that it would lead to higher inflation, particularly if the ECB were pressured to bail out irresponsible borrowers. Thus, they forced a compromise according to which the Germans gave up their cherished deutschemark and in exchange got a hawkish ECB that was run similarly to the German Bundesbank.

In retrospect, this turned out to be a disaster, re-creating many of the defects of the interwar gold standard, and one additional problem: it's far more difficult to exit a single currency like the euro than to exit the gold standard. That's because under the gold standard there was a difference between the medium of account (gold) and the medium of exchange (cash). The currency price of gold could be immediately adjusted during a crisis. That is, currencies could be sharply devalued overnight.

For countries using the euro, there was literally nothing to devalue. Their medium of account and medium of exchange were identical—euro currency notes. They could try to create a new currency from scratch, but the moment they began doing so their banking system would collapse. You can't print up billions worth of currency notes overnight, and it is almost impossible to keep such an important policy decision secret. Rumors of this decision would cause panicky savers to pull their money out of domestic banks.

We've already seen how the international commodity price shock of 2008 threw US monetary policy off course, as rising headline inflation made the Fed reluctant to cut rates during the summer of 2008 despite a weakening economy. But at least the Fed did not raise rates during this period. In contrast, the ECB did not have the sort of "dual mandate" that the Fed operated under. Thus, it refused to cut rates during late 2007 and early 2008, when the Fed was slashing its target rate from 5.25% to 2.0%. In July 2008, the ECB actually tightened monetary policy by raising rates in order to reduce headline inflation. This is why NGDP fell even more sharply in Europe than in the US; the ECB was a more hawkish institution, and hence more likely to pursue tight money during a period when supply shocks were driving consumer price inflation higher.

When the eurozone recession became severe in late 2008 and early 2009, the ECB still refused to cut rates to zero. This is harder to explain, because by 2009 inflation rates were falling sharply. Part of the problem seems to have been confusion over the nature of the problem. As in the US, many assumed that the real problem was real shocks, whereas the real problem was actually a sharp decline in aggregate demand—that is,

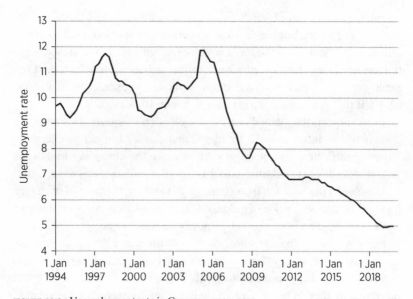

FIGURE 19.3. Unemployment rate in Germany, 1994–2019

Source: FRED via Organization for Economic Co-operation and Development, https://fred.stlouisfed.org/series
/LMUNRRTTDEQ156S.

the real problem was nominal (GDP). European economics lags the US
(and the UK) in its understanding of the importance of demand shocks.
This may be partly owing to the fact that Europe is a collection of small
countries, many of which traditionally operated under a fixed-exchange-
rate regime. Under such a regime, the only real solution for high unemployment is some sort of labor-market reform to make industry more
competitive, known as *internal devaluation.* Macroeconomic theory is and
has always been very closely linked to the policy regime that countries
operate under.

A textbook example of internal devaluation occurred in Germany during 2004. People tend to forget that in the early years of the twenty-first
century Germany was viewed as the "sick man of Europe." Unemployment
was 11%, and much of German industry was uncompetitive. A center-left
government enacted some labor-market reforms to reduce wages and increase the incentive to work, and these reforms succeeded in bringing German unemployment rates down sharply, as shown in figure 19.3.

Notice that the average rate of unemployment in Germany was about 10%
before these reforms took effect in 2004, which suggests severe structural

problems. Also note that even during the Great Recession of 2008–2009, the German unemployment rate rose only modestly. It's easy to understand how European economists might have looked at this picture and concluded that structural (real) factors were much more important than demand-side (nominal) factors. In 2004, Germans had little or no ability to reduce unemployment with demand-side policies, and hence supply-side reforms were their only option.

Unfortunately, the single-country perspective is extremely misleading when one is considering a larger currency area, where the monetary policy cannot be taken as exogenous. Germany's role within the eurozone is analogous to that of a single state in the US. Fed policy is not and should not be aimed at the needs of a single state, and ECB policy should not be aimed at the needs of only Germany.

Consider the unemployment rate for North Dakota (fig. 19.4), which looks a bit like the pattern in Germany. Notice that unemployment in North Dakota peaked at only 4.3% during the Great Recession. But that does not in any way indicate that the US did not face a shortfall of aggregate demand, or that other states could have produced the same results with the same labor-market policies. Not all states have huge reserves of shale oil. Similarly, not all European countries are loaded with firms that produce exactly the sorts of cars and machines that China is buying in vast quantities. To the demand-siders, Germany was just lucky. To the European supply-siders, Germany was smart in its public policies. The truth is that both were correct: Germany was lucky to have the right product mix and smart to liberalize its labor markets. Don't be a supply-sider or a demand-sider, be a supply-and-demand-sider.

From 2009 to 2011, eurozone inflation rose from 0% to 3%, well above the ECB's target. Even in 2011, it was obvious that the inflation surge was temporary, owing to one-off factors such as higher oil prices and increased value-added taxes in a number of European countries. The public-debt problems that were either exposed (Greece) or created (Spain) by the Great Recession led to some fiscal austerity, because the eurozone has limits both on budget deficits (no more than 3% of GDP) and on the national debt of member nations (no more than 60% of GDP). This led to value-added tax increases, which pushed the inflation rate temporarily higher.

By late 2011, the tight money had brought NGDP growth to a standstill, and NGDP was actually declining in many of the Mediterranean countries (Portugal, Italy, Greece, and Spain). As is often the case, falling NGDP led to a debt crisis. And as is also often the case, the debt crisis

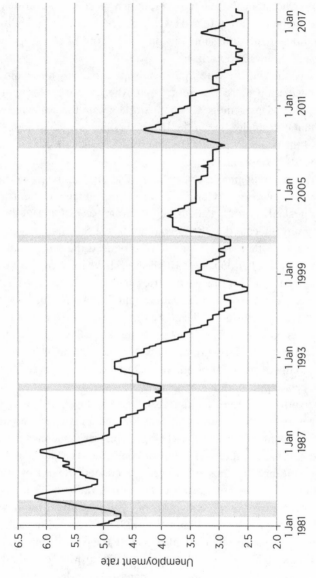

Note: Gray bars indicate periods of recession.

FIGURE 19.4. Unemployment rate in North Dakota, 1981–2017

Note: Gray bars indicate periods of recession.

Source: FRED via U.S. Bureau of Labor Statistics, https://fred.stlouisfed.org/series/NDUR.

was misdiagnosed as being mostly exogenous, unrelated to tight money. Before I explain how this misdiagnosis occurred, let's consider an analogy from the US.

In 2006 and 2007, a subprime debt crisis gradually developed in the US. By 2009, the debt crisis had gone far beyond subprime loans to include prime mortgages as well as loans to businesses, especially property developers. At any given time, there will always be a range of loans, some riskier than others. During a crisis, the riskiest loans will often get into trouble first, and the entire crisis will be seen as a sort of morality tale— foolish borrowers and lenders did not behave in a prudent fashion. And there's just enough truth in that view to make it seem plausible. People really do make foolish decisions. Some people who got mortgages in 2006 should not have done so.

But most of the bank failures that occurred during the Great Recession happened because of failed business loans, not subprime mortgages. So although it is true that foolish lending did occur, it is also true that falling NGDP made the crisis much worse. (Of course the moral hazard created by policies such as the Federal Deposit Insurance Corporation, too-big-to-fail, and Fannie Mae also contributed to that foolish lending.)

In the eurozone crisis, Greece fills the role of foolish American subprime borrowers. Not only did Greece borrow far too much, the Greek government fraudulently hid the amount of its borrowing from the ECB. Even the Greek public deserves part of the blame, because the public repeatedly voted for governments led by corrupt politicians. On the other hand, Spain is an example of a country that got into a debt crisis mostly because of the ECB's tight money policy. If the ECB had kept eurozone NGDP growing at 4% per year after 2007, then the eurozone recession would have been far milder, and the Spanish public-debt situation would have been far less dire. Indeed, Spain's public debt was actually quite low before the recession, and it became excessive only because the recession hit Spain (Europe's Sunbelt) harder than most other eurozone nations.

Fortunately, the term of hawkish ECB head Jean-Claude Trichet concluded at the end of October 2011, when the more dovish Mario Draghi took over. Policy gradually shifted in a more expansionary direction, albeit far too slowly. Although eurozone money continued to be too tight, given the constraints that Draghi operated under, he did a relatively good job, even adopting negative interest on reserves in 2014.

Countries outside the eurozone had more monetary policy flexibility and generally used that freedom to avoid the worst of the Great Recession.

For instance, compare euro member Ireland with nonmember Iceland, which has its own currency. Ireland had a severe banking crisis and suffered from years of very high unemployment. Iceland had an even more severe banking crisis, but it was able to boost NGDP growth by sharply depreciating its currency.

In Ireland, the unemployment rate peaked at more than 15% in early 2012 (10 percentage points above pre-recession levels) and did not fall below 8% until late 2016, as shown in figure 19.5. In Iceland, the unemployment rate rose to roughly 7.5% in 2010 (only 5 percentage points above pre-recession levels) and was back down to 3.2% by early 2016. Iceland saw a smaller increase in unemployment and a faster recovery.

When a country maintains adequate NGDP growth during an economic crisis, there will often be a period of high inflation. But that's actually a good thing, because it helps produce a necessary reduction in real wages, encouraging firms to boost employment. Euro member Ireland was forced into a brief period of deflation and then near-zero inflation (fig. 19.6). This was associated with low Irish NGDP growth and therefore high unemployment. In contrast, Iceland's policy of currency depreciation led to a period of high inflation, which supported stronger NGDP growth. As a result, unemployment rose much more modestly in Iceland than in Ireland.

Sometimes our puritan instincts lead us astray when we think about debt excesses and their aftermath. People instinctively feel that there ought to be a price for all the irresponsible borrowing that took place in Ireland and Iceland—as if the countries were sobering up after a wild party. Didn't Iceland take the easy way out by devaluing its currency to prop up demand? No, just the opposite! Iceland took the painful step of cutting real wages and buckling down to work harder. Work is *hard*; that's why we get paid for it.

Here it might help to consider an analogy from everyday life. Suppose your family runs up excessive debts until you reach a point at which you are in danger of bankruptcy. What is the solution? A long vacation at home watching TV? Or buckling down and working harder, perhaps with two jobs? The answer is obvious, and it also applies to nations. It makes no sense for a country to react to a debt crisis with policies that lead to high unemployment. That just makes a bad situation even worse.

The solution for the eurozone was to institute pro-growth policies, such as maintaining adequate NGDP growth while pursuing supply-side reforms. When I say "supply-side reforms," I basically mean that the southern eurozone members needed to adopt the more flexible labor-market

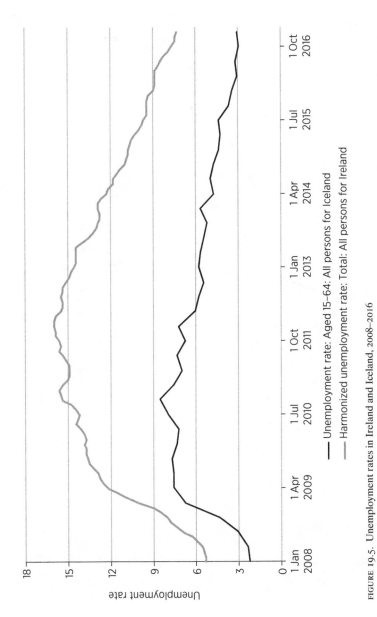

FIGURE 19.5. Unemployment rates in Ireland and Iceland, 2008–2016

—— Unemployment rate: Aged 15–64: All persons for Iceland

—— Harmonized unemployment rate: Total: All persons for Ireland

Source: FRED via Organization for Economic Co-operation and Development, https://fred.stlouisfed.org/series/LRUN64TTISA156N, https://fred.stlouisfed.org/series/LRHUTTTTIEM156S.

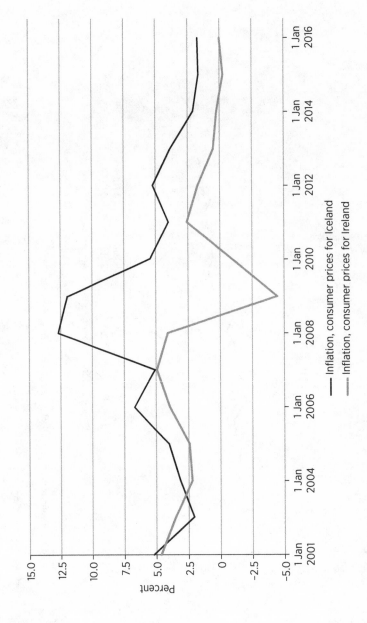

FIGURE 19.6. Inflation in Ireland and Iceland, 2002–2016

Source: FRED via World Bank, https://fred.stlouisfed.org/series/FPCPITOTLZGIRL, https://fred.stlouisfed.org/series/FPCPITOTLZGISL.

Inflation, consumer prices for Iceland
Inflation, consumer prices for Ireland

policies of northern Europe. Conservative economists often overlook the need to maintain adequate NGDP growth, while liberal economists often overlook the need for supply-side reforms. Countries such as Greece desperately needed both measures. Again, both the supply side and the demand side are important.

Inflation or Socialism? How Tight Money Leads to Big Balance Sheets

We've already seen how people tend to misjudge the stance of monetary policy, wrongly concluding that low interest rates and a big monetary base represent easy money. During recent years this confusion has been especially pronounced for two countries, Japan and Switzerland. These two countries have shared certain common characteristics: Both have had very low inflation rates, negative in some years. Both have had extremely low interest rates, often negative in even some of the longer maturities. Both have built up central bank balance sheets that are extremely large, roughly 100% of GDP.

For Japan and Switzerland, pundits have wrongly assumed that the low interest rates and big balance sheets represented extremely expansionary monetary policies, whereas these two countries have actually had some of the most contractionary monetary policies in the world. This misconception about the link between interest rates, balance sheets, and monetary policy has led pundits to wrongly conclude that to achieve higher inflation, Japan and Switzerland would need even lower interest rates or an even bigger balance sheet. Just the opposite is true.

Back in 2003, Lars Svensson suggested that currency depreciation offered Japan a "foolproof" way out of its deflationary liquidity trap.[4] In 2011, I suggested (in a blog post) that the Japanese deflation was basically intentional and that the Bank of Japan behaved exactly like a central bank that did not want rising prices. I pointed to the fact that the BOJ repeatedly raised interest rates despite a complete lack of inflation, and that it sharply reduced the monetary base in 2006. These are not the sorts of actions you'd expect from a central bank that was trying but failing to create inflation. I also suggested that if the BOJ actually wanted inflation, it could simply devalue the currency, as Lars Svensson had suggested.[5]

Paul Krugman agreed that a weaker yen might be useful but (responding to my post) questioned whether the Japanese would be able to depreciate their currency: "About the exchange rate: there's this persistent

delusion that central banks can easily prevent their currencies from ap-
preciating. As a corrective, look at Switzerland, where the central bank
has intervened on a truly massive scale in an attempt to keep the franc
from rising against the euro—and failed."[6] Krugman was right to connect
the Swiss and Japanese cases, but subsequent events pretty much confirmed my view, and contradicted his. Let's start with Japan.

In late 2012, Shinzo Abe campaigned on an explicit promise to create higher inflation. Despite the widely held view that inflation is highly
unpopular in aging societies such as Japan, Abe won a huge mandate for
his policy of inflation and was reelected by overwhelming votes on two
occasions, after he successfully ended Japan's deflation and created mild
inflation. One part of this policy was currency depreciation. The yen began falling immediately after Abe started talking about a higher inflation
target, eventually depreciating by about 35% against the dollar.

Even so, the BOJ fell short of its 2% inflation target.[7] But Abe's policy
did end deflation and achieve positive inflation, and more importantly
turned falling NGDP into rising NGDP (fig. 19.7). This sharply boosted
employment, despite a rapidly falling population. Most pundits agree that
Japan has done considerably better under Abenomics. But can we be sure
that monetary policy was the key? What about fiscal stimulus? Actually,
Abe adopted a *contractionary* fiscal policy, raising taxes and reducing the
budget deficit. Thus, more than 100% of the burden for demand stimulus
was put on monetary policy.

Just to be clear, the BOJ did not adopt an optimal monetary-policy
regime. Instead of targeting the rate of inflation, it should have targeted
the price level, or—even better—the level of NGDP. But the new policy
regime was clearly better than the previous regime, and it showed that a
determined government most certainly can depreciate its exchange rate.

To be fair, Paul Krugman would acknowledge that any government
can depreciate its currency if it supplies an unlimited quantity of domestic
currency to the foreign exchange markets and commits to peg the exchange rate at a depreciated value. As we saw in chapter 12, Krugman correctly noted that the US government had pressured the Japanese not to
depreciate their currency by purchasing large quantities of foreign exchange. The real concern is a central bank's bloated balance sheet, and
the combination of political risk and investment risk associated with the
foreign assets being purchased. That brings us to the Swiss case.

Before considering Switzerland, it will be helpful to recall countries
with the opposite problem: central banks struggling to maintain a fixed

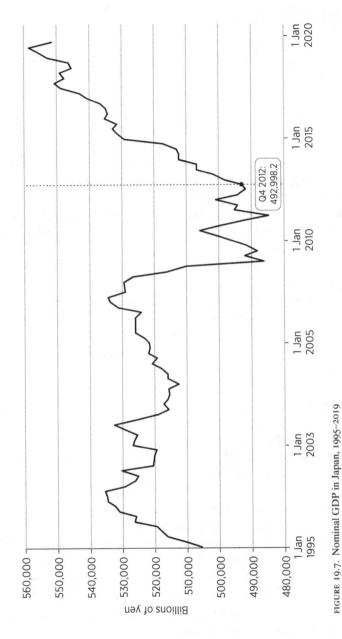

FIGURE 19.7. Nominal GDP in Japan, 1995–2019

Source: FRED via JP Cabinet Office, https://fred.stlouisfed.org/series/JPNNGDP.

exchange rate when speculators like George Soros are selling their currency in anticipation of a devaluation. In such cases there might really be nothing a central bank can do. It might run out of reserve assets to sell in an attempt to prop up the value of the currency.

But that's not the "problem" Japan and Switzerland faced: they were attempting to hold *down* the value of their currencies. Countries can run out of foreign exchange, but they can never run out of domestic currency, which can be produced at virtually zero cost (assuming they don't run out of ink and paper). The BOJ could promise to sell unlimited yen at 100 to the dollar, 500 to the dollar, or 5,000 to the dollar. There is no technical limit to the amount of currency depreciation that a central bank can do, or to the amount of inflation it can create. So what exactly is the problem?

Krugman would argue that central banks are reluctant to buy too many foreign assets. If the value of those assets were to decline, a central bank could actually become insolvent. Or the country might face criticism from its trading partners. That doesn't mean that currency depreciation is not a foolproof way of creating inflation, just that there's a risk that you might create too much inflation, and if your stock of foreign assets has declined in value, you might not be able to buy back enough of that newly created money to prevent overshooting your inflation target.

So Krugman understood that a determined central bank can always create inflation, at least in a technical sense. When he expressed skepticism about the potency of monetary policy he was making the more sophisticated argument that central banks might be unable to create inflation, given the political constraints under which they operate—especially their reluctance to engage in massive foreign exchange market intervention. That's plausible, but I'm going to argue that this more sophisticated argument was also refuted by events in Japan and Switzerland, and that Krugman's analysis was deficient in one important respect.

As is so often the case, the key intellectual error here is to assume that low rates and a big balance sheet represent an expansionary monetary policy. If you start with that assumption, then the failure of those policies to end deflation leads to a sort of fatalism with regard to monetary policy. That is, people tend to think, "If even X wasn't enough to create any inflation, just imagine how much would have been needed to push inflation up to 2%." But as we've seen, that's the wrong way to think about things. With the correct policy framework, central banks could achieve success by *doing far less*.

Consider the characteristics that Japan and Switzerland have shared, listed at the beginning of this section. Lots of people think that because the Japanese and Swiss printed so much money and still failed to achieve inflation, they must need to print much more money in order to achieve 2% inflation. But that's reasoning backward. It is *because of deflationary monetary policies* that interest rates are so low in Japan and Switzerland, and it is because interest rates are so low that the monetary base has become such a large fraction of GDP. Lots of people want to hold the base money of a country when the purchasing power of that base money is increasing over time, especially if the currency is also expected to appreciate in the foreign exchange market.

If the Japanese and Swiss adopted a much higher inflation target—say, 4%—and did whatever it takes to achieve that target, then not very many people would want to hold Swiss and Japanese currency, just as not many people want to hold Australian base money. In that case, the Japanese and Swiss monetary bases would shrink dramatically as a share of the countries' GDP (assuming Japan and Switzerland did not choose to pay interest on reserves).

Conservatives thus face a problem that they have been slow to recognize: there is a trade-off between inflation and socialism.[8] The lower the inflation rate, the larger the central bank balance sheet. Conservatives tend to dislike inflation, but they also are also uneasy when government institutions buy up massive quantities of financial assets. But they can't have it both ways—the lower the inflation rate, the larger the share of a nation's wealth that will be owned by the central bank.

Figure 19.8 shows a trade-off between nominal interest rates and the size of the central bank balance sheet. Other things being equal, the higher the trend rate of inflation (or NGDP growth), the higher the nominal interest rate, the smaller the monetary base, and hence the smaller the central bank balance sheet. Of course nominal interest rates are not the only factor that matters. For any given nominal interest rate, a higher level of interest on reserves leads to more demand for excess reserves and to a bigger balance sheet. In addition, a country viewed as a "safe haven," such as Switzerland, will tend to have a bigger balance sheet than will a country with less policy credibility. But even in Switzerland the very low level of nominal interest rates has sharply increased the demand for base money.

Interestingly, in 2011 Switzerland did adopt a policy of fixing their currency to the euro as a way of holding down their real exchange rate and ending deflation. In January 2015 it abandoned that policy and let the currency appreciate sharply. Two reasons were cited in 2015: fear of higher inflation (because the euro was weak at the time) and fear that the Swiss

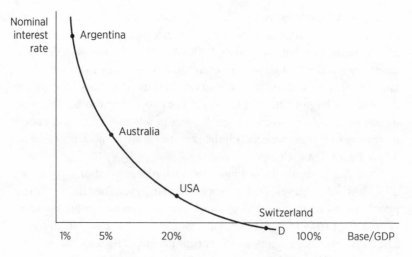

FIGURE 19.8. The trade-off between nominal interest rates (or inflation) and central bank balance sheets

National Bank would have to buy too many assets to hold down the value of the Swiss franc.

At the time I warned that the Swiss had things exactly backward, and that letting the currency appreciate would in the long run simply whet the appetite of currency speculators, who would then expect even more currency appreciation over time. When the Swiss franc was fixed to the euro in 2011, speculation gradually declined, because the franc was no longer expected to appreciate. Indeed, the balance sheet was fairly flat for two years, between August 2012 and December 2014, after the euro crises had calmed down (fig. 19.9).

But when speculators began to correctly anticipate that the Swiss National Bank would allow the currency to appreciate in early 2015, they bought Swiss francs and the balance sheet began increasing. More importantly, it increased even more strongly after the currency was allowed to appreciate in January 2015. If the Swiss authorities believed that they could avoid buying foreign assets as they allowed their currency to appreciate, then they were sadly mistaken. Again, deflationary monetary policies and near-zero interest rates both lead to big balance sheets. If the Swiss don't want their central bank to have such a large balance sheet, they will have to accept a bit more inflation.

FIGURE 19.9. The Swiss National Bank's balance sheet, 2008–2016

Source: FRED, https://fred.stlouisfed.org/series/SNBMONTBASE#0.

In early 2015 the Danish currency was also under pressure from speculators. Some pundits suggested that Denmark would be forced to revalue
its currency higher, just as Switzerland did. But no country is forced to
revalue its currency, and the Danes wisely decided to refrain from doing
so. As a result the Danish krone is still pegged to the euro, and Denmark's
monetary base increased much less than Switzerland's. Those who wish
to speculate in a currency that will appreciate over time choose the Swiss
franc, not the Danish krone.

To summarize, the same sort of monetary model that explains the
Great Recession in the US can also help us to understand the international scope of the Great Recession, as well as the variation from one
country to another. In the next chapter we will return to the US and look
at the long, slow recovery. This was also widely misinterpreted, giving rise
to at least six alternative perspectives, none of which panned out in the
end. Even so, it will be instructive to look at these various failed explanations, because doing so will help us to better understand what actually did
happen. Ideas have consequences.

CHAPTER TWENTY

Alternative Explanations of the Great Recession

If it is true that the Great Recession was caused by policy errors, then we need to explain how policy makers misinterpreted what was going on. In this chapter we'll look at how four alternative schools of thought tried to make sense out of the events of 2007–2014.

We'll begin with Keynesian economics, which is far and away the most important and influential school of thought in the field of macroeconomics. Because of its widespread support in top universities, it's a view that cannot be easily brushed aside.

In a few places, it might seem as if I am caricaturing viewpoints different from mine. I will try to avoid doing so and to provide nuance where needed, but there is simply no way to do justice to a field as vast and diverse as Keynesian economics without some simplification. When I discuss other schools of thought I'll focus on where their views are most distinctive, with the proviso that many individuals within those schools of thought hold complex views that are more nuanced than my description suggests.

Why Was the Great Recession Seen as a Triumph of Keynesian Economics?

Before the Great Recession, New Keynesian economics dominated the profession, both in academia and in government policy making. Interestingly, the recession seems to have slightly weakened the New Keynesian position while leading to a surge of interest in the original ideas of John

Maynard Keynes. Before 2008, New Keynesians had pretty much given up on fiscal policy as a stabilization tool, believing that it was enough for the central bank to target inflation and employment. New Keynesian models tended to feature rational expectations, as well as the assumption that the economy would self-correct after a shock, once wages and prices had adjusted.

The Great Recession led to a resurgence of interest in fiscal policy, theories of market irrationality, and the concept of secular stagnation, all ideas associated with the Keynesian revolution of the late 1930s (but not with New Keynesianism). It also reinforced some ideas common to both old and new Keynesianism, such as the reduced effectiveness of monetary policy at the zero bound and the importance of demand shocks in a world of sticky wages and prices. Economists such as Paul Krugman suggested that the Great Recession provided practically a textbook example of the superiority of the Keynesian model of the economy.[1]

The Keynesians certainly got some important things right. Later we'll see that critics of Keynesian economics missed the mark on several key issues. These critics exaggerated the risks of inflation from programs such as quantitative easing, and they denied that the problem of high unemployment and slow real GDP growth was caused by a lack of aggregate demand. The high inflation that some predicted never arrived, and once unemployment fell below 5% in 2016, it became apparent that the very high unemployment rates of 2009–2011 were not caused by real factors, such as government policies that discouraged people from working.

On the other hand, I believe that Keynesians made four key errors:

- They wrongly concluded that the Great Recession was evidence of the inherent instability of capitalism, whereas it was actually caused by tight money.
- They wrongly assumed that monetary policy was mostly ineffective at the zero bound.
- They wrongly assumed that fiscal stimulus is highly effective, and appropriate at the zero bound.
- They wrongly assumed that unemployment compensation programs are expansionary at zero interest rates, whereas they are actually contractionary.

The dominance of Keynesian economics partly reflects the way it lines up with common sense. When President George W. Bush tried to justify his 2001 tax cut, he pointed out that people would spend the extra money, boosting the economy. The actual rationale of Bush's Republican advisers was along supply-side lines, but it is much easier to explain things from a demand-side perspective. Indeed, all four misconceptions line up with most people's commonsense view of the world.

It certainly looked as though capitalism was an inherently unstable system during the 2008 financial crisis. The financial crisis led even former cheerleaders for free markets such as Alan Greenspan to rethink their opposition to regulation.[2] But what does it actually mean to ask: Is capitalism inherently unstable? What monetary policy is the baseline assumption here? On closer inspection, this is a meaningless question, because the instability of capitalism depends entirely on what sort of monetary regime is being followed. Under the interwar gold standard, capitalism was quite unstable; under NGDP-level targeting, it would be pretty stable. Australia had no recession between 1992 and 2020, and it is one of the world's most capitalist economies—ranking higher in "economic freedom" than the US.[3]

Some people would try to rephrase the question as: Is capitalism unstable, holding monetary policy constant? But there is no such thing as the central bank doing nothing because there are dozens of different ways of doing nothing. Recall that, in my view, expected NGDP growth is the best indicator of the stance of monetary policy. Some economists point to real or nominal interest rates, others to the monetary base or M2, and still others to the price of gold or the exchange rate. A central bank might hold the interest rate constant while dramatically changing the money supply (as the Fed did during the 1940s), or it might hold the monetary base constant while sharply cutting interest rates (as the Fed did from July 2007 to May 2008).

While the question of whether the economy is inherently unstable is meaningless, there are two very meaningful questions that are closely related: Can the central bank stabilize NGDP growth? And, could stable NGDP growth lead to a stable real economy? The basic Keynesian model implies that the answer to the second question is yes. So that leaves the first question. From a Keynesian perspective, the only way to make sense of the question, Is capitalism unstable?, is to reframe it: Can the central bank stabilize NGDP growth? The events of 2007 and 2008 led many Keynesians to assume the answer was no.

We've already seen where Keynesians went wrong. They (and most non-Keynesians as well) assumed that the Fed's interest rate cuts of 2007–2008 represented an expansionary monetary policy. Because the economy went into a deep slump despite this "easy money," it seemed as if monetary policy was not able to stabilize NGDP, even before the US hit the zero bound in December 2008.

The failure of QE to lead to rapid recovery in 2009 further confirmed the weakness of monetary policy in the eyes of Keynesians and others. Because Keynesians wrongly view interest rates as the transmission mechanism of monetary policy, they wrongly assumed that the Fed was out of ammunition once rates hit zero. This led to a renewed interest in fiscal stimulus, which does not rely on the interest-rate transmission mechanism. While QE was piling up as excess reserves in the banking system, Keynesians argued that fiscal stimulus would directly lead to higher aggregate demand.

This link to common sense, or what might be called "folk economics," makes faith in the Keynesian approach to macroeconomics so strong that it can survive lots of predictive failures. During the Great Recession in the US, there were four notable policy initiatives that Keynesians misjudged, two expansionary and two contractionary. In all four cases the economy performed far differently from what was expected.

Monetary Offset

The first Keynesian initiative during the Great Recession was the Bush tax rebates that were paid out during the spring of 2008. These led to a temporary spike in disposable income during May 2008, but they had relatively little impact on consumption, as shown in figure 20.1.

One reason for the modest impact is well understood—the permanent income theory. People with erratic incomes (e.g., farmers, realtors) tend to smooth consumption over time by saving temporary income gains. The public understood that these tax rebates were temporary windfalls, and hence people saved a large proportion of the rebates.

Keynesians will reply that careful cross-sectional studies show that many people don't behave as the permanent income theory predicts. Unfortunately, these cross-sectional studies don't actually tell us much, because they ignore a much bigger problem with fiscal stimulus—monetary offset. If the Fed is targeting inflation at 2%, then it is likely to offset the effect of any fiscal stimulus (or austerity) on aggregate demand. In a sense the Fed is legally required to offset fiscal policy, because Congress's dual mandate does not grant any sort of exception for a change in fiscal policy.

Many people find the concept of monetary offset to be bizarre and confusing. Surely Congress wouldn't want the Fed to "sabotage" its efforts at fiscal stimulus! Congress may not want that, but the legislation that the Fed operates under virtually requires monetary offset. The Fed is instructed to

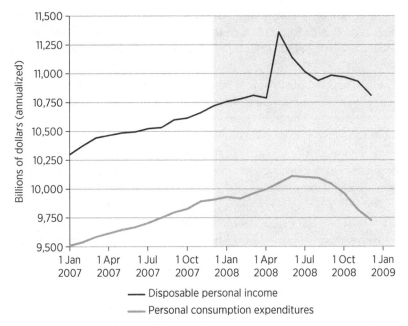

Note: Gray bar indicates period of recession.

FIGURE 20.1. US disposable income and consumption, 2007–2008

Note: Gray bars indicate periods of recession.

Source: FRED via US Bureau of Economic Analysis, https://fred.stlouisfed.org/series/DSPI, https://fred.stlouisfed.org/series/PCE.

set monetary policy at a level that produces the sort of aggregate demand that will lead to stable prices (2% inflation) and high employment (unemployment close to the natural rate). Any fiscal action that moves aggregate demand away from where the Fed was targeting it must be offset by an adjustment in Fed policy, in order to achieve its dual mandate.

As we've already seen, that's exactly what happened in 2008. Let's return to figure 20.1 for a moment. Although it might look as if the tax rebates had no effect on consumption, GDP growth (both real and nominal) did accelerate modestly during the second quarter of 2008. Fiscal stimulus probably did boost output in the second quarter. People tend to forget that while the recession officially began in December 2007, the economy was mostly flat during the first half of 2008. By midyear, it looked as though the Fed's sharp rate cuts of late 2007 and early 2008 had successfully staved off a recession. With fiscal policy providing the public with more disposable income, the Fed felt its job was done. The Fed's seemingly inexplicable refusal to cut interest rates between April and October 2008 is almost certainly at least partly related to the fiscal stimulus of May 2008, although high oil prices also played a role.

Obviously the Bush tax rebate was a spectacular failure in the long run, as the economy almost immediately plunged into the deepest recession since the 1930s. The more important question is whether it also represented a failure of Keynesian economics. Keynesians would argue that the tax rebate modestly boosted spending in the spring of 2008 and that the economy was hit by a severe financial crisis and might have done even worse without the rebates.

But this Keynesian argument overlooks the deeper problem of monetary offset. If the Fed takes fiscal policy into account when making its decisions (and it clearly does), then the Bush tax cuts might well have worsened the recession by nudging policy in a tighter-than-otherwise direction. The so-called fiscal multiplier might actually be negative, meaning that tax cuts and spending increases might actually reduce GDP when taking monetary offset into account. The Fed feared an overheating economy in mid-2008 and therefore refused to cut interest rates. Those fears were partly attributable to the Bush tax cuts. Thus, we got a bit more output in the second quarter of 2008 at the expense of a lot less output in late 2008 and in 2009.

I've argued that the baseline assumption should be that the fiscal multiplier is roughly zero. After all, if the Fed has set policy at a level expected to deliver on-target aggregate demand, then it ought to fully offset the demand-side impact of any fiscal stimulus. This does not mean that the multiplier is precisely zero in every case; it could be more or less than zero. And fiscal actions can also affect real output through channels other than aggregate demand. Monetary offset is most likely to occur when there are changes in taxes and transfers that do not impact the public's incentive to work, save, or invest (the usual supply-side channels). And neither President Bush's 2008 lump-sum tax rebate nor President Obama's fiscal stimulus package of 2009 had significant supply-side components. They were straightforward demand stimulus.

Fiscal Stimulus at the Zero Bound

The second major initiative occurred when a much larger fiscal stimulus was enacted in 2009. Recall that Keynesians believe that the case for fiscal

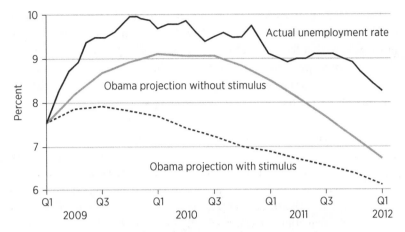

FIGURE 20.2. US actual versus projected unemployment rate, Q1 2009 to Q1 2012

Source: US Senate, Republican Policy Committee.

stimulus is strongest when the economy is at the zero bound. To give a
sense of how strong this Keynesian consensus is, consider a University of
Chicago survey of forty-four leading economists, conducted in 2014. The
economists were asked whether the unemployment rate at the end of 2010
was lower than it would have been without the 2009 fiscal stimulus. Of the
thirty-seven economists who responded, thirty-six said yes and one said
no.[4] If I had been asked, I would have said no. So why is the consensus so
strong in the other direction?

The stylized facts certainly don't provide much support for the effectiveness of the Obama stimulus packages. Not only did the unemployment rate rise above the levels projected by the Obama administration,
the rate rose well above the levels predicted *if the stimulus package had
not been enacted* (fig. 20.2).[5] At first glance, that would seem to be a rather
astounding failure. So what accounts for the consensus that the stimulus
was successful?

Perhaps the economy was hit by some sort of unexpected shock. After
all, economic forecasting is not a perfect science. Maybe the forecasters
did not anticipate the financial crisis. Unfortunately for that explanation,
these forecasts were made in January 2009, by which time the severity of
the financial crisis was clearly apparent. Some Keynesians, such as Paul
Krugman, did predict a worse outcome.[6] But even accounting for the
rosy scenario associated with government forecasts there was clearly a
failure here.

I see the continuing faith in Keynesian economics as resulting from a convergence of common sense and flawed empirical studies. Most economists believe that fiscal stimulus should be expansionary when rates are zero, and there are some cross-sectional studies that seem to indicate that this is the case. For instance, at the state level, spending on fiscal stimulus is positively correlated with economic growth. Most of the empirical studies find a positive "multiplier," meaning that more government spending or tax cuts seem to result in higher levels of aggregate demand an output.

Once again, however, the cross-sectional studies do not account for monetary offset. No one seriously denies that if the federal government spends an extra $5 billion on a military base in North Dakota, the GDP of North Dakota will likely rise somewhat. The more interesting question is whether this sort of fiscal stimulus will boost the GDP of the US as a whole, or whether it will merely transfer output from one region to another.

It may seem implausible that Ben Bernanke would have sabotaged the effects of fiscal stimulus with monetary offset. After all, Bernanke actually called for fiscal stimulus once the severity of the recession became apparent. I don't doubt for a moment that if Fed officials were asked whether they tried to sabotage fiscal stimulus, their answer would be no. But if the same question were framed a different way, the answer might well be yes. Thus, Fed officials usually say that they have set their policy instruments at a level that they think is most appropriate to the needs of the economy. And Fed officials also say that, when setting policy, they take into account all outside factors, including the stance of fiscal policy. When we combine those two statements, we end up with monetary offset, also known as sabotage.

The best argument that the Obama stimulus had a positive multiplier effect is the argument that Bernanke was unable to convince the Federal Open Market Committee to do as much monetary stimulus as he would have liked. I consider that a relatively strong argument. The best argument that there was no multiplier effect is the argument that Bernanke, as a scholar of the Great Depression, had no intention of presiding over another Great Depression, and that if Congress had failed to act he would have pushed the Fed to adopt some far more powerful medicine, such as level targeting. I also consider that to be a strong argument. Perhaps the safest conclusion is that there is no such thing as "the multiplier" in the scientific sense of a deep parameter of nature, but rather the effect of fiscal stimulus varies from one case to another, depending on the degree of monetary offset.

Fiscal Austerity at the Zero Bound

A policy initiative in 2013 led to perhaps the most spectacular failure of Keynesian theory, and the most difficult to explain away. In late 2012, the US government took a series of steps to reduce the budget deficit, including instituting a 2-percentage-point increase in the payroll tax, an increase in income taxes, and a "sequester" that reduced government spending. Importantly, most of these measures took effect in January 2013. As a result of this austerity, the budget deficit plunged by $500 billion in a single year, from $1,061 billion in 2012 to $561 billion in 2013.[7] (I use calendar-year figures rather than fiscal-year figures because most of the austerity measures began in January 1, 2013, not on October 1, 2012, when the fiscal year began.)

By 2012, the eurozone had entered a double-dip recession caused by tight money but misdiagnosed as caused by fiscal austerity. Many observers feared the same could occur in America. In late 2012, 350 Keynesian economists signed a letter warning that the expected fiscal austerity risked pushing the economy into recession: "At the end of the year, we face a congressionally-created 'fiscal cliff,' with automatic 'sequestration' spending cuts everyone agrees should be stopped to prevent a double-dip recession."[8]

At roughly the same time, the Fed adopted several more expansionary policies, including forward guidance and the third round of QE (QE3). The Fed specifically cited the need to offset the effects of fiscal austerity. Those of us in the market-monetarist camp suggested that the monetary stimulus would largely offset the fiscal austerity. After all, the asset markets were not showing any signs of an oncoming recession, and market monetarists tend to rely on market forecasts, not complex econometric models of the economy (which have proved almost useless for forecasting recessions).

This market-monetarist forecast was certainly out of the mainstream and attracted some notice from prominent Keynesian bloggers. Here's Mike Konczal in April 2013:

> We rarely get to see a major, nationwide economic experiment at work, but so far 2013 has been one of those experiments—specifically, an experiment to try and do exactly what Beckworth and Ponnuru proposed [i.e., monetary stimulus offsetting fiscal austerity]. If you look at macroeconomic policy since last fall, there have been two big moves. The Federal Reserve has committed to much bolder action in adopting the Evans Rule and QE3. At the same time, the

country has entered a period of fiscal austerity. Was the Fed action enough to offset the contraction? It's still very early, and economists will probably debate this for a generation, but, especially after the stagnating GDP report yesterday, it looks as though fiscal policy is the winner.[9]

And here's Paul Krugman in April 2013:

As Mike Konczal points out, we are in effect getting a test of the market monetarist view right now, with the Fed having adopted more expansionary policies even as fiscal policy tightens.

And the results aren't looking good for the monetarists: despite the Fed's fairly dramatic changes in both policy and policy announcements, austerity seems to be taking its toll.[10]

It turns out that Konczal and Krugman spoke too soon. When all the data were in, it became clear that GDP growth (both real and nominal) had sped up in 2013. Real GDP rose by 2.66% between the fourth quarter of 2012 and the fourth quarter of 2013, after rising by only 1.28% over the previous twelve months. It was a truly spectacular failure of the Keynesian model.

Not surprisingly, the Keynesians refused to go down without a fight. Some pundits used annual averages of 2013 GDP compared to 2012 GDP, which inappropriately mix growth in late 2012 (which was very slow) with growth in 2013, which gradually increased.[11] Austerity didn't begin until 2013. When a policy change occurs on January 1, economists use growth rates over the course of a year, not annual averages compared to the earlier year.

Some claimed that there had actually been very little austerity.[12] But notice that the claims that the austerity was a "test" of market monetarism were made well after the austerity had already been imposed. Does anyone seriously think that Keynesians would have later said the austerity was not a test of fiscal policy if there had been a recession in 2013? What does it say about a theory that the government should use fiscal policy to stabilize the economy if 350 of the most prominent advocates of that view are not even able to identify the stance of fiscal policy in real time? These excuses were not offered until late 2013, when the failure of the Keynesian model became apparent.

During 2013, state and local spending moved modestly in a more expansionary direction, so overall the government sector was not quite as contractionary as the federal data would suggest. But fiscal policy is a 100% federal responsibility. From the perspective of federal policy makers, state and local spending is just as endogenous as private investment spending. The relevant policy question is not whether changes in government spending matter for the business cycle, but whether changes in *federal* government spending and taxes matter for the business cycle. In any case, even accounting for changes in state and local spending, there was clearly substantial fiscal austerity in 2013, and Fed policy successfully offset the effects—it *more* than offset the effects.

You Get What You Pay For: Extended Unemployment Insurance

The fourth policy initiative involved the unemployment insurance program. In late June 2008, President Bush signed a law extending unemployment benefits for thirteen weeks. Classical economic theory predicts that a policy of subsidizing activity X will lead to more of X, and that includes unemployment. At the time, even relatively liberal bloggers such as Brad DeLong expected Bush's action to result in a roughly 0.6% rise in the unemployment rate by the 2008 election. This reflected the standard way that economists look at unemployment insurance. If you pay people not to work, there will be less people working.

It turns out that DeLong was almost exactly correct—the unemployment rate rose from 5.8% in July to 6.5% in October 2008, although obviously other factors were likely involved. Later, the maximum unemployment benefits were extended much further, to as many as ninety-nine weeks in some states.

The Great Recession pushed Keynesians, and the economics profession as a whole, further to the left. Keynesians were quite critical when the GOP Congress ended the extended unemployment benefit program at the beginning of 2014. This had the effect of reducing the maximum duration of unemployment benefits from seventy-three weeks to the traditional twenty-six weeks. Indeed, Keynesians predicted that ending the extended benefits could depress aggregate demand and hence actually raise the unemployment rate. This was despite the fact that academic studies showed that unemployment insurance itself raises the unemployment rate, even in areas where the unemployment rate is already high and jobs are hard to find.

Here is an excerpt from an economics textbook coauthored by Paul Krugman, Robin Wells, and Kathryn Graddy (before the 2014 unemployment benefit cuts): "People respond to incentives. If unemployment becomes more attractive because of the unemployment benefit, some unemployed workers may no longer try to find a job, or may not try to find one as quickly as they would without the benefit. Ways to get around this problem are to provide unemployment benefits only for a limited time or to require recipients to prove they are actively looking for a new job."[13] Soon after the end of extended unemployment benefits, however, Krugman was making a very different claim. Here's another prediction of his, this one from April 2014, which turned out to be just as premature as his April 2013 prediction:

> [*New York Times* reporter] Ben Casselman points out that we've had a sort of natural experiment in the alleged effects of unemployment benefits in reducing employment. Extended benefits were cancelled at the beginning of this year; have the long-term unemployed shown any tendency to find jobs faster? And the answer is no. . . .
>
> You might imagine that the long-term unemployed, through their desperation, might take jobs away from existing workers—but it's not easy to see how that might work, and there's no evidence that this is happening.
>
> So the point is that as long as you understood that we have a demand-constrained economy, you knew that cutting off the unemployed would produce all pain, no gain. And your prediction was right.[14]

Actually, your prediction would have been wrong. Once again, the final numbers undercut a key Keynesian argument, as employment growth sped up significantly in 2014. Payroll employment had grown by 2.1 million in 2012 and by 2.3 million in 2013. But in 2014, payroll employment soared by 3.0 million, rendering 2014 the best year of the recovery, as lots of desperate workers who had lost unemployment benefits flooded back into the workforce. This does not mean that workers collecting unemployment benefits are "lazy," just that they are rational. It is sensible to be pickier about what sort of job you are willing to accept if you have a cushion to fall back on.

What Keynesians Got Wrong and What They Got Right

So far I've been pretty critical of Paul Krugman and the other Keynesians, based on a series of misleading arguments they have made:

- They have made claims about the effect of fiscal stimulus and austerity in the US that were in no way supported by the evidence.

- They have blamed slow recovery in the UK on inadequate aggregate demand, even though the data clearly pointed to low productivity, and British employment actually did relatively well. In the traditional Keynesian model, aggregate demand affects output by affecting employment, not productivity.
- They have blamed the eurozone problem on the zero-bound problem even though the eurozone was not even at the zero bound during 2008–2012.
- They have ignored lots of empirical evidence that unemployment benefits reduce employment.
- They wrongly predicted that output would return to the previous trend line once the economy recovered. Back in 2008, Gregory Mankiw had a very public dispute with Paul Krugman on this issue, and Mankiw turned out to be correct.[15]
- Even though the Keynesian model predicts that depressed demand will reduce output by raising the unemployment rate, Keynesians have responded to the Great Recession with all sorts of ad hoc mechanisms that were not well supported by standard Keynesian models. These included claims that depressed aggregate demand could permanently reduce output (secular stagnation), perhaps by depressing productivity or labor-force participation. Of course it is possible, though unlikely, that these new theories are true. Far more troubling was the way these ideas were presented—as if they were standard Keynesian arguments, when in fact they were new and unconventional ideas.
- They attacked China for large current account surpluses, even though surpluses were even larger in northern Europe, and were vastly larger in per capita terms. As we saw in chapter 12, there is no persuasive evidence for the "beggar thy neighbor" view that trade surpluses steal jobs from other countries.
- They relied on cross-sectional studies of fiscal austerity that ignored the role of monetary offset. When a follow-up (unpublished) study conducted by Mark Sadowski (a commenter in my blog) controlled for having an independent monetary policy, the effect went away and the fiscal multiplier fell to roughly zero.[16] Deficit spending does not significantly boost GDP. Additional studies by Kevin Erdmann and Benn Steil reached similar conclusions.[17] The Keynesian cross-sectional studies that so many people cite include lots of eurozone countries without an independent monetary policy, and hence they are essentially useless for the key question—does fiscal policy work when there is monetary offset? If the European Central Bank engages in monetary offset (and it almost certainly did during the Great Recession), then any fiscal stimulus in one eurozone country will boost domestic spending at the expense of reduced spending in the rest of the eurozone.
- They kept insisting that the weak US economy and low inflation were due to the Fed being hamstrung by the zero-bound issue, even after the Fed was no

longer at the zero bound. If the zero bound really had been the main problem, then the Fed's performance should have dramatically improved once it was no longer constrained. In fact, the Fed continued to undershoot its inflation target after exiting the zero bound in exactly the same way as it had before the zero bound ended (in late 2015). Some Keynesians continued to insist that fiscal austerity was slowing growth even when the Fed was no longer at the zero bound. These arguments made no sense because even in the Keynesian model, monetary offset is clearly operative when interest rates are above zero. Keynesian economics became increasingly sloppy the further it removed itself from the 1990s New Keynesian consensus.

To summarize, economists were shifting from the relatively sensible New Keynesianism of the 1990s toward the much cruder "vulgar Keynesianism" of the 1930s and 1940s, where classical economic principles like opportunity cost, free trade, and the virtue of saving were thrown out the window. Keynesians revived the "paradox of thrift," an argument that increased saving can depress an economy. They argued that there was no opportunity cost to more federal spending, owing to the multiplier effect.[18] And they suggested that Chinese and German trade surpluses were reducing US employment.

On the other hand, in many respects Keynesians were ahead of the rest of the economics profession. So, while Paul Krugman was not right about everything, in my view he did get many of the big issues exactly right:

- The Great Recession was mostly caused by a drop in aggregate demand.
- Monetary stimulus was appropriate, and was not likely to lead to high inflation.[19]
- Because unemployment was mostly caused by deficient aggregate demand (with supply-side factors such as extended unemployment compensation playing only a modest role), unemployment was likely to fall back to a low rate once wages and prices adjusted.[20]

In contrast, many conservative economists were wrong on those key points, which means they were even further off course than the Keynesians. I spent the majority of the Great Recession debating with Keynesians for much the same reason that adherents to a given religion often have the most contentious disputes with one another—if economists didn't recognize the importance of deficient aggregate demand, then it was hard to even engage in productive conversations with them in the years after 2010. Their worldviews were too different.

Monetarists, Austrians, and New Classical Economists

Critics of Keynesian economics often have views that are regarded as somewhat "conservative" or libertarian. They include monetarists, Austrians, and new classical economists. The most famous critic of Keynesian economics was Milton Friedman, who passed away in 2006, right before the Great Recession. If Friedman had been alive and in good health during 2008, I believe the conservative movement might not have drifted so far off course.[21]

Friedman's revisionist take on the Great Depression was a lot like my revisionist take on the Great Recession. Furthermore, Friedman praised Alan Greenspan's policies as recently as 2006,[22] so he would not have been able to blame the Great Recession on Fed mistakes during 2003–2006 (as did many conservatives after the crash of 2008). Unfortunately, that "easy money" meme became the standard conservative explanation for the Great Recession—a sort of morality tale in which easy money by the Fed led to housing and banking excesses, which ended in a severe crisis and recession.

Because Friedman had praised Fed policy in 2006, he would have been left with two other explanations for the Great Recession, the inherent instability of capitalism or excessively tight money in 2008. Almost certainly he would have chosen the latter option. After all, he was on record as far back as 1997 arguing that money was excessively tight in Japan despite the near-zero interest rates. Friedman would have been particularly outraged by interest on reserves, which he would have (correctly) seen as a repeat of the Fed's misguided decision to raise reserve requirements in 1937. Unfortunately, for a decade after Friedman's death in 2006, this sort of criticism of tight money largely disappeared from the right.[23]

In their *A Monetary History of the United States*, Friedman and Schwartz had been quite critical of the Austrian explanation of the Great Depression, which focused on monetary excesses during the 1920s. They argued that monetary policy was not excessively expansionary during the 1920s, and that the real problem was tight money after 1929. By 2008, however, Anna Schwartz was drifting in an Austrian direction, as was Allan Meltzer, another well-known monetarist. In 2008 and 2009, there were only a very few voices on the right claiming that money was too tight.[24]

It is from this vacuum that market monetarism emerged, a sort of "third way" between the Keynesians and the more conservative anti-Keynesian schools of thought. The problem was a lack of aggregate demand—as the Keynesians argued—but it was caused by tight money at the major central banks. Unfortunately, we market monetarists were not high-profile economists, and the press paid much more attention to the prominent conservative economists who signed a letter in 2010 suggesting that monetary stimulus could lead to high inflation: "We believe the Federal Reserve's large-scale asset purchase plan (so-called 'quantitative easing') should be reconsidered and discontinued. We do not believe such a plan is necessary or advisable under current circumstances. The planned asset purchases risk currency debasement and inflation, and we do not think they will achieve the Fed's objective of promoting employment."[25]

To be fair, the letter refrained from a straightforward prediction of high inflation, rather warning of "risks" and also suggesting that the economy's problems called for supply-side solutions. That's not an absurd claim, given that productivity and labor-force participation were also problems, not just high unemployment. Still, inflation ended up undershooting the Fed's target over the following nine years, and in retrospect it looked like this group of economists was far off base in their judgment about the proper stance of monetary policy. Rather than doing too much, in retrospect the Fed was clearly doing too little. Keynesians like Paul Krugman frequently reminded their readers just how far off base the conservative establishment was during the Great Recession—and with good justification.[26]

During the twenty-first century, the Austrian perspective gradually took over from monetarism as the most popular macroeconomic perspective on the right. The Austrians had argued that an easy money policy during the 1920s had prevented prices from gradually falling back to pre–World War I levels, and that this pumped up a stock market bubble, as well as excessive investment in sectors such as New York office buildings.[27] The stock-market crash and subsequent downturn were seen as necessary corrections, until the malinvestment in the economy could be absorbed.

At first glance, the Great Recession also looked like it had been caused by previous excesses, particularly in the housing and banking sectors. Add in very low interest rates after the 2001 recession, and you have a set of stylized facts that nicely fits the Austrian narrative of easy-money-driven excesses leading to a subsequent slump. Interestingly, during the first year of the Great Depression the Austrian perspective was also quite popular, especially the views of F. A. Hayek, for much the same reason that the Great Recession led to a surge of interest in Austrian economics. But later the Austrian perspective went out of style. What went wrong?

In 2008, Lawrence White (an economist sympathetic to the Austrian tradition) revisited Hayek's policy views during the Great Depression.[28] During the Depression period, Hayek generally favored a monetary policy aimed at stable nominal income, similar to the market-monetarist proposal for NGDP targeting. But Hayek's actual policy advice during the Great Contraction of 1929–1933 did not match his theoretical model. Even though prices and output were falling, Hayek opposed stimulus, hoping that the slump would lead workers to accept more wage flexibility. Much later in his life, Hayek admitted that he had been wrong and that monetary stimulus would have been appropriate during the early 1930s. But by then it was too late: as the Depression got much worse, those who had opposed stimulus gradually lost favor with the public. Keynesian economics became the consensus view.

I've emphasized the role of cognitive biases in monetary economics, and I wonder whether these biases affected some right-leaning economists after 2008. Unlike Milton Friedman, many conservatives seem to have a sort of visceral distaste for any form of "stimulus" even when the logic of their model calls for it. For instance, some conservatives now argue that central banks should ignore their employment mandate and focus like a laser on hitting the inflation target. When the European Central Bank was founded, it adopted a single mandate to control inflation. And yet when inflation fell below that central bank's target, conservatives in Europe and elsewhere seemed reluctant to accept the implications of their long-held views—monetary stimulus was needed to push inflation up to the target. No longer were central banks to focus like a laser on inflation control; new objectives such as preventing asset price bubbles were suggested.

By the twenty-first century, it was liberals who most frequently pointed to the work of Friedman and Schwartz on the Great Depression. After all, Friedman had argued that additional monetary stimulus would have been appropriate. In contrast, while conservatives revered Friedman as a great economist and a powerful advocate of free markets, they seemed to ignore his frequent claims that money was too tight in the US and in Japan.

The following metaphor may help to distinguish between Austrian and Keynesian economics. Think of a stable economy as like a flat plain—say, Kansas or Oklahoma. In the Keynesian view, the business cycle occurs when this flat plain is interrupted by deep ravines. The Great Depression is like the Grand Canyon. The goal is to get the economy back up to the flat plain, which is boom conditions. In the Austrian view, the business cycle occurs when the flat plain is interrupted by tall mountains. When the economy rises up to a peak (a boom), economic activity is unsustainable and a subsequent decline is inevitable.

Keynes thought that policy makers should always try to keep the economy in boom conditions. Keynesians want to fill in the canyons. His Austrian critics argued that those conditions were unsustainable, and would lead to a relapse. Austrians want to prevent mountains from forming. Thus, the Keynesians' geographic metaphor for the business cycle might look like northern Arizona, whereas the Austrians' metaphor might look like Colorado. In my view there is some of each type of topography. There are times where the economy is too strong (mountains) and times when it is too weak (canyons).[29]

While Keynesians and Austrians disagree about the nature of the business cycle, they do agree that demand shocks affect output in the short run and that an easy-money policy involves low interest rates. In my view, both groups put too much weight on interest rates as an indicator of the stance of monetary policy. Thus, Austrians complained that the Fed policy of 1% interest during 2003 was easy money, and also that it was destabilizing. Many Keynesians agreed that it was easy money but thought it appropriate. In my view, it wasn't especially easy money, and both groups were engaged in reasoning from a price change. The low rates mostly reflected a weak economy, not easy money.

In contrast with both Keynesian and Austrian economists, new classical economists were skeptical of the idea that monetary policy had much impact on the business cycle. In their view, the weak economy early in the second decade of the twenty-first century reflected bad supply-side policies. During 2012 and 2013, the economist Casey Mulligan wrote several papers showing how the expansion of the welfare state (including the Affordable Care Act) had reduced the incentive to work.[30] Supply-side factors almost certainly played some role in the Great Recession; indeed, I've already argued that the extended unemployment benefit program modestly boosted the unemployment rate, until the program was ended in 2014.

At the same time, it is important not to overstate the importance of supply-side factors in the business cycle. There is no plausible argument that the collapse in employment during 2008–2009 was caused by reduced incentives to work. Not when falling NGDP is a much more plausible explanation. Note that sharply falling NGDP also caused a deep recession in 1921, when the US had relatively few welfare programs. On the other hand, the recovery from the 1921 recession was much quicker than the recovery from the Great Recession of 2007–2009, perhaps because the modern welfare state makes the labor market less flexible.

In the end, however, unemployment did come down sharply, despite the failed attempt to repeal the Affordable Care Act. In 2013 (when unemployment was still 7.4%), I published a blog post suggesting that the next few years would be a test of Mulligan's hypothesis.[31] If unemployment fell sharply, it would suggest that the major problem was deficient demand. If the US got stuck at a high rate of unemployment, as often happens in European countries after a recession, then it would suggest that various welfare programs were sharply reducing the incentive to work. In fact, unemployment did fall sharply, which suggests that demand-side (i.e., monetary) factors were the dominant cause of the Great Recession, although taxes and subsidies that reduce employment also played a modest role.

Another possible real shock was the tightened regulation of credit markets, including the Basel III rules that raised capital requirements, and also the Dodd-Frank Wall Street Reform and Consumer Protection Act, which tightened regulation of banking in the US. The economist Steve Hanke has argued that these regulations slowed the recovery from the Great Recession.[32] This type of real shock can also reduce growth in the broader monetary aggregates, which include bank credit.

When credit regulation is tightened, it can have an impact on both aggregate demand and aggregate supply. Less bank lending might reduce business investment. Even if growth in aggregate demand is maintained, the resources used in business investment cannot be immediately reallocated to other sectors. That's a negative supply shock. Tightening credit regulation may also reduce aggregate demand if the Fed fails to offset the reduction in bank credit by boosting the monetary base. In other words, regulations that reduce bank lending will reduce aggregate demand where there is no monetary offset, just as with fiscal austerity.

Note that even if the tighter banking regulations were appropriate after the financial crisis, it certainly doesn't help to have a pro-cyclical regulatory regime—lax rules during booms and tightened regulations during slumps. When the economy entered a boom in the late 2010s, regulations were once again relaxed somewhat.

Banking regulation is a difficult issue for free market economists. In a perfect world, there would be absolutely no regulation of banking. But given interventions such as deposit insurance (the Federal Deposit

Insurance Corporation), the government-sponsored enterprises (Fannie Mae and Freddie Mac), and the implicit policy of too big to fail, the banking system suffers from a problem of moral hazard—the incentive to take excessive risks. Because of the Federal Deposit Insurance Corporation, banks that are not taking socially excessive risks are not acting in the interests of their shareholders. This creates an argument for banking regulation as a "second best" policy. The best banking policy is laissez-faire. But if governments insist on protecting bank creditors from their folly, then one can make an argument for rules that limit the ability of banks to take on excessive risks. As an analogy, the best policy to mitigate flood risk is no federal flood insurance. But if policy makers insist on this sort of subsidized insurance program, then there may need to be restrictions on building homes in flood-prone areas.

The Neo-Fisherian Heresy

During the recovery from the Great Recession, years of low interest rates failed to produce high inflation. This led prominent academic economists such as Stephen Williamson and John Cochrane to experiment with models that turned Keynesian economics on its head. These Neo-Fisherian models suggest that perhaps low interest rates were actually a *tight* money policy. After all, many prominent macroeconomic models included a Fisher effect, and in these models a long period of low nominal interest rates generally coincides with low inflation. So, the argument went, perhaps the way to create higher inflation is to *raise* interest rates.

There's much that could be said about the Neo-Fisherian hypothesis. For example, it's slightly embarrassing for the field of economics if we as a profession cannot decide whether low rates are easy money or tight money. Imagine if physicists couldn't decide whether gravity attracted or repelled objects. Also, mainstream economists immediately mocked the Neo-Fisherians, using metaphors like, "Do umbrellas cause rain?" Yes, a period of high inflation is often associated with high interest rates, but surely the high rates don't *cause* the high inflation.

I shared some of this dismay, but over time I've developed a somewhat more nuanced view. I believe that Neo-Fisherians are reasoning from a price change in exactly the opposite way from which Keynesians and Austrians reason from a price change. Keynesians often wrongly assume that low rates are easy money, and Neo-Fisherians wrongly assume that low rates are tight money. Either could be true, depending on whether the liquidity effect or the Fisher effect is more powerful at the point in time in question. What makes me slightly sympathetic to the Neo-Fisherian position is that this small group of economists has been harshly attacked (even mocked) for views that are *less wrong* than those of many mainstream New Keynesians and Austrians.

In chapter 16, we saw that the reaction of asset markets to money announcements suggests that in some cases lower interest rates represent an easy-money policy that will lead to higher inflation, and in some cases lower interest rates represent a tight money policy that will lead to lower inflation. In defense of the Neo-Fisherians, over any extended period of time the most common outcome is that low rates represent a tight-money policy that will lead to lower inflation. Most people find this very confusing, because on any given day, an unexpected decision by the central bank to cut interest rates will generally represent an easier money policy. Nonetheless, most of the time when interest rates are falling, money is actually getting *tighter*.

As an analogy, most of the time when nominal wage growth is slowing, it is also true that nominal wages are *too high*, and vice versa. That's because wages are sticky, and the slowing wage growth indicates that wages are falling to the new and lower equilibrium value with a time lag.

Here it will be helpful to return to Ben Bernanke's observation that NGDP growth and inflation are better measures of the stance of monetary policy than interest rates. When money is tight, both inflation and NGDP growth tend to decline. That puts downward pressure on interest rates, and it's what we saw happen in 2007–2008. So the Neo-Fisherians have a point. Where they go off course is assuming that interest rates are a policy, not the outcome of various potential policies. Consider two monetary policy shocks: a one-time increase in the money supply and a permanent change in the growth rate of the money supply. Figure 20.3 illustrates how the price level might respond in each case.

In the case of the one-time increase of the money supply (left graph), the price level adjusts upward and there is no permanent increase in the rate of inflation. This sort of expansionary monetary shock is likely to produce lower interest rates in the short run; indeed, it might be caused by the Fed cutting its fed funds target. A permanent increase in the money supply growth rate (right graph) will lead to permanently higher inflation. This will likely push interest rates higher, and it is the sort of policy change the Neo-Fisherians have in mind. Unfortunately, in the short run,

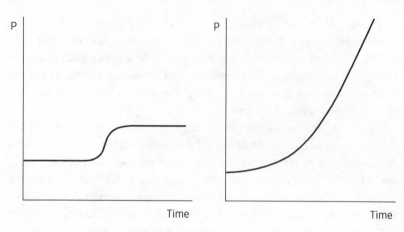

FIGURE 20.3. Two monetary policy shocks

this sort of shock is less common than the one-time change,[33] and hence the Neo-Fisherian hypothesis doesn't really provide a very good road map for understanding day-to-day changes in Fed policy.

Just as the longest journey begins with a single step, a shift to a permanently higher growth rate in the money supply (M) begins with a one-time increase in M. Only rarely, however, do one-time changes lead to permanent growth rate changes, and when they do it is usually only apparent in retrospect. Thus, a central bank decision to reduce its interest rate target unusually leads to higher commodity prices—an odd result for a policy the Neo-Fisherians view as contractionary.

The best way to understand the Neo-Fisherian view is to consider a policy shock that actually does conform to this view. One example occurred in Switzerland in January 2015. For three years the Swiss government had been holding down the value of the Swiss franc by pegging the franc at 1.2 to the euro. Speculators occasionally bought francs, anticipating an eventual revaluation upward. On January 15, 2015, the Swiss suddenly cut interest rates sharply (to −0.75%). Recall that according to the interest parity condition, these lower interest rates should have led to a higher expected rate of appreciation in the Swiss franc, which is deflationary. At the same time, lower interest rates are usually expansionary. How did the Swiss National Bank make sure this particular rate cut was contractionary? The solution was simple: it simultaneously revalued the Swiss franc sharply higher. That revaluation was contractionary enough to prevent the lower interest rates from boosting Swiss inflation.

Ironically, this sort of Neo-Fisherian policy mix (in the opposite direction) was anticipated by noted New Keynesian economist Lars Svensson in a paper describing a "foolproof" escape from a liquidity trap. When Svensson wrote the paper in 2001, his focus was on Japan, which at the time was the only country stuck in a liquidity trap. Svensson's proposal had two parts: keep the exchange rate stable against the dollar, and before fixing the exchange rate, do a one-time devaluation of the yen.[34]

Let's think about how these two parts fit together. When a country has persistent deflation, its currency will usually appreciate over very long periods of time, owing to purchasing power parity. By fixing the yen to the dollar, Japanese inflation will gradually move up from zero or negative (in 2001) to something closer to 2% (the US inflation rate). So far, so good.

Unfortunately, purchasing power parity only works in the very long run. And pegging the yen to the dollar will also have the side effect of raising nominal interest rates in Japan from near zero up to American levels (which were well above zero in 2001). How can Japan avoid letting those higher interest rates depress the Japanese economy? That's where the second part of Svensson's plan comes in. By first depreciating the yen by enough to offset the contractionary effect of higher interest rates, the combined policy will lead to higher inflation both in the short run and in the long run.

The Swiss experiment of 2015 was essentially the mirror image of Svensson's proposal for Japan, with tighter money and lower interest rates instead of easier money and higher interest rates. This is the sort of policy combination that the Neo-Fisherian model implicitly features.

Svensson noticed that under his proposal easier money would be associated with higher nominal interest rates, but when he wrote his paper there was as yet no Neo-Fisherian hypothesis.[35] You might wonder what makes this case so different from the standard case in which higher rates mean tighter money. The key is that the use of exchange rates as a policy instrument allows monetary policy makers to control the future path of policy in a way that is much more credible than when they use the (Keynesian) fed-funds rate as a policy instrument.

For instance, Keynesians sometimes advocate a policy of "forward guidance," according to which the central bank promises to hold interest rates at a low level for many years. On occasion this might even work. But it's actually not much different from a tight-money policy that results in slow NGDP growth and near-zero interest rates. In other words, when the Fed promises to hold rates near zero for many years, it's not clear whether it is promising years of easy money or promising that America will become like (deflationary) Japan.

I hope that by now you recognize that interest rates are an ambiguous indicator of the stance of monetary policy—that is one of the most important themes of this book.

In contrast, when monetary policy causes the exchange rate to depreciate, the impact is unambiguously expansionary. The price approach to monetary policy is much less ambiguous than the interest-rate approach to monetary policy. Making promises about the future path of exchange rates is a way of telling the public that we are in the second panel of figure 20.3, not the first panel. It doesn't just shift the line, it changes the slope.

Although using an exchange rate policy instrument is superior to using the fed-funds rate as a policy instrument, it's still not optimal. Real exchange rates move around for many reasons (never reason from an exchange rate change). It would be even better to use something tied more directly to the goals of monetary policy, something that measures the inflation of NGDP expectations.

Interestingly, while real-world examples of the Neo-Fisherian hypothesis playing out are relatively rare in the US, monetary policy tends to be at its most effective at precisely those times when it is best described by the Neo-Fisherian model. Recall the contractionary monetary policy surprise of December 2007 (discussed in chapter 16) that led to lower Treasury yields on bonds with maturities from three months to thirty years. This happened because a highly effective monetary policy action is one that is likely to materially shift the expected future path of NGDP, and it is major shifts in NGDP growth expectations that have the biggest impact on nominal interest rates. A shift toward easier money might make nominal interest rates fall for a time, but a truly dramatic shift toward much easier money is likely to lead to higher interest rates. This is well known to Latin Americans, who have experienced repeated bouts of rapid money creation, extreme devaluation, and hyperinflation.

Like the Keynesian, (traditional) monetarist, and Austrian perspectives, the Neo-Fisherian critique has some flaws, but it also contains important ideas. It reminds us to be very skeptical of the conventional wisdom that low rates are easy money. In the next chapter, we'll see why market monetarism provides the best road map to a much more effective monetary-policy regime.

PART VI

What Does It All Mean?

CHAPTER TWENTY-ONE

Policy Implications of Market Monetarism

In the preceding chapters, I've pushed back against the notion that monetary policy is a series of "gestures," which supplement other gestures being made by fiscal policymakers, as well as shocks from the private sector. I've argued that a better analogy for monetary policy makers is a ship captain who steers a large vessel that is constantly being affected by wind and waves. In this view, the captain (i.e., the Federal Open Market Committee) is responsible for the ship's course and is expected to push back against outside factors.

If we frame things this way, then the root cause of destabilizing demand-side shocks is monetary-policy instability. For instance, the root cause of the Great Contraction of 1929–1933 was central banks' failure to prevent a big fall in nominal GDP. Of course you can always look for even deeper root causes, such as the failure of those with political power to appoint the right officials, or the failure of the interwar economics profession to correctly analyze what was going wrong. But the most *useful* definition of a root cause focuses on the role of policy—if we can figure out how to get policy right, then we can prevent economic problems caused by NGDP instability.

If the market-monetarist analysis is correct, then what are the implications for policy? People who have some familiarity with our ideas often immediately think in terms of NGDP targeting. It's true that the Fed allowed NGDP to fall sharply during 2008–2009, and that this policy failure was the proximate cause of the Great Recession. But it's equally true that the Fed failed to achieve its dual mandate of 2% PCE inflation and high employment. So pointing to a lack of NGDP targeting is not enough—the policy failures went much deeper.

Market monetarists are sometimes associated with unconventional policy tools such as quantitative easing and negative interest on reserves. Once again, however, this association misses the bigger picture. It's nice to know how to clean up the mess after a large bridge collapses, but the real goal is to prevent the bridge from collapsing in the first place. It's useful to have policy tools for a severely depressed economy, but the real goal is to prevent events such as the Great Recession. We all would prefer a policy regime in which those tools are not needed. If market monetarism has anything useful to offer, it will lead to a regime in which there is much less use of extraordinary policy tools such as QE and negative IOR. The goal is to keep NGDP growing strongly enough that the public and banks don't choose to hoard enormous quantities of base money (cash and reserves).

What Remains to Be Done?

Regarding money, I am sympathetic to the "Whig interpretation of history"—that is, to the view that we are learning from previous mistakes and that policy is improving over time.[1] After the Great Depression, the Federal Reserve was gradually given additional flexibility to prevent sharp declines in nominal spending. Unfortunately, it took many years for the Fed to adapt to the nearly unlimited discretion available under a pure fiat money regime. The decision to allow gold prices to float after March 1968 was the monetary equivalent to giving a sixteen-year-old boy the keys to his dad's Maserati. There is a learning curve—in that case, it became known as the Great Inflation.

By the 1980s, central bankers had absorbed the "Taylor principle": the central bank needs to raise its interest-rate target even faster than any increase in inflation.[2] This ensures that even the real interest rate will rise when money is tightened, putting downward pressure on inflation. Once central banks had figured this out, high inflation was no longer a problem. In the US, this success was attributed to the wizardry of Alan Greenspan, but in fact foreign central banks were equally successful. It's not difficult for a determined central bank to prevent high inflation.

More recently, central banks have struggled with the issue of how to deal with excessively low inflation. It is still unclear how much central bankers have learned from the mistakes made during Great Recession, but surely they have learned *something*. I'm actually pretty optimistic about the future, at least once the COVID-19 crisis is over.

One way of thinking about the optimal monetary policy is to look at what went wrong during the Great Recession and how the next iteration of policy rules can further improve the Fed's performance. I see three lessons coming out of the policy failures of 2008–2009:

- *Policy needs to target the market forecast.* In 2008, Fed officials relied too much on economic models and not enough on market forecasts. An optimal monetary policy is one that results in the market consensus expecting success. If the Fed is targeting nominal GDP growth of 4%, then the market should forecast 4% nominal GDP growth.
- *We need some sort of level targeting regime.* Preferably this would be a level targeting of NGDP, but even price-level targeting would be far superior to the current "let bygones be bygones" inflation-targeting regime. The purpose of level targeting is not just to correct past mistakes and provide long-term predictability for the path of NGDP, although that's a worthy goal. More importantly, level targeting would help stabilize the economy by reducing the volatility of nominal spending when the economy is hit by a shock.
- *Policy makers need to adopt a "whatever it takes" approach to monetary policy.* The primary tool should be open-market purchases and sales of government securities. If not enough securities are available, it would be better to adopt unconventional policies such as purchases of alternative assets or the adoption of negative interest on reserves (or both), rather than just having policy makers throw up their hands and ask for assistance from fiscal authorities. Congress is simply not equipped to implement an effective countercyclical fiscal policy regime. Exhibit A is the major tax cut implemented in 2018, a period of only 4% unemployment.

Although NGDP targeting is often viewed by outsiders as the core of market monetarism, I regard the three principles listed here as the most important tenets of market-monetarist policy. After all, today even many Keynesian economists have shifted their support to NGDP targeting. The primary goal today should be the adoption of a "whatever it takes" policy of targeting the forecast, combined with level targeting.

The adoption of these three policy principles has the potential to greatly moderate the business cycle while continuing to minimize the so-called welfare cost of inflation, which is actually the welfare cost of excessively high and unstable NGDP growth. But of course the devil is in the details, and we need to think about two specific issues: what is the appropriate policy target, and how can we best ensure that the stance of monetary policy leads to on-target market forecasts of growth in aggregate demand?

Is NGDP Targeting Optimal? If So, at What Rate?

Throughout this book I've assumed, either implicitly or explicitly, that unstable nominal GDP growth creates economic problems, especially for the labor and financial markets. But this does not necessarily mean that NGDP targeting is desirable. Indeed, I very much doubt that the optimal monetary policy target is precisely equal to NGDP.

To see why NGDP targeting is not always optimal, consider a country such as Kuwait, where oil production makes up a large share of GDP. Obviously a small country like Kuwait has relatively little impact on the global price of oil. If the global price of oil were to suddenly rise from $50 a barrel to $100 a barrel, and if Kuwait's oil output remained fairly stable, then the nominal expenditure on Kuwaiti oil would roughly double. If the Kuwaiti central bank were engaged in NGDP targeting, then the nominal expenditure on goods other than oil would have to plummet sharply, perhaps triggering a depression.

This thought experiment demonstrates that NGDP targeting is not some sort of a magic bullet that solves all macroeconomic problems. The standard argument is that NGDP instability creates problems for the labor market because changes in NGDP are closely correlated with changes in total labor compensation in countries like the US. Because hourly nominal wage rates are sticky in the short run, any change in total labor compensation is likely to produce similar changes in total hours worked. In a country like Kuwait, however, there is much less correlation between changes in NGDP and changes in total labor compensation. The oil industry is not very labor intensive, relying more heavily on natural resources and physical capital. When oil prices soar, so do profits for the state-owned Kuwaiti oil company.

My own view is that a monetary policy aimed at targeting total nominal labor compensation per capita may be slightly preferable to an NGDP target. However, in the US there is not likely to be much difference between the expected growth rate of NGDP and the expected growth rate of total nominal labor compensation. In the US, NGDP targeting may be relatively close to the optimal monetary policy. Keep in mind, however, that NGDP targeting is likely to be less effective in countries where unstable commodity markets represent a larger share of GDP. Thus, NGDP is a slightly less reliable indicator of monetary stability in a major commodity producer such as Australia than it is in a highly diversified economy such as the United States.

If we take NGDP as a reasonable approximation of the optimal policy target, the next task is to choose an appropriate growth rate. And should the growth rate be adjusted occasionally in order to offset shocks to productivity, thus keeping inflation stable in the long run? Here I can't emphasize enough that with NGDP targeting, unstable inflation is a feature, not a bug. Most economists think of inflation and real GDP as the key variables, whereas NGDP growth (the sum of these variables) is a sort of ungainly hybrid, like a minotaur—half man and half beast. To market monetarists, NGDP is the "real thing" whereas inflation is an almost meaningless data point created by government bureaucrats lacking any coherent economic model for their work.

Given how often economists talk about inflation and how much effort central banks put into targeting that variable, you might assume that economists have a pretty clear idea about what the CPI is supposed to measure. Nothing could be further from the truth. Consider the example of entry-level luxury cars. How rapidly did they rise in price between 1986 and 2016? In fact, there is no way to answer that question—or, more precisely, there are many different ways, and no clear way of determining which approach is correct. Consider these two approaches:

- An entry-level luxury car like the Acura Legend sold at a sticker price of $22,500 in 1986. By 2016 the Legend was no longer being produced, but a Honda Accord selling for roughly the same sticker price that year was better than the 1986 Legend in almost every possible way quality can be measured: it was bigger, safer, more powerful, more luxurious, and more durable; it had more features; and so on. So in that sense the price of an entry-level luxury car has fallen since 1986—you get more for your money today.
- Now let's think of an entry-level luxury car not as just a bundle of mechanical attributes but as a fashion statement. In 1986, a person could have impressed the neighbors by parking an Acura Legend in the driveway for $22,500. By 2016 this person might have had to spend at least $33,750 to get a car considered "entry-level luxury." So in that sense the price of an entry-level luxury car has risen.

So which is it? Which do economists consider to be the "correct" way of measuring inflation? In fact, there is no consensus on this issue at all;

indeed, I wonder how many economists even understand the problem. To the average American, 50% inflation in entry-level luxury cars between 1986 and 2016 would be the right figure. The average person is unimpressed by economists' claims that TV prices have fallen by more than 90%, owing to the enormous improvement in picture quality. To most Americans, the concept of cost of living means something like "the cost of living the way we live now." As quality improves, people expect to have better TVs, cars, cell phones, and so forth. They want to know how much more they need to make to keep up with the Joneses.

Most economists are slightly condescending about the public's view of inflation and would insist that you need to adjust prices for quality changes. And there are cases where that makes sense. If automobile tires now last for thirty thousand miles instead of ten thousand miles, then looking at just the price of tires will overstate the inflation rate for tire services. But the economists' view also has its flaws. After all, in economics the ultimate barometer of value is supposed to be utility. And because humans are social animals, it may well be that a psychological concept like utility is more accurately described by the second approach described above than the first. Maybe you need to buy a $33,750 car in 2016 to get the same utility that someone could have derived from a $22,500 car in 1986. Maybe it's prestige that determines utility—where you are in the pecking order, not the physical attributes of a car.

But if utility is what matters, as economic theory seems to imply, then what are we to make of the fact that surveys of Americans don't indicate any increase in average levels of happiness since the 1950s? This would seem to imply that there has been no increase in real income, properly defined, and that all of our nominal gains have been pure inflation. I'm not at all sure that's correct, but these thought experiments do raise a real issue—there is no *objective* measure of inflation, because the variable has never been properly defined. Thus it's not just a question of "biased" estimates; we wouldn't be able to come up with an objective measure of inflation even if we had perfect information about the world. We don't know what we are trying to measure.

Interestingly, John Maynard Keynes had the same intuition, as this passage from his *General Theory of Employment, Interest and Money* demonstrates:

But the proper place for such things as net real output and the general level of prices lies within the field of historical and statistical description, and their purpose should be to satisfy historical or social curiosity, a purpose for which perfect precision—such as our causal analysis requires, whether or not our knowledge of the actual values of the relevant quantities is complete or exact—is neither usual nor necessary. To say that net output to-day is greater, but the price-level lower, than ten years ago or one year ago, is a proposition of a similar character to the statement that Queen Victoria was a better queen but not a happier woman than Queen Elizabeth—a proposition not without meaning and not without interest, but unsuitable as material for the differential calculus. Our precision will be a mock precision if we try to use such partly vague and non-quantitative concepts as the basis of a quantitative analysis.[3]

Keynes suggested some alternative variables. One key variable in *General Theory* is, of course, aggregate demand, which we can proxy with nominal GDP. And then Keynes points to two other important variables:

> In dealing with the theory of employment I propose, therefore, to make use of only two fundamental units of quantity, namely, quantities of money-value and quantities of employment. . . .
>
> We shall call the unit in which the quantity of employment is measured the labour-unit; and the money-wage of the labour-unit we shall call the wage-unit.[4]

The "wage-unit" is what I've been calling nominal hourly wages. Recall that nominal GDP, total hours worked, and nominal hourly wages are the key variables in my musical-chairs model of the business cycle. Keynes correctly understood the instability of capitalism as caused by unstable NGDP combined with sticky wages, resulting in unstable employment levels. You can toss in prices and output if you like, but they don't really add anything substantive to the model.

If NGDP targeting is politically infeasible, it is certainly possible to create a hybrid of NGDP and inflation targeting by gradually adjusting the trend rate of NGDP growth to match changes in the trend rate of real GDP growth. That would still deliver at least 90% of the benefits of NGDP targeting, and it would keep inflation close to 2% over the entire business cycle. But it would be an entirely unnecessary tweaking of the model, done merely to placate people who are unaware of the underlying logic of NGDP targeting.

One common criticism of NGDP targeting is that the public understands the logic of inflation targeting but doesn't know anything about NGDP. I would argue that almost the exact opposite is true. Back in 2010, inflation fell below 1% and Ben Bernanke discussed the need to boost the rate of inflation back to 2%. There was a firestorm of criticism on talk radio, and many Americans wondered why the Fed was trying to raise the cost of living when the public was already suffering from a housing crash and high unemployment. In fact, not one American in a hundred understands the logic of inflation targeting. Most people assume that the lower the rate of inflation, the better.

The problem here is that Americans don't understand the distinction between supply-side inflation and demand-side inflation. When picturing the effects of inflation, people tend to hold their own nominal income fixed. Thus, inflation seems like something that would lower their real income. In practice, they are envisioning supply-side inflation, which really does reduce the real income of Americans. But in 2010 Bernanke was proposing higher demand-side inflation, and in a depressed economy an increase in aggregate demand boosts both prices and real output. That means that the real income of Americans *rises* when there is demand-side inflation, at least in the short run. Yet very few Americans understand this distinction.

In contrast, suppose Bernanke had made the following statement in 2010: "The Federal Reserve has determined that the US economy is healthier if the average income of Americans grows by roughly 5% per year. In recent years income growth has been far lower, and we are implementing an expansionary monetary policy to raise the average income of Americans." Would that statement have caused as much confusion as Bernanke's call for a higher cost of living for Americans? Almost certainly not, but most economists overlook this messaging problem and continue to assume that the public understands inflation targeting, despite overwhelming evidence to the contrary. Economists are too close to their abstract models, and often lose sight of how average people think about macroeconomic concepts.

So let's say the Fed does decide to target NGDP, maybe even to adopt level targeting. What trend rate of NGDP growth should policy makers shoot for? Like almost everything in economics, there are costs to and benefits of higher and lower NGDP growth. The major cost of rapid NGDP growth results from distortions in the US tax system. Higher NGDP growth raises nominal returns on capital, and this leads to higher taxes on capital income. In many public finance models the optimal rate of taxation of capital income is zero. Thus, the higher the rate of NGDP growth, the higher is the rate of taxation of capital and the lower is the level of saving and investment.

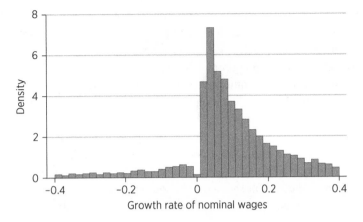

FIGURE 21.1. The distribution of nominal wage gains
Source: Barattieri, Basu, and Gottschalk (2010), https://www.nber.org/papers/w16130.

There are two primary problems with excessively low NGDP growth, both associated with a zero-bound problem. As the trend rate of NGDP growth slows, the percentage of workers who need nominal pay cuts to stay employed will increase. Because there is a psychological barrier to nominal wage cuts (because of money illusion), excessively slow NGDP growth makes the labor market less efficient. Unemployment is higher than optimal, because of downward sticky wages. How do we know that there is money illusion? If money illusion did not exist then the distribution of wage gains would be roughly bell-shaped. Instead, there is a sharp break at 0%, as shown in figure 21.1.

Normally a market becomes more efficient as irrational individuals are punished with financial losses. That is why financial markets are so efficient. But the labor market is different. Most of the social costs from sticky wages are external costs, not borne by the individual workers with money illusion.

There is also a zero-bound problem for interest rates. Contrary to the claim of the Keynesians, the zero-bound issue does not make monetary policy ineffective. But it can lead to a dramatic increase in the size of the central bank balance sheet, forcing central banks in places like Japan and Switzerland to buy vast quantities of assets. This is the "inflation or socialism" dilemma discussed in chapter 19. If we assume that the public doesn't want central banks to hold vast quantities of private-sector assets, then it is important to set the trend rate of growth in NGDP high enough to keep the economy above the zero bound for interest rates.

I'm not certain exactly which rate of NGDP growth is optimal, but something on the order of 3% or 4%, per capita seems like a reasonable compromise in view of the costs of excessively low or excessively high NGDP growth. In the long run, this sort of growth rate should keep both zero-bound problems (nominal wages and nominal interest rates) at manageable levels while also avoiding the extremely high tax rates on capital seen in high-inflation periods such as the 1970s.

The most important goal should be maintaining stable growth in NGDP—the exact rate chosen is far less important. Indeed, the optimal growth rate for NGDP will depend on how heavily capital income is taxed—any model of the "welfare costs of inflation" that excludes that issue should be heavily discounted.

NGDP Futures Targeting

Let's say the Fed decides on 4% NGDP growth, level targeting. It commits to do whatever it takes to hit this target—or at least to achieve a situation in which the market expects it to hit this target. How does the Fed decide where to set its policy instruments? And what policy instrument should it use?

Let's work backward from the second question. It's easy to describe what policy instrument it should *not* use—interest rates. Interest rates are one of the very worst possible policy instruments because the instrument becomes ineffective when rates fall slightly below zero. Using interest rates is like buying a car with steering that works fine 90% of the time but locks up on twisty mountain roads. The interest-rate instrument locks up when rates fall slightly below zero, but that's likely to be in the midst of a deep recession, when you most need an effective monetary policy.

Almost any alternative would be superior to interest rates, including the monetary base, the exchange rate, or even the price of gold. While exchange rates seem to work fine for small economies like Singapore, they are probably not a practical tool for the US. If the Fed tried to adjust exchange rates in such a way as to hit its policy goals, there would be howls of outrage from other countries that experience what they view as undesirable moves in their exchange rate against the dollar. Of course any monetary policy will influence the exchange rate, but the politics of directly targeting the exchange rate make this tool an unlikely choice for the US.

As much as I oppose the use of interest rates as a policy instrument, most central banks are committed to the use of this policy tool. Thus, any proposed monetary policy rule should be flexible enough to allow for using the short-term interest rate as a policy tool.

So let's move on to the first question: How does the central bank decide where to set the policy instrument? To many people this is all there is to monetary policy: deciding where to set interest rates. In fact, it's a less important decision than determining the policy goal (e.g., NGDP-level targeting), but it is nonetheless a significant issue, worthy of careful thought.

The most famous model for setting the policy instrument is the Taylor rule, which uses a formula for setting the fed funds target based on recent levels of output and inflation. For a period of several decades, the Taylor rule provided a plausible approximation of the method by which the Fed set interest rates. But during the first decade of the twenty-first century, the rule seemed increasingly misleading. The basic problem is that the Taylor rule assumes that the natural real rate of interest is stable, whereas in fact it has been gradually declining over time. Thus, adherence to the Taylor rule would have led to excessively contractionary monetary policy after 2002. Indeed, policy became too contractionary after 2007, even though during 2008 it was more expansionary than was recommended by the Taylor rule.

Interestingly, the Taylor rule was supposed to fix some of the problems associated with simpler monetary supply rules proposed by monetarists such as Milton Friedman, who favored a steady increase in the M1 or M2 money supply, at roughly 3% per year.[5] When velocity became unstable during the early 1980s, these sorts of rules fell out of favor. The problems with the Taylor rule after 2002 are eerily similar to the problem with previous monetarist proposals—it is dangerous to rely on the assumption that key parameters in a model will remain stable after a new monetary regime is adopted.[6]

Despite the problems with previous policy rule proposals, I do believe that some sort of rule is necessary. But the rule needs to focus more on the policy goal and less on the instrument. Instead of requiring central banks to set their instrument according to some sort of rigid formula, we need a rule that requires central banks to set their policy instrument at a position that is expected to achieve their publicly announced policy goals. Thus, if the goal is 4% NGDP growth, the central bank should be required to set the policy instrument at a position expected to achieve 4% NGDP growth.

In 1989, I proposed using futures markets to target NGDP. Over the years, this proposal has been widely misunderstood, even by prominent economists such as Ben Bernanke and Michael Woodford.[7] So it will be useful to consider the intuition behind this proposal, one step at a time.

Let's start with the twelve-member Federal Open Market Committee and assume that the committee wishes to target NGDP growth at 4.0% per year. How can we motivate them to set the policy instrument (the monetary base or the fed funds rate) at the correct position? One idea is to reward FOMC members who made the correct decision with a monetary bonus and punish those who made a poor decision by docking their pay. If this proposal had been in effect during 2008–2009, then the hawks would have been punished for being too contractionary to hit the target. If it had been in effect during the 1970s, the doves would have seen their pay docked for being too expansionary.

Here's how the system might work. Each member votes on a policy instrument setting. The actual policy instrument setting is determined by the median FOMC voter. Those who took a more dovish position can be viewed as predicting below 4.0% NGDP growth, while those who took a more hawkish than average position are implicitly forecasting above 4.0% NGDP growth. When the actual numbers are announced one year later, those who guessed right might get a $1,000 bonus, and those who guessed wrong would pay a $1,000 fine.

This is just the first step. The wisdom-of-crowds principle suggests that we should expand the FOMC to more than twelve members—why not allow all 7.6 billion humans to have a vote on the FOMC? Obviously most people would choose not to participate, because they have little interest in risking $1,000 on an issue that they know little about. But surely some people would be willing to vote on the appropriate instrument setting for monetary policy.

The next step is to move beyond "one man, one vote" to a regime of "one dollar, one vote," which is how things are done in "efficient" asset markets. Now the Fed would stand willing to buy and sell unlimited quantities of NGDP futures at a given price, say, $4,000. The policy instrument is set at a position where the longs and shorts roughly balance out. When the actual NGDP is announced a year later, the speculators are paid off on the basis of the difference between the actual NGDP growth and the Fed's policy goal (assumed to be 4.0% NGDP growth). Thus, if actual growth comes in at 4.2%, then the contracts are valued at $4,200 at maturity, and those who took a long position make a $200 profit on each contract, while those who took a short position incur a $200 loss. If NGDP comes in at 3.7%, then the short sellers earn a $300 profit and those who took a long position lose money.

Later I'll describe a modified version of this proposal that addresses four common criticisms of this plan. Before doing so, however, I want to emphasize that I believe that even this simple version of NGDP targeting would work fine, and that the following four criticisms do not raise any important objections. Let's consider each criticism in turn.

First, let's consider the circularity problem. In 1997, Ben Bernanke and Michael Woodford published a paper arguing that NGDP (and CPI) futures targeting was subject to a "circularity problem."[8] If central bankers used futures markets to guide policy decisions, and if markets had faith that the central bank would take whatever steps are needed to offset the effect of economic shocks, then futures prices would never move in a way that provided the sort of signals that the central bankers would need in order to adjust policy. The NGDP futures price would stay at $4,000, providing no market signal to the Fed that easing or tightening is needed. The term *circularity problem* refers to the fact that central bankers would be looking to markets for guidance and markets would be looking to central bankers for guidance.

But this criticism does not apply to my 1989 NGDP targeting proposal. In that regime, the important point is not that the markets are predicting the future level of NGDP (although they are); rather, it's that they are predicting the instrument setting that would lead to on-target NGDP growth. The actual price of NGDP futures is always exactly $4,000 during the period when they are being targeted, because the central bank promises to buy and sell unlimited quantities of these futures contracts at the target price. If this scheme were subject to a circularity problem that makes it infeasible, then this would have been equally true of the classical gold standard (when the Treasury pegged gold prices at $20.67 per ounce from 1879 to 1933), or of the Bretton Woods fixed-exchange-rate system. The system I proposed in 1989 would effectively elicit market forecasts of the optimal instrument setting, which does not involve any circularity problem.[9]

Second, while the circularity problem undercuts the utility of price data from actively traded NGDP futures contracts, some critics go even further and point to the current nonexistence of an NGDP futures market as an argument against NGDP futures targeting—let's consider this argument next. What if no one traded NGDP futures contracts, and hence there was no market price to react to? My response is that if no one traded NGDP futures, then policy would be on the right track. During late 2008, I certainly would have been frantically selling NGDP futures short, in anticipation of what was obviously going to be a sharp decline in actual NGDP. If I had been the only one trading the contracts with the Fed, I could have become quite wealthy.

This is one of the features I like best about NGDP targeting. No, not the idea that I could become fabulously wealthy—indeed, just the opposite. I'm quite fatalistic about get-rich-quick schemes; I don't ever expect to win the lottery. What I like about this sort of thought experiment is that it shows that if NGDP futures targeting failed then *it would be easy to become wealthy*. Because I am skeptical that it will ever be easy for me to become wealthy, I don't expect NGDP targeting to fail.

Third, let's consider the inefficient market critique. Not everyone accepts my claim that the efficient-market hypothesis is approximately true, and that asset markets are efficient. What if there were a speculative bubble in NGDP futures prices? In that case, the price of NGDP futures might diverge from the optimal forecast of future NGDP, leading to a risk premium in NGDP futures prices. Anything is possible, but I'd argue that NGDP futures are about the least likely market to suffer from speculative bubbles. Indeed, there is so little interest in trading NGDP futures contracts that this sort of market does not even exist, despite the fact that NGDP is not even currently being targeted. So there's not much demand to hedge against NGDP risk. Any risk premium embedded in NGDP futures prices is likely to be quite small, far less than 100 basis points. While the NGDP risk premium might be regarded as significant from a financial market perspective, it would be of little consequence from a macroeconomic stability perspective. Furthermore, only a time-varying risk premium would cause macroeconomic instability.

In addition, research suggests that bubbles are more likely to occur when the market consists of people with similar perspectives rather than a large and diverse set of traders. A small FOMC is much more prone to the dangers of groupthink than a large and diverse asset market.[10]

Fourth, some people argue that an NGDP futures market might be subject to market manipulation. Suppose a wealthy person bought lots of NGDP futures contracts. That would trigger a contractionary monetary policy response (because going long on NGDP is an implied prediction that NGDP growth will overshoot the target). The worry is that a speculator might then make side bets in other markets affected by monetary policy—say, going short on equities. Tight money might depress stock prices. Then even if the speculator lost money in NGDP futures, the speculator could profit in the side bet on stocks.

This sort of scheme is much harder to pull off than it might appear.[11] After all, these contracts are likely to be traded by big institutions. Which institutions are going to make the money-losing trades that allow a market manipulator to profit? If one speculator did succeed in making monetary policy too contractionary to achieve the policy target, then other speculators could profit at this speculator's expense by taking a short position on NGDP futures, thus pushing policy in the opposite direction.

If market manipulation were a feasible strategy, then why didn't this sort of manipulation occur under a fixed exchange rate regime? George Soros could have sold large quantities of a currency, forcing a tightening of monetary policy and perhaps triggering a decline in domestic equities. And yet I don't recall people using the market-manipulation hypothesis as an argument against fixed-exchange-rate regimes, including the gold standard. People who worry about market manipulation think they have found a special flaw in NGDP futures targeting, but the argument proves too much, because the same objection would apply to numerous other systems that seemed to work just fine over a period of decades.

Even though I don't find any of the preceding criticisms of NGDP targeting to have merit, it turns out that there is an alternative approach that delivers almost all the benefits of NGDP futures targeting without any of the problems that critics have pointed to.

Setting Guardrails on Monetary Policy

It turns out that there is a much simpler and less controversial way of using NGDP futures contracts in monetary policy than the regime I proposed in the previous section.[12] Let's start with the assumption that central banks are worried about unforeseen events and thus are reluctant to give up all discretion. But let's also assume that they are open to rules that make their job easier. Here's an analogy: you might like having the freedom to drive your car wherever you wish but also appreciate the safety provided by guardrails, which put constraints on where you can drive your car.

Imagine the following conversation with a central banker:

MARKET MONETARIST: Why not set a 4% NGDP growth rate target?

CENTRAL BANKER: There might be times when a 4% growth rate is not appropriate.

MARKET MONETARIST: OK, but surely there is some range of NGDP growth that, if breached, would not be consistent with your dual mandate?

CENTRAL BANKER: Yes, I suppose an NGDP growth rate of below 2% or above 6% would be pretty clearly destabilizing.

MARKET MONETARIST: Then why don't you offer to sell unlimited NGDP futures
   contracts at a price implying 6% NGDP growth, and buy unlimited contracts at
   a price implying 2% NGDP growth?
CENTRAL BANKER: I'm not sure we can trust this futures market to set monetary
   policy. Markets are occasionally prone to irrational behavior—to bubbles.
MARKET MONETARIST: You don't have to let the NGDP futures market set policy;
   you are free to set monetary policy wherever you wish, as long as you promise
   to buy and sell NGDP futures contracts at the two extremes.
CENTRAL BANKER: But what if most investors took either a long or a short position? We might lose lots of money.
MARKET MONETARIST: You just told me you think you are smarter than markets,
   which are occasionally irrational. In that case, you'll make money on average.
   But if deep down you don't believe that you are smarter than the markets, then
   don't set policy at a position where almost everyone thinks NGDP growth is
   going to be far too high, or far too low.

I see this as a way for central banks to dip their toes in the water, to
get used to markets taking a modest role in directing policy. Actually,
markets already play a role, but in a far less efficient way. The Fed already
pays attention to TIPS spreads, which offer a crude forecast of inflation. It
already pays attention to the fed-funds futures market, which forecasts future policy settings by the Fed. It even reacts to the stock market. NGDP
futures are a far more efficient way of bringing market expectations into
the policy-making process, because they reflect market expectations about
the variable that policy makers *actually care about*—aggregate demand.

Setting the guardrails at 2% and 6% would still allow a fair bit of discretion—too much, in my view. (Excluding extremely rare cases where
NGDP instability may be optimal, as during the COVID-19 lockdown period.) Recessions would still occur, as when NGDP growth suddenly slowed
from 5.5% to 2.5%. But once this framework is in effect, it will be easy to
gradually narrow the guardrails. Perhaps in the second year the limits could
be set at 2.1% and 5.9%. After two years they could be narrowed to 2.2%
and 5.8%. After ten years, the guardrails might be 3% and 5%, which is
narrow enough to dramatically moderate the business cycle. Recall that in
mid-2008 the growth rate of NGDP slowed from the usual 5% to below
negative 3%, the sort of dramatic slowdown that would be nearly impossible under a 3%–5% guardrails regime.

These sorts of NGDP futures guardrails would be sort of like the beep-
ing sound that your car makes when you back up too close to an object.

You can override those beeps and continue backing up, but you are incurring a risk of accident. The central bank can ignore the fact that 99% of speculators are selling 2% NGDP growth contracts, expecting even lower than 2% growth, but the central bank will have been warned, and policy makers had better have a very good excuse ready if there is a deep recession and Congress asks why they recklessly ignored the market forecast.

Here's another way of thinking about the policy. If a 3%–5% guardrails regime had been in place in 2008, then one of two things would have happened: The Fed would have noticed lots of speculators taking a bearish position, and eased policy enough to support adequate NGDP growth. Or, the Fed would have ignored the futures markets, and I would have become very wealthy taking a short position in NGDP futures. Because I don't ever expect to become very wealthy, I do expect NGDP futures targeting to successfully stabilize NGDP expectations.

One Rule to Rule Them All

There's a long-standing debate in economics centered on the issue of rules versus discretion in monetary policy. Should central banks be free to choose the policy that they think best, or should their policy be constrained by a clearly-spelled-out policy rule?

Both sides of the debate are better at seeing the flaws of the other side than the weaknesses of their own view. Previous proponents of policy rules often sought out a mechanical formula that the Fed could use to set the policy instrument. Thus, the monetary base might grow at a fixed rate, or respond in some predictable fashion to changes in velocity. Alternately, interest rate targets might be set on the basis of a formula such as the Taylor rule.

Critics pointed out that a formula might work at one point in time but not at another. They argued that policy makers must have discretion to deal with unforeseen circumstances. But discretion has its own problems, leading to increased uncertainty, which can destabilize the economy. We need policy rules, but they must be the right kind of rules—robust enough to work under changing conditions.

There is only one type of policy rule that is truly robust—Lars Svensson's "target the forecast." Policy should always be set in a position where it is expected to succeed. Any other policy rule will be fragile, likely to be abandoned when conditions are not favorable.

Rules that rely on market expectations to guide policy are likely to be especially robust. One can view all previous policy rule ideas as being embedded within NGDP futures targeting. If monetarists are correct and NGDP growth is driven by money supply growth, then speculators will take money supply data into account when they invest in NGDP futures contracts. If John Taylor is right about how interest rate targets should be set to stabilize inflation and employment, then his insights will factor into expectations of NGDP growth. As we learn more about the relationship between policy instruments and the macroeconomy, the policy rule will automatically adjust to incorporate those new insights.

In the field of monetary policy making, the market-based approach can be seen as a sort of "end of history." It's almost impossible to imagine a policy superior to NGDP futures targeting, because if such a policy existed it could be used to get rich trading in NGDP futures. I don't expect to be proved wrong about NGDP futures targeting for the same reason that I don't ever expect to become a billionaire—markets are scarily efficient.

Fortunately, the Fed is already gradually moving in the direction of market monetarism. In early 2019, the Fed suddenly backed off from predictions of two rate increases during 2019, and instead ended up cutting rates three times. The change was not motivated by the output of macroeconomic models, which tend to rely on dubious concepts such as the Phillips curve. There was no new macroeconomic data that would have justified this sudden policy change. Rather, the Fed was responding to clear market signals that two rate increases risked pushing the economy into recession. The Fed is already moving from Keynesian Phillips-curve policy making toward market monetarism.

And while the Fed has not yet adopted NGDP targeting as an official policy goal, more and more Fed officials are discussing the importance of keeping NGDP growing along a stable path. After this manuscript was completed, the Fed adopted a policy similar to level targeting, called *average inflation targeting*. Over the past decade, market monetarism has made enormous progress, and I expect policy to continue moving in this direction.

CHAPTER TWENTY-TWO

Why Should You Believe in Market Monetarism?

The interpretation of the Great Recession presented in this book runs counter to the prevailing wisdom both within and outside the economics profession. In this final chapter I'd like to review the key tenets of market monetarism, and then make a case for why you should take this counterintuitive theory seriously.

Market monetarism has two components: the market part and the monetarism part. Monetarism is the school of thought that focuses on how shifts in the supply and demand for money drive two of the most important types of macroeconomic phenomena—nominal aggregates, such as inflation and nominal GDP growth, and business-cycle movements in real GDP and unemployment. The market aspect of the theory adds efficient markets and rational expectations theory to late-twentieth-century monetarism.[1] Because of the wisdom of crowds, asset markets provide the optimal forecast of key macroeconomic variables and thus represent the best way of judging whether monetary policy is too easy or too tight.

Some would point to NGDP targeting as a third key component of market monetarism. But it's not what makes market monetarism distinctive; NGDP targeting is totally compatible with mainstream macroeconomics.

The next two sections explain the intuition behind the monetarism and market aspects of market monetarism. I'll try to show that these two approaches offer the best foundation for macroeconomic analysis.

Nominal Aggregates Are Monetary Phenomena:
An Island Parable

Monetarists believe that other schools of thought reify various contingent epiphenomena—that is, they confuse side effects with core mechanisms. Thus, nonmonetarists are inclined to look at phenomena such as inflation through the lens of changes in interest rates, bank credit, or the Phillips curve. They see interest rates as *representing* "monetary policy" and tight labor markets as *causing* inflation.

To a monetarist, those epiphenomena are the side effects of changes in the supply and demand for money in an economy with sticky wages and prices. But they are not the core mechanism. Increases in the money supply or decreases in money demand are inflationary even if they don't move interest rates at all, and even if they don't result in product-market or labor-market tightness. Let's review the intuition behind monetarism with a parable of an island economy lacking a financial system, where prices are flexible and the economy is always at full employment.

Imagine an island with one hundred thousand people who are all self-employed. They produce forty-three commodities, such as food, clothing, and shelter, and exchange the commodities with one other. There is no financial system and obviously there is 0% unemployment—how could a self-employed person be unemployed? To avoid the inconvenience of barter, they adopt some form of money. They could use shells or fish, but let's say they use currency from a huge crate containing $1 billion of Monopoly money that washed up on the beach after a shipwreck.

How do we model the price level? Certainly not with interest rates or a Phillips curve! There are no interest rates and there is no unemployment. It's easiest to start with NGDP and then work backward to prices. Suppose people prefer to hold 12.5% of their annual output or income in the form of money balances. This 12.5% represents the inverse of velocity (i.e., $1/V$). In our island economy, V will be 8 and NGDP will be eight times the money supply. Thus, if the money supply is $1 billion, then NGDP will be $8 billion, or $80,000 per person. Now let's model the rate of inflation:

$$\text{inflation} = \text{NGDP growth} - \text{RGDP growth}.$$

NGDP growth will equal growth in the money supply plus growth in velocity. RGDP growth is determined by nonmonetary factors. There's your basic model of inflation in the simple island economy.

Of course the real world is much more complicated, and this makes it difficult to model velocity. Workers are usually not self-employed—they work for companies and have sticky wages. Labor markets don't always clear. There are also financial markets, and the nominal interest rate can have a big impact on velocity (especially at the zero bound). But no matter how important these extra factors seem, they are still basically epiphenomena—at its core, monetary economics is all about shifts in the supply and demand for money. The equilibrium price level and NGDP is not determined by the Phillips curve or the liquidity effect from interest rate changes.

Let's call the supply and demand transmission mechanism in my simple model the hot-potato-effect mechanism. It's still the core transmission mechanism in our modern economy; it doesn't go away just because you add sticky wages and interest rates. It's just harder to see.

For instance, let's say our island economy with one hundred thousand people and $1 billion in Monopoly money does just fine for 273 years, with NGDP fluctuating above and below $8 billion as velocity moves around due to random minor shocks. Then another crate of Monopoly money unexpectedly washes up on the beach, doubling the money supply to $2 billion. The public is not stupid; people understand the implications of this monetary shock. They know that prices will double in equilibrium, so they immediately start charging twice as much for the commodities they sell.

Is this "rational expectations" assumption realistic? In this case I think it is. When the Mexican government does a 100-to-1 currency reform, a woman in Oaxaca selling strawberries to tourists will immediately cut the peso price of her strawberries by 99%, even though the Mexican government has no law requiring strawberry sellers to charge any particular price.

Now let's say I am wrong about rational expectations and flexible prices. Then what? Let's say the people who live in my island economy are a bit "slow" and don't understand that the extra $1 billion in Monopoly money that washed up on the beach will soon cause the price level to double. In this case you get an overheated economy, with excess demand created by the hot-potato effect. The price level does not immediately double; rather, it doubles over a period of weeks or months, as people eagerly spend their newfound wealth on goods and services.

Notice that it would be exceedingly strange to argue that this excess demand is *causing* the inflation. Indeed, if there were no excess demand we'd be back in the currency reform case, where prices immediately double. The excess demand resulting from sticky prices is actually *slowing* the upward adjustment in prices. The inflation is clearly caused by a doubling of the money supply in both the rational-expectations case and the sticky-price case: the hot-potato effect. It's just that with sticky prices it takes a bit longer for inflation to occur, and excess demand for goods is a side effect. But it would be silly to claim that this excess demand causes the inflation. It's a symptom of price stickiness, which actually *slows* the rise in prices.

Now let's add hourly wage earners with sticky wages to our island economy. After the second crate of Monopoly money washes up on the beach, firms eagerly produce more as demand for their goods rises and wages are temporarily fixed. Hours worked increase. But it would be silly to argue that the tight labor market is *causing* the inflation. If wages were not sticky and the labor market cleared, then the inflation would actually happen even more rapidly; indeed it would happen immediately if both wages and prices were flexible and people had rational expectations. Sticky wages slow the inflation process and lead to labor shortages. Labor shortages are a symptom of sticky wages.

Now let's add a financial market and interest rates. After the second crate of money washes up, the lucky islanders who first discover the crate have more money than they wish to hold. They exchange this money for other assets, which depresses interest rates. Of course eventually prices will double and then they really will be happy to hold twice as much cash as before. Interest rates will return to normal. But during the transition period the excess cash balances cause the interest rate to fall, which depresses the velocity of circulation. The reduced velocity slows inflation. So money is not neutral in the short run. But it would be silly to argue that the lower interest rates *cause* the inflation. Indeed, if interest rates did not decline and velocity stayed the same, then prices would rise *much faster.*

The tendency for interest rates and velocity to initially decline because of sticky prices actually *slows* the upward adjustment in prices. It's merely a symptom of price stickiness, not an underlying cause of inflation. The inflation is caused by the hot-potato effect resulting from a doubling of the money supply. Lower interest rates are a symptom of sticky prices.

I'm a market monetarist, not a new classical economist. So obviously I think sticky wages and nominal debt contracts are really important. But they are important not because they explain how money causes inflation—the flexible price classical model does just fine in that regard—they are important because they help us to understand all the nasty side effects of unstable money. Those real-world side effects are extremely important, far more important than the inflation itself. (Hitler's rise to power occurred during the German tight-money policy of 1929–1933, not the hyperinflation of 1920–1923.)[2] But these side effects are not the underlying cause of the inflation (or of the NGDP growth); they are symptoms. This makes theories of inflation that focus on excess demand, the Phillips curve, or the interest rate doubly wrong. Not only do these factors not cause inflation; to the extent that they are important, they actually slow the inflation process resulting from monetary shocks (shocks to the money supply or to money demand).

Why do so many conventional economists fall into the trap of confusing symptoms and causes? First, because these symptoms often result from inflationary monetary shocks (confusing correlation with causation). And second, because economists are confusing demand shifts with "excess demand." Think about a microeconomic analogy: If there is a shortage of bottled water in Florida after a hurricane and water prices are gradually rising to equilibrium, the rising water prices are not caused by the shortage of water; prices would be even higher if there were no excess demand, no shortage. The rising water prices are caused by more demand for water. The shortage occurs because the prices do not rise fast enough. Similarly, inflation is caused by either more supply of money or less demand for money. All the rest is symptoms—epiphenomena.

Where did modern macroeconomic theorists go wrong? Perhaps when they built these liquidity-effect and Phillips-curve epiphenomena into the center of their models of the transmission mechanism. We don't need Phillips curves or interest rates to explain why a greater supply of peaches or less demand for peaches reduces the relative value of peaches, nor do we need Phillips curves or interest rates to explain why more money supply or less money demand reduces the relative value of money. We need to go back to basics: supply and demand for the medium of account.

Japan has kept interest rates very low for a very long time, and it still has low inflation. Its unemployment rate was only 2.2% in late 2019. Sorry, but interest rates and the Phillips curve are not reliable models of inflation.

Now of course elite macroeconomists are very smart people, and they did not develop these models for no reason at all. In the short run, an easy-money policy often (not always) leads to lower short-term interest rates. But over longer periods of time it often leads to higher nominal interest rates. The point here is that it's the easy-money policy that matters, not the interest rates. An easy-money policy will lead to higher inflation *regardless* of whether it causes lower or higher interest rates. The easy money policy of 1965–1981 led to both higher interest rates and higher inflation in the US. Switzerland's tight-money policy of January 2015 led to lower inflation and lower interest rates—even in the short run. (Yes, the Neo-Fisherians are occasionally correct.)

The same is true of the Phillips curve. It worked OK for many years, especially under the gold standard. The Phillips curve still "works" in places like Hong Kong, as we saw in chapter 10. A low rate of unemployment is indeed often associated with higher inflation. But it did not work during the 1970s in America, when unemployment and inflation rose at the same time, or in 2019, when inflation stayed low despite unemployment falling to 3.5%. And that's because it is not part of the core transmission mechanism for inflation: the core mechanism is the supply and demand for money. Changes in inflation may or may not be related to interest rates or unemployment, but they are always related to what's going on with the supply and demand for money.

Armed with this market-monetarist perspective, we reinterpret macroeconomic history, trying to zero in on the core mechanism without getting distracted by the various side effects of monetary shocks. What are some of these distracting side effects? Changes in interest rates (due to sticky prices), shocks to the financial system (due to sticky nominal debt), and shocks to the labor market (due to sticky nominal hourly wages). These side effects are important, but the core message of market monetarism is that these side effects are just that: side effects. They do not drive the process. That's why one can find examples of inflation that cannot be explained by conventional models. A good example can be seen in 1933–1934, when (wholesale) prices rose by 20% after a monetary shock that produced almost no change in either interest rates or the money supply. Instead, a sharp devaluation of the dollar dramatically reduced current money demand (by increasing the future expected money supply), creating rapid inflation despite 25% unemployment, and even though much of the banking system was shut down.

How an NGDP Futures Market Can Revive Macroeconomic Theory

The previous section explained the intuition behind the monetarism part of market monetarism. But what about the market part of the theory? I believe that the biggest flaw in modern macroeconomics is that the efficient markets hypothesis is not deeply embedded into all our models. Thus, when there is a policy initiative such as quantitative easing, mainstream economists adopt a "wait and see" attitude. They say that after observing a year or two of macroeconomic data, we will have a better idea about the policy's effectiveness.

A market monetarist says that within five minutes we'll know everything that we will ever know about the effectiveness of the policy move. Inflation, RGDP, and NGDP futures prices will immediately adjust to reflect the optimal forecast of the effect of the policy initiative. If those markets don't exist, then other proxies such as TIPS spreads, exchange rates, commodity prices, and stock prices will tell us all that we can know about the effectiveness of the policy. The actual future performance of the economy will be affected by that policy shock, but also by myriad other unrelated factors. Waiting and observing the actual future course of events won't tell us anything that we don't already know. We need to study the way shocks have an impact on the expected path of the economy, not the actual path.

Here's an analogy. If a star quarterback breaks his arm three days before the Super Bowl, the change in the Las Vegas point spread will tell us all we'll ever know about the injury's impact on the outcome of the game. The actual outcome of the game will depend on many random factors— the injury to the quarterback being only one.

Market monetarists see market-driven regimes for "targeting the forecast" as a sort of "end of (macroeconomic) history." They are the final stage in the long process of discovering an optimal policy rule. How can any policy ever be better than the policy stance expected by markets to reach the policy goal? How can any macroeconomic model's forecast ever reliably beat the market forecast? Sure, some models might outdo the market occasionally, but the key word here is *reliably*.

Market monetarists also argue that market forecasts of the goal variable are the most useful measure of the stance of monetary policy. Other economists look at a wide variety of epiphenomena, especially interest rates. But the response of interest rates is dependent on any number of contingent factors and cannot possibly serve as a reliable indicator of whether money is easy or tight. Interest rates are never higher than during hyperinflation, when money is actually quite expansionary. In the final analysis, the only useful definition of easy and tight money is that they describe the actual stance of monetary policy relative to the stance expected to achieve the policy goal: Is money too easy or too tight? Easy money is a policy expected to produce excessive NGDP growth, and tight money is a policy expected to produce too little NGDP growth. And again, it's market expectations that will ultimately provide the optimal forecast.

Why Should You Be Persuaded by Market Monetarism?

In twenty-two chapters, I've described my market-monetarist approach to macroeconomics and explained how this model can account for the Great Recession. But why should you believe any of my claims? After all, mine is a decidedly heterodox view of recent events, and of monetary policy more broadly. What distinguishes me from one hundred other monetary cranks, all making grand claims that they have reinvented macroeconomics, attached to policy nostrums that can supposedly cure all our ills?

When I was a teenager, I was impressed by bold, heterodox thinkers. "Yeah, how *could* those pyramids have been built without the assistance of aliens from outer space?" As an adult, I've come to appreciate the efficiency of intellectual markets. If most mainstream physicists say that cold fusion is implausible, I go with the consensus view. It's very unlikely that any heterodox theory I have read about will survive the test of time. So why should you be persuaded by the ideas in this book? Why shouldn't you regard me as just another monetary crank?

I'm not sure I have a pat answer to this objection. I could point out that there was a period when a number of other commentators thought that my arguments had held up well over time.[3] They seemed to think that recent innovations in Fed policy had somehow validated the arguments I have been making since 2008. But that success occurred at a pretty modest level; I certainly didn't convince the overall profession.

Another answer is that my theory is not at all like cold fusion. As we saw in chapter 13, it was built on the foundations of some very boring mainstream macroeconomic ideas, circa 2007. So if I am a rebel, I'm a very strange kind of rebel—a heterodox defender of orthodoxy at a time when many mainstream economists have lost faith in textbook economics.

Paul Krugman once made a similar observation. In a 1996 essay entitled "Ricardo's Difficult Idea," Krugman provided four recommendations for becoming a public intellectual. This one caught my eye: "*Adopt the stance of rebel:* There is nothing that plays worse in our culture than seeming to be the stodgy defender of old ideas, no matter how true those ideas may be. Luckily, at this point the orthodoxy of the academic economists is very much a minority position among intellectuals in general; one can seem to be a courageous maverick, boldly challenging the powers that be, by reciting the contents of a standard textbook. It has worked for me!" That's also what I've been doing for the past decade.[4]

Also keep in mind that even if markets are efficient, it is only because each trader is willing to take a fresh, independent look at the situation and do his or her best to make accurate forecasts. Similarly, the market for ideas does tend toward efficiency in the long run, but only because intellectuals are willing to continually probe weaknesses in existing theories, and seek better ones. I view myself as just one tiny component of the wisdom of crowds, which means I can't do my job if I blindly accept the conventional wisdom.

In 2017, a blogger named Scott Alexander reviewed a new book by Eliezer Yudkowsky, which wrestles with the question of when should we be willing to reject the expert consensus. I was intrigued by Alexander's summary of one of Yudkowsky's examples:

> Eliezer spent a few years criticizing the Bank of Japan's macroeconomic policies, which he thought were stupid and costing Japan trillions of dollars in lost economic growth. Everyone told Eliezer he couldn't be right, because he was an amateur disagreeing with professionals. But after a few years, the Bank of Japan switched to Eliezer's preferred policies, the Japanese economy instantly improved, and now the consensus position is that the original policies were deeply flawed in exactly the way Eliezer thought they were. Doesn't that mean Japan left a trillion-dollar bill on the ground by refusing to implement policies that even an amateur could see were correct?[5]

Of course other people that I view as monetary cranks, such as advocates of modern monetary theory, also see events confirming their worldviews. But the following Alexander observation offers a bit of evidence beyond "he said, she said":

> Why was Eliezer able to out-predict the Bank of Japan? Because the Bank's policies were set by a couple of Japanese central bankers who had no particular incentive to get things right, and no particular incentive to listen to smarter people correcting them. Eliezer wasn't alone in his prediction—he says that Japanese stocks were priced in ways that suggested *most investors* realized the Bank's policies were bad. Most of the smart people with skin in the game had come to the same realization Eliezer had.[6]

If I have the serene confidence of a monetary crank, it is founded on one bedrock principle—it's really hard to get rich. And it's hard to get

rich because markets are scarily efficient. If markets systematically reacted the wrong way to economic news, then it would be easy to profit on
that market flaw. But it isn't easy to earn excess returns. At its core, market monetarism is about the view that the best estimate of the way that
the world works is roughly the way that the markets believe it works. In
other words, always take the asset-market consensus over the intellectual-
market consensus.

The specifics of market monetarism will always be a work in progress.
Market participants will continually discover new perspectives on the
economy and incorporate those perspectives into their mental models of
the economy. I hope that future market monetarists disprove some of my
claims and come up with better versions of the theory. Maybe they'll discover that markets believe that fiscal stimulus is effective.

Nonetheless, the basic market-monetarist framework for thinking
about the economy is likely to survive:

- Shocks to the supply and demand for money drive the nominal aggregates.
- Unexpected movements in the nominal aggregates drive fluctuations in real
  output and employment. They also contribute to financial instability.
- The market forecast of key macroeconomic variables provides the optimal
  way of understanding what's going on with the economy, predicting its future
  course, evaluating the stance of monetary policy, and indeed setting the policy
  instruments.

There's no objective reason to rely on my pronouncements, as my creden-
tial are less impressive than those of many other economists. I was just
lucky; my set of research interests dovetailed almost perfectly with what
was needed to make sense out of the 2008 crisis. But the asset markets are
another story. If the asset markets and I ever diverge on some core issue,
then by all means believe the asset markets, not me.

How to See Past Framing Effects

I once came across a book by Jonathan Lopez that discussed forgeries
of Vermeer paintings that were produced during the 1920s by the Dutch
painter Han van Meegeren. I was struck by the way Lopez describes how
van Meegeren could fool the experts with paintings that today look so
mediocre, so unlike the work of Vermeer:

He was to discover, first and foremost, that a fake doesn't necessarily succeed or fail according to the fidelity with which it replicates the distant past but on the basis of its power to sway the contemporary mind. Although the best forgeries may mimic the style of a long dead artist, they tend to reflect the tastes and attitudes of their own period. Most people can't perceive this: they respond intuitively to that which seems familiar and comprehensible in an artwork, even one presumed to be centuries old. It's part of what makes forgeries so seductive.

Van Meegeren put this principle to work early and did so with notable style and grace, although, at the time, even he was probably unaware of his anachronisms. Van Meegeren's lovely Vermeer-esque girls from the 1920s resemble, on the one hand, the genuine article, but on the other, the highly fashionable portraits that the forger was doing under his own name at roughly the same moment. To the eyes and expectations of the day, what could possibly have been more appealing, on a subliminal level, than an art deco version of Vermeer's delicate aesthetic? Indeed, Van Meegeren's *Lace Maker* looks as though she would gladly cast aside her labors and fox-trot the night away if only someone would ask her.[7]

Now let's compare this to the way *Time* magazine described the 1991 recession, and then look for parallels:

Why are Americans so gloomy, fearful and even panicked about the current economic slump? . . .

. . . The slump is the longest, if not the deepest, since the Great Depression. Traumatized by layoffs that have cost more than 1.2 million jobs during the slump, U.S. consumers have fallen into their deepest funk in years. "Never in my adult life have I heard more deep-seated feelings of concern," says Howard Allen, retired chairman of Southern California Edison. "Many, many business leaders share this lack of confidence and recognize that we are in real economic trouble." Says University of Michigan economist Paul McCracken: "This is more than just a recession in the conventional sense. What has happened has put the fear of God into people."

. . . U.S. consumers seem suddenly disillusioned with the American Dream of rising prosperity even as capitalism and democracy have consigned the Soviet Union to history's trash heap. "I'm worried if my kids can earn a decent living and buy a house," says Tony Lentini, vice president of public affairs for Mitchell Energy in Houston. "I wonder if this will be the first generation that didn't do better than their parents. There's a genuine feeling that the country has gotten way off track, and neither political party has any answers. Americans don't see any solutions."

... The deeper tremors emanate from the kind of change that occurs only once every few decades. America is going through a historic transition from the heedless borrow-and-spend society of the 1980s to one that stresses savings and investment.[8]

Today, the van Meegeren forgeries of Vermeer paintings look almost laughably inept, and the *Time* magazine description of the 1991 recession seems absurdly histrionic. The 1991 "slump" was about as ordinary a business cycle as you can imagine. Tight money slowed NGDP growth, triggering a quite typical recession. The economy did fine during the remainder of the 1990s.

I see a common theme in these two seemingly unrelated examples. In both cases, people had trouble looking past the way current details showed up in the object of their analysis. They had trouble seeing the *timeless elements* in the picture.

Recall that it wasn't until several decades after the beginning of the Great Depression that Milton Friedman and Anna Schwartz were able to look past the 1929 stock-market crash, the subsequent banking panics, and the international monetary crisis of 1931–1933 and see that the root cause of the Great Depression was a severe decline in NGDP caused by excessively tight money. I used to wonder why it took the profession so long to come up with this explanation. Now I know why. I lived through the Great Recession. I remember the powerful sway of headline news stories in late 2008. When the financial system was collapsing, it took a determined effort to look beyond the headlines, to look beyond the framing effects, and to understand that tight money was driving NGDP growth sharply lower. The Great Recession certainly looked like a story about a housing bust and a banking crisis.

I'd like my readers to come away from this book armed with the cognitive skills needed to see past framing effects—to get to the heart of what's going on with the macroeconomy. Here's my advice to readers who want a clearer understanding of what's really going on. Focus like a laser on a couple of key principles, and don't be distracted by the headlines.

The first principle is that monetary policy drives NGDP, and NGDP instability drives most of the business cycle in large, highly diversified economies. So how do we determine whether a recession is the Fed's fault? If the downturn in real GDP is not accompanied by a sharp decline in NGDP growth, then it is not the Fed's fault. If NGDP also falls sharply over an extended period, then it is almost always the Fed's fault. Surely it can't be that simple! Don't we need to consider *why* there was a decline in NGDP? Actually, no. If NGDP growth falls sharply for an extended period then it is the Fed's fault. (Yes, one exception is that the Fed did not cause the initial COVID-19 slump, but monetary policy may yet end up prolonging the recession.)

Here's why people get confused about this issue. Fed policy errors don't happen in a vacuum; they occur when the Fed takes its eye off the ball—say, because of an oil shock or a financial crisis. These distractions may cause the Fed to lose focus on maintaining adequate NGDP growth (as both shocks did in 2008), triggering a recession. But even in that case, the recession would probably be caused by the fall in NGDP growth, not by the oil shock or the financial crisis. Real shocks by themselves can occasionally cause a mild recession in a large, diversified economy like the US, but this happens very rarely.[9]

Consider this analogy. Someone is given a slow-acting poison, which may or may not be a fatal dose. Then an assassin comes up and shoots the same person in the heart. The gunshot wound is the cause of death, regardless of the poison in the victim's system. In this analogy, the poison is like a real shock and the gunshot wound is like a monetary shock. With sticky wages, a sharp fall in NGDP growth means higher unemployment—always.

Some people have a very odd belief that a tight money policy instituted during a period when the economy is healthy can cause a recession, but a tight money policy instituted during a period of financial turmoil cannot cause a recession. In the latter case, they see the financial turmoil as the "real cause" of the recession. That's like claiming that a gunshot to the heart will kill a healthy person but will not kill someone who is being poisoned.

A sharp fall in NGDP growth is *always* contractionary, regardless of what else is going on in the economy. If NGDP falls sharply, then the Fed has fired a gun into the body of the economy. That body might or might not also have (financial) poison in its system—but if NGDP growth plunges, then the Fed is holding a smoking gun. It's that simple.

The second principle is that supply-side factors determine longer-term RGDP growth and play a rather modest role in the business cycle. Real shocks are most likely to be responsible for recessions when inflation is countercyclical.

In the longer term, supply-side factors begin to dominate. Being a good macroeconomist means being able to think on two levels at once. We need to understand the difference between NGDP and RGDP, and why these variables are often highly correlated and yet remain radically different. We need to understand the difference between nominal exchange rates and real exchange rates, and why these variables too are often highly correlated and yet remain radically different. And we need to understand the difference between short-run and long-run factors affecting real GDP. Each day, the economy is affected by demand shocks from the recent past as well as by supply shocks extending much further back in time.

Some economists are famously known as supply-siders. Others are demand-side economists. I'm a supply-and-demand-sider; I regard both factors as highly important. When NGDP and RGDP both fall sharply at almost exactly the same time, it makes sense to look first for demand-side factors. Conversely, when there is a very long period of "secular stagnation," it's a mistake to focus on demand-side factors.

The best way to look past the noise is to use a natural-rate version of the AS-AD model, and let the data speak for itself. Don't form a preconceived idea about what must be happening and then look for data to confirm your view. People who do that tend to make really bad forecasts. Let the data lead the way.

Always remember that the real world is complex, constantly buffeted by both demand and supply shocks. Slow growth in aggregate demand caused relatively high unemployment early in the second decade of the twenty-first century, but the extended unemployment insurance program (a negative supply shock) also played a modest role. The economy can be shot and poisoned at the same time.

This second principle was written before the recent COVID-19 depression. In retrospect, the claim that deflationary recessions have monetary causes seems somehow wrong. Rather than rewrite this section, I'd like to think about why this principle doesn't seem to apply to the 2020 recession.

First, recessions can have multiple causes, and it seems plausible that both real and nominal factors played a role in 2020. More importantly, the nature of this real shock was quite unusual, perhaps unique in American history. During the typical adverse supply shock, the production of key commodities like oil is disrupted. In this case, it was the ability to *consume* oil that was inhibited while the ability of oil companies to produce the commodity remained almost uninterrupted. That doesn't mean that a suitably expansionary monetary policy couldn't have prevented the accompanying disinflation and thus moderated the depression, just that it would have required a much more aggressive stimulus than is typically the case.[10]

I'd like to conclude with a few comments on the future prospects for market monetarism. I'm actually pretty optimistic on this score, but not because I'm under any illusions that we market monetarists have much influence on the economics profession. I believe we'll win in the long run, but only after our ideas are independently rediscovered by much more eminent economists.

The increasing spread and growing sophistication of financial markets will inevitably lead to the creation of an NGDP futures market. Technological changes such as big data will eventually lead to real-time estimates of NGDP at a monthly, and perhaps even a daily, frequency. It's only a matter of time until all money is electronic and the power of computers provides us with good estimates of the aggregate daily purchases of goods and services in the US economy.

This brave new world will have many downsides, including a loss of privacy. On the positive side, however, it's almost inevitable that NGDP market expectations will become increasingly easy to measure and thus an increasingly important indicator of the state of the economy. And once we reach that point, it's easy to see how NGDP futures prices could eventually replace interest rates as the preferred indicator of the stance of monetary policy. They would be far more reliable.

I've always thought that an NGDP futures price is what has been needed to complete macroeconomics. Once *TheMoneyIllusion* blog got some attention, I was able to raise enough money to fund an NGDP prediction market.[11] With this market we finally have real-time estimates of expected NGDP growth, the most important single variable in macroeconomics, or at least in business-cycle theory.

Someday we'll have a much more liquid version of this market, and monetary policy can focus on stabilizing NGDP expectations. The ultimate goal is to make the economy act as if classical economic theory is true, as if supply creates its own demand (sometimes referred to as "Say's law"). The goal is an economy in which politicians don't have to worry about maintaining adequate aggregate spending, but they do have to worry about opportunity costs, in which case it is obvious that more spending in one area means less in another. In other words, the goal is a world in which policy makers don't view fiscal stimulus or the bailout of bankrupt firms as a way of "saving jobs," but rather as a sort of crony capitalism that favors one sector over another. We are not there yet, but the arrow of history is certainly pointing in the right direction.

I started this book with a famous Richard Dawkins quotation involving Ludwig Wittgenstein. Let's conclude with the same anecdote, reimagined to illustrate market monetarism:

> "Tell me," the great twentieth-century philosopher Ludwig Wittgenstein once asked a friend, "why do people always say it was natural to assume that the Great Recession was caused by a housing crash and subsequent financial crisis?" His friend replied, "Well, obviously because it just looks as though the Great Recession was caused by a housing crash and subsequent financial crisis." Wittgenstein responded, "Well, what would it have looked like if it had looked as though a tight money policy had sharply depressed NGDP growth, causing lower nominal interest rates, higher unemployment, and a wave of defaults on nominal debts?"[12]

Acknowledgments

I'd like to thank Charles Meyer and Chad Zimmerman at the University of Chicago Press, who gave me the opportunity to publish my views. Two peer reviewers for the University of Chicago Press provided valuable suggestions and constructive criticism of both the content and the style of the initial manuscript.

I'd like to thank a number of people who directly contributed to this project, especially my colleagues at the Mercatus Center at George Mason University. Patrick Horan and Craig Fratrik provided invaluable research support and pointed to areas that needed improvement. Marc Dupont assisted on the graphs, and both he and Jacob Fishbeck provided feedback on an early draft. Line editor Corrie Schwab provided very detailed editorial comments that greatly improved the manuscript. Garrett Brown guided me in all the steps needed to get a manuscript in acceptable shape for a top-flight publisher.

Over the past decade, I've learned a lot from reading other bloggers who are sympathetic to some of the market-monetarist ideas, including David Beckworth, Nick Rowe, George Selgin, David Glasner, Marcus Nunes, Kevin Erdmann, Josh Hendrickson, and Lars Christensen, from whom I have learned a great deal. But I've also benefited from reading bloggers outside the market-monetarist community, including Paul Krugman, Tyler Cowen, Brad DeLong, Tim Duy, John Cochrane, Greg Mankiw, John Taylor, and many others, and wrestling with their insights, even when we have disagreed on particular issues. The internet has enabled so much fruitful interaction over the past decade that it is now difficult for me to detect exactly where these bloggers' ideas end and mine begin. Although I have done my best to give credit where it is due, undoubtedly there are places in this book where other researchers do not receive the credit they deserve.

I'd also like to thank Ken Duda, Gabe Newell, and a number of other generous donors who had the vision to support my efforts to create a nominal GDP futures market. And, finally, I'd like to thank my wife, Bi, and my daughter, Isabella, for putting up with my fanatical devotion to this project over a number of years.

Notes

Preface

1. Christina Romer, "Dear Ben: It's Time for Your Volcker Moment," *New York Times*, October 29, 2011.

Introduction

1. Ben Bernanke's *The Courage to Act: A Memoir of a Crisis and Its Aftermath* (2015) provides an excellent mainstream account of the financial crisis and the Great Recession.

2. Hall, "Why Does the Economy Fall to Pieces?," 3.

3. See Friedman and Schwartz, *Monetary History*.

4. In addition, the GDP growth data from 2008 were revised downward in later revisions.

5. Milton Friedman, "Rx for Japan: Back to the Future," *Wall Street Journal*, December 17, 1997.

6. Friedman looked at broader monetary aggregates such as the M2 money supply when he evaluated the stance of monetary policy. Unfortunately, the monetary aggregates have not proved to be reliable indicators in recent years.

7. Mishkin, *Economics of Money*, 8th ed., 606–7.

8. Bernanke, "Japanese Monetary Policy."

9. Bernanke, "Remarks by Governor Ben S. Bernanke."

10. In chapter 17, I'll show that the 1999 Bernanke critique of the Bank of Japan mirrors the criticisms of the Fed provided in this book.

11. Ben S. Bernanke, "Temporary Price-Level Targeting: An Alternative Framework for Monetary Policy," *Brookings* (blog), October 12, 2017, https://www.brookings.edu/blog/ben-bernanke/2017/10/12/temporary-price-level-targeting-an-alternative-framework-for-monetary-policy/.

12. Bernanke, "Remarks by Governor Ben S. Bernanke."

Chapter One

1. The eleven-minute segment that discusses this issue has interesting implications for the question of whether the Fed "caused" the Great Recession. John Horgan and Joshua Knobe, "Science Saturday: Experimental Philosophy," *Bloggingheads.tv*, posted February 16, 2008, video, starting at 20:47, https://bloggingheads .tv/videos/1460?in=20:47.

2. That's not to say that one cannot develop sophisticated models, using game theory or behavioral economics, in which firms raise prices a bit faster than they cut prices. The point is that students were basing their reasoning on the false assumption that cutting prices means doing some sort of favor to consumers at the expense of profits.

3. I say "most" because if the money shortage is severe enough, it can disrupt business to some extent. The Indian economy slowed modestly in early 2017 after the government invalidated most of the currency stock, in an ineffective attempt to flush out illegal hoards of cash.

4. Here I'm actually referring to the monetary base, which also includes bank deposits at the Fed. In 2007–2008, the base was roughly 98% currency.

5. My book on the Great Depression, *The Midas Paradox: Financial Markets, Government Policy Shocks, and the Great Depression* (2015), focuses on flaws in how the major central banks managed the international gold standard.

Chapter Two

1. Fisher, *Money Illusion*, 3.

2. In fact, the term *pound sterling* refers to the fact that in the distant past the British pound was one pound of silver.

3. Gas cost about $.17 a gallon in 1931. Silver has recently been worth about $20 per ounce in the commodity markets, which means that $.17 worth of old silver coins would sell for $2.45 today—roughly the cost of a gallon of gasoline when I was writing this book.

4. See Sumner, *Midas Paradox*.

5. Fisher, *Money Illusion*, 6.

Chapter Three

1. Many people mistakenly focus on August 1971, when President Nixon raised the official price of gold. But what matters is the market price of gold, which began rising in 1968. That was the final break with the gold standard.

2. Keynes, *Tract on Monetary Reform*, 172.

3. See Barro, "Money and the Price Level."

4. In recent years, the value of gold has been much less stable.

5. See Sumner, *Midas Paradox*.

6. With unit-elastic demand, the price times the quantity is always constant along a given demand curve.

7. Hume, "Of the Balance of Trade," 62–63.

Chapter Four

1. The relationship is precisely true when changes are expressed as first differences of logs, which is the approach used in upper-level economics.

2. Hume, "Of Interest," 56.

3. I suppose Singapore can stand in for Hume's imaginary Pacific nation, except that it is certainly not free of foreign trade!

4. Of course this counterfactual is only approximately true and is based on the assumption that price levels show relatively little long-run change under the gold standard.

Chapter Five

1. The ideas in this chapter are partly based on Phillip Cagan's analysis, in "Monetary Dynamics of Hyperinflation," of money demand during hyperinflation.

2. See Sumner, "Model of the Transactions and Hoarding Demand."

3. See Sumner.

Chapter Six

1. For an overview of the debate, see Celia and Grubb, "Non-Legal-Tender Paper Money"; Grubb, "Is Paper Money Just Paper Money?"; Michener, "Re-examination of the Empirical Evidence."

2. Sumner, "Colonial Currency."

3. Krugman, "It's Baaack!"

4. Krugman.

5. Krugman.

6. Krugman.

7. Krugman.

8. Krugman.

9. Krugman.

10. Krugman.

11. See Ireland (2014).

12. Nick Rowe, "E(NGDP) Level-Path Targeting for the People of the Concrete Steppes," *Worthwhile Canadian Initiative* (blog), October 20, 2011, https://
worthwhile.typepad.com/worthwhile_canadian_initi/2011/10/engdp-level-path
-targeting-for-the-people-of-the-concrete-steppes-.html.

13. Nick Rowe, "Two (Probably) Unstable Macroeconomic Equilibria," *Worthwhile Canadian Initiative*, September 25, 2012, https://worthwhile.typepad.com
/worthwhile_canadian_initi/2012/09/two-probably-unstable-macroeconomic-equi
libria.html.

Chapter Seven

1. Bernanke, "Remarks by Governor Ben S. Bernanke."

2. Bernanke, *Courage to Act*.

3. See Meltzer, *Keynes's Monetary Theory*.

4. Some argue that the post–World War I reparations imposed on Germany, as
well as the German hyperinflation of 1920–1923, also contributed to the success
of the Nazis. It is worth noting, however, that the Nazi Party was still relatively
small as late as 1929 and then rapidly gained support during the severe depression
of 1929–1933. In *The Midas Paradox*, I argued that flaws in the international gold
standard contributed to the deflation and depression of the early 1930s, which was
especially severe in Germany. Thilo Nils Hendrik Albers used an international
data set to show that economic recovery tended to occur after a country left the
gold standard. Albers, "Prelude and Global Impact of the Great Depression."

5. Krugman, "Who Was Milton Friedman?"

6. Hume, "Of Money," 37–38.

7. Hume, 40.

8. Hume, 40.

9. Hume, 41–42.

10. Hume, 42.

11. I use these figures to make the math easier; the actual figures were slightly
different.

12. Research by Jakob Madsen, in "Length and the Depth," confirms that
wages and prices in the US were *sticky*, or slow to adjust, during the Great Depression. Jonathan Rose, in "Hoover's Truce," showed that President Hoover's policy
of discouraging wage cuts during the Great Depression made nominal wages especially sticky.

13. My book *The Midas Paradox* summarizes twenty years of my research on
the Great Depression.

14. A study by Timothy Hatton and Mark Thomas, "Labour Markets," confirms that changes in labor-market institutions explain why the US recovery during the 1930s was slower than the recovery after the 1920–1921 depression.

15. In a similar fashion, those who came of age during the Great Inflation tended to be overly concerned about inflation during the period after 2008. Unfortunately, the economics profession has a lot of "generals fighting the last war."

Chapter Eight

1. Keynes, *Treatise on Money*, 1:170.

2. Keynes, *Collected Writings*, 21:186. (The selection quoted here was originally published in March 1933.)

3. Friedman, "Role of Monetary Policy"; Phelps, "Phillips Curves."

4. There had been previous examples of fiat money, such as the Civil War–era greenbacks, but these were temporary policies until the US could return to a commodity money standard.

5. Here I am using changes in the GDP deflator price index for inflation. CPI inflation was a bit higher.

6. Freidman and Schwartz, *Monetary History*.

7. I say "seems to" because on closer examination a policy of targeting the money supply is just as interventionist as a policy of targeting interest rates, exchange rates, the price of gold, or any other variable.

8. Friedman, "Mr. Market."

9. Friedman, "25 Years after the Rediscovery of Money," 177.

Chapter Nine

1. Friedman, "Role of Monetary Policy."

2. Friedman.

3. Lucas, "Econometric Policy Evaluation."

4. Walters, "Consistent Expectations."

5. Lucas, "Econometric Policy Evaluation."

6. Spiegel, "Central Bank Independence."

7. Keynes, *Collected Writings*, 13:518. Emphasis in original. (The selection quoted here was originally published in February 1935.)

8. The new classical economists did not deny that some price stickiness exists; rather, they claimed that this factor was not significant enough to explain why nominal shocks played an important role in the business cycle.

9. I'm cheating a little here. One of the "real shocks" that might cause depressions is bad government policies, including higher taxes, changes to regulations, and price controls. But while bad policies did lengthen the Great Depression, there is little evidence that the typical business cycle is actually caused by government intervention in the economy.

10. "Open Letter to Ben Bernanke," *Wall Street Journal*, November 15, 2010.

Chapter Ten

1. Sumner, *Midas Paradox*.

2. Dan Weil, "Shiller: Why Negative Rates Aren't Sparking More Investment Is 'Puzzle of Our Time,'" *Newsmax Finance*, February 12, 2015.

3. See Silver and Sumner, "Nominal and Real Wage Cyclicality."

4. This is not to deny that public policies can increase wage stickiness. But even without minimum wages and pro-union legislation, deflationary shocks would tend to boost unemployment, as in 1921.

5. See Bils, "Real Wages."

6. Sumner and Silver, "Real Wages." For a theoretical explanation for procyclical real wages during supply shocks, see Hoehn, "Procyclical Real Wages."

7. See Selgin, *Less Than Zero*.

8. This may need to be revised slightly going forward, as interest rates seem to be trending a bit lower, even accounting for NGDP growth.

9. Koenig, "Like a Good Neighbor"; Sheedy, "Debt and Incomplete Financial Markets." More recently, James Bullard, president of Federal Reserve Bank of St. Louis, made a similar argument in a 2019 paper he coauthored with Riccardo Di-Cecio, "Optimal Monetary Policy." In "Better Risk Sharing," David Beckworth provided empirical support for the view that NGDP targeting promotes financial stability.

Chapter Eleven

1. There is conflicting research on this issue. See Nelson, "Was the Deflation of 1929–1930 Anticipated?"; Hamilton, "Was the Deflation during the Great Depression Anticipated?"; Cecchetti, "Prices during the Great Depression"; Evans and Wachtel, "Were Price Changes during the Great Depression Anticipated?"

2. Keynes, *Tract on Monetary Reform*, 80.

3. Friedman, "Reviving Japan."

4. Mishkin, *Economics of Money* (8th ed.), 606–7.

5. Mishkin, *Economics of Money* (10th ed.), 617–18.

6. Bernanke, "Some Thoughts on Monetary Policy in Japan."

7. Steve Matthews and Jeff Kearns, "Bernanke Says Accommodative Policy Needed," *Bloomberg*, March 26, 2012.

8. Bernanke, "Japanese Monetary Policy," 10. Emphasis in original.

Chapter Twelve

1. Japan's currency may have needed to depreciate because Japan "missed the boat" on the high-tech boom of the twenty-first century, even relative to East Asian firms such as South Korea's Samsung.

2. Dornbusch, "Expectations and Exchange Rate Dynamics."

3. Dornbusch.

4. Lars Svensson pointed out that the impact of currency depreciation is ambiguous, because there is a both an income and a substitution effect. Svensson, "Escaping from a Liquidity Trap."

5. Sinead Carew, "Global Stocks Slammed by ECB; Euro Jumps Most since 2009," *Reuters*, December 2, 2015.

6. Svensson, "Escaping from a Liquidity Trap"; McCallum, "Theoretical Analysis."

7. Svensson, "Escaping from a Liquidity Trap."

8. Bernanke, Reinhart, and Sack, "Monetary Policy Alternatives," 10–11.

9. John Taylor, "Not a Repeat of the Great Intervention," *Economics One*, September 18, 2010.

10. Taylor.

11. Paul Krugman, "Reckonings; Purging the Rottenness," *New York Times*, April 25, 2001. The Mellon allusion is a reference to the claim by President Hoover's Treasury secretary that excesses needed to be purged from the economy during the Great Depression.

12. See Bergsten and Gagnon, *Currency Conflict*.

13. A recent paper by Peter Navarro and Wilbur Ross, "Scoring the Trump Economic Plan," cited the expenditure equation for GDP (GDP = C + I + G + NX) to argue that current account deficits reduce output:

> The growth in any nation's gross domestic product (GDP)—and therefore its ability to create jobs and generate additional income and tax revenues—is driven by four factors: consumption growth, the growth in government spending, investment growth, and net exports. When net exports are negative, that is, when a country runs a trade deficit by importing more than it exports, this subtracts from growth. . . .
>
> In 2015, the US trade deficit in goods was a little under $800 billion while the US ran a surplus of about $300 billion in services. This left an overall deficit of around $500 billion. Reducing this "trade deficit drag" would increase GDP growth.

14. Autor, Dorn, and Hanson, "China Shock." Paul Krugman shares my view that monetary policy would have offset any impact of the China shock on aggregate employment. Paul Krugman, "Trade and Jobs: A Note," *New York Times*, July 3, 2016.

15. Autor, Dorn, and Hanson, "China Shock."

Chapter Thirteen

1. Sumner, "Comment on Brad DeLong." See also Scott B. Sumner, "About This Blog," *TheMoneyIllusion*, February 2, 2009.

2. Sumner, "Using Futures Instrument Prices."

3. Thompson, "Free Banking"; Hall, "Optimal Fiduciary Monetary Systems"; Glasner, *Free Banking*; Hetzel, "Maintaining Price Stability."

4. See Svensson, "What Is Wrong with Taylor Rules?"

5. Eichengreen, *Golden Fetters*.

6. Research by Gabriel Mathy in "Stock Volatility" confirms that stock indices were unusually volatile during the 1930s, and that major price movements were often linked to monetary factors, such as banking crises and instability in the international gold standard.

7. We later learned that interest rates can actually go slightly negative, but there is still presumably an effective lower bound, perhaps at around −1%. In "Great Expectations," Eggertsson cited three of my Depression papers in his influential 2008 *American Economic Review* paper on the role of policy expectations during the Great Depression.

8. Sumner, "Comment on Brad DeLong."

9. Scott B. Sumner, "Hume and Hall Call Out the Fed," *TheMoneyIllusion*, February 2, 2009.

10. Cassel, "Memorandum of Dissent"; Hawtrey, "Gold Standard."

11. See Bernanke, "Remarks by Governor Ben S. Bernanke."

12. See Sumner, *Midas Paradox*.

13. Research by Gabriel Mathy offers an alternative view, because uncertainty shocks were highly correlated with economic decline during the Great Depression. Establishing causation going from increased uncertainty to falling output, however, is quite difficult. Uncertainty is also a side effect of an unstable monetary environment. Mathy, "How Much Did Uncertainty Shocks Matter."

14. Keynes, *Treatise on Money*, 1:170.

15. Jon Hilsenrath, "Fed Chief Gets Set to Apply Lessons of Japan's History," *Wall Street Journal*, October 12, 2010.

16. The small upticks in 1997 and 2014 occurred when the sales tax was increased, whereas the tiny bump in 2008 happened when oil soared to $147 per barrel. Otherwise, these decades show an amazing record of stability.

17. Krugman, "It's Baaack!"

Chapter Fourteen

1. As of early 2019, *The Economist* magazine reports that real housing prices in the US are down 10% from the 2006 peak, and in Ireland they are down 15%. But real housing prices are up 5% in the UK, 36% in Australia, 56% in New Zealand, and 75% in Canada. "Global House-Price Index," *The Economist*, June 27, 2019.

2. Erdmann, *Shut Out*.

3. Saunders, "Stock Prices."

4. "Really Tough Times for Chicago," *The Economist*, January 14, 2010.

5. Dean Baker, "Bursting Bubbles," *In These Times*, May 9, 2003; David Leonhardt, "Beware, Mr. Bubble's Worried Again," *New York Times*, August 21, 2005.

6. See Greasley and Madsen, "Housing Slump."

7. Most of the bank failures were caused by bad commercial loans (caused by the recession), not bad subprime mortgages.

8. Rorty, *Contingency, Irony, and Solidarity*.

Chapter Fifteen

1. Quoted in "The Perils of Forecasting," *Wall Street Journal*, January 26, 2006.

2. Stekler and Talwar, "Economic Forecasting."

3. Samuelson, "Living with Stagflation, 972.

4. Nick Rowe, "Did Inflation Targeting Destroy Its Own Signal?," *Worthwhile Canadian Initiative*, January 12, 2015.

5. In June 2008, the Fed forecast real GDP growth in 2009 to be in the range of 2.0% to 2.8%. It forecast PCE inflation in the range of 2.0% to 2.3%. Although no explicit NGDP growth forecast was provided, these figures suggest that the Fed expected roughly 4.5% NGDP growth, the sum of real growth and inflation. Minutes of the Federal Open Market Committee, June 24–25, 2008.

6. More specifically, Australia had a target range of 2% to 3%.

7. See Woodford, "Methods of Policy Accommodation."

8. Keynes, *General Theory*.

9. Yes, the Fed targets inflation and employment, not NGDP, but as a practical matter any policy that is expected to achieve the dual mandate will also result in a fairly stable path for NGDP.

10. Bernanke, "Japanese Monetary Policy"; Svensson, "Escaping from a Liquidity Trap."

Chapter Sixteen

1. Gretchen Morgenson, "Dr. Greenspan Chases Gloom of Investors' Chill Winter," *New York Times*, January 4, 2001.

2. Morgenson, "Dr. Greenspan Chases Gloom."

3. Fleming and Remolona, "What Moves the Bond Market?"

4. John Parry, "Treasury Prices Plummet as Stock Prices Soar on Earlier-Than-Expected Fed Interest-Rate Cut," *Wall Street Journal*, January 4, 2001, C16.

5. Edmund L. Andrews, "Fed Cuts Rate Half Point, and Markets Soar," *New York Times*, September 19, 2007.

6. Ellen Freilich, "Treasuries—Prices Fall on Inflation Worries, Stock Strength," *Reuters*, September 19, 2007.

7. E. S. Browning, Michael Hudson, and Joanna Slater, "Markets Get a Jump-Start from Fed," *Wall Street Journal*, September 19, 2007.

8. Cúrdia, "Why So Slow?"

9. Mishkin, *Economics of Money*, 606.

Chapter Seventeen

1. Bernanke, "Japanese Monetary Policy," 17–18.

2. Bernanke, 20.

3. Bernanke, 3–4. Emphasis added.

4. Bernanke, 7.

5. Bernanke, 10–11.

6. Bernanke, 12. Emphasis added.

7. Bernanke, 13.

8. Bernanke, 25–26.

9. Hawtrey, *Century of the Bank Rate*, 145.

10. Bernanke, "Some Thoughts on Monetary Policy."

11. Bernanke.

12. Bernanke.

13. See Matthew Klein, "Central Bankers Have One Job and They Don't Know How to Do It," *Financial Times*, October 17, 2017.

14. This is not to suggest that the Fed had explicitly adopted Lars Svensson's criterion but rather that the consensus forecast never strayed far from the implicit policy goals.

Chapter Eighteen

1. Woodward and Hall, "Options for Stimulating the Economy."

2. Woodward and Hall's critique was written later on, after the target rate had been cut to 1.0%.

3. See Ireland (2014).

4. David Beckworth, "Repeating the Fed's Policy Mistake of 1936–1937," *Macro Musings Blog*, October 29, 2008.

5. Sumner, "Comment on Brad DeLong"; Sumner, "Comment on Dolan."

6. Scott B. Sumner, "Hume and Hall Call Out the Fed," *TheMoneyIllusion*, February 2, 2009.

7. That is currently the rate in Switzerland, but in April 2019 a Swiss central bank official indicated a willingness to go even lower, if necessary.

8. Louis Woodhill, "Why the Fed's QEII Will Not Work," *RealClearPolitics*, November 11, 2010.

9. Michael M. Grynbaum, "Stocks Soar 11 Percent on Aid to Banks," *New York Times*, October 13, 2008.

10. Sharon Otterman, "Wall Street Soars on Bargain Hunters and Possible Federal Reserve Rate Cut," *New York Times*, October 28, 2008.

11. See "Market Meltdown," YouTube video posted by claytonia8, August 6, 2007, 3:13, https://www.youtube.com/watch?v=SWksEJQEYVU.

Chapter Nineteen

1. David Beckworth and Christopher Crowe argued that America is a "monetary superpower," with a disproportionate impact on global monetary conditions. I think that's right; however, it remains true that the biggest impact of Fed policy occurs within the US. Beckworth and Crowe, "Great Liquidity Boom."

2. Scott B. Sumner, "Why Are Economists in Denial about the Eurozone?," *TheMoneyIllusion*, October 14, 2014. Emphasis in original.

3. Beckworth, "Monetary Policy Origins."

4. Svensson, "Escaping from a Liquidity Trap."

5. Scott B. Sumner, "Expectations Traps: They're Even More Applicable to Fiscal Policy," *TheMoneyIllusion*, June 3, 2010.

6. Paul Krugman, "Japanese Monetary Policy (Wonkish)," *New York Times*, July 30, 2010.

7. Inflation averaged roughly 1% per year during Abe's first seven years. The rate was higher when he raised the national sales tax in early 2014 and lower when global oil prices fell in half during 2014–2015.

8. Obviously the term *conservative* covers a wide range of views. Here I'm referring to people who are opposed to governments owning lots of private-sector assets but who also favor a very low inflation target.

Chapter Twenty

1. More specifically, it was seen as confirming what Keynesians call the "IS-LM model" of the economy.

2. Michael M. Grynbaum, "Greenspan Concedes Error on Regulation," *New York Times*, October 23, 2008.

3. See the 2019 Index of Economic Freedom complied by the Heritage Foundation.

4. Chicago Booth IGM Forum, July 29, 2014.

5. "The Obama Stimulus: Three Years of Failure," US Senate Republican Policy Committee, February 17, 2012.

6. Paul Krugman, "Romer and Bernstein on Stimulus," *New York Times*, January 10, 2009.

7. "A History of Surpluses and Deficits in the United States," *DaveManuel .com*, accessed February 7, 2020, https://www.davemanuel.com/history-of-deficits -and-surpluses-in-the-united-states.php.

8. "350 Economists Warn Sequester Cuts Could Kill the Recovery," *Our Future* website, February 26, 2013. This letter was uncannily reminiscent of a 1981 letter signed by 364 British Keynesians, warning that Thatcher's policies would be disastrous. In fact, Thatcher was so successful that even the Labour Party accepted many of her policies when it finally took office in 1997. Philip Booth, "How 364 economists got it totally wrong," *Telegraph*, March 15, 2006.

9. Mike Konczal, "The Great Economic Experiment of 2013: Ben Bernanke vs. Austerity," *Washington Post*, April 27, 2013.

10. Paul Krugman, "Monetarism Falls Short (Somewhat Wonkish)," *New York Times*, April 28, 2013.

11. Scott B. Sumner, "Keynesianism: It's Not Just Resting," *Econlog*, January 4, 2014.

12. Paul Krugman, "Happy New Year? The Conscience of a Liberal," *New York Times*, January 4, 2014.

13. Krugman, Wells, and Graddy, *Essentials of Economics*.

14. Paul Krugman, "Supply, Demand, and Unemployment Benefits," *New York Times*, April 15, 2014.

15. Greg Mankiw, "Wanna Bet Some of That Nobel Money?," *Greg Mankiw's Blog*, March 4, 2009.

16. Scott B. Sumner, "Mark Sadowski on Fiscal Austerity, with and without Monetary Offset," *TheMoneyIllusion*, June 18, 2015.

17. Kevin Erdmann, "More on Austerity, Growth and Monetary Policy," *Idiosyncratic Whisk*, October 19, 2013; Benn Steil, "So What Did the Great Recession Teach Us about the Power of Public Spending? Revisiting Paul Krugman," *Geo-Graphics* (Council on Foreign Relations), September 22, 2017.

18. Matthew O'Brien, "Why More Stimulus Now Would Pay for Itself— Really!," *The Atlantic*, March 26, 2012.

19. Paul Krugman, "Beliefs, Faith and Money," *New York Times*, July 6, 2014.

20. Paul Krugman, "The Roots of Evil (Wonkish)," *New York Times*, March 3, 2009.

21. In 2016 I published a piece describing how I believe Friedman would have reacted to the Great Recession. Sumner, "What Would Milton Friedman Have Thought?"

22. Milton Friedman, "He Has Set a Standard," *Wall Street Journal*, January 31, 2006.

23. After the election of Donald Trump in 2016, an increasing number of conservatives became concerned that monetary policy was too tight.

24. Both Robert Hetzel and Tim Congdon began making this claim in 2008. Hetzel, "Monetary Policy"; Tim Congdon, "The Unnecessary Recession: A Flawed Economic Doctrine Led Gordon Brown and Alistair Darling to Plunge Britain into Its Worst Postwar Crisis," *Standpoint*, May 29, 2009. In "What Would Milton Friedman Have Thought," I discuss the views of Schwartz and Meltzer.

25. "Open Letter to Ben Bernanke," *Wall Street Journal*, November 15, 2010.

26. Paul Krugman, "Beliefs, Faith and Money," *New York Times*, July 6, 2014.

27. Under a gold standard, prices would normally revert back to prewar levels after a war ended.

28. See White, "Did Hayek and Robbins Deepen the Great Depression?"

29. To be fair, Keynesians and Austrians accept that there can be excesses in either direction—their differences are a matter of emphasis.

30. This research is summarized in Mulligan, *Redistribution Recession*.

31. Scott B. Sumner, "The 'New Claims' Puzzle," *TheMoneyIllusion*, August 15, 2013.

32. See Hanke, *On the Paradox of Excessive Bank Regulation*.

33. That is, it is less common in the United States. In Latin America a Neo-Fisherian outcome is much more common.

34. Svensson, "Zero Bound."

35. Here's what Svensson said in "Zero Bound":

> It is technically feasible for the central bank to devalue the currency and peg the exchange rate at a level corresponding to an initial real depreciation of the domestic currency relative to the steady state. (2) If the central bank demonstrates that it both can and wants to hold the peg, the peg will be credible. That is, the private sector will expect the peg to hold in the future. (3) When the peg is credible, the central bank has to raise the short nominal interest rate above the zero bound to a level corresponding to uncovered interest rate parity. Thus, the economy is formally out of the liquidity trap. In spite of the rise of the nominal interest rate, the long real rate falls, as we shall see.

Chapter Twenty-One

1. See Butterfield, *Whig Interpretation*.

2. The Taylor principle was developed by John Taylor, and the related "Taylor rule" for setting the interest rate target is widely used as a benchmark to evaluate the stance of monetary policy.

3. Keynes, *General Theory*, 40.

4. Keynes, 41.

5. Friedman, "Role of Monetary Policy."

6. Goodhart's law (named after Charles Goodhart) says that a monetary policy indicator will become less reliable as soon as the central bank begins to target that indicator.

7. See Bernanke and Woodford, "Inflation Forecasts."

8. Bernanke and Woodford.

9. Even Bernanke and Woodford, in "Inflation Forecasts," acknowledged that having the market forecast the appropriate policy instrument setting was a way to circumvent the circularity problem.

10. See Chappell, McGregor, and Vermilyea, *Committee Decisions*; Battaglini, "Policy Advice"; Lombardelli, Talbot, and Proudman, "Committees versus Individuals."

11. See Hanson, Oprea, and Porter, "Information Aggregation."

12. I got the basic idea for this approach from Woolsey, "Index Futures Targeting."

Chapter Twenty-Two

1. This is similar to how Milton Friedman added the Fisher effect and the natural rate hypothesis to earlier versions of the quantity theory of money.

2. This doesn't prove that tight money led to fascism, but it is worth noting that the Nazi Party was quite small in 1929, and its vote share soared as Germany fell into deflation and depression.

3. See, for example, Derek Thompson, "The Blogger Who Saved the Economy," *The Atlantic*, September 14, 2012; Joe Weisenthal, "Meet the Blogger Who May Have Just Saved the American Economy," *Business Insider*, September 14, 2012; Matthew Yglesias, "The Scott Sumner Rally," *Slate*, September 13, 2012; Tyler Cowen, "It's Not Just Monetary Policy, It's Scott Sumner Day," *Marginal Revolution*, September 13, 2012.

4. Ironically, Krugman moved away from that approach a few years after he wrote "Ricardo's Difficult Idea."

5. Scott Alexander, review of *Inadequate Equilibria: Where and How Civilizations Get Stuck*, by Eliezer Yudkowsky, *Slate Star Codex*, November 30, 2017.

6. Alexander, review of *Inadequate Equilibria*. Emphasis added.

7. Lopez, *Man Who Made Vermeers*, 6.

8. John Greenwald, "Recession, Why We're So Gloomy," *Time*, January 13, 1992.

9. Prior to COVID-19, 1974 offered probably the closest example to a "real recession" in the United States. And even in that case, NGDP growth slowed somewhat. Real recessions are more common in smaller economies.

10. In terms of the AS-AD model, the COVID-19 pandemic caused the AS curve to both shift to the left and become much less elastic (i.e., steeper.)

11. It is operated by Hypermind, a French organization that has created prediction markets for various political and economic outcomes.

12. The unaltered Wittgenstein quotation can be found in Dawkins, *God Delusion*, 411.

Bibliography

Albers, Thilo Nils Hendrik. "The Prelude and Global Impact of the Great Depression: Evidence from a New Macroeconomic Dataset." *Explorations in Economic History* 70 (2018): 150–63.

Autor, David H., David Dorn, and Gordon Hanson. "The China Shock: Learning from Labor Market Adjustment to Large Changes in Trade." Working Paper No. 21906, National Bureau of Economic Research, Cambridge, MA, January 2016.

Barattieri, Alessandro, Susanto Basu, and Peter Gottschalk. "Some Evidence on the Importance of Sticky Wages." Working Paper No. 16130, National Bureau of Economic Research, Cambridge, MA, June 2010.

Barro, Robert. *Macroeconomics*. 4th ed. New York: Wiley, 1993.

———. "Money and the Price Level under the Gold Standard." *Economic Journal* 89, no. 353 (1979): 13–33.

Battaglini, Marco. "Policy Advice with Imperfectly Informed Experts." *Advances in Theoretical Economics* 4, no. 1 (2004): 1–32.

Beckworth, David. "Better Risk Sharing through Monetary Policy? The Financial Stability Case for a Nominal GDP Target." Working paper, Mercatus Center at George Mason University, Arlington, VA, 2018.

———. "The Monetary Policy Origins of the Eurozone Crisis." *International Finance* 20, no. 2 (2017): 114–34.

Beckworth, David, and Christopher Crowe. "The Great Liquidity Boom and the Monetary Superpower Hypothesis." In *Boom and Bust Banking: The Causes and Cures of the Great Recession*, edited by David Beckworth, 95–126. Oakland, CA: Independent Institute, 2014.

Bergsten, C. Fred, and Joseph E. Gagnon. *Currency Conflict and Trade Policy: A New Strategy for the United States*. Washington, DC: Peterson Institute for International Economics, 2016.

Bernanke, Ben S. *The Courage to Act: A Memoir of a Crisis and Its Aftermath*. New York: Norton, 2015.

———. "Japanese Monetary Policy: A Case of Self-Induced Paralysis?" Working paper, Princeton University, December 1999.

———. "Remarks by Governor Ben S. Bernanke." Speech at the Federal Reserve Bank of Dallas Conference on the Legacy of Milton and Rose Friedman's *Free to Choose*, Dallas, October 24, 2003. https://www.federalreserve.gov/board docs/speeches/2003/20031024/default.htm.

———. "Some Thoughts on Monetary Policy in Japan." Speech before the Japan Society of Monetary Economics, Tokyo, May 31, 2003. http://www.federalre serve.gov/boarddocs/speeches/2003/20030531/default.htm.

Bernanke, Ben S., and Kevin Carey. "Nominal Wage Stickiness and Aggregate Supply in the Great Depression." *Quarterly Journal of Economics* 111 (August 1996): 853–83.

Bernanke, Ben S., Vincent R. Reinhart, and Brian P. Sack. "Monetary Policy Alternatives at the Zero Bound: An Empirical Assessment." *Brookings Papers on Economic Activity* 2 (2004): 1–100.

Bernanke, Ben S., and Michael Woodford. "Inflation Forecasts and Monetary Policy." *Journal of Money, Credit and Banking* 29 (1997): 653–84.

Bils, Mark J. "Real Wages over the Business Cycle: Evidence from Panel Data." *Journal of Political Economy* 93 (August 1985): 666–89.

Blanchard, Olivier J., and Daniel Leigh. "Growth Forecast Errors and Fiscal Multipliers." *American Economic Review* 103, no. 3 (May 2013): 117–20.

Bullard, James, and Riccardo DiCecio. "Optimal Monetary Policy for the Masses." Working Paper 2019-009C, Federal Reserve Bank of St. Louis, April 2019.

Butterfield, Herbert. *The Whig Interpretation of History*. New York: Norton, 1965.

Cagan, Phillip. "The Monetary Dynamics of Hyperinflation." In *Studies in the Quantity Theory of Money*, edited by Milton Friedman, 25–117. Chicago: University of Chicago Press, 1956.

Cassel, Gustav. "Memorandum of Dissent." In *Report of the Gold Delegation*. Geneva: League of Nations Financial Committee, 1932.

Cecchetti, Stephen G. "Prices during the Great Depression: Was the Deflation of 1930–32 Really Unanticipated?" *American Economic Review* 82, no. 1 (1992): 141–56.

Celia, James, and Farley Grubb. "Non-Legal-Tender Paper Money: The Structure and Performance of Maryland's Bills of Credit, 1767–75." *Economic History Review* 69, no. 4 (2016): 1132–56.

Chappell, Henry W., Jr., Rob Roy McGregor, and Todd A. Vermilyea. *Committee Decisions on Monetary Policy: Evidence from Historical Records of the Federal Open Market Committee*. Cambridge, MA: MIT Press, 2005.

Cúrdia, Vasco. "Why So Slow? A Gradual Return for Interest Rates." Economic Letter 2015-32, Federal Reserve Bank of San Francisco, CA, October 12, 2015.

Dawkins, Richard. *The God Delusion*. Boston: Mariner, 2006.

DeLong, J. Bradford. "The Triumph of Monetarism?" *Journal of Economic Perspectives* 14, no. 1 (2000): 83–94.

Dornbusch, Rudiger. "Expectations and Exchange Rate Dynamics." *Journal of Political Economy* 34, no. 6 (December 1976): 1161–76.

Eggertsson, Gauti B. "Great Expectations and the End of the Depression." *American Economic Review* 98, no. 4 (2008): 1476–516.

Eichengreen, Barry. *Golden Fetters: The Gold Standard and the Great Depression, 1919–1939.* New York: Oxford University Press, 1992.

Eichengreen, Barry, and Jeffrey Sachs. "Exchange Rates and Economic Recovery in the 1930s." *Journal of Economic History* 45, no. 4 (December 1985): 925–46.

Erdmann, Kevin. *Shut Out: How a Housing Shortage Caused the Great Recession and Crippled Our Economy.* Lanham, MD: Rowman & Littlefield, 2018.

Evans, Martin, and Paul Wachtel. "Were Price Changes during the Great Depression Anticipated? Evidence from Nominal Interest Rates." *Journal of Monetary Economics* 32 (August 1993): 3–34.

Fisher, Irving. "The Business Cycle Largely a 'Dance of the Dollar.'" *Journal of the American Statistical Association* 18, no. 144 (1923): 1024–28.

———. *The Money Illusion.* New York: Adelphi, 1928.

Fleming, Michael J., and Eli M. Remolona. "What Moves the Bond Market?" *Economic Policy Review* (Federal Reserve Bank of New York), December 1997, 31–50.

Friedman, Milton. "Mr. Market." Interview by Gene Epstein. *Hoover Digest*, no. 1 (January 30, 1999).

———. "Reviving Japan." *Hoover Digest*, no. 2 (April 30, 1998).

———. "The Role of Monetary Policy." *American Economic Review* 58, no. 1 (1968): 1–17.

———. "25 Years after the Rediscovery of Money: What Have We Learned? A Discussion." *American Economic Review* 65, no. 2 (1975): 176–79.

Friedman, Milton, and Anna J. Schwartz. *A Monetary History of the United States, 1867–1960.* 1963. Reprint, Princeton, NJ: Princeton University Press, 1971.

Gagnon, Joseph E. "Quantitative Easing: An Underappreciated Success." Policy brief, Peterson Institute for International Economics, Washington, DC, April 2016.

———. "We Know What Causes Trade Deficits." Peterson Institute for International Economics, Washington, DC, April 27, 2017. https://piie.com/blogs /trade-investment-policy-watch/we-know-what-causes-trade-deficits.

Glasner, David. "The Fisher Effect under Deflationary Expectations." Working paper, January 2011. Available at the Social Science Research Network, http:// papers.ssrn.com/sol3/papers.cfm?abstract_id=1749062#.

———. *Free Banking and Monetary Reform.* Cambridge: Cambridge University Press, 1989.

Greasley, David, and Jakob B. Madsen. "The Housing Slump and the Great Depression in the USA." *Cliometrica* 7 (2013): 15–35.

Grubb, Farley. "Is Paper Money Just Paper Money? Experimentation and Variation in the Paper Monies Issued by the American Colonies from 1690 to 1775."

388 BIBLIOGRAPHY

388 BIBLIOGRAPHY

388 BIBLIOGRAPHY

388 BIBLIOGRAPHY

388 BIBLIOGRAPHY

388 BIBLIOGRAPHY

388 BIBLIOGRAPHY

388 BIBLIOGRAPHY

388 BIBLIOGRAPHY

388 BIBLIOGRAPHY

388 BIBLIOGRAPHY

388   BIBLIOGRAPHY

In *Research in Economic History*, edited by Susan Wolcott and Christopher Hanes, 147–224. Bingley, UK: Emerald Group, 2016.

Hall, Robert E. "Optimal Fiduciary Monetary Systems." *Journal of Monetary Economics* 12 (1983): 33–50.

———. "Why Does the Economy Fall to Pieces after a Financial Crisis?" *Journal of Economic Perspectives* 24, no. 4 (2010): 3–20.

Hamilton, James D. "Was the Deflation during the Great Depression Anticipated? Evidence from the Commodity Futures Markets." *American Economic Review* 82, no. 1 (1992): 157–78.

Hanke, Steve H. *On the Paradox of Excessive Bank Regulation*. Washington, DC: Cato Institute, 2011.

Hanson, Robin, Ryan Oprea, and David Porter. "Information Aggregation and Manipulation in an Experimental Market." *Journal of Economic Behavior and Organization* 60 (2006): 449–59.

Hatton, Timothy J., and Mark Thomas. "Labour Markets in the Interwar Period and Economic Recovery in the UK and the USA." *Oxford Review of Economic Policy* 26, no. 3 (2010): 463–85.

Hawtrey, Ralph G. *A Century of the Bank Rate*. London: Longmans, Green, 1938.

———. *The Gold Standard in Theory and Practice*. London: Longmans, Green, 1947.

Hetzel, Robert L. *The Great Recession: Market Failure or Policy Failure?* Cambridge: Cambridge University Press, 2012.

———. "Maintaining Price Stability: A Proposal." *Economic Review* (Federal Reserve Bank of Richmond), March–April 1990, 53–55.

———. "Monetary Policy in the 2008–2009 Recession." *Economic Quarterly* (Federal Reserve Bank of Richmond) 95 (Spring 2009): 201–33.

Hoehn, James G. "Procyclical Real Wages under Nominal-Wage Contracts with Productivity Variations." *Economic Review* (Federal Reserve Bank of Cleveland) 24, no. 4 (1988): 11–23.

Hume, David. "Of Interest." 1752. In *David Hume Writings on Economics*, edited by Eugene Rotwein, 47–59. Madison, WI: University of Wisconsin Press, 1970.

———. "Of Money." 1752. In *David Hume Writings on Economics*, edited by Eugene Rotwein, 33–46. Madison, WI: University of Wisconsin Press, 1970.

———. "Of the Balance of Trade." 1752. In *David Hume Writings on Economics*, edited by Eugene Rotwein, 60–77. Madison, WI: University of Wisconsin Press, 1970.

Ireland, Peter N. "The Macroeconomic Effects of Interest on Reserves." *Macroeconomic Dynamics* 18 (September 2014): 1271–1312.

Keynes, John Maynard. *The Collected Writings of John Maynard Keynes*, edited by Donald Moggridge. Cambridge: Cambridge University Press, 1982. See particularly volumes 13 and 21.

———. *The General Theory of Employment, Interest, and Money*. 1936. Reprint, New York: Harcourt, Brace & World, 1964.

———. *A Tract on Monetary Reform*. London: Macmillan, 1923.

———. *A Treatise on Money*. 1930. Reprint, London: Macmillan, 1953.

Koenig, Evan. "Like a Good Neighbor: Monetary Policy, Financial Stability, and the Distribution of Risk." *International Journal of Central Banking* 9, no. 2 (2013): 57–82.

Krugman, Paul. "It's Baaack! Japan's Slump and the Return of the Liquidity Trap." *Brookings Papers on Economic Activity* 2 (1998): 137–87.

———. "Ricardo's Difficult Idea." 1996. https://web.mit.edu/krugman/www/ricardo.htm.

———. "Time on the Cross: Can Fiscal Stimulus Save Japan?" Working paper, Massachusetts Institute of Technology, 1999.

———. "Who Was Milton Friedman?" *New York Review of Books*, February 15, 2007.

Krugman, Paul, Robin Wells, and Kathryn Graddy. *Essentials of Economics*. 2nd ed. New York: Worth Publishers, 2010.

Lombardelli, Clare, James Talbot, and James Proudman. "Committees versus Individuals: An Experimental Analysis of Monetary Policy Decisionmaking." *Bank of England Quarterly Bulletin* 42, no. 3 (2002): 262–73.

Lopez, Jonathan. *The Man Who Made Vermeers: Unvarnishing the Legend of Master Forger Han van Meegeren*. Boston: Houghton Mifflin Harcourt, 2009.

Lucas, Robert. "Econometric Policy Evaluation: A Critique." *Carnegie-Rochester Conference Series* 1 (1976): 19–46.

Madsen, Jakob B. "The Length and the Depth of the Great Depression: An International Comparison." *Research in Economic History* 22 (December 2004): 239–88.

Mankiw, N. Gregory. *Macroeconomics*. 4th ed. New York: Worth, 2000.

Mankiw, N. Gregory, and Ricardo Reis. "Pervasive Stickiness." *American Economic Review* 96, no. 2 (2006): 164–69.

Mathy, Gabriel P. "How Much Did Uncertainty Shocks Matter in the Great Depression?" *Cliometrica*, August 2, 2019.

———. "Stock Volatility, Return Jumps and Uncertainty Shocks during the Great Depression." *Financial History Review* 23, no. 2 (2016): 165–92.

McCallum, Bennett T. "Theoretical Analysis Regarding a Zero Lower Bound on Nominal Interest Rates." *Journal of Money, Credit and Banking* 32, no. 4, pt. 2 (November 2000): 870–904.

Meltzer, Allan. *Keynes's Monetary Theory: A Different Interpretation*. Cambridge: Cambridge University Press, 1988.

Michener, Ronald W. "Re-examination of the Empirical Evidence Concerning Colonial New Jersey's Paper Money, 1709–1775: A Comment on Farley Grubb." *Econ Journal Watch* 16, no. 2 (2019): 180.

Mishkin, Frederic. *The Economics of Money, Banking, and Financial Markets*. 8th ed. Boston: Pearson, 2007.

Mishkin, Frederic. *The Economics of Money, Banking, and Financial Markets.* 10th ed. Boston: Pearson, 2013.

Mulligan, Casey. *The Redistribution Recession: How Labor Market Distortions Contracted the Economy.* Oxford: Oxford University Press, 2012.

Navarro, Peter, and Wilbur Ross. "Scoring the Trump Economic Plan: Trade, Regulatory, & Energy Policy Impacts." Unpublished paper issued by the Donald Trump presidential campaign, September 29, 2016.

Nelson, Daniel B. "Was the Deflation of 1929–1930 Anticipated? The Monetary Regime as Viewed by the Business Press." *Research in Economic History* 13 (1991): 1–65.

Phelps, Edmund S. "Phillips Curves, Expectations of Inflation and Optimal Unemployment over Time." *Economica* 34, no. 135 (August 1967): 254–81.

Rorty, Richard. *Contingency, Irony, and Solidarity.* Cambridge: Cambridge University Press, 1989.

Rose, Jonathan D. "Hoover's Truce: Wage Rigidity in the Onset of the Great Depression." *Journal of Economic History* 70, no. 4 (December 2010): 843–70.

Samuelson, Paul. "Living with Stagflation." 1979. In *The Collected Scientific Papers of Paul A. Samuelson, Volume 5,* edited by Kate Crowley. Cambridge, MA: MIT Press, 1986.

Saunders, Edward M., Jr. "Stock Prices and Wall Street Weather." *American Economic Review* 83, no. 5 (December 1993): 1337–45.

Selgin, George. *Less Than Zero: The Case for a Falling Price Level in a Growing Economy.* 1997. Reprint, Washington, DC: Cato Institute, 2018.

Sheedy, Kevin. "Debt and Incomplete Financial Markets." *Brookings Papers on Economic Activity,* Spring 2014, 301–61.

Silver, Stephen, and Scott B. Sumner. "Nominal and Real Wage Cyclicality during the Interwar Period." *Southern Economic Journal,* January 1995, 588–601.

Spiegel, Mark M. "Central Bank Independence and Inflation Expectations: Evidence from British Index-Linked Gilts." *Economic Review* (Federal Reserve Bank of San Francisco) 1 (1998): 3–14.

Steil, Benn, and Dinah Walker. "Correcting Paul Krugman's Austerity Chart for Monetary Effects Yields Very Different Results." *Geo-Graphics* (Council on Foreign Relations), January 13, 2015.

Stekler, Herman O., and Raj M. Talwar. "Economic Forecasting in the Great Recession." Research Program on Forecasting Working Paper No. 2011-005, Center of Economic Research, George Washington University, Washington, DC, August 5, 2011.

Sumner, Scott B. "Colonial Currency and the Quantity Theory of Money: A Critique of Smith's Interpretation." *Journal of Economic History* 53, no. 1 (1993): 139–45.

———. "Comment on Brad DeLong: Can We Generate Controlled Reflation in a Liquidity Trap?" *Economists' Voice* 6, no. 4 (2009): 1–2.

———. "Comment on Dolan and Recent Fed Policy." *Economists' Voice* 6, no. 1 (2009): 1–2.

———. "Measurement, Accountability, and Guardrails: Nudging the Fed towards a Rules-Based Policy Regime." *Cato Journal* 36, no. 2 (Summer 2016): 315–35.

———. *The Midas Paradox: Financial Markets, Government Policy Shocks, and the Great Depression.* Oakland, CA: Independent Institute, 2015.

———. "A Model of the Transactions and Hoarding Demand for Currency." *Quarterly Review of Economics & Business* 30 (Spring 1990): 75–89.

———. "Nominal GDP Futures Targeting." *Journal of Financial Stability* 17 (April 2015): 65–75.

———. "Using Futures Instrument Prices to Target Nominal Income." *Bulletin of Economic Research* 41 (1989): 157–62.

———. "What Would Milton Friedman Have Thought of Market Monetarism?" In *Milton Friedman: Contributions to Economics and Public Policy*, edited by Robert A. Cord and J. Daniel Hammond, 246–64. Oxford: Oxford University Press, 2016.

Sumner, Scott B., and Stephen Silver. "Real Wages, Employment and the Phillips Curve." *Journal of Political Economy* 97, no. 3 (1989): 706–20.

Svensson, Lars E. O. "Escaping from a Liquidity Trap and Deflation: The Foolproof Way and Others." *Journal of Economic Perspectives* 17, no. 4 (2003): 145–66.

———. "What Is Wrong with Taylor Rules? Using Judgment in Monetary Policy through Targeting Rules." *Journal of Economic Literature* 41 (2003): 426–77.

———. "The Zero Bound in an Open Economy: A Foolproof Way of Escaping from a Liquidity Trap." *Monetary and Economic Studies*, February 2001, 277–312.

Thompson, Earl. "Free Banking under a Labor Standard: A Perfect Monetary System." Working paper, Department of Economics, University of California, Los Angeles, January 8, 1982.

Walters, Alan A. "Consistent Expectations, Distributed Lags, and the Quantity Theory." *Economic Journal* 81 (June 1971): 273–81.

White, Lawrence H. "Did Hayek and Robbins Deepen the Great Depression?" *Journal of Money, Credit and Banking* 40, no. 4 (2008): 751–68.

Woodford, Michael. "Methods of Policy Accommodation at the Interest-Rate Lower Bound." Working paper, Columbia University, 2012.

Woodward, Susan, and Robert E. Hall. "Options for Stimulating the Economy." *Financial Crisis and Recession*, December 8, 2008.

Woolsey, William. "Index Futures Targeting and Monetary Disequilibrium." Unpublished manuscript, January 2013.

Yeoman, R. S. *A Guide Book of United States Coins 2020.* 73rd ed. Florence, AL: Whitman Publishing, 2019.

Index

Page numbers in italics refer to figures or tables.

federal funds. *See* reserves, federal
Federal Open Market Committee, 200–201, 314, 344–45, 346
Federal Reserve: announcements, interpreting market responses to, 247–49, *248*; on average inflation targeting, 350; coin production, M2 money supply and, 26; dual mandate, 171–72, 310, 311, 377n9; Great Contraction and, 96–97; Great Recession and, vii–viii, 4, 15, 99, 226–27, 244–45, 250–55; interest on reserves and, 82–83, 164, 276–84; level targeting and, 241–42; monetary base and, 45; monopoly on production of money, 49–50; nominal quantity of money in US economy and, 48–49; policy, income and Fisher effects and, 166; reserve balance at banks of, *84*, 271–72; RGDP and NGDP decline and, 362–63; targeting the forecast by, 243–44, 273–75; tools of, 90. *See also* monetary policy
Feldstein, Martin, 125, 128
fiat money: central bank monopoly on production of, 49–50; in Europe, 42; indeterminacy problem of, 78; liquidity traps and, 208–10; market test of, 89–91; *Monetary History* as description of, 97; monetary theory and, 85–87; supply and demand for, *46*, *157*; understanding, 42–43; in the US, 42, 110, 373n4; value of, 87–89
financial markets: news media on monetary policy moving, 282–83
Fischer, Stanley, 128
Fisher, Irving, 34, 70, 117, 205–6
Fisher effect: Great Recession and, 252; money and interest rates and, 156, 159; money supply and, 74; one-time change in money supply and, 165–66, *165*; Phelps and Friedman on, 110–11; theory of, 72–73
Fisher equation: defined, 71–72; TIPS spread and, 89–90
Fleming, Michael, 249
foreign assets, government purchases of, 190–91
Friedman, Milton: on easy money, 256; on expected rate of inflation, 118; on interest-rate movements, 168–69; on interest rates in Japan, 7, 369n5;

as Keynesian economics critic, 321; monetarism and, 114–17, 245, 373n5; Mundell debate with, 125; natural-rate hypothesis, 109–11, 122–23
Friedman, Milton, and Anna Schwartz. See *Monetary History of the United States, A*
futures markets: NGDP futures targeting and, 343–47; prices, as guide to monetary policy, 197, 199

gasoline, 24, 370n3. *See also* oil price shocks
GDP (gross domestic product): downward revision of 2008 data, 369n4; terminology of, 151. *See also* nominal GDP; real GDP
General Theory of Employment, Interest and Money (Keynes), 208, 338–39
Germany: gold standard and, 98, 372n4; internal devaluation in, 292–93; real exchange rate and, 189–90, 192; tight money and Nazi Party in, 355, 382n2
Glasner, David, 199
gold: as dollar unit of account, 41–42, 43, 45, 370n1, 371n4; FDR depreciating dollar against, 42, 203; fluctuations in price of, 198; prices, Great Depression and, 36; prices, Great Inflation and, 24, 28; as standard, circularity problem and, 345; as standard, Great Depression and, 202; unstable value of, 35; US abandons as dollar unit of account, 110
Goodhart's law, 382n6
Graddy, Kathryn, 317–18
Great Contraction (1929–1933), 96–99, 202–3
Great Depression: author's research on, 197, 201–3, *204*, 205; coin production and, 24–25, 26–27; costs of, New Keynesianism and, 98; economic theory on causes, vii; explanations for, 27–28, 224–25, 370n5; financial crisis following, 2, 3; Hayek on stimulus during, 323; history of economic thought and, 205–8; Hume's description of, 100; uncertainty shocks and, 376n13; US wages and prices during, 372n12. *See also* Roosevelt, Franklin D.
Great Inflation (1966–1981): coming of age during, 373n15; equation of exchange and, 53–54; factors in, 111, 113, 235–36,

1. (107) What is the Phillips curve, and why did it have such a hold on policymakers in the 60s-70s?

2. (109) Natural Rate Hypothesis, citizens rarely respond positively to swings in the economy. Why do we view fluctuations as bad and not natural? Are they "bad"?

3. Efficient Market Hypothesis (EMH) — financial markets are efficient and that asset prices reflect all available info at any given time. Believe? Yes or no? If yes, should central banks adopt EMH in their monetary policy?